THE AUTHOR Richard Tames read history at Cambridge and took his Master's Degree at the University of London. He now lectures at Syracuse University and the University of Maryland in London and is a London Tourist Board Blue Badge guide. He is the author of *A Traveller's History of London* and *A Traveller's History of Japan*.

SERIES EDITOR Professor Denis Judd is a graduate of Oxford, a Fellow of the Royal Historical Society and Professor of History at the University of North London. He has published over 20 books including the biographies of Joseph Chamberlain, Prince Philip, George VI and Alison Uttley, historical and military subjects, stories for children and two novels. His most recent book is the highly praised *Empire: The British Imperial Experience from 1765 to the Present*. He is an advisor to the BBC *History* magazine.

Other Titles in the Series

THE TRAVELLER'S HISTORY SERIES

'Ideal before-you-go reading' *The Daily Telegraph*

'An excellent series of brief histories' *New York Times*

'I want to compliment you ... on the brilliantly concise contents of your books' *Shirley Conran*

Reviews of Individual Titles

A Traveller's History of Japan

'It succeeds admirably in its goal of making the present country comprehensible through a narrative of its past, with asides on everything from bonsai to *zazen*, in a brisk, highly readable style ... you could easily read it on the flight over, if you skip the movie.' *The Washington Post*

'... dip into Richard Tames's literary, lyrical *A Traveller's History of London*'. *The Sunday Telegraph*

A Traveller's History of France

'Undoubtedly the best way to prepare for a trip to France is to bone up on some history. *The Traveller's History of France* by Robert Cole is concise and gives the essential facts in a very readable form.' *The Independent*

A Traveller's History of China

'The author manages to get 2 million years into 300 pages. An excellent addition to a series which is already invaluable, whether you're travelling or not.' *The Guardian*

A Traveller's History of India

'For anyone ... planning a trip to India, the latest in the excellent Traveller's History series ... provides a useful grounding for those whose curiosity exceeds the time available for research.' *The London Evening Standard*

A Traveller's History
of Oxford

A Traveller's History of Oxford

RICHARD TAMES

Series Editor   DENIS JUDD
Line Drawings   PETER GEISSLER

PHOENIX
PRESS

A Windrush Press Book

5 UPPER SAINT MARTIN'S LANE
LONDON WC2H 9EA

A PHOENIX PRESS PAPERBACK published in association with
THE WINDRUSH PRESS

First published in Great Britain
by Phoenix Press in association with The Windrush Press in 2002
A division of The Orion Publishing Group Ltd,
Orion House, 5 Upper St Martin's Lane,
London WC2H 9EA

Set by DP Photosetting, Aylesbury, Bucks
Printed and bound in Great Britain by Clays Ltd, St Ives plc

ISBN 1 84212 684 9

The Windrush Press, Windrush House, Adlestrop, Moreton-in-Marsh,
Gloucestershire GL56 0YN
Tel: 01608 658758   Fax: 01608 659345
www.windrushpress.com

Contents

Preface

There are at least three Oxfords. One is, of course, the ancient and illustrious university; another is the city itself, from posh North Oxford to the outer council housing estates; the third is the once powerful industrial Oxford, based on the motor car manufacturing factories of Cowley, the Oxford of the Morris Minor, the Mini, the MG and many other classical automobile names.

There is however a fourth Oxford, a place of fantasy, of myth and legend, and some significant truths. This is the Oxford of 'the dreaming spires' and of 'lost causes'. It is a staple, not merely of the English-speaking imagination, but also of that of much of the rest of the world. It is a place associated with 'an accent', an annual boat race with the great rival university of Cambridge, eccentric dons, academic excellence, a symphony by Haydn, a dark blue colour, snobbery, the nurturing of national and, indeed, international leaders, a particular brand of mar-malade, and the production of brilliantly innovative ideas and theories – from religion to politics, science, literature, economics and the arts.

The point is that the history of Oxford is so long, so complex so distinguished, so controversial that it is like a great quarry to be mined, a treasure house to be plundered or a rambling repository of Englishness and Britishness waiting to be used and abused. So, in the end, Oxford becomes all things to all people. The trick is to sift the truth and reality from the whimsy and the hyperbole.

This is what Richard Tames has so triumphantly achieved in this exceptionally thorough, beautifully written and comprehensive his-tory. As an Oxford man myself, it gives me great pleasure to say this of a Cambridge man. Perhaps I am also a touch relieved. Or are these comments simply another irritating example of the inevitable mock-rivalry, the wry in-jokery of the whole Oxbridge inter-relationship, and thus further proof of the cosy collusion at the heart of the system?

On the other hand, Tames might have written so well about Oxford rather than Cambridge because, as A.A. Milne once said, 'What distinguishes Cambridge from Oxford, broadly speaking, is that nobody who has been to Cambridge feels compelled to write about it.'

Oxford University boasts some of the most beautiful and sumptuously endowed colleges in the world, as well as the Bodleian Library and the Sheldonian Theatre. It is small wonder that it attracts so many eager, respectful visitors from overseas each year. When not being flooded with tourists, however, there is a loveliness and a tranquillity at its heart that renders it other worldly.

The story of Oxford is, of course, more than the sum of its architecture; it is essentially the history of who went there. The list of its alumni is so distinguished, so awe-inspiring that it is hard to know where to begin. A quick glance at Britain's political leadership would reveal that the twenty-five Prime Ministers, including Tony Blair, have been Oxford graduates. Among its overseas alumni are ex-President Bill Clinton, Benazir Bhutto, Bob Hawke – formerly Australian PM, Rupert Murdoch, and the Crown Prince and Princess of Japan. There are 30,000 overseas graduates in all, a third of them in the United States, and nearly all of them the beneficiaries of the scholarships endowed by Cecil Rhodes, himself an Oxford graduate.

Not merely government and administration, but the sciences and the arts, publishing and medicine, the academic and business worlds are all heavily influenced by Oxford. Indeed, as Richard Tames points out, 'Oxford can fairly claim to be the birthplace/midwife/crucible/catalyst of: the Arthurian legends, the English Bible and the Douai Bible, Anglicanism and Methodism, the Royal Society, the pre-Raphaelites and Aestheticism, *Alice in Wonderland, the Chronicles of Narnia*, and *The Lord of the Rings*, the OED and the DNB, Oxfam and Mensa, penicillin, the sub-four minute mile and Inspector Morse.' As if this was not enough, 'Five founders of American states were Oxford men and it was an Oxford man who founded the Smithsonian.'

Richard Tames's book contains one of the most comprehensive, attractive, readable and intriguing histories of Oxford to date. It should be in the suitcase, back-pack, and pocket of anyone who visits this beautiful, bustling, distinctive English city.

Denis Judd, 2002

Introduction

'Does he actually know anything about Oxford? Has he set eyes on the place? Never. He's taken good care not to. He only knows the things about Oxford that everybody knows. The things that everybody knows about Oxford are mostly myths and illusions...'

John Wain *Hungry Generations* (1994)

I declare a lack of interest. This is not an insider's account. I went to 'the Other Place'. I have visited Oxford to organise conferences, stay with friends, guide groups of American students, buy books and attend a wedding and a baptism; but I have never lived there. This is not, therefore, a book for Oxford people who already know quite enough about each other. (I leave it to them to try the preceding sentence – with and without a comma.) This book aims to take the reader *around* Oxford, rather than claiming to penetrate it. Tourist buses take the visitor around Oxford, so the walking tour guides make a point of emphasising that you can't see inside the colleges properly from the top of a bus; and the colleges *are* Oxford – of which, more anon. The walking tour can take the visitor into some quads and gardens, though probably not the *sanctum sanctorum* of a Fellows' Garden. They can probably escort the visitor into a chapel and a dining-hall, but probably not into a library or a don's or student's room. To the latter the outsider may have access as a member of a summer course or weekend conference; but it will be a student room with the 'character' stripped out of it – hopefully. The well-connected or merely fortuitously lucky may be invited to dine at a High Table but may retain little of the experience beyond a hazy impression of sybaritic excess and humanistic brilliance, which will suit Oxford very

1

well. This is, therefore, rather a book to lead the reader outward than
inward, to illustrate the impact of Oxford on the world, rather than
Oxford's interest in itself, though its complexity and competitiveness
make it a perfect place for gossip. An 'Oxford secret' = telling only
one person at a time.

There is, in any case, far, far too much to tell. The university's history
of itself runs to eight hefty volumes. I had intended to start this book
with a chapter entitled 'Approaches', following the routes into the city
that converge at Carfax to show how each side-turning reveals a different facet of Oxford's past, tranquil Turl Street contrasting with
commercialised Cornmarket Street. Take the Woodstock Road, for
example. Who would not be diverted by the very name of Squitchey
Lane? – once Green Way, then more grandly Victoria Road, but
named by those who used it from the couch-grass (quitch) which grew
beside it in profusion. Polstead Road was the childhood home of
Lawrence of Arabia and St Margaret's Road, the next turning off to the
right, was once known as Gallows Walk, being the site of Oxford's
gibbet in the seventeenth century. On the left is St Hugh's, the first
custom-built college for women, named for a medieval bishop of
distant Lincoln, of whose vast diocese Oxford formed a part until the
Reformation. Next comes the church of St Philip and St James, built in
1862 by G.E. Street, William Morris's mentor and consecrated by
Bishop Wilberforce, who was famously rebuked by T.H. Huxley
during a celebrated public debate on Darwinism. John Betjeman hailed
'Phil and Jim' as 'the cathedral of . . . laburnum-shaded North Oxford'
but it finally closed in 1982 and became the Oxford Centre for Mission
Studies in 1988. North Oxford is, of course, a subject in itself: Oxford's
swankiest suburb, the embodiment of John Ruskin's enthusiasm for the
Gothic and consequently a showcase of Victorian villadom by local
architect William Wilkinson. Next comes cosmopolitan St Anthony's
College, housed in what was once an *Anglican* convent, founded by a
French/Lebanese/Yemeni shipping magnate. It is followed by St
Anne's, housed in handsome inter-war buildings by the designer of the
classic red telephone kiosk. Opposite, housed in an eighteenth century
observatory which was modelled on the Tower of the Winds in
Athens, is postgraduate Green College, founded by a Mancunian-

Canadian-Texan millionaire. To its south stands the Radcliffe Infirmary, built with the bequest of a royal physician. Opposite that stands the Acland Home, named for the founder of the University Museum and re-founder of Oxford as a respected centre of medical education. South of the infirmary is a third college which began for women only, Somerville, virtually embracing St Aloysius church, where Gerard Manley Hopkins once served. Sir William Beveridge, architect of the post-war welfare state lived at 104 Woodstock Road ... The draft of the first 'Approach' soon became a chapter in itself and so the enterprise was abandoned.

Oxford's Gifts to the World

Not being from Oxford I can boast on its behalf unrestrained by any feigned modesty. Oxford's name has been attached to an accent (supposedly posh), a colour (dark blue) and a symphony (by Haydn), as well as styles of shoe, shirting, trousers, cloth, chair, bath, picture-frame and philosophical discourse. In the 1830s the university was riven by the Oxford Movement. In the 1920s Frank Buchman's moralising mission became known as the Oxford Group, though it had little indeed to do with either the university or the city. (The university's extensive website is entirely devoid of reference to either Buchman or his group, later known as Moral Rearmament.) Oxford can fairly claim to be the birthplace/midwife/crucible/catalyst of: the Arthurian legends, the English Bible and the Douai Bible, Anglicanism and Methodism, the Royal Society, the Pre-Raphaelites and Aestheticism, *Alice in Wonderland*, *The Chronicles of Narnia* and *The Lord of the Rings*, the OED and the DNB, Oxfam and Mensa, penicillin, the sub-four minute mile and Inspector Morse. Oxford alumni include twenty-five British prime ministers and almost a hundred archbishops, plus four winners of the Nobel Prize for Literature (Galsworthy, Eliot, Golding and Naipaul) and three winners of the Nobel Peace Prize – which has also been awarded to two of its faculty. Christ Church alone has produced sixteen prime ministers, not to mention John Locke, Lord Shaftesbury and Lewis Carroll. University College can boast prime ministers Attlee and Wilson of Britain, Dr K.A. Busia of Ghana, Bob

Hawke of Australia and President William Jefferson Clinton of the United States.

The permanent academic community includes over seventy Fellows of the Royal Society and over a hundred Fellows of the British Academy. Oxford graduates account for over a fifth of the entries in Britain's *Who's Who*. Its roll-call of international alumni includes Benazir Bhutto, Rupert Murdoch and the Crown Prince *and* Crown Princess of Japan. There are over 30,000 overseas Oxford alumni, a third in the USA, over 2,000 in Canada and the same number in Australia, plus more than a thousand in each of Germany and France. Whether or not Britain can claim to have a 'special relationship' with the United States, Oxford certainly has. The Founding Fathers of the United States didn't go to Oxford but they read Locke and Blackstone – who did. Five founders of American states were Oxford men and it was an Oxford man who founded the Smithsonian. American generosity has made possible the founding of entire colleges – Ruskin, St Catherine's, Green and Templeton, not to mention funding the New Bodleian extension and the Law Library. The Rhodes Scholarship programme inspired the equally influential Fulbright programme and nowadays Americans account for some 10 per cent of all Oxford students.

Oxford as a city, rather than as a university, can claim credit for Frank Cooper's Oxford marmalade, the MG, the Morris Minor and the 'Mini' car. It is the birthplace of the thriller writer P.D. James and of master art forger Eric Hebborn. Ironically, but perhaps inevitably, as an unanticipated 'Motopolis' Oxford was an early pioneer of the Park-and-Ride system. It followed York in producing a citizen's charter to improve the quality of public service delivery. In Helen House, opened in 1982 in the grounds of All Saints' Convent, Leopold Street, the city established the first ever hospice specifically for children.

THE OTHER PLACE

'What distinguishes Cambridge from Oxford, broadly speaking, is that nobody who has been to Cambridge feels compelled to write about it.'

A.A. Milne

The portmanteau term 'Oxbridge' may seem to imply a certain parity but the fact that the equally plausible 'Camford' has never caught on does suggest a degree of disparity. The Dictionary of National Biography's selection of *Brief Lives* includes a hundred and fifty significant Britons of the twentieth century. Of these thirty-four were graduates of Oxford, against twenty-one from Cambridge; though perhaps more to the point is the fact that almost a hundred of the entrants went to neither. In 2001 the BBC asked the British public to vote for its Greatest Briton. Narrowing the nominations down to a final thirty yielded three from Cambridge – Sir Isaac Newton, Alan Turing and William Wilberforce – as against two from Oxford – Margaret Thatcher and Sir Christopher Wren. Of the rest Sir Alexander Fleming went to medical school, John Logie Baird had his course at Glasgow cut short by the war and only birth-control pioneer Marie Stopes actually graduated from a conventional university course. But, insofar as there is an 'Oxbridge conspiracy' to stitch up British public life, it is Oxford which is disproportionately guilty. An Oxford don, asked why this should be so, offered the opinion that Oxford had always seen itself as a preparation for public life, whereas at Cambridge 'they've always been more interested in . . . (long, thoughtful pause) . . . always been more interested in . . . truth.'

EXPLAINING OXFORD

'I speak not of this college or of that, but of the University as a whole; and gentlemen, what a whole Oxford is!'

Lord Coleridge (1820–94)

Few matters seem more perplexing to outsiders than the relationship between the 'The university' and 'The colleges'. The exposition offered by Sir William Hamilton in the *Edinburgh Review* in 1831 still has much to recommend it:

> Oxford and Cambridge . . . consist . . . of the Universities proper and of the Colleges. The former . . . is founded, controlled and provided by public authority, for the advantage of the state. The latter . . . are created, regulated and endowed by private munificence, for the interest of certain favoured individuals. Time was when the Colleges did not exist, and the University

was there; and were the Colleges again abolished, the University would remain entire. The former, founded solely for education, exists only as it accomplishes the end of its institution; the latter, founded principally for aliment and habitation, would still exist, were all education abandoned within their walls.'

The university may be thought of for most of its history as an affiliation of colleges. A college, like a regiment, is an undying corporation and a focus of individual and collective loyalty, membership of which combines aspects of both equality and inequality. Its surrounding walls represent closure, continuity and camaraderie, its gardens an Arcadia preserved and reserved for the few. Each has a unique institutional personality, often represented by peculiar, some *very* peculiar, customs, such as the sounding of a horn to summon diners at Queen's College or the legend of a mallard which induces the fellows of All Souls to hazard life and limb processing by night and well fortified with alcohol across the roofs of their college buildings.

Sometimes Oxford does endeavour to explain itself, though not always with excessive frankness. Matthew Arnold confessed that 'I find I am generally thought to have buttered her up to excess for the sake of parting good friends; but this is not so, though I certainly kept her best side in sight and not her worst.' The same criterion appears to have guided the editors of the otherwise admirably comprehensive *Encyclopaedia of Oxford* in failing to include an entry on the publishing tycoon/swindler Robert Maxwell. While not formally connected with the university as such his abrasive spirit and 'buccaneering' commercial morality touched the lives of many of its members over several decades.

One of the wittiest expositions of Oxford is J.C. Masterman's *To Teach the Senators Wisdom* (1952). Set during the summer vacation, it chronicles a gently panic-stricken week during which half a dozen dons discuss how they should introduce a visiting group of American VIPs to the essence of Oxford. Each attempts in turn to define this elusive notion by focusing on the architecture, the gardens, the river, the collegiate system, the tutorial method of teaching, the complementarity of the sporting and the academic etc. When the visitors turn out to be very different from anything they had anticipated (i.e. young women) and to ask questions they cannot answer about topics they have never considered they are totally bemused – until two undergraduates come brilliantly and effortlessly to their rescue. Thus does Oxford re-invent itself in each generation, which Masterman suggests, is its true essence.

Another way of explaining Oxford would be to consider a 'typical' Oxford product, such as, perhaps, Belfast-born, Glasgow-educated James Bryce (1838–1922) – 'that awful Scotch fellow who outwrote everybody' to win a scholarship to Trinity, where, coming from a Presbyterian background, he successfully defied official pressure to sign up to the Thirty-Nine Articles as a condition of receiving his award. Firsts in classics, law and history, the Gaisford prize for Greek prose, the Chancellor's prize for Latin essay, theVinerian and Craven scholarships all followed, along with the Presidency of the Union. Bryce's Arnold Historical Prize essay on the Holy Roman Empire, the most famous of the century, was published as a book. A Fellow of Oriel at twenty-four and subsequently a barrister, education commissioner, Regius Professor of Civil Law, MP, co-founder of the *English Historical Review*, a champion of Armenian rights and of Irish Home Rule, Bryce became President of the Board of Trade and such a hugely successful ambassador to the United States that he was assigned Abe Lincoln's former pew in Washington's Old Presbyterian church as a signal mark of honour. Bryce, ultimately a Viscount, OM and GCVO, was also President of the Alpine Climb, having ascended the last 5,000 feet of Mount Ararat alone, climbed peaks from Basutoland to Japan and nearly fallen into the volcano of Mauna Loa on Hawaii. Doubtless these experiences helped him keep Oxford in its proper perspective. His in-depth analysis of US politics, *The American Commonwealth*, was treated in the States as his masterpiece. He was awarded thirty-one honorary degrees, fifteen of them American. Canada went one better and named Mount Bryce in the Canadian Rockies after him. Scarcely an 'average' career – 'Oxford average', possibly. Oxford's history shows that it is by no means necessary to win university prizes, like Bryce, to win the 'glittering prizes' of life itself. Many of its most famous graduates never actually graduated. The poet Shelley, the adventurer and poet Walter

Savage Landor and the orientalist and pornographer Sir Richard Burton, were all 'sent down' in disgrace. Edmund Halley, Pitt the Elder, Samuel Johnson, Charles James Fox, Thomas de Quincey, Algernon Swinburne, Max Beerbohm, Terence Rattigan, Stephen Spender and John Betjeman all left without a degree. Even mediocrity is not invariably fatal. John Ruskin, W.H. Auden and Evelyn Waugh all got thirds. Waugh was particularly annoyed as he made very clear through the mouth of one of his characters in *Brideshead Revisited* – 'You want either a first or a fourth. There is no value in anything between. Time spent on a good second is time thrown away . . .'

DECLAIMING OXFORD

Oxford, very aware of itself as Oxford, can seldom be accused of selling itself short. The fifteenth century panegyrist who boasted that '*If God himself on earth abode would make, He Oxford sure would for his dwelling take*' has remained anonymous to history. But, writing in 1932, Oxford historian Sir John Marriott could blithely assert that 'Few cities in the world, none in England, have been so written about as Oxford.' He remembered himself a page later to qualify his claim in a grudging aside – 'London, of course, always excepted.' Marriott did, however, have a point. In 1989 Judy Batson's *Oxford in Fiction: An Annotated Bibliography* was able to list 533 novels written about or set in Oxford, over four times as many as have a Cambridge background.

Apart from being the setting for much writing, Oxford has also been the chosen residence of many writers. While her husband was commandant of Cowley Barracks, Bury Knowle House at Headington was once the home of now forgotten Adeline Kingscote (1860–1908), an accomplished swindler who bankrupted herself and the vicar of Cowley and wrote over sixty titles, ranging from *The English baby in India and how to rear it* to romances, up to eight a year, with such highly appropriate titles as *What a woman will do, The indiscretion of Gladys* and *The love letters of a faithless wife.* Joyce Cary, Elizabeth Bowen, Ian McEwan and Brian Aldiss, sometime bookseller and literary editor of the *Oxford Mail* are all Oxford residents. Oxford novelist alumni include Winifred Holtby, Rose Macaulay, Mary Renault, Brigid Brophy, Margaret Forster, Barbara Pym, Joanna Trollope, supreme mistress of the 'Aga Saga' and Helen Fielding, author of *Bridget Jones's Diary*. 'Dr. Seuss' (Theodor Seuss Geisel) author of *The Cat in the Hat* was a graduate student in the 1920s when the Rev.W.W. Awdrey, creator of *Thomas the Tank Engine*, was an undergraduate. Kenneth Grahame was educated in Oxford and wrote *The Wind in the Willows* for the beloved son, later an undergraduate at Christ Church, who shares his tomb in the graveyard at St Cross. In 2002 local resident Philip Pullman became the first ever children's author to be awarded the prestigious Whitbread Prize.

In literary terms Oxford seems to have a close affinity with crime. Afficionados disagree about whether Sherlock Holmes went to Cambridge or Oxford. Dorothy Sayers' creation, the insouciant Lord Peter Wimsey, was indubitably an Oxford man.The success of the television versions of the curmudgeonly Inspector Morse (from Latin *mors*, death) has made Oxford and crime synonymous to many and even inspired Morse walking tours around the city. His creator, local resident Colin Dexter, was awarded an OBE and the freedom of the city. A Cambridge man and former examiner in Classics for Oxford's schools examination board, Dexter stands in an august tradition. Writing detective stories has long been considered a respectable diversion for the overburdened donnish mind, affording opportunities to indulge in elegant puzzle-setting, stylish word-play and displays of esoteric knowledge, invariably antiquarian or literary, rather than scientific. Dons were essentially inhabitants of a closed world of insider jokes and feuds which closely paralleled the classic country house setting of the traditional detective story in which a brilliant amateur upstages the bumbling police. The otherwise austere Monsignor Ronald Knox and socialist historian G.D.H. Cole and the worldy J.C. Masterman were all accomplished exponents of the genre. Some dons, however, took refuge behind pseudonyms – J.I.M. Stewart wrote prolifically as Michael Innes. Modern practitioners include John Fuller, Peter Levi and Veronica Stallwood, a former Bodleian employee, whose Kate Ivory stories are invariably set in Oxford. Other recent examples include Michael Dibdin's *Dirty Tricks*, Tony Strong's *The Poison Tree* and the best-selling *An Instance of the Fingerpost*, set in the 1660s by art historian Iain Pears, an Oxford graduate and another local resident.

OXFORD FOR OUTSIDERS

> 'Oxford is on the whole more attractive than Cambridge ... and the traveller is therefore recommended to visit Cambridge first or to omit it altogether if he cannot visit both.
>
> Baedeker's *Great Britain* (1887)

Oxford's touristic history began with medieval pilgrims but, unlike many other places, did not end with the destruction of that tradition at the Reformation. The city's geographically central location would always have brought it some passing traffic, as would the desire of alumni to revisit scenes of youthful endeavour or dissipation. But Oxford's enterprising inhabitants can take much credit for actively promoting its attractions. One Victorian 'booster' boldly proclaimed that a first visit to Oxford was 'A Thing to Remember for Life', no less. A *satire* on Oxford guide-books appeared as early as 1760. One of the earliest of that genre, the *Microcosmography* of J. Earle (died 1665) sketched out a range of 'university types' for the benefit of visitors. The 'Plodding Student', good at logic, hopeless at poetry; the 'Downright Scholler' whose 'mind is somewhat too much taken up with his mind'; the 'Pretender to Learning', a name-dropper of

Gowns in 1813. From the left: scholar, gentleman-commoner and Bachelor of Arts

authors who keeps the same book open on his table for six months at the same page; and the 'Young Gentleman of the University' who 'comes there to wear a gown and to say thereafter that he has been at the University'.

The building of the Sheldonian Theatre and Ashmolean Museum added two first-class visitor attractions. Breezy, free-spending Samuel Pepys enjoyed his visit, as did the doughty Celia Fiennes. but hyper-critical Zacharias von Uffenbach couldn't wait to get back to London. Another German, C.P. Moritz, arrived much fatigued late at night, having been picked up on the road at Nuneham Courtney by an English clergyman, who introduced him to a midnight drinking session of fellow pastors at the Mitre. The beer flowed until first light when the bemused visitor's new acquaintance abruptly abandoned him with the announcement 'Damn me, I must read prayers this morning at All Souls'. Moritz was less than exhilarated by his first sight of the much-praised thoroughfares of Oxford which he found 'dingy, dirty and disgusting'.

The advent of the railway introduced a new species of visitor, the day-tripper, who represented a welcome market for Abel Hayward's *Penny Guide to Oxford*. The reactions of the enraptured Nathaniel Hawthorne and the reverential Henry James confirmed, however, that the spirit of pilgrimage was not entirely dead. American awe, however, eroded with the years. In the 1920s a Christ Church porter, personification of collegiate *hauteur*, was shaken to hear a transatlantic voice enquire 'Say, usher, is this a purely literary establishment or can I get a snack here?'. Oxford responded to such vulgarisms characteristically, a pedantic notice in Queen's Lane frostily proclaiming *No Chars-a-Banc Allowed Here*.

Over the past quarter century attitudes have changed markedly. The university itself backed 'The Oxford Story' 'dark ride'. Specialised tours of the locations associated with the grumpy, beer-swilling genius of Inspector Morse and the very differently talented Harry Potter became available. The city's highly qualified Blue Badge guides offer others on such themes as Architecture, 'American Roots', 'Alice', Science, Literature, Ghosts, Gardens and Waterways. Enterprising undergraduates offered their services as rickshaw drivers.

OXFORD FOR INSIDERS

> 'Who can ... walk up the Oxford High Street on a sunny morning or linger on a clear night in Radcliffe Square and not be aware of something more authentic than the life of everyday?'
>
> *The Character of England* (1950)

In 1918 C.S. Lewis observed candidly that 'People talk about the Oxford manner and the Oxford life and the Oxford God knows what else ... As if the undergraduates had anything to do with it... The real Oxford is a closed corporation of jolly, untidy, lazy, good-for-nothing humorous old men who have been electing their own successors since the world began.' Things were about to change – at least outside the university itself.

In the second and third quarters of the twentieth century it seemed to many that Oxford as a city had made an historic break away from its traditional domination by the university to achieve a more 'normal' dependence on manufacturing. In the closing decades of the twentieth century the more traditional pattern reasserted itself. Oxford is once again a city of students, though not all of them are 'at Oxford' in the sense in which that has generally been understood. Oxford University itself has over 16,500 students, over a quarter at postgraduate level and almost a quarter from overseas, representing some one hundred and thirty nationalities. The city's other university, Oxford Brookes, has nearly 15,000 students and the College of Further Education some 14,000. Smaller institutions include Plater College, a Catholic residential college for students aged over twenty, a dozen language schools and tutorial colleges plus the overseas campus programmes of American universities, catering for those who wish to say that they, too, were 'at Oxford'.

The whole history of Oxford is an attempt to answer the question of its own purpose. The masters who ran and taught in the earliest student halls sought to replicate themselves. The medieval founders of colleges aimed to turn out servants of the church and indirectly of the state. The author of that enduringly successful mid-Victorian spoof *The Adventures of Mr Verdant Green* was, for once, probably being serious when he made his protagonist announce that 'it is formation of character that I regard as one of the many great ends of a university system'. Cardinal Newman in *The Idea of a University*, published in 1873, conceived of it as ideally constituting a community for the moral development of its members and not in any way vocational. Jowett, Master of Balliol in the following generation, saw its prime function as breeding a mandarinate to oversee nation and empire like platonic guardians. His near contemporary, Mark Pattison, thought it should be a powerhouse of research. Cecil Rhodes looked to Oxford as a finishing-school for supermen. Quite possibly there isn't a right answer, certainly not a single one. Perhaps the nearest comes from a novelist (Oxford, of course) – 'it doesn't matter what the professors teach, it's what the *place* teaches ...'

Mea Culpa

At Cambridge they tried to teach us 'Oxford history' – getting the dates right. I have tried to get the dates right. (*Pace* that oracle for American tourists – Fodor's – the Radcliffe Camera is of the eighteenth century, not the seventeenth and Christ Church is *never* referred to as Christ Church College.) It is, of course, perfectly possible to get all the facts right and the story wrong. The reader must judge. This is a book to introduce you to those who can take you further and to discover Oxford as a starting-point for endless odysseys, to show that Oxford remains true to its origins – not so much an institution as an adventure of the mind.

CHAPTER ONE

Beginnings

Oxford is so beautiful still that only those who know her history are sensible of any loss...

E.A. Greening Lamborn 1936

Apollo. Brutus. Olenus Calenus. Mempric. Vortimer. Merlin. King Alfred the Great. Take your pick for the founder of Oxford. All have been claimed to be at some time. In 1381 University College forged a charter from Alfred to win a legal case. Three and a half centuries later the forgery was upheld in an English court of law as genuine. In 1872 the same college solemnly celebrated the millennium of its foundation. E.A. Freeman, the Trinity College historian, declined to attend but sent over a burnt piece of cake by way of congratulation. The mysterious Alfred Jewel (genuine) does, however, remain one of the great treasures of the Ashmolean Museum.

Oxford's origins – defensive, religious, cultural and commercial – have defined its characteristics: traditionally defensive of religion and more recently commercially cultural. Its setting between two rivers has made Oxford periodically liable to severe flooding but by the same token has inhibited city centre building to preserve an archipelago of open green spaces, which provide enchantment to visitors and a relief to residents.

Romans and Saxons

The University of Oxford has no founder as such. The town of Oxford ditto, though Alfred's claim to that honour would be more plausible. Port Meadow and the University Parks area have yielded neolithic tools and arrowheads and evidence of Bronze and Iron Age barrows and ditches. There are fragmentary Roman remains along the line of the present Banbury Road but there was no significant settlement nearer than the present Blackbird Leys housing estate to the south-east, though there was large-scale pottery production below Shotover. Wares produced there have been discovered as far away as Paris, Bruges and Scotland. A pot to be seen in the Museum of Oxford bears a legend incorporating what may claim to be the earliest local name – TAMESIBUGUS FECIT ('Thamesdweller made [this]').

No major route traversed the site of today's city, Romans preferring to build along higher ground. The nearest artery was a mere by-road, six miles to the east, linking Dorchester to Bicester. When the Roman foundations of York, Chester, Bath and Lincoln were flourishing cities, Dorchester had also been a cathedral city for centuries and Abingdon was home to a great abbey but Oxford was still a swamp.

Headington may have been the locus of a Saxon royal estate. In 2001 preliminary excavations were made there to locate the site of a palace referred to in the *Anglo-Saxon Chronicle* as having been built there by Ethelred II ('the Unready' r.978–1016). But Oxford is first mentioned in the *Anglo-Saxon Chronicle* in 912 as *Oxnaforda*, the place where oxen are forded – hence the present city arms showing an ox above wavy blue lines. The ford referred to, though, may not have been, as is widely assumed, where Folly Bridge now stands, but at Hinksey Ferry. The city of Oxford itself took the date as canonical, celebrating its official millennium in 1912.

In that *Chronicle* entry the town of Oxford is bracketed with London in a single sentence as both being under the authority of King Edward the Elder (r.899–924), son and successor of Alfred the Great (r.871–99). While this need not imply anything like equality of size or importance between London and Oxford it does suggest that Oxford was already a well-established settlement when its existence was first documented. It was Edward the Elder who was probably responsible for strengthening the fortifications and laying out a rudimentary grid-plan of streets; a coin of his reign has been found in New Inn Hall Street. The streets of the Saxon city, smaller and squarer than the medieval walled settlement which succeeded it, centred on Carfax, which has remained Oxford's notional centre ever since. Carfax, which manages to sound both antique and hi-tech at the same time, takes its name from the Latin *quadrifurcus*, four forks; in French the same etymology yields *carrefour*, crossroads.

Low-lying land was more attractive to the Anglo-Saxons than it had been to the Romans. Lacking the engineering and organisational skills to build Roman-style roads, they regarded rivers as useful transport links, as well as potential boundaries or barriers. The site of Oxford, with the Thames and Cherwell bounding it on three sides, may have been valued both for its accessibility and its potential defensibility. It certainly for some considerable time marked the border of the large contending kingdoms of Mercia and Wessex, although scholars have disagreed about whether the original core settlement was south or north of the Thames. The Saxon layer of settlement lies roughly four metres below the present street-level for those who would settle the matter.

As a confluence of rivers and roads marked by a defensible settlement the site would also have commercial potential as a place for consumption and exchange.

The fact that King Athelstan (r.924–39) established a mint at Oxford in 925 would certainly imply this. The later Anglo-Saxons used the word 'port', borrowed from Charlemagne's empire, to mean not a seaport but a market centre, whether on the coast or inland. When a visiting American scholar asked E.A. Freeman to show him Oxford's 'most ancient monument' he pointed to Port Meadow. While nowadays this may constitute what archaeologists call 'a significant void' a thousand years ago it was busy with barter and banter and significant enough to be mentioned in Domesday Book (1086) as where 'all the burgesses of Oxford have a pasture outside the city wall in common, which pays 6s. 8d.'

A Saint and Second Sight

The existence of a local saint might also have helped Oxford grow as a place of pilgrimage. St Frideswide (?680–735) (pronounced to rhyme as Fried-swide) appears to have been cast in the mould of those Saxon touch-me-not princesses, like Etheldreda (d.679), foundress of Ely Abbey, who accepted their duty to marry for political purposes – but only on condition that they could remain virgins. Etheldreda pulled this off twice without apparent recourse to supernatural intervention. For Frideswide the story was a little different. Pursued by a particularly persistent prince, Algar (aka Ulfgar), the Dark Age Turandot fled to the forest (or a pigsty by other account) at Binsey. As Algar closed in on his marital quarry he was suddenly struck blind by a thunderbolt – until Frideswide gave new meaning to the term 'second sight' by restoring his vision with water from a holy well – allegedly the one in Binsey churchyard – which appeared in response to her prayers. Taking this heavy hint to heart, the prince decamped and Frideswide encamped, allegedly founding a double monastery, where monks and nuns lived side by side, though in separate communities. The earliest surviving account of these happenings dates from some four centuries later, in the chronicle of William of Malmesbury, written *c.* 1125. Stripped of the legend's fanciful trimmings even the sceptical doyen of early historians of university life, Dr Hastings Rashdall, found in it a 'germ of historical fact', suggesting that Oxford was already a settled site by the eighth century. More modern scholarship inclines to the view that Frideswide was a real person and that there was a monastery where Christ Church now stands from *c.* 700. The supposed healing qualities of the holy well in Binsey churchyard attracted medieval pilgrims, among whom such miraculous waters were generically known as 'treacle' – hence Lewis

St Frideswide, patron saint of the city and university

Carroll's fanciful appropriation of the notion for the story told by the Dormouse in *Alice* in which three little sisters lived at the bottom of 'a treacle-well'. Frideswide's tomb in what is now Christ Church Cathedral marks the *likely* site of her religious foundation, given that her relics were translated in 1180 and again in 1289, the probable date of her once elaborate tomb.

Frideswide's career was no less eventful in death. The invocation of her name by an Oxford carpenter in Chaucer's *Miller's Tale* shows the strength of her reputation six and a half centuries after her demise. The attribution of miracles at her shrine led to the emergence of a significant twice-yearly cultic celebration (Feast, 19 October, Translation 12 February) and her adoption as patron of the university some time before 1434. The dissolution of the monasteries led to the trashing of her tomb in 1538. Briefly restored under Mary, the grave was even more thoroughly desecrated in 1558 when her relics were deliberately mixed with those of Catharine Dammartin, ex-nun and late wife of former Austin canon and Regius Professor of Divinity, Peter Martyr Vermigli. The mixed remains remain as remaindered. Part of the shattered shrine has been reconstructed from fragments found in a well at Christ Church. Its carvings of oak and ivy, sycamore and vine recall the saint's sylvan refuge. In the Latin Chapel an early (1859) example of the work of Burne-Jones commemorates Frideswide in stained-glass.

Danes and Normans

As a fortified *burh* Oxford was part of a chain of thirty-such established by Alfred to mark the contested boundary between the realms of the Anglo-Saxons to the south and west and the Viking-occupied Danelaw to the north and east. Initially the rivalry was religious as well as ethnic and political. The Christianisation of the Danes encouraged an intermingling of populations but removed only one strand of friction. In 979 Danes raided and fired Oxford. In 1002 on St Bryce's Day, at the behest of Ethelred II 'the Unready' (the 'Redeless', i.e. without wise advice), the inhabitants of Oxford slaughtered their local Danish neighbours, burning down St Frideswide's when they sought refuge there. The Danes obligingly reciprocated with two massacres of Oxford townsfolk in 1009 and 1013.

Despite such unpromising beginnings Oxford was then launched on a career – now approaching its millennium – as a conference centre. Ethelred held an Oxford *gemot* (great council) in 1015, at which hospitality was conspicuous by its absence, two great lords, Sigeferth and Morcar, being impeached for treason and put to death. In 1016 King Edmund Ironside (r.1016) died in Oxford after a reign of months. In 1018 the Danish Knut (Canute) also held a *gemot*, at which both leading Danes and Englishmen vowed to live in peace under the good laws of King Edgar's day. Knut's son Harold, usurping the throne from his absentee half-brother Harthacanute, was crowned at Oxford in 1037 and also died there three years later. In 1065 Edward the Confessor met rebels supporting Earl Morcar (another one) at Oxford to conduct negotiations. The only surviving architectural remnant of this turbulent era, and the oldest extant building in Oxford, is the rubble tower of St Michael's, Northgate, at the northern end of Cornmarket, which doubled up as a look-out point and part of the city defences.

Domesday Book records a still desolated community. Although it covered 127 acres and had eight churches and a population upwards of 2,000, of Oxford's thousand-plus houses, three hundred were exempt from local taxes in return for labour service to repair and maintain the city's defences. Of the seven hundred and twenty-one houses deemed 'geldable' (i.e. liable to taxes) no less than four hundred and seventy-eight were in ruins. One suggestion is that, rather than representing the impact of yet another fire or epidemic, these surplus properties witness a restoration of order to the region and its consequent abandonment by many who had taken refuge within its defences. Whatever the cause of the ruins, it was rapidly remedied. The Norman governor, Robert d'Oilly, was a proactive, if peremptory, rebuilder. The castle mound, raised in 1071, was achieved at the cost of levelling Oxford's western suburb and diverting a road. The castle eventually built on it was encircled by five towers and a moat. D'Oilly also built bridges where Magdalen and Folly (a corruption of his name) bridges now stand, the latter approached by an arched stone causeway of impressive length, one of the earliest in medieval Europe. The defences of Oxford castle

The Norman tower of the castle begun in 1071 by Robert d'Oilly

were to be slighted by Parliamentary forces after the expulsion of the Royalist garrison in 1646 and much that remained after that was cleared to make way for the county gaol in 1805. The road beside it was cut through in 1770, obliterating what had once been the castle's outer courtyard. The mound remains, however, as do the tower and crypt of the vanished church of St George-in-the-Castle (1074), one of the first to be dedicated to England's future patron saint.

The Normans came not only as conquerors but as religious reformers, whose zeal solidified into stone. A college of canons was attached to the chapel of Oxford castle. St Frideswide's was refounded in 1122. In 1129 at Osney, more or less where Oxford's first railway station would stand, another Robert d'Oilly, nephew of the first, founded a priory, which was to be up-graded to an abbey, the third largest in the country, in 1154. It figures in the memorial to its last abbot, Robert King, in the south choir aisle of Christ Church Cathedral. A Binsey anchoress founded a Benedictine nunnery at Godstow around 1133. At St Cross, Holywell, part of the Norman chancel survives, as does the chancel and crypt of St Peter-in-the-East in Queen's Lane and there are Norman chancel arches at St Andrew, Headington and St James,

Cowley. But the most complete and, perhaps in view of its suburban location unexpected, Norman survivals – west front, south door and chancel arch – are at St. Mary, Iffley (1175–82).

While the Normans claimed to be bringing a renewed rigour to Christianity, they also brought in their wake a community of Jews. Banned from landownership and most trades, the Jews were virtually confined to money-lending, a sin for Christians, but the Christian God would consign them to Hell anyway as murderers of Christ. As Greening Lamborn drily observed in his sketch of Oxford's history 'they appear to have served the useful and still not obsolete function of advancing the expenses of a university course, to be repaid with interest when the borrower had taken his degree'. The interest rate was eventually capped at 43 per cent. Oxford's Jews built its earliest stone houses, doubtless for self-protection and to secure bonds of debt from the risk of fire. (A major fire in 1138 did inflict severe damage on the city.) Ironically, the Jews probably also helped finance the cathedral and Osney Abbey. The street running down from Carfax to the city's southern gate, now St Aldate's, was known as Great Jewry, being the heart of the community. The site of the Jews' cemetery is now covered by the Botanic Gardens. The path between the two is now known as Deadman's Walk. England's Jews were expelled by Edward I in 1290 and their general readmission as a community was not secured until 1656 under Cromwell. Oxford, however, by then already boasted England's first coffee-house, courtesy of its proprietor Jacob the Jew.

Royal Residents

Towards the end of his reign Henry I (r.1100–35) built a royal palace, Beaumont, immediately to the north of Oxford's city walls, where the Ashmolean Museum faces onto Beaumont Street. Henry certainly celebrated Easter there in 1133. Of that palace all that remains is the memory of its bowling green in the name of Gloucester Green, where Oxford's main Tourist Information Centre now stands and from which the walking tours of the Blue Badge guides depart. Henry also founded St Bartholomew's hospital, for lepers, out at Cowley Marsh, a prudent distance from the town; its surviving remains are seventeenth century, with fourteenth century details in the chapel.

Henry's literacy, a highly unusual monarchical achievement for the time, won him the nickname 'Beauclerk' and he is said to have enjoyed the conversation of learned men. Nor was literacy Henry's only conspicuous talent. Regrettably his prodigious output of bastards – at thirty-five an all-time British royal record – failed to give him a legitimate male heir and his attempt to secure the throne for his daughter Matilda by obliging the leading nobles to accept her succession on oath led, after his death, to broken oaths and civil war. The first surviving document relating to Oxford's Jews dates from 1141 and refers to a levy to help pay for the fighting. In 1142 Matilda's cousin and rival, Stephen of Blois, based himself in Beaumont during a three month siege of Oxford castle, where Matilda was immured. One snowy December night, however, the resourceful queen, wrapped in white, was lowered by ropes from the tower of St George-in-the-Castle and evaded Stephen's sentries to escape across the frozen river to Abingdon and safety.

Mutual exhaustion eventually brought the contending parties to a compromise, registered at Oxford, which put Matilda's son on the throne as Henry II (r.1154–89). A fiery, fidgety, fretful man, Henry ruled an empire stretching from the Pyrenees to the Scottish border and needed to be constantly on the move to assert his authority. But Beaumont remained a favoured residence, witnessing the birth of his son and successor, Richard I 'Coeur-de-Lion' (r.1189–99) in 1157. Richard's younger brother and successor John 'Lackland' (r.1199–1216) may also have been born at Beaumont or at the nearby hunting-lodge of Woodstock in 1166. Henry II's mistress 'Fair Rosamund' (? d.1176) was buried at Godstow, which proved to be the making of the place. What had been an insignificant nunnery acquired a new church in 1179 – consecrated in the presence of Henry II and the Archbishop of Canterbury – and was richly endowed with estates by the king and Rosamund's family, the Cliffords. St Hugh, Bishop of Lincoln, visited her grave in 1191 (after the king was safely dead) and found it adorned with silken hangings, lamps and candles. Given her openly adulterous relationship with the late king, the bishop ordered her resting-place to be removed from before the high altar and translated to the chapter house, where it was marked by a grimly punning Latin inscription to the effect that she might have been called Rosamund but she was not the Rose of the World – '*Hic jacet in tumulo Rosa mundi non Rosa munda; Non redolet sed olet quae redolere solet.*' (In this tomb lies a Rose fair but not pure. She no longer smells as sweetly as once she did.) Godstow nunnery eventually became a sort of finishing school for the daughters of Oxford's upper bourgeoisie. Whether its most famous 'old girl' was held up as an example to them must remain unknown

The year after John's birth Henry II was embroiled 'in a spat with his feudal overlord, the king of France, then protecting the exiled and recalcitrant Archbishop of Canterbury, Thomas Becket. As a result of this the 'nation' of English students at university in Paris was obliged to repatriate – either expelled or recalled or quite possibly both – most being attracted to Oxford.

STUDENTS BEFORE UNIVERSITY

As a university Oxford may lack a founder but it had several attractions as a focus. It lay at the heart of Britain's central lowlands, relatively easy to traverse by the standards of the time and not too far from international ports such as London to the east, Southampton to the south and Bristol to the west. It also had a royal residence, with its promise of patronage and preferment, and a significant concentration of religious houses, producers as well as consumers of learning or, at least, of books. Significantly this concentration of ecclesiastical wealth and manpower was located at the western extremity of the vast diocese of Lincoln, a factor which limited the scope for direct episcopal interference and left local churchmen that much more autonomy. Finally, it was a thriving town in its own right, the conclusive factor in Rashdall's eyes – 'Oxford must be content to accept its academic position as an accident of its commercial importance.' The Victorian historian J.R. Green was equally emphatic that 'Oxford had already seen five centuries of borough life before a student appeared. The university found it a busy, prosperous borough and reduced it to a cluster of lodging-houses.'

One Theobald of Etampes (Theobaldus Stampensis), who actually appears to have come from Caen, is known to have given lectures at

Oxford around 1117 and Robert Pullen (d.?1147) also did so *c.* 1133–8, before flying higher still to teach at Paris and gain a cardinal's hat in Rome. Around 1136 Geoffrey of Monmouth, then a canon of the college at Oxford castle, wrote his *History of the Kings of Britain*, which became a prime source for the legends of King Arthur. Giraldus Cambrensis (Gerald of Wales, Gerald de Barri) (?1146–1223) went to Oxford around 1186 to publicise his pioneering ethnography of Ireland because there 'more clerks were to be found and more clerkly than elsewhere.'

The clerical character of this society was all-embracing, as John Dougill has stressed – 'Learning took place solely within the parameters set by the church: teachers were all drawn from the ranks of the clergy, and students were essentially seminarists who wore the clerical tonsure and enjoyed the right to be tried by church courts.' J.R. Green invited his readers to imagine the decidedly 'unacademic' atmosphere of the days when academia was as anarchic as the kingdom under Stephen and Matilda – 'thousands of boys, huddled in bare lodging houses, clustering round teachers as poor as themselves in church porch and house porch, drinking, quarrelling, dicing, begging at the corners of streets.' Many students were indeed boys, barely into their teens. Finds of bone ice skates, whistles and chess pieces imply that youthful minds were not always bent on study.

Books, painfully copied by hand, were astronomically expensive. Even writing materials were beyond the reach of many. Lecturing, primarily the exegesis of theological texts, and disputation, complemented by rote learning and prodigious feats of memorisation, lay at the core of pedagogic orthodoxy. Latin was the universal language of learning in every subject, the *lingua franca* of every place of higher education in western Europe and, for the lucky few, the passport to earthly success in church and state. The fact that members of the university invariably spoke to one another in Latin, a language both incomprehensible to the townsfolk and indicative of social superiority, was, however, a source of irritation and friction between the two communities.

The medieval curriculum classically consisted of the 'seven liberal arts' arranged in two tiers. Students began with the *trivium* (three ways)

– whence our word 'trivia' – which consisted of grammar, logic and rhetoric and was intended to perfect the student's grasp of Latin and mastery of approved techniques of reasoning and persuasion. From this he proceeded to the *quadrivium*: arithmetic, geometry, astronomy and music. The Bachelor's degree was granted after four years and the Master's, giving licence to teach, after another three. All examinations took the form of verbal expositions and interrogations. Having covered this comprehensive grounding the graduate was ready to devote the next decade of his life to study law or 'the queen of sciences' – theology. This culminated in the achievement of a doctorate.

The most eminent of Oxford's early academics was also the university's first saint. Known as Edmund of Abingdon (*c.*1175–1240), he was the son of Reginald Rich, a wealthy merchant who became a monk. Devout from youth, Edmund studied grammar at Oxford then took the Arts course at Paris, returning to teach 'the new logic' (i.e. Aristotle) at Oxford. He subsequently became Archbishop of Canterbury (1233–40) and was canonised in 1246. St Edmund is depicted in a late thirteenth century window to be seen in St Michael, Northgate. A cult developed at his birthplace, Abingdon and St Edmund Hall is named for him. In 1269 'Teddy Hall' passed under the control of Osney Abbey and later became an adjunct of Queen's College. It finally achieved autonomy in 1957.

There were as yet no colleges as autonomous, self-governing institutions in which teachers exercised discipline over those they taught. Instead students congregated in 'halls' which were much more like 'dorms', offering cheap living through sharing chores, and also mutual protection against often hostile townsfolk. Unlike the future colleges, halls might be very transitory establishments. Some were run like co-operatives, with students electing their leadership. Others were run by graduate teachers seeking a subsidiary income. Still others were run as commercial enterprises, notably Jacob's Hall and Moyses' Hall, whose owners, as Jews, would have been excluded from teaching. The Jewish-owned halls were often superior, often up-graded from lath-and-plaster to stone. The number of halls probably peaked in the early fourteenth century when there were about one hundred and twenty of them. There were still over seventy in 1450, as against nine colleges. A century later only eight survived, as against thirteen colleges. Surviving halls, albeit much altered, include Beam Hall, Merton Street and Tackley's Inn at 90 High Street.

If Oxford began obscurely and evolved uncertainly it nearly ended ignominiously. In 1209 a student killed a townswoman with his bow and arrow, accidentally or otherwise. Enraged townsfolk strung up two students by way of retribution and the rest fled to Paris, to Reading and to Cambridge. For five years student life in Oxford was in limbo. In 1214 it was reinstated by a Papal Legate. Henceforth a Chancellor would be appointed to exercise authority over students and enforce reasonable rents and prices. In due course he acquired proctors, first mentioned in 1248, to assist him. Robert Grosseteste (d. 1253) became Chancellor *c.* 1224 and in 1240 began to issue interest-free loans to students. Of humble origins, Grosseteste was to prove a formidable scholar and an even more formidable churchman and protector of the infant University – in the commendatory words of the St Albans chronicler Matthew Paris 'the blamer of prelates, the corrector of monks, the director of priests, the instructor of clerks, the support of scholars, the preacher to the people, the persecutor of the licentious. . .'. In 1229 a further exodus of English students from Paris reinforced the re-established student body but by then an even more potent force than mere numbers had arrived to reinvigorate the stumbling rebirth of academic life – the friars.

Enter the Friars

Monks, supposedly at least, lived in closed communities, dedicating their lives to worship and study. The friar represented an ecclesiastical innovation, a response to the twin challenges of heresy and the growth of urbanism, neither of which the traditional church structure, organised for an overwhelmingly rural society, seemed capable of meeting. Where scholars congregated in an urban setting – such as Oxford – the challenge was redoubled by its compound nature.

Friars, fortified by a renewed dedication to the ancient monastic ideal of personal poverty, were intended to combine an exemplary life-style with, in the case of the Dominicans, finely honed communication skills, and, in the case of Franciscans, the healing touch, to win vulnerable laymen from the temptations of materialism, sin, despair and error. It is a tribute to Oxford's standing that both Dominicans, known as Blackfriars from the colour of their robes, and Franciscans, known similarly as Greyfriars, arrived in Oxford in the same year as they arrived in London, 1221 and 1224 respectively. Indeed, the Dominican house in Oxford was the first in England. A generation later came the Augustinian (Austin) friars (1252), who in 1268 founded a priory where Wadham College now stands. The Carmelites or White Friars (1256), settled on the west side of Stockwell Street until they were given the by then decayed royal palace of Beaumont in 1318. They were followed by the Trinitarians (1286), as well as by less durable brotherhoods, such as the Friars of the Sack (1262) and the Crutched Friars (1342), whose name came from the cross (Latin *crux*) which was their mark.

The Dominicans, having settled in St Edward's parish, built a small oratory and school dedicated to that patron saint and targeted their efforts towards the Jewish community. In 1233 Dominican Robert Bacon (d.1248), preaching before Henry III in Oxford, boldly told him to clear out the parasitic foreign clique at his court. The still youthful king rolled with the punch, although he ignored the advice, to his later cost. But he does not seem to have borne a grudge. In 1244, on the death of its Jewish owner, David of Oxford, Henry III gave the Dominicans the financier's former home, where the Town Hall now stands, as a *Domus Conversorum*, a refuge hostel for converts shunned by their former co-religionists, congregating in their synagogue a minute's walk to the south on the same side of the road. Royal favour bred further favours. From 1246 onwards a Dominican was appointed Royal Confessor. Four Oxford Dominicans went on to become cardinals. Of these Robert Kilwardby (d.1279) was the first friar to become Archbishop of Canterbury. By 1305 the Dominicans in Oxford numbered ninety-six but by the dissolution they had dwindled to fifteen.

The Franciscans, true to form, established themselves in St Ebbe's, the city's poorest and most wretched quarter, where they could minister to outcasts, lepers and the sick. The original four Greyfriars became forty by 1233. In 1317 there were eighty-four and by 1377 a hundred and three. Their large church, now beneath the Westgate shopping centre, was prestigious enough to be chosen as the burial-place of Richard, Earl of Cornwall, would-be king of Sicily and brother of Henry III.

Outstanding among the early Franciscans was *doctor illustris* Adam de Marisco (Adam Marsh) (?d.1247) from Somerset, whose sound judgment of men and matters made him the trusted adviser of figures as eminent as Boniface, Archbishop of Canterbury, Simon de Montfort and Grosseteste. Roger Bacon (see below) praised him as 'perfect in all knowledge and worthy to be classed with Solomon, Aristotle and Grosseteste'. Grosseteste, who himself, though not a friar, had taught Greyfriars for a decade, was an enthusiastic patron of the efforts of both Orders and wrote warmly of them to Pope Gregory IX. Spirituality apart – if that is not to miss the main point of the friars' mission – they also had a profound impact on the conduct of study, cheapening it by multiplying the number of teachers, and regularising it by obliging pupils to adapt their often chaotic ways to the disciplined and ordered routines of their mentors.

Considering that the Dominicans set themselves up as the intellectual vanguard of the new movement, it is ironic that the three most celebrated friar scholars at Oxford were all Franciscans – all of whom fell foul of authority. Roger Bacon (*c.*1214–?1294), possibly a nephew of Robert Bacon, who has been much confused with him, was a pupil of St Edmund of Abingdon. After studying in Paris, where his teaching won him the accolade *doctor admirabilis*, Bacon returned to Oxford around 1250, determined to summarise all science in the service of religion. He believed passionately that *Sine experientia nihil sufficienter scire potest* – Without experience nothing can be sufficiently known. Nearly six centuries later Charles Daubeny, Professor jointly of Botany and Rural Economy, had those words inscribed over the entrance of the laboratory he had had built at his own expense at the Botanic Gardens.

Bacon regarded the neglected study of mathematics as the key to all other science – 'he who knows not mathematics cannot know any other sciences: and what is more he cannot discover his own ignorance or find its proper remedies'. Making optics his own specialism, he studied rainbows and eclipses and described spectacles. Bacon was also the first European to describe how gunpowder is made and foresaw the possibility of motorised vehicles and flying machines. He is also credited with a wicked sense of humour by a traditional Oxford story which tells how a group of Cambridge scholars came to hold a disputation, intent on proving themselves more learned than their Oxford rivals. Bacon, warned of their approach, went to Oxford's outskirts disguised as a common thatcher and when they stopped to ask for directions, replied in Latin with a challenge to extempore versifying. Alarmed at such erudition in a common labourer the Cambridge men at once fled back to the Fens.

Living apart from his brethren, supposedly in the house on Folly Bridge which survived until 1779, Bacon was vulnerable to gossip. The daring of his speculations opened him to charges of heresy and dabbling in the black arts. He scarcely helped his case by an aggressive contempt for those he considered his intellectual inferiors. Franciscan discipline consigned him to Paris and confined him to physical imprisonment for long years, deprived of books and equipment, but he did eventually return to Oxford, where he died. His grave is unknown but there is a memorial plaque on a north wall of the car park in St Ebbe's. He was subsequently demonised in English literary tradition as Friar Bacon, conducting necromantic discourses with a brazen head and trouncing a rival 'Nigromancer' in Robert Greene's *Frier Bacon and Frier Bongay* (1594). In 1668 Samuel Pepys paid a shilling to see round 'Friar Bacon's Study' on Folly Bridge. Three centuries later Bacon was revived as the central character of *Doctor Mirabilis* (1964) a novel by *Star Trek* author James Blish, who had settled in Oxford as a would-be acolyte of C.S. Lewis.

John Duns Scotus (?1265–1308) taught at Oxford, Paris, Cambridge and Cologne, his movements being as much determined by potential persecution as by promotion. Commenting critically on the prevailing reliance on Aristotle, he pioneered the doctrine of the Immaculate Conception, holding that will is superior to intellect and love to knowledge. The function of reason was less to prove God's existence than to explicate its consequences. Theology should thus be ranked as a practical science. Scotus also pioneered the comparative study of grammar beyond the confines of a single language. His dialectical skills won him the title '*doctor subtilis*' in his own lifetime but his philosophical disciples were to be ridiculed by sixteenth century English Reformers as 'dunses' for their defence of papal pretensions. Gerard Manley Hopkins and Martin Heidegger were among later admirers who thought otherwise. Hopkins, serving at the church of St Aloysius on the Woodstock Road in 1878 celebrated his metaphysical mentor in a poem, *Duns Scotus's Oxford*, whose opening lines have become a favourite invocation:

'Towery city and branchy between towers;
Cuckoo-echoing, bell-swarmed, lark-charmed, rook-racked, river-rounded;'

William of Ockham (or Occam) (?1285–?1349) – *doctor invincibilis* – was probably a pupil of Duns Scotus. He published many works on logic and is identified with the principle of 'Ockham's razor': whenever a simple theory explains a problem satisfactorily don't try to complicate it further.

By the fourteenth century the friars were increasingly on the defensive. Other academics accused them of scaring off students because parents had heard stories of friars trapping young lads into unwittingly swearing oaths which bound them to become friars on pain of damnation. And while the friars may have maintained their poverty in personal matters their piety and learning had attracted gifts which made them increasingly wealthy as communities. Richard Fitzralph of Balliol complained bitterly, with scarcely concealed jealousy, of the 'endlese wynnynges that thei geteth by beggyng' so that 'alle bookes beth y-bouht of freres' and 'everech covent of freres . . . and . . . everech frer . . . hath an huge librarye'. The brilliant controversialist John Wyclif likewise blamed the friars for driving him out of Oxford.

The 'Graye Fryars Paradise' (i.e. enclosed garden) of five acres, given to them by Henry III in 1244, survived to serve as a nursery during the food-pinched civil war years of the 1640s. By 1710 it was one of the few features of Oxford to please the hypercritical visitor von Uffenbach, having metamorphosed yet again to become the beer garden of a tavern – 'at the back of which, on the water, are countless little boxes, partitioned by hedges, where the fellows drink in summer'. It was later built over to become Paradise Square and finally disappeared under the

Westgate shopping development, remembered only by a plaque in Old Greyfriars Street. The Carmelites echo only in Friar's Entry, the passageway beside Debenham's department store.

The Greyfriars returned to Oxford in 1905 as Capuchins, a reformed branch of the Order, the colour of whose hoods is now familiar to students as cappucino. Their friary, St Anselm's in St John Street, was recognised by the university as a House of Studies in 1910. In 1919 they moved to new premises, Grosseteste House, in the Iffley Road and in 1931 built a new Greyfriars on the other side of the road. Since 1957 this has been recognised as a Permanent Private Hall. As a self-governing college it selects its own students, giving priority to Franciscans but accepting members of other Orders and secular students.

The Dominicans returned through the extraordinary efforts of Father Bede Jarrett, a graduate of St Benet's Hall, who enlisted a string of supporters ranging from wealthy Americans like Mrs Jefferson Tytus to King Alfonso XIII of Spain and Pope Benedict XV and was thus able to buy 62–64 St Giles and build a chapel next to it. Blackfriars, the Priory of the Holy Spirit opened in 1929 but was not completed until 1954.

The Coming of the Colleges

'For an Oxford man, Oxford is primarily his college'
Dacre Balsdon *Oxford Then and Now* (1970)

Three colleges dispute precedence as the oldest. Generations of tourist guides have memorised them by the convenient acronym BUM – Balliol, University and Merton. Resolving the contention as to which came first is confused by the question 'first what?' – first proclaimed? first with actual scholars? or statutes? or permanent buildings? or buildings on the same site still occupied?

Balliol supposedly traces its origins to an insult. John de Balliol, lord of Barnard Castle in the then wild north-east, disputed some lands with the Prince-Bishop of Durham, who was not, as his imposing title implies, a figure to cross lightly. Impatience gave way to insult which was rewarded with the penance of an act of charity – viz. the main-

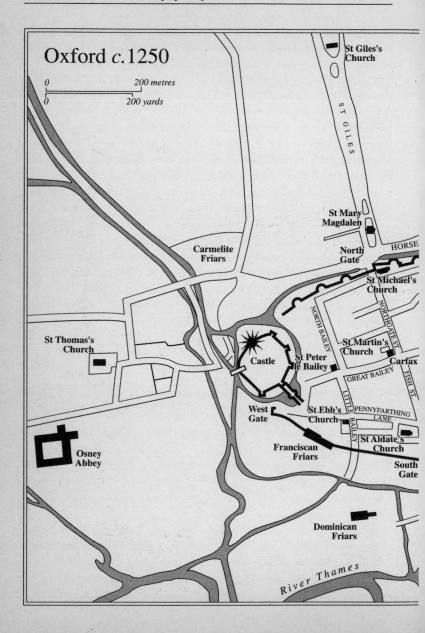

Oxford *c.* 1250

0   200 metres
0   200 yards

St Giles's
Church

ST GILES

St Mary
Magdalen

HORSE

North
Gate

Carmelite
Friars

St Michael's
Church

NORTH BAILEY

NORTHGATE ST

St Thomas's
Church

Castle

St Peter
le Bailey

St Martin's
Church

Carfax

FISH ST

GREAT BAILEY

LITTLE BAILEY

West
Gate

St Ebb's
Church

PENNYFARTHING
LANE

St Aldate's
Church

Franciscan
Friars

Osney
Abbey

South
Gate

Dominican
Friars

River Thames

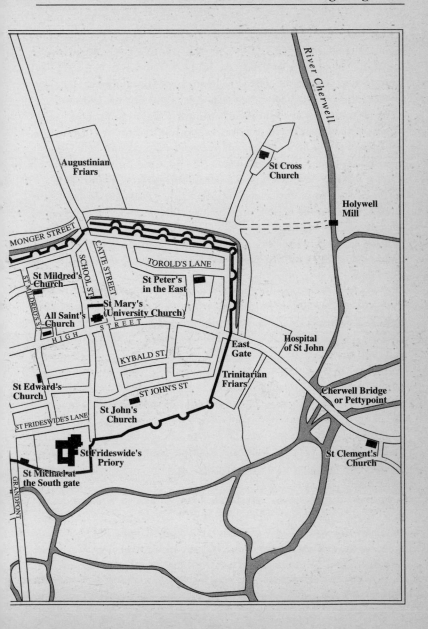

tenance of poor scholars in Oxford. Tradition claims this originally involved renting a house in 1263, just outside of the city walls where the Master's lodging now stands. By 1266 there were certainly scholars living where the present college is. In terms of continuous occupation of site it thus ranks oldest. Balliol died in 1269 but his widow Dervorguilla remained an enthusiastic patroness of the venture and secured its future by further grants, the formulation of statutes of organisation (1282) and the building of accommodation, New Balliol Hall (1284), near the site of the present chapel.

University College also originated from the north-east, with William of Durham's munificent bequest of 310 marks (£206.13s.4d.) in 1249 to buy property, the rents from which were to support ten or twelve Masters of Arts studying Divinity. A property known as *Aula Universitatis* (University Hall) was acquired in 1253. In terms of having the earliest benefactor and first property University College thus ranks as the oldest.

It was Walter de Merton (d.1277), possibly a pupil of Adam Marsh and twice Chancellor of England and Bishop of Rochester, who first recognised that students could disperse and buildings decay or be sold off . What would in fact secure the permanence of an institution and its autonomy as fully self-governing, with control of its own administration and assets, was the seemingly flimsy device of words on paper (actually vellum) with legally binding force. In terms of Merton's first statutes of 1264 his college therefore ranks as the oldest. The statutes also set a model for others and were immediately imitated in the foundation of Peterhouse at Cambridge and by Exeter, Oriel and Queen's later at Oxford. Merton's example doubtless also prompted Balliol and University College to set their own houses in order, legally speaking.

Merton was, moreover, far better funded than its peers and was already supporting over thirty fellows by 1300, whereas 'Univ.' remained so poor that its very existence seemed imperilled at times. Built on the site of a stone house bought from Jacob son of Moses, Merton further boasts Oxford's oldest library, its first tower, its first quadrangle, Mob Quad (the name, of unknown origin, dates from the eighteenth century) and a chapel on a scale to dwarf most parish churches of the period. Admittedly Mob Quad was achieved piecemeal between 1304 and 1378 but the quadrangle became fundamental to college design. It moderated outside noise and the worst effects of wind and rain and offered privacy and security. The quadrangle concept was later extended from colleges to hospitals and almshouses, as at Ewelme (see below).

By 1300 Oxford's academic community numbered perhaps fifteen hundred, still mostly operating in hired premises. Three more colleges were to be founded in the first half of the fourteenth century, all still for masters and graduates. Exeter (1314) was the creation of the bishop of that city, Walter de Stapledon, a Devon man and Oxford graduate, who rose high in the service of Edward II until he was murdered by the enemies of that feckless, luckless monarch. The college statutes restricted recruitment to the diocese of Exeter and the field of study to philosophy, the founder's intentions being to provide trained manpower for his poor native province rather than a springboard for academic stardom. Inadequately funded into the bargain, Exeter was, therefore, compared with Merton, long doomed to a marginal role in the life of the university as a whole, forcing its best talents to switch

The university seal showing the Chancellor in academic dress with three scholars on either side of him and six below. It dates from the late thirteenth century

allegiance to other, better-financed, less restrictive colleges. Oriel (1326) was initially founded by another servant of Edward II, Adam de Brome, and subsequently re-founded by the king himself, thus becoming the first Oxford college with a royal founder. Basing his statutes on those of Merton, de Brome specifically directed Fellows towards the higher faculties, Law and Theology, barred to Exeter men, and thus clearly intended to groom high-flyers for careers in the service of church and state.

Queen's (1341) was named for Philippa of Hainault, Flemish consort of Edward III, by its founder and her chaplain, Robert Eglesfeld, a Cumberland man. His statutes went into very elaborate detail, down to matters of dress, diet and accounting and reveal a clear bias towards those, like himself, who were from a poor background and from Cumberland and the neighbouring county of Westmorland – or were his actual kin or their descendants or were natives of places where the college held property. Despite the founder's skill in acquiring a spacious site and mobilising an impressive line-up of sponsors and donors Queen's got off to a slow start thanks to the very legal entanglements that the gifts of its supporters brought in their train. By excluding most of the available pool of national talent the 'two counties' bias condemned the college to a somewhat somnolent existence.

Whatever their differences all these colleges shared one fundamental characteristic: they were only for graduates. Undergraduates still lived in the halls which continued to proliferate.

The newfangled colleges were complemented by the establishment of study centres to house Benedictine communities then attempting to revive the ancient but decayed tradition of monastic scholarship. Gloucester College (1283), technically a cell of Gloucester Abbey, was situated where Worcester College now stands and served the fifteen houses of the Order's southern province. A row of fifteenth century *camerae* (chambers) can still be seen in the gardens at Worcester. Durham College (1291), on the site of Trinity, served the Benedictines' northern province, supported by the Prior of Durham. Canterbury College (1331) was exclusively for clergy from that Cathedral Priory; the site it occupied from 1362 was subsequently absorbed by Christ Church. The Augustinians sent monks to Oxford long before they had a college, holding chapter-meetings in St Frideswide's from 1371 onwards. In 1435 they were finally given a large detached townhouse in what is now New Inn Hall Street as St Mary's College, though its adaptation only seems to have been completed just in time for the dissolution. In 1899 the Benedictines were re-established, as an off-shoot of Ampleforth Abbey, now better known as an outstanding Roman Catholic school. From 1918 their re-instituted establishment in Oxford was known as St Benet's Hall, finding a permanent home in a former Ursuline convent at 38–9 St Giles in 1922. Basil Hume, much-beloved Cardinal Archbishop of Westminster, graduated from St Benet's in 1947.

Expansion

For the two centuries after Henry II's accession the expansion of the university boosted the expansion of a town which was already bene-fiting from the expansion of the English economy as a whole. Oxford also continued to benefit from its role as an occasional conference centre and royal residence. Henry II summoned the Welsh princes to appear before him at Oxford in 1177. King John held councils at Oxford in 1204, 1205 and 1215. In 1264 Henry III passed most of Lent in the house of the Dominicans. Edward I was in residence in 1275, 1280, 1283 and 1290.

As far as its non-academic inhabitants were concerned Oxford was also a major market centre for a thriving agricultural region whose products generated the usual processing industries of brewing, baking, tanning and clothmaking. The town's guilds of weavers and shoe-makers were among England's earliest. In 1155 Henry II confirmed Oxford's right to a guild merchant, dating from the reign of Henry I, to control its commerce and to have 'all other customs and liberties and laws of their own which they have in common with my citizens of London.' In 1199 King John granted the townsmen of Oxford a charter vesting the government of the town in a Mayor and two aldermen. Oxford's Mayor, moreover, was to share with the Lord Mayor of London the honour of serving as butler at the Coronation Feast of all future kings of England. Oxford's municipal rights became something of a model, adopted as the basis of corporate charters by places as far apart as Marlborough, Bedford, Portsmouth and Great Yarmouth.

Thirteenth century Oxford had some eighteen churches and a population in the region of five thousand. Growing local wealth funded the rebuilding of St Frideswide's (*c.*1180–1210) and Osney Abbey (1247), the reconstruction of stout city walls (1226–40), the relocation and rebuilding (1232–57) of the Hospital of St John the Baptist by the Jews' cemetery, the building of the still surviving tower of St Martin, Carfax, the erection of the tower and spire on the university church of St Mary's in the High Street and the construction next to it of the Congregation House, which served as an embryonic administration centre and treasury for the expanding university. Henry III's brother, Richard of Cornwall, founded Rewley Abbey in about 1280, beyond Gloucester College, as a scholarly retreat for Cistercian monks. Even the Mitre Hotel boasts a rib-vaulted cellar dating back to the expansive thirteenth century.

Oxford's ambitious building projects employed stone-masons, carpenters, metal-workers and makers of stained-glass. In addition the peculiar demands of university life supported bookbinders, parchment-makers and manuscript painters. One of the latter was William de Brailes, who worked *c.* 1230–60 in Catte Street, the heart of the Oxford book trade. A property deed names him with three illuminators, three bookbinders and a parchment-maker. William headed an *atelier* which produced the earliest surviving fully illustrated English *Book of Hours*. His workshop is the first known example to be dated and located of the sort of establishment which emerged to challenge the monastic monopoly on manuscript decoration and to accept commissions from lay as well as ecclesiastical patrons. Increasingly the specialist crafts would marginalise the everyday ones. In twelfth century Oxford there were sixty weavers, by 1270 only fifteen. The clothiers of the Cotswolds were taking over the woollen trade and the academic cuckoo was taking over the urban nest.

CONTRACTION

The Black Death, a global pandemic of bubonic and pneumonic plague which devastated Europe in 1348–9, may have carried off a third of the population, though in Oxford itself the death-rate may only have been a quarter. The number of students, however, is estimated to have fallen from perhaps 1,500 in the thirteenth century to six hundred by the 1350s – and the plague came again in 1361. The mortality rate of literate clergy may also have been disproportionately high. This might reflect either an heroic willingness to minister to the dying, involving a correspondingly higher risk of exposure to infection, or it may have been a consequence of monastic confinement, which meant that when a single member of a community was struck down, his fellows soon followed. In Oxford disputatious Trinitarian friars seem to have succumbed to the unarguable force of infection in 1349. The 1361 outbreak evidently created such a critical shortfall in literate manpower that the courts of the land were induced to drop archaic law French in favour of plain English. In the longer run the impoverishment of university life, intellectually if not materially, would be compounded by the debilitating Hundred Years War (1338–1453) with France, which disrupted scholarly ties between English and foreign universities and greatly diminished the inflow of foreign students and teachers. Nor could the colleges, as estate-holders, entirely escape the impact on their rental incomes of a diminished and discontented rural labour force. Oxford itself would slip far behind as a provincial centre. In terms of taxable wealth Oxford ranked eighth after London in 1344. By 1523 it was twenty-ninth. The lay subsidy of 1380 reveals the extent to which the city's economic profile had already become subservient to the needs of the university. The most numerous occupations, as elsewhere, were naturally related to sustenance and apparel. The former gave employment to forty manciples, thirty brewers, seventeen bakers and seven grocers and spicers. The fact that there were more fishmongers (18) than butchers (16) suggests a large clerical population observant of the dietary laws which made half the days of the year 'fish days'. Keeping up appearances employed forty-one tailors, eleven drapers and mercers, eight glovers and ten barbers, complemented by an unstated number of laundresses and 'sutrices' (sewing-women). The business of keeping folk shod was divided between a dozen cordwainers, who worked in fine (Cordovan) leather and nine cobblers who serviced the proletarian end of the trade. Building employed nine masons and a dozen slaters.

Specialised collegiate and ecclesiastical needs were met by two dozen parchment makers, ten booksellers and stationers, ten chandlers (suppliers of candles) and half a dozen goldsmiths. Other specialised trades included three bowyers, daubers (plasterers), harpers, leeches (doctors), limneours (manuscript painters) and 'Garlic-mongers'.

'Slay! Slay! Havoc! Havoc!'

Even when Oxford was thriving and prosperous the concentration within its walls of a large number of young men, many possessed of what the Scots call 'a guid conceit' of themselves, plus a proclivity for alcohol, always contained the potential for large-scale disorder. The imposition of price controls implicitly subsidised the student body and was thus another permanent source of grievance among those whose main concern was simply to get a living. Blood was drawn in a Town/Gown skirmish in 1228 and arson ensued in another in 1236. In 1238 Chancellor Grosseteste was obliged to offer his protection to students involved in an affray at Osney Abbey, where the papal legate was staying. The legate had to flee and his brother was killed. In 1244 the Jews became the focus of attack. As a result the Chancellor's jurisdiction was enlarged to give him exclusive jurisdiction over student debts and contracts, interest rates and the prices and quality of goods sold to scholars. He also gained the powers of a justice of the peace, to fine, banish or imprison in the royal gaol in Oxford castle. Another pogrom occurred in 1268, allegedly caused by a Jewish insult to a Christian religious procession, which seems somewhat unlikely, the more so as the Jews were already on the defensive, losing royal favour and subjected to increasingly arbitrary mulcts as their numbers dwindled. In 1298 another major Town/Gown dispute led to several deaths, townsmen having complained to the king that many who passed themselves off as Oxford 'clerks' were in fact outlaws on the run. Given the limited extent of the collegiate structure, the rudimentary nature of the university's embryonic 'central administration' and the anarchic profusion of halls there is nothing inherently improbable in this.

Students were also quite capable of brutal quarrels amongst themselves, usually on North vs South lines, as in 1252, 1274 and 1334.

Scots naturally allied themselves with the North, while the Welsh and Irish ranked themselves with the South. As a result it became customary to choose proctors from North and South in alternate years to assure visible impartiality in the enforcement of order. The worst ever such incident in Oxford's history is referred to as a riot but in terms of scale and ferocity it was more like a civil war in miniature. The year was 1355, in the immediate aftermath of the Black Death, with the town and surrounding villages still severely dislocated. Official attempts to stabilise conditions by reimposing strict wage and price controls created further tension. The trouble began on Tuesday 10 February, the Feast of St Scholastica the Virgin. Scholars drinking in the Swyndelstock tavern at the corner of Queen Street and St Aldate's exchanged 'snappish words' and 'saucy language' with John de Croydon over the quality of the wine he served them. The disgruntled patrons then threw both the wine – and the jug it came in – at their host's head. Family and neighbours rallied round the outraged tavern-keeper and soon the town bell at St Martin's was ringing a call to arms, while townsmen set about any unarmed student within reach. The Chancellor 'perceiving what great danger they were in caused the University bell at St Mary's to be rung out, whereupon the Scholars got bows and arrows and maintained the fight till dark night, at which time the fray ceased, no one Scholar or Townsmen being killed . . .'. Yet.

The long chilly February night failed to cool passions thus roused. Overnight the town bailiffs forewarned householders to turn out again when the town tocsin next rang out. They also called in reinforcements from the surrounding countryside. On the Wednesday morning a band of townsmen broke up a theology lecture and eighty bowmen attacked scholars strolling around St Giles. Both bells then rang out, summoning the respective sides to combat. Scholars managed to block some of the gates to keep out rural reinforcements until early evening, when they at last poured in at the west gate and the defenders fled to their lodgings as the invaders cried 'Slay! Slay! Havoc! Havoc! . . . Smite fast. Give good knocks.' Five student hostels were broken into 'with fire and sword', their residents 'killed or maimed or grievously wounded' and their contents stolen, smashed or trampled. Once again the violence ended only at nightfall.

On Thursday morning the scholars, completely cowed, feared to venture into the streets and the townspeople, scenting victory, gathered in even greater numbers to continue the ransack, forcing their way into fourteen locked lodgings 'with iron bars and other engines'. Resisters were dealt with mercilessly and their corpses 'scornfully cast into houses of easement, others they buried in dunghills'. Chaplains were a particular target, several being scalped of their tonsures. By early afternoon, the terror had run its course, 'all the Scholars being fled divers ways'. Sixty-three students and an unknown number of townspeople had died. Given the power and privileges of the university, royal retribution was certain and severe. Control over the town's inns and market was transferred to the university, as was the power to police the streets by night. In addition the Mayor and sixty-two townsmen were ordered to attend a solemn memorial service for the souls of the dead on St Scholastica's day the following year – and every year thereafter. They were also obliged to swear an annual oath to acknowledge the university's rights and privileges, confirmed and extended by a new charter dated 27 June 1355. The penitential ceremony was amended in form at the Reformation and suspended during the Civil War but not finally abolished until 1825. St Scholastica, interestingly, is the patron saint of convulsive children.

A New Beginning

In Oxford, as elsewhere, repeated visitations of disease led to economic depression and depopulation, so much so that a substantial tract of land in the very heart of the town became available for redevelopment. A panel of townsmen 'swore that it was not to the damage of the King or the said town if certain void plots of ground lying under the town wall were procured ... (being) ... full of filth, dirt and stinking carcasses to the great detriment of all men that passed that way, and that also there was a concourse of malefactors, murderers, harlots and thieves to the great damage of the town and that scholars and others were often wounded, killed and lost, and that all the said plots of ground amounting to several acres lay waste and had been for a long time deserted from the inhabiting of any person.'

William of Wykeham, Bishop of Winchester and Chancellor of England, who founded New College in 1379

New College (1379) was originally dedicated to the Virgin Mary, as was Oriel, so the distinguishing epithet 'New' has survived ever since. Its creator William of Wykeham (1324–1404), Bishop of the country's richest see, Winchester, and Chancellor of England, was explicitly concerned to address the crisis of educated manpower afflicting the realm by producing 'men of learning fruitful to the church'. To this end he introduced two revolutionary innovations. Undergraduates would be admitted to live alongside graduates and fellows and a secondary foundation, in Winchester, would be simultaneously established as a 'feeder' to supply those undergraduates. Winchester grew to become one of the great public schools which was to dominate Oxford's undergraduate intake in later centuries. It certainly dominated New College, providing all its undergraduates until the middle of the nineteenth century.

William of Wykeham was, moreover, insofar as the profession existed, a trained project manager, having supervised extensive building work at Windsor Castle. As a result, whereas Merton evolved, New College was designed and, in its ordered design set a widely followed model for succeeding centuries. All major buildings were set round a single quadrangle. Hall and chapel were built back-to-back. The distinctive T-shaped chapel provided an ante-chapel to be used for meetings or formal academic disputations. There was a brewhouse, a bakehouse, a bell-tower and a garden. The cloister, another distinctive innovation, surrounded a central garden intended to double as orchard and graveyard, a perpetual *memento mori* for perambulating residents on days when it was too wet to use the garden for gentle exercise. The gateway, the only entrance and exit, was surmounted by rooms for the Warden who could thus cast an eagle eye over the comings and goings of his charges and colleagues.

Another novel feature of New College was the Long Room, a range of first-floor latrines built over a huge cesspit. Writing in the late seventeenth century Robert Plot, first superintendent of the Ashmolean Museum, still regarded it as 'stupendous . . . so large and deep that it has never been emptied since the foundation of the College, which

New College: Entrance gateway

was above three hundred years since, nor is it ever like to want it'. Actually he was wrong. College records show that it was emptied in 1485. The official visitors appointed to check over conditions in 1567 thought it needed scouring again. They also ordered that the practice of jettisoning urine from upper windows should cease forthwith. A century after this the University's gardener, Jacob Bobart was still praising the by-product of New College's 'house of office' as 'an excellent soil to fill up deep holes to plant young vines'.

Even with William of Wykeham's new foundation the combined membership of the colleges still numbered less than a hundred out of a total university population of perhaps fifteen times that many. Had all the colleges perished the University would have remained, though it would have developed a very different character. As it was the colleges expanded, often by fits and starts, but inexorably. A guide can point to dozens of sites where houses were demolished to make way for a college building but none where defunct college property was permanently returned to town use.

A Turbulent Priest

Beyond the fact that he was a Yorkshireman the origins of John Wyclif (?1330–84) are obscure. He was at Oxford by 1356 and became Master of Balliol by 1361 but soon resigned to take the living of Fillingham in Lincolnshire, then the choicest position in Balliol's gift. He may also have become warden of Canterbury College. In 1362 the university certainly petitioned the Pope to 'provide' for him and in 1363 and again in 1368 the Bishop of Lincoln permitted him to absent himself from Fillingham to study at Oxford, much of which time he appears to have passed in impoverished Queen's College – a fitting setting, given how his views were to unfold. In the latter year Wyclif exchanged his vicarage for the living at Ludgershall, Bucks. which was much nearer Oxford. By 1372 he had become a doctor of divinity and in 1374 was awarded the rectory of Lutterworth in Leicestershire. He was also appointed by Edward III (r.1327–77) as a member of a delegation sent to Bruges to contest with representatives of Pope Gregory XI the thorny question of papal rights of taxation and appointment in England. Wyclif took the royalist line, buttressing patriotic interests with a complex and subtle line of theological reasoning. Wyclif's theological sincerity need not be doubted but his arguments could obviously be politically useful to secular princes who judged themselves the appropriate instruments to rid the Church of the surplus assets which undermined its spiritual authority. One such was Edward III's son, John of Gaunt (i.e. Ghent) (1340–99), who increasingly protected Wyclif from the consequences of utterances which scarcely endeared him to more worldly churchmen, such as William of Wykeham – who happened to be a political opponent of John of Gaunt. In 1377 king and parliament consulted Wyclif on the legality of withholding taxes from the Pope. Wyclif affirmed its legality. Unsurprisingly the Pope condemned his teachings and ordered his arrest. The English authorities, royal and academic, declined to act and Wyclif responded with a treatise, *On the Truth of Holy Writ* (1378), declaring the Bible to be the only true guide to the Divine Will. By implication this posited the need for a Bible in English which the laity could read for themselves rather than rely on its transmission via the agents of a corrupt Church. In 1379 Wyclif's *De Eucharistia* denied the doctrine of transubstantiation; even after its consecration bread remained bread and not the literal body of Christ, though Christ was present at the Mass, if not in bodily form. This attack on a central teaching of the Church, unlike the assault on its wealth, was in no one's material interests. Wyclif compounded his exposure by further venomous invective against ecclesiastical fat cats of every stripe, from cardinals to droning chantry priests. In 1380–1, back at Queen's, he planned an English translation of the Bible and envisaged an order of Poor Preachers who would shun churches to find their pulpits in highways and hedges, bringing God's Word to the simple folk.

In 1381 the simple folk rose in rebellion, from Hampshire to Cheshire. The epicentre of the great Peasants' Revolt lay along either side of the Thames estuary, in Essex and Kent, whence armies of peasants, enraged by the third poll tax in five years, and ex-servicemen, disgruntled by the incompetent conduct of the French wars, converged on London. Wyclif's teachings, as yet known only to the learned, cannot have been a cause of the revolt, but its slogans of millennarian egalitarianism were a dangerous echo of them and Wyclif's sympathy for the poor was well known. The rebels dragged the Archbishop of Canterbury, Simon of Sudbury, out of the Tower of London and struck off his head. Once the ruling class had recovered its nerve, tricked the rebels into dispersing and then relentlessly hunted down the ringleaders, the ill-fated Sudbury's youthful and vigorous successor, William Courtenay (1347–96), an Oxford man and later Chancellor, moved inexorably against Wyclif – even though Wyclif himself had openly condemned the revolt. A synod at Blackfriars, London, condemned Wyclif's works in 1382 and this time Oxford capitulated, banning his writings and expelling those who remained faithful to them. Wyclif suffered a stroke but no further punishment than exile from Oxford and carried on writing prolifically at Lutterworth until a second stroke carried him off in 1384. Opponents vowed that the name Wyclif surely meant 'wicked life'. Nor did they let him find rest, even in his grave.

That, however, was by no means the end of it. Wyclif's disciples carried through an English translation of the Bible and spread their teachings as unauthorised hedge-priests. The orthodox denounced them as Lollards (from the Dutch *lollaerd*, mumbler i.e. speaker of nonsense) and in 1401 the Church invoked the assistance of the state in their suppression. By the authority of the statute *De heretico comburendo* dozens were brought to the stake. Lollardy was driven underground but never entirely extinguished. Nor was it confined to England. Probably via some sympathiser in the entourage of the royal consort, Anne of Bohemia, it reached central Europe, where it inspired Czechs to the creation of a short-lived revolutionary, religious republic. Its leader Jan Hus went to the stake in 1415, having written 'Wyclif, Wyclif, you will unsettle many a man's mind.' It is noteworthy that many of Wyclif's Latin works survive as manuscripts in the libraries of Prague and Vienna and that in Bohemia he was revered as the 'fifth Evangelist', no less. Through Hus Wyclif might thus even be claimed as an influence on Luther. A century and a half later John Foxe, the martyrologist of Magdalen College would write 'When all the world was in most desperate and vile estate this man stepped forth like a valiant champion, even as the morning-star in the midst of a cloud.'

In Oxford Wyclif's name is remembered in Wycliffe Hall, Banbury Road, established in 1877 as an evangelical theological college to offset the then rising tide of Anglo-Catholicism within the university. In 1879 it became the birthplace of the Oxford Inter-Collegiate Christian Union.

CHAUCER'S OXFORD

In his *Prologue* to the *Canterbury Tales* Geoffrey Chaucer (?1340–1400) presents a panorama of medieval English society through the characters of twenty-nine pilgrims – warts and all. Few escape some censure. The poor parish priest, however, toiling selflessly for his flock, emerges as a paragon; some discreet authorial sympathy with Lollardy there? Or a reminder of the influence of John of Gaunt among Chaucer's audience at the court of Richard II? The threadbare, malnourished 'Clerk of Oxenford', whose only materialism is a lust for books, is portrayed with almost equal sympathy as a man driven by the love of learning – 'gladly wolde he lerne and gladly teche'. But what are we to make of the fact that Chaucer credits him with possessing no less than twenty books – equal in value to two or even three common dwelling-houses ? The Clerk also claims to have travelled as far as Padua and to have met the great Italian poet Petrarch in person.

The other learned man in Chaucer's motley band was a 'Doctor of Physick', among whose authorities is mentioned John of Gaddesden (?1280–1361), a member of Merton, who may even have been Chaucer's model for the Doctor himself. Both Gaddesden and the Doctor revered Muslim polymaths, such as Averröes (Ibn Rushd) and Avicenna (Ibn Sina), whose knowledge of ancient Greek learning had come to northern Europe via translations made in Spain, rendering their Arabic manuscripts into universally accessible Latin. Chaucer and Avicenna, though separated by centuries, oceans, deserts and religions, shared a passion for astronomy. Chaucer even wrote *A Treatise on the Astrolabe*, in which the tables are 'compownded after the latitude of Oxenforde'. Merton claims to have in its collections an astrolabe which belonged to the poet.

Chaucer's son Lewis did go to Merton and the poet's works reveal other Oxford connections. *Troilus and Criseyde* is dedicated jointly to the poet John Gower and to 'Philosophical Strode', i.e. Ralph Strode (fl.1350–1400) who taught philosophy and logic at Merton. *The Nun's*

Priest's Tale mentions 'Bisshop Bradwardyn', a Merton mathematician and theological controversialist who became Edward III's personal confessor and Archbishop of Canterbury, though the Black Death carried him off within days of landing in England from attendance at a papal coronation. The *Miller's Tale*, the second in the sequence of stories told by the pilgrims, deals with the sexual shenanigans of an Oxford student, Nicholas the Gallant, who lodges with a rich old carpenter who has a pretty teenage wife. One day, while the husband was over in Osney ... Chaucer's sympathies are clearly with roistering Nicholas, despite his greater dedication to seduction than scholarship. The fact that the hero gets away with cuckolding the carpenter with no worse a penalty than a burnt backside – you'll have to read the *Tale* to find out how – is symbolic of the mastery of Gown over Town in the aftermath of the St Scholastica riots. Even the third Oxford scholar mentioned by Chaucer, Jankyn, toy boy fifth husband of the man-eating Wife of Bath, manages to get a paid berth as the assistant to a parish priest, despite being a university drop-out. It was to curb the excesses and idleness of such students that in 1410 the university tightened up its supervisory procedures, requiring formal enrolment with a hall.

In the church at the west end of the picture-postcard village of Ewelme, mid-way between Oxford and Henley-on-Thames, Chaucer's grand-daughter, Alice, lies in a handsome canopied tomb, her dress, that of a nun, belying her marriage to the Duke of Suffolk, while her coronet and Order of the Garter confirm it. In St John's Chapel nearby can be seen the brass of Chaucer's son, Thomas, donor of the finely carved font cover. Outside in the churchyard lies Jerome K. Jerome, author of that sardonically silly celebration of the timeless Thames, *Three Men in a Boat*, whose riparian adventures terminated so appropriately at Folly Bridge. The church and adjacent almshouses and school, all dating from 1430–50, were all endowed by Alice and her husband.

Three More Colleges

Lincoln College, taking its name from the bishop who founded it and in whose diocese Oxford long stood, was established in 1427. Its founder, Richard Fleming, had been unjustifiably suspected of Lollard sympathies and explicitly defined the purpose of his foundation as being to 'defend the mysteries of the sacred page against those ignorant laics who profaned with swinish snouts its most holy pearls'. As if to underline the vehemence of his conviction he had Wyclif's body exhumed and the bones burned and the ashes scattered in the River Swift. Fleming's death soon afterwards, however, left his would-be bastion of orthodoxy on initially shaky foundations.

The College of All Souls of the Faithful Departed was nominally co-founded in 1438 by the teenage Henry VI and his Archbishop of Canterbury, Henry Chichele (?1362–1443), an experienced diplomat and enterprising accumulator of ecclesiastical wealth, well able to endow his creation generously. Thanks to Oxford's still-decayed state he was also able to purchase a fine central site for it. Chichele was a product of the Winchester–New College conveyor-belt. Like Fleming he gave his college an anti-Lollard mission but, as its name implies, it was also to serve as a memorial and a chantry for the dead of the Hundred Years War, then entering its hundred and first year. In recruiting members All Souls was bound to reject all not born within the province of Canterbury and bidden to give preference to Founder's kin and those born on college lands. Chichele also founded (1437) St Bernard's College for monk-students of the Cistercian Order. It remains largely intact as the front quadrangle of St John's College.

All Souls was to develop a distinctive character among colleges as the one without students. In *English Hours* (1905) Henry James would depict its Fellows as residents of an academic Elysium 'having no dreary instruction to administer, no noisy hobbledehoys to govern, no obligations but toward their own culture, no care save for learning as learning and truth as truth'.

Magdalen was founded in 1458 by William of Waynflete, whose very long and distinguished career had included spells as Master of Winchester, Provost of Eton and Chancellor of England. A long life – he died in 1486 aged 88 – enabled Waynflete to persist against many disruptions and uncertainties occasioned by the 'Wars of the Roses' (1455–85) to ensure the successful development of his creation, which he left so well endowed that only Christ Church would surpass it.

Far more of the early colleges at Oxford were founded by bishops than was the case at Cambridge and their careerist orientation was reflected in the output they produced. Some 57 per cent of bishops between 1216 and 1500 were Oxford men, but only 10 per cent came from Cambridge, with almost exactly the same proportions pertaining to cathedral deans. It is ironic to reflect that Oxford foundations were the legacy of churchmen whose careers were defined by two principles, pluralism and celibacy. Pluralism, the accumulation of church appointments from which the incumbent drew the income but whose duties he paid a deputy to perform or neglected altogether, was excoriated by Wyclif. But pluralism was the mechanism for the accumulations of wealth which made the foundation and secure maintenance of colleges possible. And it was celibacy which denied the founders of colleges the families amongst whose members they might otherwise have dispersed their wealth. Both principles – pluralism and celibacy – were to be roundly condemned by the Protestant zealots of the following century. Cash to fund the next round of college foundations was to be drawn from plundering not the livings of the church but the living church itself.

THE END OF THE BEGINNING

Given the depopulated and frequently disordered state of fifteenth century England even the founding of yet more colleges might be taken as evidence of Oxford's growing maturity and a mark of its significance in the life of the nation at large. But there were also other portents, albeit hesitant, of an era of renewed expansion.

In the exquisite Divinity School Oxford acquired its first fully detached university building. Begun around 1420 it took over sixty years to complete. The dramatic, intricate vault was the work of William Orchard (d.1504) the master-mason also responsible for the vault of Christ Church Cathedral and much of Magdalen. Among the hundreds of roof-bosses almost a hundred coats-of-arms can be identified, early evidence of sponsors' desire to exhibit their corporate logo as they exercised their public-spirited generosity. Although the financial net to support the project was clearly cast wide the main contributors were Cardinal Beaufort and the philanthropic Duke Humfrey.

Humfrey, Duke of Gloucester (1391–1447) was the younger brother of Henry V (r.1413–22). A Balliol man and a veteran of Agincourt, he preferred manuscripts to marching and in searching them out and deciding which to purchase was advised by the Italian Piero del Monte, who had come to England as a papal tax collector. The Duke was donating books to the University Library as early as 1411. Between 1439 and 1444 he gave no less than two hundred and eighty volumes. Generosity oft breeds influence and at the Duke's behest the university was persuaded to introduce the works of Cicero, Ovid and Virgil to its curriculum. The Duke also helped pay for the building of a new library above the Divinity School. The central part is still known as Duke Humfrey's Library in memory of his gifts.

Generations of English schoolchildren were taught that the Middle Ages ended with the Battle of Bosworth in 1485 and the inauguration of the glorious Tudor dynasty. More sophisticated interpreters than the writers of elementary school textbooks have emphasised the continuities of the following half century, epitomised by the glories of late Gothic architecture and the obedience still generally given to the Catholic Church, despite its manifold abuses and self-evident shortcomings. But for Oxford, at least, the Middle Ages ended before Bosworth. In 1475 an Italian expatriate began giving lectures on Greek and in 1478 Oxford produced its first printed book.

CHAPTER TWO

Renaissance and Reformation

The Humanists

'When I listen to Colet it seems to me that I am listening to Plato himself. Who could fail to be astonished at the universal scope of Grocyn's accomplishments? Could anything be more clever or profound or sophisticated than Linacre's mind? Did Nature ever create anything kinder, sweeter or more harmonious than the character of Thomas More? ... It is marvellous to see what an extensive and rich crop of ancient learning is springing up here in England.'

Desiderius Erasmus 1499

In England the Renaissance was a literary phenomenon long before it extended to art. At its heart was a rediscovery of ancient Greek texts. This broadened into an invigoration of those studies we now call the humanities and an acceptance of those secular values of the classical world which did not conflict with Christian teachings. 'Humanism' became accepted as the short-hand term for a cultural phenomenon with a sharp educational focus and agenda promoted by a close clique of humanists, focused on New College, where the classic textbooks of the medieval commentators were actually burned in Front Quad. Naturally, the 'Greeks' faced a rearguard action from Oxford colleagues wedded to Latin as the sole language of learning – but they had powerful friends at court, quite literally. Although much of the 'new learning' was transmitted indirectly, via France and the Low Countries, there was also much direct contact with Italy itself, despite the perils and expense such scholarly odysseys necessarily involved. It was Thomas Chaundler, Warden of New College (1454–75) who invited the

Italian Cornelio Vitelli to become the first teacher of Greek at Oxford. Vitelli's most important pupil was William Grocyn (1446–1519) who became the first English teacher of Greek at Oxford, after perfecting his mastery of the language under a Greek exile in Italy. Grocyn's later career took him to London, where Erasmus was often his house guest. Grocyn's pupils included St Thomas More (1478–1535), future Chancellor of England and William Warham (?1450–1532), future Archbishop of Canterbury and Chancellor of Oxford. As far as Oxford itself was concerned, however, two other pupils, John Colet (1467–1519) and Thomas Linacre (?1460–1524) were to prove even more important.

JOHN COLET

Colet also studied in Italy before giving lectures at Oxford on the Epistles of St Paul; these proved to be a revelation and a revolution. Whereas traditional biblical exegesis had become lost in minutiae, commenting at inordinate length on single sentences or even words, Colet, adopting an historical perspective and a contextual method, explained to his eager audiences the personality of St Paul, the circumstances of the apostle's career and the nature of the early Christian communities in Corinth, Ephesus and Rome whose concerns Paul was addressing. Elsewhere in Oxford Duns Scotus still provided the main tools of biblical criticism. Colet left Oxford (1505) for London to become Dean of St Paul's. His standing was such that he was chosen to preach at the installation of Wolsey as a cardinal. Lasting glory, however, lay in his foundation of St Paul's school (1508-10) 'to the erudition and profite of children: my countrymen Londoners especially'. Colet founded it to have 153 pupils, more than twice as many as Winchester or Eton. St Paul's was not only significant in its own right as a leading London school but even more so as a milestone in English educational history, providing the model for the hundreds of grammar schools, founded in the sixteenth century, whose products created the literary explosion of the Elizabethan era. The first high master of St. Paul's was William Lily (?1468–1522), Colet's own pupil and Grocyn's godson. Lily's own pupils included John Leland but he is chiefly remembered for 'Lily's Grammar' – much of it the work of Colet and

Erasmus – which became a standard text. In 1543 Henry VIII ordained its use in schools throughout his realm, conferring on it the status of 'the King's Grammar'.

THOMAS LINACRE

The name of Thomas Linacre has been commemorated in Oxford by two medical lectureships of his own foundation, and, much later by professorships in physiology and zoology and a college for postgraduate students. In the wider world Linacre is remembered as the founder and first president of the Royal College of Physicians (1518). Another pupil of Vitelli and a fellow of All Souls, he spent six years studying in Italy, qualifying as a doctor at Padua, then the foremost medical school in Europe. Linacre lectured at Oxford on his return, probably on medicine, but his reputation stood, if anything, even higher as a literary stylist and grammarian. Erasmus said that Galen, in Linacre's translation, spoke better Latin than he had Greek in the original. Linacre's expertise and versatility plucked him from Oxford to London as royal tutor to Prince Arthur and later Princess Mary and physician to Bishop Foxe, Archbishop Warham, Cardinal Wolsey and Henry VIII.

The Oxford humanists shared a profound dissatisfaction with current abuses in the Church but had no intent to subvert the Church itself. They believed that studying the Gospels in their original Greek would illuminate a path by which a godly reformation might become self-evident. They enjoyed disputation but were aware of its dangers. As Colet put it – 'let divines, if they like, dispute . . . A bad life is the worst heresy.'

BRASENOSE AND CORPUS

The limited and uneven impact of humanism in Oxford is reflected in the contrasting character of two colleges founded at the height of the 'war of the grammarians' between the 'Latin only' and 'Greek too' factions.

Of the foundation of Brasenose (1509) by two Lancashire men, William Smyth, Bishop of Lincoln and lawyer Sir Richard Sutton, the popular Oxford historian Sir John Marriott wrote with typical brusque felicity 'there is much that is picturesque but nothing that is historically

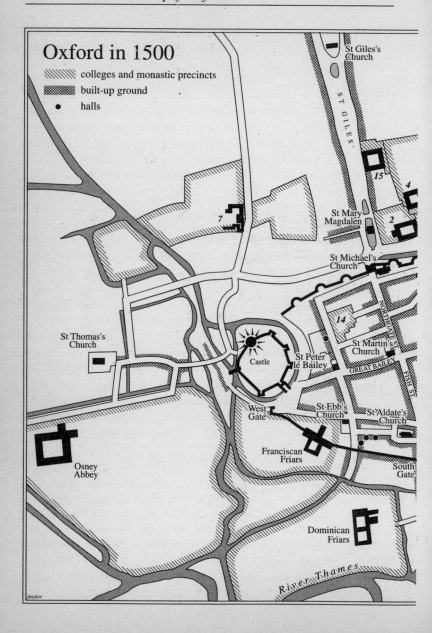

Oxford in 1500

▨▨▨	colleges and monastic precincts	
▓▓▓	built-up ground	
●	halls	

St Giles's Church

ST GILES'

15

4

7

St Mary Magdalen

2

St Michael's Church

NORTHGATE

14

St Thomas's Church

Castle

St Peter le Bailey

St Martin's Church

GREAT BAILEY

FISH ST

West Gate

St Ebb's Church

St Aldate's Church

Osney Abbey

Franciscan Friars

South Gate

Dominican Friars

River Thames

jtaylor

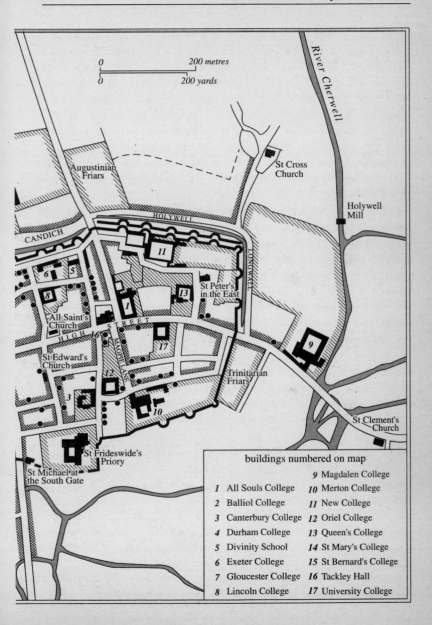

0   200 metres
0   200 yards

River Cherwell

Augustinian
Friars

St Cross
Church

Holywell
Mill

HOLYWELL

CANDICH

LONGWALL

11

St Peter's
in the East

6 *5*

8

13

All Saint's
Church

1

S T R E E T

HIGH

16

17

St Edward's
Church

MAGPIE LANE

St Michael at
the South Gate

12

Trinitarian
Friars

3

9

10

St Clement's
Church

St Frideswide's
Priory

buildings numbered on map

		9	Magdalen College
1	All Souls College	*10*	Merton College
2	Balliol College	*11*	New College
3	Canterbury College	*12*	Oriel College
4	Durham College	*13*	Queen's College
5	Divinity School	*14*	St Mary's College
6	Exeter College	*15*	St Bernard's College
7	Gloucester College	*16*	Tackley Hall
8	Lincoln College	*17*	University College

significant', except, perhaps, that Sutton was the first lay founder of a college, kings apart. The King's Hall and College of Brasenose (aka BNC) evolved from ancient Brasenose Hall whose members had once migrated briefly, in search of greater tranquillity, to the charming market town of Stamford in Lincolnshire in 1334, supposedly taking with them the famous brass knocker from which the college takes its name. As they omitted to bring it back the college was eventually obliged to buy an entire house in Stamford in 1890 simply to repossess the treasured icon – assuming that it actually was the same one. Another quixotic consequence of their brief exile was the requirement, sustained until 1827, for every Oxford MA candidate to swear that he would never give or attend lectures in Stamford. As well as representing a continuation of its eponymous ancestor, the development of BNC's site also represented the absorption of eight other former halls as well. Bishop Smyth's main legacy was the dissolved Augustinian priory of Cold Norton in the Cotswolds, which proved to be a handy refuge in times of plague. The Lancastrian origins of the founders favoured recruitment from the north, especially Lancashire, Cheshire and Yorkshire but, that apart, it lacked a distinctive mission. The statutes of the college did, however, explicitly provide for the birching of students found guilty of 'speaking English in public'.

Corpus Christi, by contrast, was founded (1517) by Richard Foxe (?1448–1528), blind Bishop of Winchester, with its own professors of Greek, Latin and Theology. Using a site previously occupied by five decayed academic halls, Foxe had originally begun to build a monastic house until upbraided by his friend Hugh Oldham, Bishop of Exeter – 'shall we build houses and provide livelihoods for ... monks whose end and fall we ourselves may live to see; no, no ... we should have care to provide for the increase of learning and for such as by their learning shall do good in the Church and the Commonwealth'. Oldham, who also founded Manchester Grammar School, reinforced his argument with a donation of £4,000. Foxe's statutes envisaged the college as a busy hive, where 'the scholars like clever bees night and day may make wax and sweet honey to the honour of God and the advantage of themselves and all Christian men'. Although Fellows were limited to forty days vacation a year provision was made for one Fellow at a time to take a three-year leave of absence to enable him to study in Italy. Erasmus prophesied that the Corpus library would bring more scholars to Oxford than once flocked to Rome. In the quad still stands a six-teenth century sundial surmounted by the college emblem, a pelican, symbolic of Christian self-sacrifice.

The Printed Page

The first book printed in Oxford bears the date 1468 – a misprint for 1478. This blunder may have brought some fleeting but deceptive comfort to the tribe of hand-scribes. Even allowing for the occasional error, though, the progress of printing was unstoppable on economic grounds alone. A single hand-copied Bible would take a scribe up to four years to complete. In the first year of production of Gutenberg's Bible twenty men produced 450 copies. Each copy was therefore produced ninety times faster and, even more to the point, at a tenth of the cost of a hand-copied version.

Oxford's interest in printing came close on the heels of Caxton's pioneering London establishment of 1476, but failed to establish itself as a permanent presence. The printer of Oxford's first book, an exposition of the Apostles' Creed incorrectly attributed to St Jerome, was Theodoric Rood, from Cologne. Rood's private press undertook commissions from the University but was suppressed as part of a general closure of provincial presses in 1486. A second press, run by the appropriately named John Scolar, was operating in 1517–18, and taken over by Charles Kyrforth in 1519–20. It may have been a subsidiary venture of the London press run by Wynkyn de Worde, Caxton's technical assistant and successor. The Tudors, however, had become keenly aware of the subversive potential of printed material and made strenuous efforts to confine the craft to London, where it could be policed by the Stationers' Company. In Oxford a hiatus of over half a century consequently supervenes. Not until 1585 and by special per-mission of Elizabeth I, did Joseph Barnes re-establish a press in Oxford. with a £100 loan from the University. University and municipality jointly regulated the activities of local printers henceforth, limiting entry to the trade until such powers of restriction were abolished by the

Municipal Reform Act of 1835. Printers to the University were further bound by being technically enrolled as academic members and thus subject to academic discipline.

The Perils of Patronage

Even by the standards of a turbulent and luxury-loving age the meteoric career of Thomas Wolsey (?1475–1530) was extraordinary. Derided by his enemies as the son of a mere butcher, Wolsey in fact was the offspring of a well-to-do Ipswich grazier and cattle-dealer. A graduate of Magdalen at sixteen, he became its Bursar at twenty-six, thus giving early evidence of his extraordinary capacity for administration. Rising on the coat-tails (more strictly cope-tails) of Bishop Foxe, Wolsey through tireless drudgery and shrewd diplomacy made himself indispensable to Henry VIII. Within five years of Henry's accession Wolsey was Archbishop of York. A cardinal's hat and the post of Lord Chancellor in succession to Warham followed a year later, as

The founder of Christ Church, Cardinal Thomas Wolsey

Wolsey began building a fabulous palace for himself at Hampton Court. He intended as his crowning glory the foundation of an Oxford college to outshine all others, complemented by a feeder school in his native Ipswich. Between 1524 and 1529 Wolsey dissolved thirty religious houses to appropriate their revenues for his projected Cardinal's College. He envisaged a permanent staff of professors, chaplains, choristers, canons, 'censors' and servants totalling a hundred and seventy six. Foxe averred that Wolsey 'gathered into that College whatsoever excellent thing there was in the whole realm'. Absorbing the existing buildings of St Frideswide's Priory and Canterbury College, Wolsey's foundation had acquired its palatial kitchens and majestic hall but only three sides of its projected Great Quadrangle when his sensational fall from power (1529) halted all building work on the king's orders. Henry halfheartedly re-started the project as a very much reduced King's College in 1532 but in 1545–6 resolved instead to combine it with a new bishopric of Oxford as 'the Cathedral Church of Christ in Oxford of the Foundation of King Henry the Eighth'. It became known as *Aedes Christi*, the House of Christ, or, more simply, 'The House'. Of the Ipswich feeder school only an arched gateway was ever built.

As Henry VIII neglected to give this greatest of all Oxford foundations any statutes it became governed by self-evolved custom. In 1561 Elizabeth I established a link with the school of Westminster Abbey which she had re-founded and which was to become a major source of Christ Church undergraduates for succeeding centuries.

ENTER THE PROFESSORS

Would-be benefactors whose resources ran short of founding a whole college could, from this period onwards, make a more modest contribution by endowing a chair to promote the advanced study of a particular subject. The first was the Lady Margaret Professorship of Divinity, established in 1502 with a stipend of twenty marks a year by Lady Margaret Beaufort (1443–1509), Countess of Richmond and Derby and mother of the then monarch, Henry VII (r.1485–1509) – though she was in fact wealthy enough to found two colleges, both at Cambridge. In 1546 her grandson, Henry VIII, founded the first five

Regius Professorships – in Divinity, Civil Law, Medicine, Hebrew and Greek – with an annual stipend of £40. Although professorships, especially the Regius appointments, became highly prestigious this was to be a much later development. In a collegiate university a Fellowship remained the key to comfort and security for centuries to come.

Dissolution and Reformation

The comprehensive suppression of religious foundations in 1536–9 is conventionally referred to as the dissolution of the monasteries but it embraced far more than monasteries and also had a substantial pre-history. William of Waynflete had not hesitated to suppress religious houses to use their assets for the grammar school he founded to complement Magdalen College. One local casualty had been the Hospital of St John the Baptist, whose buildings were demolished or converted to Magdalen's use in 1456. Wolsey had done likewise, only more so, for Christ Church. By the 1530s only about half the houses originally founded in England and Wales yet remained to be dissolved.

Oxford was fortunate in that Henry VIII explicitly ordered his commissioners to keep their hands off the assets of the colleges of the university, judging 'no money better bestowed than that which is given to our Universities, for by their maintenance our Realm shall be well governed when we are dead and rotten'. But the religious houses at Osney, Rewley and Godstow all went. So did the monastic colleges – Gloucester, Durham, Canterbury and St Bernard's. St Bartholomew's Hospital was at least converted into an almshouse for the city. St Edmund Hall, a property which had been acquired by Osney was eventually acquired by its neighbour, Queen's.

The assault on ecclesiastical property initiated by the Crown was the largest and most concentrated redistribution of wealth since the Norman Conquest. As such it was bound to upset many, but it enriched others and Oxford was to gain from their beneficence. Where Oxford lost badly was in the succeeding reign, in the plundering of its chapels and libraries, purged by Protestant zealots of 'Papist' symbols and books in 1549 under the authority of a Commission authorised by Lord Protector Somerset. The majestic reredos in the chapel of All Souls was smashed to pieces. Cartloads of missals and manuscripts were burned with glee. Duke Humphrey's great library was swept clean not only of its books but even of its fittings. Only three of its hundreds of manuscripts were ever recovered. Books not deemed heretical and therefore burned were either kept for their own use by the 'Reformers' or sold off to booksellers 'or to glovers to press their gloves or to tailors to make measures (patterns) or to bookbinders to recycle their bindings.'

RECOVERY

Mention of these crafts is a reminder of local economic recovery after the stagnation of the fifteenth century. A brewers' guild was officially incorporated in 1521, the butchers followed in 1536 and the glovers in 1562. The manufacture of gloves and cutlery were two local specialisms whose products were known well beyond the Oxford area itself. The cordwainers were strong enough to refuse membership to mere cobblers and workers in old leather. The numbers of mercers and drapers increased to meet the needs of increasingly fashion-conscious undergraduates. In 1570 the bakers found it sensible to split into separate white and brown branches, while shortly afterwards the mercers merged with the woollen drapers to create a heterogeneous retail association taking in haberdashers, milliners, grocers, salters and ironmongers. Less formally one might note the existence of a distinctive community of watermen whose inter-related families were to inhabit Fisher Row into the twentieth century.

By 1524–5 Oxford had a population of about 4,000, making it about half the size of Norwich, England's leading provincial city. Local infrastructure and services also improved. In 1536 Dr Claymond, President of Corpus Christi, paid for the erection of a stone-pillared, lead-roofed canopy in Cornmarket 'that thereby in wet seasons sacks of corn might be preserved from the violence of the weather'. The first common scavenger was appointed in 1541. In 1556 a range of permanent butchers' shops was built in Queen Street. A workhouse for the poor was erected in 1562. The 1576 Mileways Act bound inhabitants within a five mile radius to help repair roads within a mile of the city. In 1610 Otho Nicholson, a Christ Church man who had done well as a lawyer and diplomat, paid for an elaborately carved water conduit to be put up at Carfax. The first piped water supply was laid on in 1615 although it was not until 1654 that the city acquired a fire engine.

'A Laborious Journey and Costely Enterprise'

John Leland (?1506–52), a pupil of William Lily at St Paul's, was educated at Christ's, Cambridge, All Souls and Paris before becoming a sub-librarian and chaplain to Henry VIII. In 1533 he was given power to search out manuscripts in religious institutions and diligently devoted the spring and summer months of almost the entire period 1533–45 to systematically searching out manuscripts and making copious notes about the places he passed through en route. In doing this he performed a priceless service to posterity by having 'conservid many good autors, the which otherwise had beene like to have perischid' in the holocaust of destruction which accompanied the dissolution. Leland was duly, if rather modestly, rewarded with the rectory of Haseley in Oxfordshire and a canonry at King's College, until it became Christ Church. Having collected a veritable archive of source materials, he planned an immensely ambitious history and topography of England and Wales, plus a multi-volume *Who's Who* of British writers, but the enormity of the task drove him incurably insane in 1547. Leland's *Itinerary* of his travels survives, though incomplete, as an invaluable picture of Tudor England, though it was not published until Thomas Hearne edited a nine-volume edition in 1710–12. Revised versions of Leland's works, based on careful study of the original manuscripts, were edited by Lucy Toulmin Smith (1838–1911), librarian (1894) of Manchester College, Oxford, the first woman in England to hold such a post.

The Oxford Martyrs

The first thing to make clear about the 'Oxford Martyrs' is that they were all Cambridge men, that university having been the crucible of English Protestantism. The accession to the throne of devoutly Catholic Queen Mary in 1553 led to the arraignment in reliably reactionary Oxford of the senior churchmen prominent in promoting

Protestantism in the reign of her deceased brother Edward VI (r.1547–
53): Thomas Cranmer (1489–1556), Archbishop of Canterbury;
Nicholas Ridley (?1500–55), Bishop of London; and Hugh Latimer
(?1485–1555), Bishop of Worcester. Cranmer was already under sentence of death for treason for having supported Lady Jane Grey's
abortive bid for the throne at Mary's accession but Mary wanted him
condemned for heresy as well. Cranmer's instrumental role in securing
the divorce of Henry VIII from Mary's mother, Katherine of Aragon,
twenty years before was never to be forgotten or forgiven. In April
1554 the accused were required to defend their beliefs, in Latin, in the
Divinity School. Afterwards they were paraded before their tormentors
in the university church of St Mary's on 20 April, to be informed,
unsurprisingly, that they were in error. They were offered, and refused,
the opportunity to recant. Condemned as heretics, they awaited
execution by fire while Parliament was persuaded to re-enact the
necessary legislation for this. As an archbishop, Cranmer, author of the
incomparable prose of the *Book of Common Prayer*, was subject only to
the jurisdiction of the Pope and in September 1555 was therefore
formally tried for heresy in St Mary's before special papal commissioners. Communication with Rome necessitated a delay of at least
eighty days before the verdict could be ratified and the sentence carried
out. Ridley and Latimer were dealt with more summarily. Tried and
condemned for heresy and excommunicated, they refused again to
recant and were burned at the stake on 16 October 1555.

Their *auto da fé* took place in what is now Broad Street but was then
the town ditch outside the northern city wall, opposite Balliol. Cranmer was forced to watch, probably from the tower of St Michael's. As
Ridley flinched at the slow heat from faggots too damp to blaze up
Latimer is reported to have said 'Be of good comfort, Master Ridley,
and play the man, we shall this day light such a candle, by God's grace,
in England as I trust shall never be put out.'

Cranmer, having been excommunicated, fell prey to his solitude and
the relentless interrogations of his persecutors and wrote out multiple
recantations of his beliefs. His sentence, however, remained in force.
On 21 March the disgraced archbishop was taken to St Mary's yet again
and called upon to declare his adherence to the Catholic faith before

the whole congregation. Instead Cranmer stunned them by repudiating his recantations.

> '... now I come to the great thing, which so much troubleth my con-science, more than any thing that ever I did or said in my whole life, and that is the setting abroad of a writing contrary to the truth; which now here I renounce and refuse, as things written with my hand, contrary to the truth which I thought in my heart, and written for fear of death ... And for-asmuch as my hand offended in writing contrary to my heart, therefore my hand shall first be punished therefore; for, may I come to the fire, it shall first be burned.'

Cranmer was then degraded from Holy Orders by the vengeful Bishop Bonner in a ceremony of finely calculated humiliation, arrayed in mock vestments so that they could be torn from him. When Cranmer at last went to the stake he did exactly as he had vowed, holding his right hand steadily in the fire as he stood chained, bareheaded and barefoot, until, in the words of Foxe's *Book of Martyrs*, 'in the greatness of the flame he gave up the ghost'.

The Martyrs' Memorial, erected in 1841–3, stands not on the site of their execution but in St Giles, on the site of the Robin Hood Inn,

The Martyrs' Memorial

where it can immediately be seen by travellers arriving down the Woodstock or Banbury Roads. It is an early work of Sir George Gilbert Scott, who would go on to build the biggest architectural practice in the country, as well as much of Oxford. Scott took as his inspiration the thirteenth century Eleanor Cross erected at Waltham, Essex on the orders of Edward I, in memory of his beloved consort, Queen Eleanor of Castile. The statues are by Henry Weekes (1807–77), who also sculpted William Harvey for the new Ashmolean and a bust of Dean Buckland now in the National Portrait Gallery. The figure of Cranmer is depicted holding a Bible marked May 1541, the month in which the scriptures in English were first circulated generally on the orders of Henry VIII – as a result of Cranmer's persistent pleading. Generations of undergraduates have irreverently attempted to convince gullible visitors to the city that the Memorial is in fact the spire of a huge, subterranean cathedral.

Three New Colleges

Established in the reign of Mary, Trinity College (1555) reflects her fervent Catholicism both in its name and coincidentally in that of its founder, Sir Thomas Pope (?1507–59), but it was founded for secular aims, for the benefit of poor scholars and the service of the state. Unusually no provision was made for the recruitment of the founder's kin. As Pope, an Oxfordshire lawyer, was a sympathiser with the old religion it is more than slightly ironic that he had accumulated his fortune by serving as Treasurer (i.e. deputy-head) of the Court of Augmentations, the government department established to deal with plundered monastic properties. Ideally placed for insider dealing he acquired some thirty manors, many of which were in his native county and thus convenient for his foundation to supervise. Trinity incorporated the site and buildings of Durham College, bought from Henry VIII's physician, George Owen (d.1558), a Merton man who also sold Rewley Abbey to Christ Church and himself lived at Godstow Abbey. Pope and Owen knew each other well, both having been executors of Henry VIII's will. Pope himself now lies in Trinity's chapel. As his monument jarred with the taste of the following century it has been consigned to an elegant sort of glass-fronted wardrobe, immediately to the left of the altar.

St John's – dedicated to the patron saint of tailors – was founded by Sir Thomas White (1492–1567) Master of the Merchant Taylors' Company and Lord Mayor of London, who had led the pro-Marian faction in the capital when her succession was disputed by supporters of the doomed rebellion of Sir Thomas Wyatt. White, a friend of Sir Thomas Pope, followed his example of capitalising on redundant monastic property and bought from Christ Church the site of the dissolved St Bernard's College, having apparently seen it in a dream. The college was expressly founded to 'strengthen the orthodox faith' and after Mary's Catholic Counter-Reformation ended with her death several of its fellows and ex-fellows fled abroad, notably Edmund Campion, who gave the oration at White's funeral. St John's statutes were modelled on those of Corpus Christi and after a short while modified to give preference to recruits from the Merchant Taylors' school in London. The fortunes of the college were well secured when White's widow, dying childless, bequeathed it her fortune, which was used to buy large estates north and west of Oxford.

Jesus is by origin and tradition the Welsh college and also the first established as a distinctly Protestant foundation. Its nominal founder was Queen Elizabeth I who, as a Tudor, was herself of Welsh descent, but the money for the college was put up by Hugh Price (1495–1574), Treasurer of St David's Cathedral, who endowed it with Welsh estates. Like Wolsey, he was a butcher's son who had been educated at Oxford. Despite its royal patronage Jesus got off to a slow start. Price's bequest of £60 a year failed to materialise and the college statutes, modelled on those of Brasenose, also failed to materialise until 1622.

Exeter College was two and a half centuries old when it was virtually refounded by one of its own alumni, Sir William Petre (pronounced Peter) (?1502–72) who had managed to survive four reigns and, through government office and the opportunities for recycling his income afforded by the dissolution, had managed to accumulate a fine fortune. Acquiring 36,000 acres in his native Devon alone, he built himself a handsome home, Ingatestone Hall in Essex (still the home of the Petres) and set himself to sorting out his old college as a retirement project. His gift of four church livings in Oxfordshire stabilised its finances, and created seven new Fellowships, enlarging its potential intake beyond Devon to other counties where he held lands, notably Dorset, Somerset, Oxfordshire and Essex. His new (1566) statutes matched this by providing for greater institutional stability, by means of a Rector elected for life instead of annually and making Fellows also eligible for life tenure. A Sub-Rector, Dean and Lector were appointed to tighten up teaching arrangements and enforce regular timetables for study.

Settlement

The see-saw years of zealously Protestant Edward and staunchly Catholic Mary gave way to the reign of pragmatic Elizabeth. Upholding her father's repudiation of Papal authority, she rejected the title of Head of the Reformed Church in favour of Supreme Governor. Its liturgy and creed were too Catholic to please those who looked to Calvinist Geneva for inspiration and too Protestant for those who looked to Spain for deliverance but its prayer book left a large latitude to ministers and believers. What Elizabeth insisted on was outward conformity in the interests of political stability and to this end Parliament passed the Act of Uniformity (1559) and reinstated the 1534 Act of Supremacy, confirming the sovereign's authority in matters ecclesiastical. Nine Heads of Houses and the Dean and two canons of Christ Church were ejected from their posts for refusing to acknowledge the royal Supremacy. At New College alone thirty-nine fellows were ejected between 1560 and 1576 for holding to the old faith. For the next half century the crown looked to Cambridge men for its archbishops, although the definitive statement of the Anglican settlement was formulated in eight volumes *Of the Laws of Ecclesiastical Polity* by Richard Hooker (1554–1600), a former Fellow of Corpus Christi.

In 1564 the Queen's favourite, Robert Dudley, Earl of Leicester, who had never attended either university, was appointed Chancellor. This was meant, and taken, as no sinecure. His hands-on attitude was soon made clear in a brusque letter to the university's senior officers, written in plain – very plain – English, the first time a communication had been received from a Chancellor in anything other than Latin. Dudley bade them repair their 'want of instructing your youth in the Principles of Religion, the little care that Tutors have that waye, and most especially the suffering of secret and lurking Papists amongst you, which seduce your youth and carry them over by flocks to the Seminaries beyond Seas'. Other points he deemed worthy of attention included 'Excess in apparell, as silk and velvet, and cut doublets, hose, deep ruffs and such like' and 'Ale-houses, grown to great number ... with Scholars tippling, dicing, carding' – with the result that they were graduating 'less learned than when they came thither and worse mannered than if they had been so long conversant amongst the worst sort of people?' 'No, this is not the old University order ...' he concluded ominously.

Leicester may not have restored a supposed Golden Age of undergraduate industriousness and civility but under his prodding and long tenure of twenty-four years the university became increasingly an Anglican stronghold. In 1571 Parliament endorsed the Thirty-Nine Articles, summarising the Anglican creed. In the same year the university was at last legally incorporated as a body. Other administrative adjustments shifted the initiative in the university's internal legislation from resident teachers meeting as a body in Congregation House to a much smaller council of Heads of Houses and proctors, chaired by the Vice-Chancellor. In 1576 undergraduates were required to register with a specific college tutor, responsible for supervising their conduct and progress. From 1581 onwards all students were required on matriculating (formally entering the university) to take the Oath of Supremacy. The oath was, not, however, enforced until the age of sixteen, which explains why the poet John Donne, like many others, entered Oxford at twelve. Matriculants were also obliged to subscribe in writing to the Thirty-Nine Articles, a requirement which remained in force for almost three centuries. Intended to exclude committed Catholics, as the centuries passed this measure discriminated even more against Nonconformists, most of whom came from a bourgeois background. Coupled with the dissolution, which had cut off the stream of poorer students once talent-spotted among the peasantry by the church, this had the unintended effect of giving the undergraduate body an increasingly aristocratic character. William Harrison, author of a wide-ranging *Description of England* (1587) wrote indignantly that Oxford's colleges 'were erected by their founders at the first only for poor men's sons, whose parents were not able to bring them up into learning; but now they have the least benefit of them by reason the rich do so encroach upon them. And so far has this inconvenience spread itself that it is in my time a hard matter for a poor man's child to come by a fellowship (though he be never so good a scholar and worthy of that room) . . .'

Certainly there was a growth in the proportion of sons of the gentry coming up from Elizabeth's reign onwards, though it is difficult to say how many took a degree and how many treated university, like the Inns of Court in London, as a sort of finishing school where one could pass the time pleasantly enough while networking useful contacts for later life. Tudor historian John Guy admits that 'attempts to plot the social origins of matriculants have proved inconclusive' and also notes that the apparent rise in student numbers in this period may just be apparent, a by-product of more tightly enforced registration regulations. That said, Professor Lawrence Stone's calculations show an expansion in the annual figure of entrants from around three hundred in the 1560s to *c.* 366 in the 1580s. The dynamic Elizabethan state needed more clergy, more lawyers, more schoolmasters. Oxford provided them.

The Real Oxford Martyrs

For many Catholics who fled Oxford their exodus meant permanent exile, for others, who dared to return, it meant execution. William Allen (1532–94) an Oriel Fellow from staunchly Catholic Lancashire fled in 1561 but came back in 1562 to live on the run for three years. In 1568 he founded the English College at Douai as a bastion and base to train missionaries for the reconversion of his native country. He later founded parallel establishments in Rome (1575–8) and Valladolid (1589). Allen also inspired and helped to translate the 'Douai' Bible (1582, 1609) as a vernacular version for Catholic use. He was created cardinal in 1587. Edmund Campion (1540–81) of St John's fled to

Douai soon after its foundation and became a member of the Jesuit order in Bohemia before returning to England in 1580. After circulating a refutation of Anglicanism '*Decem Rationes*' (Ten Reasons) he was arrested and racked three times so cruelly that he could not physically hold up his hand to indicate his plea in court. Yet, speaking for himself and two co-accused, Campion still summoned the resources to reprove his judges and tormentors in language of majestic dignity. '. . . if our religion do make us traitors we are worthy to be condemned, but otherwise are and have been true subjects as ever the queen had. In condemning us you condemn all your own ancestors – all the ancient priests, bishops and kings – all that was once the glory of England, the island of saints and the most devoted child of the see of Peter. . . God lives; posterity will live; their judgment is not so liable to corruption. . .'.

Campion and his companions, Briant and Sherwin, both Oxford-Douai Jesuits, all suffered the agonising fate prescribed for traitors, being hanged, drawn and quartered. Campion and Sherwin were finally canonised in 1970 as being among the Forty Martyrs of England. Cuthbert Payne and John Roberts of St John's were also to be likewise martyred and canonised. Campion is memorialised in Campion Hall (1918), the Jesuit study centre in Brewer Street. It was first (1895) established as Clarke's Hall, is the only Oxford work of Sir Edwin Lutyens, designer of the Cenotaph, and is adorned with works by Eric Gill and Frank Brangwyn.

Physic and its Limits

Linacre's efforts to improve medical teaching at Oxford found successors at New College. In 1518, when Oxford suffered a severe outbreak of 'sweating sickness', Linacre's friend Thomas Bentley (?1485–1549), qualified as a doctor and on Linacre's death succeeded him as second President of the College of Physicians and physician to Henry VIII. Another New College medic Walter Bayley (1529–93) became physician to Elizabeth I in 1561 and also Regius Professor of Physic, in which post he was succeeded by his collegiate colleague, Anthony Aylworth. Bayley's only publications, on medicinal baths in

Warwickshire and the value of eyebright in ale for preserving the sight, seem remarkably commonplace and unoriginal.

If Oxford physicians were judged eminent enough to win royal appointments and senior office in their emerging profession, they yet remained as helpless as any other in the face of epidemics. The Oxford plague outbreak of 1577 is said to have infected three hundred victims in three days 'and within twelve days space died an hundred Scholars, besides many Citizens.' Even survivors must have been terrified as sufferers 'occasioned by the rage of their disease and pain, would beat their keepers and nurses, and drive them from their presence. Others like mad men would run about the streets, markets, lanes and other places. Some again would leap headlong into deep waters.' Some accused closet Catholics 'who used the Art Magick' for the outbreak, while a more rationalist school of thinking blamed the overcrowding of prisoners in the town gaol, awaiting trial at the quarterly assizes. 'The Doctors and Heads of Houses almost to one fled ... in the country where they depended upon safety.' Even so, there were numerous distinguished victims, such as Thomas Gwyn and Thomas Carpenter, both teachers of medicine at All Souls. Thomas Cogan (?1545–1607), a Fellow of Oriel (1563-74) who broke new ground in composing *The Haven of Health* (1584) as a handbook 'for the comfort of students', concluded it with a section on *Preservation from the Pestilence with a short censure of the late sickness at Oxford*, which he clearly felt could have been better managed.

ROYAL FAVOUR

Elizabeth I's closest advisers – William and Robert Cecil, Walsingham, Bacon, Mildmay – were all Cambridge men, as were such adornments of her court as poet Edmund Spenser and the dashing Earl of Essex. So also was her astrologer John Dee, who turned down a handsome offer from Oxford to lecture on mathematics. Although there were distinguished Oxford men around her, such as Sir Walter Raleigh, Sir Philip Sidney and her 'dancing Chancellor', Sir Christopher Hatton, nevertheless the Queen visited Cambridge (1564) before she came to Oxford. By doing so she unwittingly sparked an historical controversy which refused to go away. In welcoming the monarch the public orator of Cambridge claimed that it was older than Oxford. Within *a week* Thomas Caius (pronounced Keys) (d.1572) of All Souls had produced a treatise to prove the contrary. A rejoinder was duly composed by John Caius (1510–73) – no relation – co-founder and Warden of Gonville and Caius College, Cambridge and Elizabeth's chief physician. The controversy rumbled on long after both men were dead. In 1730 the Oxford antiquary Hearne still thought it worthwhile to publish Thomas Caius' manuscript rejoinder to his Cambridge opponent's rejoinder to his rejoinder to the original Cambridge contention.

When at last Elizabeth I visited Oxford in 1566 her arrival had been eagerly anticipated for two years. A welcoming oration was made outside the North Gate, after which the Queen rode down Cornmarket through a human corridor of kneeling students shouting '*Vivat Regina!*' (Long Live the Queen!). At Carfax the Regius Professor of Greek made a second oration in that language – to which the queen replied in Greek. Almost as proud of her learning as of her looks, Elizabeth spoke half a dozen languages fluently. The queen was also notoriously vain about her long, slender fingers, which are a prominent feature of her portraits. The Vice-Chancellor's gift of half a dozen pairs of gloves, locally made and exquisitely embroidered was therefore knowing in its flattery. (The Ashmolean displays what is claimed to be one pair of the six.) The following days were filled with public disputations of points of law, divinity, physic and philosophy. A play was performed for her at Christ Church, though the proceedings were somewhat overcast by the collapse of the stage, killing three people and injuring five more. The queen helpfully 'sent forthwith the Vice-Chancellor and her Chirurgeons to help them ... that they wanted nothing for their recovery'. Elizabeth herself made a flawless Latin oration to the assembled faculty in St Mary's. The queen was at last escorted out of the city by a cavalcade of mounted academics, resplendent in robes of scarlet and hoods lined with fur. At Shotover Hill, the limits of the university's jurisdiction, the departing monarch was treated to a final oration, delivered in Latin by twenty-five year old Roger Marbeck, who would shortly be appointed the university's first public orator for life and unanimously elected Provost of Oriel by its Fellows. Decades later the queen made him chief of her physicians.

The queen's state visit of 1592 was even more extravagant. The fabulous sum of £7,560 was spent on entertainment, contributions being shared out between colleges in proportion to their wealth. Christ Church put up a lordly £2,000, Magdalen £1,200, New College £1,000 and All Souls £500, while newly founded Jesus got away with just £70. The bishop offered a Latin oration so overlong that the queen twice ordered him to cut it short but he could not, fearing that he would become hopelessly confused. The following day the queen showed him how such things should be managed, pointedly interrupting herself in mid-flow to call for a chair for the ageing and visibly flagging Lord Burleigh, and then resuming her own Latin declamation without pause. Once again she was escorted out in state and treated to a farewell oration at Shotover – 'Which being done, she gave them many thanks and her hand to kiss; and then looking wistfully towards Oxford. said to this effect in the Latin tongue "Farewell. Farewell, dear Oxford, God bless thee, and increase thy sons in number, holiness and virtue . . . ." '

Oxford in the World

The mere mention of More, Wolsey and Raleigh confirms that the greatest impact Oxonians have made with their talents and ambitions reverberates far beyond Oxford itself. Space requires the mention here of only an illustrative few. William Tyndale (?1493–1536) of Magdalen suffered exile, persecution and eventual execution to create a version of the New Testament in English so plain and direct that it could be understood even by 'the boy that driveth the plough'. Tyndale excelled 'especially in the knowledge of the Scriptures, whereunto his mind was singularly addicted' and coined such immortal phrases as 'the powers that be', 'the fat of the land' and 'eat, drink and be merry'. Such was the accuracy of his translation and the power of his prose that 90 per cent of the text of the King James Authorised Version, produced by a committee of forty learned scholars and divines two generations later, is still Tyndale's.

Robert Recorde (?1510–58) of All Souls actually taught mathematics, music, medicine, anatomy, astrology, cosmography and rhetoric and was also renowned for his expertise in mineralogy, natural history, theology and Anglo-Saxon. Despite being an expert on coinage and one time comptroller of the mint at Bristol, he was so hopeless with his own finances that he died as a debtor in King's Bench prison, Southwark. Recorde deserves to be remembered less for his astonishing versatility than for being among the first in England to acknowledge the correctness of the Copernican view of the universe and as being the first to introduce algebra as a branch of mathematics and to popularise the use of the signs $+$, $-$ and $=$.

John Foxe (1516–87) a Fellow of Magdalen, fled to the Continent in the reign of Queen Mary but returned to compose his celebrated and monumental, if opaquely titled, *History of the Acts and Monuments of the Church*, recounting in detail the persecutions and executions of Protestants which took place in her reign and railing against 'the great Antichrist of Europe or Pope of Rome'. Foxe's words have been quoted above in respect of the Oxford Martyrs. In Elizabeth's reign only the Bible itself was more widely owned than Foxe's *Book of Martyrs*. On the orders of the new Anglican church itself a copy was placed in every cathedral and in the home of every church official.

Richard Hakluyt (?1552–1616) of Christ Church, Oxford's first lecturer in geography, pioneered the study of the history of exploration and introduced the use of the globe into English schools. It was Raleigh himself who commissioned Hakluyt's *Divers Voyages touching the Discovery of America* (1582) which advocated English colonisation of that continent. Hakluyt's best known work, the *Principal Navigations, Voyages and Discoveries of the English Nation* first appeared in 1589 and was expanded to three volumes in 1598–1600. Centuries later Oxford historian J. A. Froude hailed that work as 'the prose epic of the modern English nation'. Hakluyt can, therefore, be claimed as the first ideologue and chronicler of British imperialism. The Hakluyt Society, founded in 1846 to promote interest in geographical writings, perpetuates his memory.

THE WORLD IN OXFORD

The universality of Latin as the language of academic discourse had long facilitated the mobility of both students and faculty but in the sixteenth century Oxford attracted intellectual talent from beyond England's shores by being a centre of refuge as well as a centre of learning.

Florentine friar Nicholas de Burgo (d.1537) who began lecturing on divinity in 1517 was exempted from a customary academic fee seven years later on the grounds that he still could not speak English, although he became naturalised in 1530. Burgo's early support for Henry VIII's projected divorce won him royal favour, an appointment at Cardinal College and a year as Vice-Chancellor but he was so unpopular with the generality that he was pelted in the streets and prudently retired to Italy in 1535.

Pietro Martire Vermigli (1500–62), another Florentine, was named for Dominican saint Peter Martyr (d.1252) and rose to become Visitor-General of the Augustinian order before his own deep scholarship undermined his orthodoxy. Fleeing to France, he married ex-nun Catharine Dammartin, a corpulent but comely matron with an unusual talent for 'carving plumstones into curious faces'. Accepting Cranmer's invitation of refuge in England, Vermigli was appointed Regius Professor of Divinity and first canon of Christ Church, where his wife became the first female to reside, legally at least, in an Oxford college.

Outraged Papists broke Vermigli's windows so often by night that he was forced to remove his lodgings to a rear set and build himself a two-story stone study-tower in the garden (demolished by Dean Aldrich). Catharine's death from fever was followed by her burial in the newly established cathedral. Queen Mary's accession was followed by Vermigli's permitted flight back to the Continent. In 1557, on royal orders, Catharine's body was disinterred and transferred to a dung-heap in the Dean's stable. In 1558, following the accession of Elizabeth I, it was reinterred with due ceremony, the bones being deliberately mixed with the supposed relics of St Frideswide enabling the preacher on that occasion to pronounce that henceforth 'religion and superstition should rest together'.

The family of Alberico Gentili (1552–1608) had been chased out of Italy by the Inquisition. Recommended somewhat imperiously by the Earl of Leicester, Gentili was appointed to teach law at Oxford and by the age of thirty-five was Regius Professor. By sheer intellectual zest he rescued the study of Roman law from the taint of Popery and simultaneously pioneered the novel field of international law, establishing general basic principles for the conduct of embassies and warfare, as well as ruling on specific issues such as piracy and the taking of prizes.

The arrival of Nicholas Kratzer (1487–1550?) of Munich predated the religious turbulence which was to punctuate the careers of so many. As one of the earliest appointments to the teaching staff at Corpus Christi, he was responsible for mathematics and astronomy. Kratzer developed horology as his special field, erecting splendid sun-dials at Corpus Christi and in the churchyard of St Mary's. The latter vanished in the eighteenth century, the former still stands. A friend of Erasmus and Dürer, Kratzer was one of the first to befriend Holbein when he arrived in England. Holbein's portrait of Kratzer is now in the Louvre.

The Bodleian Library

Sir Thomas Bodley (1545–1613), a student at Magdalen at thirteen, Fellow of Merton at nineteen and Proctor at twenty-four, initially specialised in Greek and Hebrew before exploiting his linguistic pro-

Sir Thomas Bodley, 1598, after a miniature by Nicholas Hilliard

wess to master modern languages and launch himself on a twenty year career as a diplomat. Retiring from public life in 1596 he returned to Oxford to devote his remaining years to the restoration of the university library. He had no very great fortune but he had no children to inherit what he did have. And he believed that he could bring to his self-imposed task certain relevant qualifications – 'knowledge, as well in the learned and modern tongues ... some purse-ability ... (and) very great store of honourable friends'. Since the library's plundering in 1549 'in every part it lay ruined and waste' for almost half a century. Bodley undertook to restore it 'to its proper use and to make it fit and handsome with seats and shelves and desks'. Refitting Duke Humfrey's library took two whole years. Its stock of books was replenished by Bodley's own gifts as well as those of other benefactors solicited by him from his wide circle of acquaintance. The library, with a renewed stock of 2,000 volumes, was finally reopened on 8 November 1602 with great pomp. King James VI and I (r.1603–25) visited in 1604 and decreed that the library should henceforth bear Bodley's name. The first catalogue, of 655 pages, appeared in 1605. In 1610 Bodley achieved a master-stroke when the Stationers' Company pledged that the library should ever after receive a copy of every newly published book, making it Britain's first 'copyright library'. In that same year it became necessary to build an extension, known as Arts End, to accommodate the ever-expanding stock. This was completed by 1612. Bodley also succeeded in persuading the university to rebuild the two-storey quadrangle outside, whose 'ruinous little Rooms' had long been used for lectures. Adding a third storey for 'stowage of books' provided further much-needed space for the Bodleian and at the same time gave lofty dignity to the handsome Schools Quadrangle when it was completed in 1624. In accordance with his wishes Bodley was buried in Merton chapel in splendid style, having left the staggering sum of two thousand marks (£666. 13s 4d.) to defray the expenses. Sixty-seven poor scholars, one for each year of his life, attended his corpse. A monument by master-mason Nicholas Stone, the foremost funerary sculptor of the day, was added at the cost of a further £200. Bodley left most of his remaining fortune for the benefit of his library, rather to the disgust of his relatives, but not to poet Henry Vaughan (1622–95).

Most noble Bodley! we are bound to thee
For no small part of our eternity.
Th' hast made us all thine Heirs: whatever we
Hereafter write, 'tis thy Posterity.
This is thy Monument! here thou shalt stand
Till the times fall in their last grain of Sand.
And whereso'er thy silent reliques keep,
This tomb will never let thine honour sleep.
Still we shall think upon thee; all our fame
Meets here to speak one Letter of thy name.
Thou canst not dye! Here thou art more than safe
When every Book is thy large Epitaph.

CHAPTER THREE

Classicism and Crisis

A Friend at Court

Whatever his political or personal shortcomings, James VI and I was a monarch of genuinely scholarly tastes and talents, the author of treatises in favour of Sunday sports and against tobacco and witchcraft. When the king visited Oxford in 1605 he knighted Henry Savile, Warden of Merton and later took a personal interest in the founding of both Wadham and Pembroke College. Touring the Bodleian James once observed somewhat fancifully 'were I not a king, I would be a university man; and if it were that I must be a prisoner . . . I would have no other prison but this library. . .'. In 1620 he presented the university with a copy of his collected works. In recognition of the importance the king attached to the universities he also granted both Oxford and Cambridge the right to send their own separate Members to the House of Commons, a privilege not abolished until 1948.

NEW COLLEGES, NEW STUDENTS

Wadham College was nominally founded by Nicholas Wadham (1532–1609) a childless Somerset landowner, lavish in his hospitality but so reclusive that he was determined to steer clear of even local politics. Despite an annual income of £3,000, greater than many peers of the realm enjoyed, he was never knighted, never sat as a Member of Parliament, never even served as a Justice of the Peace. The real driving force behind the establishment of 'his' college was his forceful widow, Dorothy, daughter of that acquisitive *arriviste* Sir William Petre. Nicholas Wadham's own sojourn at Oxford was allegedly at Corpus

Christi but is unconfirmed by documentation. His will, however, decreed the foundation of a new Oxford college, leaving Dorothy to draw on his accumulated fortune of £14,000, £6,500 in capital and £400 in income being allocated to the project. In fact the buildings alone were to cost £11, 360, the over-run being financed by Dorothy herself from her interest in her late husband's estate. She also added a further £500 to the college's annual income. Shrewdly enlisting the involvement of the scholar *manqué* on the throne, Dorothy extracted from King James a supportive letter which enabled her to purchase from Oxford corporation a suitable site – the demolished college of the Augustinians – at a much reduced price, £600 instead of the £1,000 originally posted – and within less than six months of her husband's death. Dorothy thereafter not only controlled the building programme (1610–13) and drew up the statutes but also selected or approved its personnel, right down to the servants, immersing herself in every detail of college organisation until her death, aged eighty-four, in 1618 – without ever visiting Oxford itself. Her involvement was sustained entirely by correspondence. Twenty-seven of her letters from the period 1613–18 still survive.

Wadham's statutes derive broadly from those of Corpus Christi but made some limited preferential provision for founder's kin and recruits from Somerset and Essex. In fact two-thirds of the founding establishment came from Somerset, Devon and Dorset and the college was to remain oriented towards the West Country thereafter. A significant innovation was the omission of the requirement that Fellows be in holy orders. In addition two were to be allowed to take study-leave abroad on half-pay for up to two years.

Wadham was unique among pre-modern Oxford colleges in having been built all of a piece, rather than piecemeal over decades or centuries. The architect was one of the Wadhams' own West Country men, William Arnold, which may account for its partial resemblance to a very grand Somerset manor house. Most of his masons were also from the West Country, selected by him and almost certainly cheaper than local men into the bargain. Writing in 1938 John Betjeman could enthuse over Wadham unreservedly – 'a complete college of the very latest phase of Gothic or earliest of Renaissance, whichever you like to

Wadham College gateway showing a statue of James I and the two founders, Nicholas and Dorothy Wadham below

call it. Except for a few scattered buildings to the south, it is complete in itself and is remarkable as having not a single ugly or modern building in its make up.' The hall retains its contemporary woodwork and the T-shaped chapel has an east window by Bernard Van Linge the Elder, assembled in the garden *c.*1621–2. Pevsner, writing in 1974, was more grudging viz. – 'fanaticism for symmetry ... windows have tracery not correctly Gothic but Gothic only in moód ... founder and foundress have over their heads ridiculous, flat, horizontally placed shells'. An unbridled enthusiast for the 'modern movement', Pevsner reserved his warmest approval for the 1971–2 'additions and adjustments along Holywell Street ... they are a delight' – except for the disappointing facade of the shop built for Blackwell's as a specialist music outlet.

   In contrast to the single-minded drive which created Wadham, Pembroke College (1624) came into being by stages. On his death

Thomas Tesdale (1547–1610) a rich maltster of Abingdon, left in trust £5,000 to maintain seven fellows and six scholars at Oxford, selected from his kin or poor boys of Abingdon school where he had himself been in the first intake of pupils. Arrangements were made for the selected beneficiaries to attend Balliol until Richard Wightwicke, a former Balliol man, offered to increase Tesdale's bequest so that an entirely new college could be established. Murmurs of royal approval forwarded the project and a founding commission to draw up statutes was appointed under the chairmanship of the chancellor, William Herbert, third Earl of Pembroke (1580–1630), the college being named in compliment to him. Pembroke looked more the statesman than he was. Hubert le Sueur's statue of him, based on a design by Rubens, now stands in the Old Schools Quadrangle. Dressed in armour, he projects a martial air, but, tournaments apart, never saw action. A womaniser and an early addict of tobacco in his youth, the third Earl was recklessly extravagant but with an annual income of £22,000 could afford to be. A nephew of Sir Philip Sidney and a close friend of John Donne, he was a generous patron to Jonson, Massinger and Chapman. He also paid for the Cockney Welshman Inigo Jones to study architecture in Italy and was responsible for introducing him to Charles I, who raised Jones high in his service. The first folio of Shakespeare's plays is dedicated to Pembroke and his brother jointly.

Pembroke College was established on the premises of fourteenth century Broadgates Hall, previously Segrene Hall, in Beef Hall Lane. Once the property of St Frideswide's Priory, the hall had passed to Christ Church. The college also absorbed some almshouses which were begun, but not finished, by Wolsey and were ultimately converted to become the Master's Lodgings in 1927. The last Principal of Broadgates Hall, Thomas Clayton of Balliol, became first Master of Pembroke. Chancellor Pembroke appears to have promised a generous benefaction but his sudden death at fifty meant that nothing came of this. Fortunately the Tesdale and Wightwicke bequests were supplemented in 1636 through the generosity of Charles I, who presented the college with the living of St Aldate's adjacent and a scholarship to bring boys from the Channel Islands.

GENTLEMEN COMMONERS

It would be misleading to present the foundation of new colleges as purely a 'supply side' phenomenon, the consequence only of individual acts of munificence. There was also a 'demand side' pressure for extra provision as gentry families pressed their sons to seek, if not formal qualifications, at least the polish that the universities were thought capable of providing. Ignorance of polite literature and history marked a man as a buffoon. Extra-curricular activities such as music, dancing and fencing were also valued by parents as well as students and they were well provided for at Oxford by a small army of private teachers. Even academics sympathised with such concerns, one tutor assuring a father in 1624 that 'when you left him here I took upon me the Charge of a Gentleman, I shall blush to returne him you again a meeere Scholler'.

A new type of undergraduate appears, characterised by John Earle (?1601–65), Fellow of Merton, in his *Microcosmographie* (1628) as 'A Young Gentleman of the University' who comes 'to weare a gown, and to say hereafter, he has been at the University. His Father sent him thither, because he heard there were the best Fencing and dancing schooles. His main loitering is at the Library, where he studies Arms and Books of Honour ... Of all things he endures not to be mistaken for a Scholar ...'

Professor Lawrence Stone's examination of the matriculation registers show that the average annual admission to Oxford of sons of peers, baronets and knights rose from seven in the 1570s to a peak of forty-five in the 1630s. The number of aspirant professionals also increased, with double the number graduating in medicine between 1600 and 1650 as had in the previous half century, despite the fact that teaching virtually collapsed in the 1640s. At Queen's the overall undergraduate intake rose from about seventy in the 1580s to a hundred and ninety-four in 1612, making it the largest college at that time. Overall annual enrolments appear to have risen from *c.* four hundred and eleven in the decade 1610–19 to *c.* five hundred and seventy-five in 1630–9. In terms of the percentage of the national population receiving higher education this represented a peak not surpassed until the inter-war years of the twentieth century.

Accommodation became a pervasive problem, spurring much building and rebuilding by the colleges, which meant new quads where possible and new attic storeys where not. Exeter rebuilt its hall (1618) and chapel (1623–4) and there were other major upgradings or extensions at Trinity, Merton, Jesus, Magdalen, Oriel, University and St John's. Municipal ordinances of 1615 and 1616, requiring house-holders to put out a lamp at night and sweep their frontages on pain of a fine, imply a heightened concern with environmental standards under the impact of rising numbers. Estimates suggest a doubling of the Oxford's overall population in half a century, from 5,000 in the 1580s to 10,000 by the 1630s.

Having no ambitions for the clerical career for which theological studies had been the traditional preparation, gentry students required instruction – such as they were prepared to tolerate – in the humanities rather than the divinities. Literary talent and linguistic skills were to be refined through the study of Greek and Roman classical authors organised in a curriculum known as *Literae Humaniores*, or, more briefly, 'Greats'. Oxford was becoming a new kind of academy, no longer a seminary but not quite willing to become a finishing school, though the tone of the institution was clearly tending in that direction. In 1614 a posthumous publication of Sir Thomas Overbury (1581–1613) sneeringly satirised his former collegiate colleagues as 'meer' scholars or fellows, puny and pedantic, uncritically prideful of their college, arrogant in their pretended learning, but bores in social settings and tongue-tied in the presence of women.

The admission of larger numbers of 'gentlemen commoners', with no serious intent to take degrees, posed new challenges to traditional codes of discipline since recalcitrant aristocrats were often impervious to sanctions. When the senior Fellows of Exeter decided that its tra-ditional super-strength ale should be weakened the teenage Anthony Ashley Cooper (1621–83) organised a mutiny, advising scholars who would have 'to get their livelihood by their studies to rest quiet and not appear' and to leave the actual confrontation to 'myself and all the others that were elder brothers (i.e. heirs to estates) or unconcerned with their angers'. He further secured the general support of the student body by taking as his target the destruction of the current records of their food and drink consumption, used to compute their college battels (bills). Cooper, 'not being strong of body' regularly employed a personal retinue of hefty fellow-students as bodyguards, repaying them by letting them 'eat upon his expense' and bailing them out of prison when required. During Charles II's reign the student rebel would become first Earl of Shaftesbury and founder of the Whig party.

Privilege was normally accommodated by prudently pre-emptive concessions. At Trinity the sons of peers and knights dined at High Table with senior Fellows. At Lincoln, where undergraduate numbers rose from fifty-four in 1604 to a hundred and nine in 1612, gentlemen commoners were excused lectures. The presence of a privileged elite at least extended the market for the labour of poor students who could earn tips from their 'betters' by keeping their fires made up, emptying their chamber pots and rousing them from their beds when some social or sporting occasion made this imperative.

The co-existence of rich and poor scholars bred temptations as well as tensions. One Welsh squire admonished his son, Cadwalader, that it had taken much family sacrifice to send him to 'the fountain and well head of all learning' and that he was therefore under an obligation to stick to his studies and avoid companions who squandered their allowances on tobacco and drink 'to their own loss and discredit of their friends and parents who sent them to the University for better purposes'. He should expect no fine clothes but make do with a countryman's russet coat and certainly not expect to be waited on by a servitor. Above all he should cultivate the friendship of the English, not the Welsh – 'thereby you may attain and freely speak the English tongue perfectly. I had rather that you should keep company with studious, honest Englishmen, than with many of your own countrymen, who are more prone to be idle and riotous than the English.'

The Physic Garden

Oxford's 'Physic Garden', founded in 1621 by hard-fighting, much-honoured Henry Danvers, Earl of Danby, is the third oldest in Europe, after Padua and Leyden. It was created on the site of the ancient Jews' cemetery after the five acre site had been raised in height by the addition of four thousand cartloads of muck and walled in at a total cost of £5,000. The imposing gateway, named for the founder, was added in 1632, designed by Inigo Jones and carved by master-mason Nicholas Stone. Primarily intended, as its name suggests, as a resource for the teaching of medicine in the university, it soon became as important for students of horticulture and botany, though it was not renamed the Botanic Gardens until 1840. Its advent also gave a major stimulus to gardening in the colleges. Royal gardener and plant-hunter John Tradescant was initially intended by Danby as '*Horti Praefectus*' to supervise the new establishment but his illness and demise prevented this. Instead the post was assigned by Danby to his temporary landlord, Jacob Bobart (1599–1680), a German-born veteran of the Thirty Years War who had settled in Oxford as publican of the Greyhound Inn, opposite Magdalen, making this a very local appointment indeed. Bobart turned out to be an excellent choice. He constructed what may well have been England's first conservatory. Excelling not only as a practical gardener, he also managed, despite all the disruptions and distractions visited on Oxford by the civil wars, to publish (1648) a first alphabetical, bi-lingual (Latin-English) catalogue of the garden, listing some 1,600 different plants under his care. Within a quarter of a century the number had doubled, thanks in part to the importation of many new species from abroad, a by-product of Britain's expanding efforts in colonisation and international commerce. The London plane tree (*platanus acerifolia*), which became the most common tree in England's capital, is a hybrid, dating from *c.* 1670, of American and Oriental varieties, and probably the most celebrated of the many plants to owe its introduction and acclimatisation to Oxford. A direct descendant of Bobart's hybrid can be seen in Magdalen, opposite New Buildings. Another incomer is the yellow ragwort (*senecio squalidus*), introduced from the volcanic slopes of Sicily in 1794, which was by slow decades to spread along clinkered railway tracks to colonise the bomb-sites of London after the Blitz.

The formal lay-out of the Physic Garden was the work of Robert Morison, appointed as the first Professor of Botany in 1669. Morison claimed in his autobiography to have conceived an entirely new and original way of classifying plants 'known to myself only', though 'written on plants from the creation'. Regrettably, he was knocked down and killed by a coach in the Strand near his London home before he communicated his taxonomic breakthrough to anyone else.

Bobart's younger son, also Jacob (1641–1719), succeeded his father as superintendent of the garden and in 1683 himself became Professor of Botany, despite a distinctly ungentlemanly persona and the overall appearance of a spectacularly grubby farmhand. Cosimo, third Grand Duke of Tuscany, visiting the gardens in 1699, found them distinctly unimpressive but Linnaeus complimented the Bobarts' efforts by naming the genus *Bobartia* in their honour. There still survive a yew dating from the Bobart's day and a gingko and hornbeam dating from the eighteenth century. Many foreign plants were to be added as a result of the botanical expeditions of John Sibthorp.

Collegiate Characters

Oxford's Heads of Houses, variously titled as Master, Warden, Rector, President or Provost, lack a convenient collective noun. Wadham's Maurice Bowra once slyly suggested 'a lack of Principals'. Some, at least, of his seventeenth century predecessors seem worthy recipients of this *double entendre*. Virtually unmovable, many enjoyed decades in power and were thereby subject to the usual temptations to abuse it.

Robert Hovenden (1544–1614), Warden of All Souls from 1571 until his death, was a superbly efficient manager of the college estates. He had them systematically mapped, organised the college's muddled mountain of muniments into a proper archive and reformed the accounting procedures. He also rearranged the library, completed the Warden's Lodgings, enlarged the college garden and wrote a biography of Archbishop Chichele, the college founder. A stickler in scrutinising claimants for admission as 'founder's kin', Hovenden was nonetheless himself guilty of blatant nepotism in granting both his brothers church livings in the gift of the college and unduly favourable leases on college properties. He likewise insisted that any Fellow wishing to practise law or medicine in London should renounce his college post, but he also regularly connived at corrupt resignations, whereby Fellows accepted bribes in return for the early surrender of their positions.

The tenure of the eccentric Ralph Kettell (1563–1643) at Trinity was even longer – from 1599 to 1643, when he was so roughly ejected by Cromwellian troopers his death was undoubtedly hastened – 'that was wont to be absolute in the college, to be affronted and disrespected by rude soldiers'. Kettell was admitted to Trinity on the personal recommendation of its founder's widow. As President he followed Hovenden's example as a sedulous manager of the college rental and was powerfully effective at chivvying college members into donating plate or money. In 1618–20 he had the college dining hall rebuilt and added Kettell Hall to its frontage as extra student accommodation. Kettell also pursued an obsessive personal crusade against long hair, constantly carrying a pair of scissors to take instant action against offenders, though on one occasion he had recourse to the buttery bread knife as the nearest implement to hand. Not averse to spying through keyholes, quite literally, to see that his boys were at their books, he would also drop coins anonymously through the windows of the poorest pupils. Under Kettell's leadership Trinity produced some of the century's most talented men, including Archbishop Sheldon, four bishops, James Harrington, author of *The Commonwealth of Oceana*, John Aubrey, the antiquary, gossip and author of the biographical classic *Brief Lives* and George Calvert, Lord Baltimore, the founder of Maryland. When, three years after Kettell's death, Oxford finally yielded to the besieging Parliamentary armies, the surrender was offered by one of Kettell's charges, Thomas Glemham, and accepted by another, Henry Ireton.

At Brasenose the tenure of the autocratic Dr Radcliffe, from 1614 to 1648, was tainted by nepotism and embezzlement, for which he posthumously atoned by bequeathing money for a new library and chapel, built (1656–66) by John Jackson, chief mason of Canterbury Quad, at St John's.

While still an undergraduate at Broadgates Hall, Richard Corbet (1582–1635), Dean of Christ Church (1620–9), had won notoriety as an actor, prankster, poet and wit, but by 1612 he was a proctor and chosen to give the oration at Bodley's funeral. As Dean he often entertained his bosom friend Ben Jonson at Christ Church, continued to indulge in practical jokes and regularly locked himself in the college wine-cellar to get drunk with his chaplain. Eased out of the deanery by aristocratic patrons, he was consoled with the bishopric of Oxford and then of Norwich.

John Prideaux (1578–1650) one of twelve children of a poor Devon family, was sent to Exeter College by a local well-wisher but still had to walk all the way there, clad in the leather breeches of a common labourer. Prideaux worked his way through his course as a part-time kitchen porter 'yet all this while he minded his book and what leisure he could obtain from the business of the scullery, he would improve it all in study.' His rise was satisfyingly rapid. Appointed chaplain successively to Henry, Prince of Wales and King James, he became Rector of Exeter College (1612) and Regius Professor of Divinity (1615), as well as accumulating five church livings. As Vice-Chancellor he was required to settle an acrimoniously disputed election for Principal at Jesus. In his own college he faced an even more indecorous, if less weighty, crisis. It was the custom of the day for freshmen to be hazed by having their face, from lip to chin, deprived of its skin by the nail, grown specially long for the purpose, of the right thumb of one of their 'superiors', after which they were expected to drink a beer-glass of salt water while thrusting their raw face out towards a blazing fire. In 1638 the freshmen, a particularly burly intake, led by Anthony Ashley Cooper (as above) and four of his burly cousins, declined to submit. Appearing in hall as bidden, Cooper stepped smartly forward when called by 'my lord of Pembroke's son' (i.e. the grandson of the former Chancellor) and to his very great surprise, signalled the freshmen to a general attack on their would-be tormentors by 'striking him a box on the ear'. Having the advantage of surprise the young rebels 'easily cleared the buttery and hall' until their opponents called up reinforcements and they retreated to 'a ground chamber in the quadrangle'. As the older students pounded on the door it was suddenly flung open, letting in only a limited quota of victims, before it was forced closed again by the defenders – 'those let in they fell upon and had beaten very severely' until Cooper called a halt. At this point 'Dr Prideaux being called out to suppress the mutiny, the old Doctor, always favourable to youth offending out of courage ... gave us articles of pardon for what had passed, and an utter abolition in that college of that foolish custom'.

Prideaux was doubtless grateful to pass on to the tranquillity of the see of Worcester shortly afterwards. Cooper switched to Lincoln College the following year.

Unlike Prideaux, who worked his way up from poverty, by the time Sir Eubule Thelwall (1562–1630) was chosen Principal of Jesus in 1621 he had already had a brilliant legal career which enabled him to lavish £5,000 on its hall, the chapel and the Principal's Lodgings, where his handsome panelling of 1623 still survives. As a meticulous lawyer, Thelwall was also a valued member of the commission which devised the statutes for Pembroke College.

An undergraduate at Brasenose at twelve, Yorkshireman Henry Savile (1549–1622) became a Fellow of Merton at sixteen and its Warden in 1585, holding that position until the year before his death and serving the sovereign as her personal tutor in Greek. In 1589 he rebuilt the whole north wing of the college and in 1608–10 had the Fellows' Quadrangle built. Autocratic in style, but a good judge of academic talent, he also secured for himself, by constant wheedling, the simultaneous position of Provost of Eton. Savile established his own intellectual reputation with a four volume translation of the *Histories* of Tacitus, with notes which revealed an unrivalled knowledge of Roman warfare, even down to the details of soldiers' pay and rations. Savile devoted years of his later life and the fabulous sum of £8,000 to compiling and printing a definitive ten volume edition of the writings of St Chrysostom. In terms of scholarship it was a triumph, in terms of sales pretty much a disaster. In 1619 in a further act of munificence he founded the Savilian Professorships in Astronomy and Geometry. New chairs of Natural Philosophy and Moral Philosophy were also founded in 1621 by Sir William Sedley and Dr Thomas White respectively.

Wider Horizons: Faculty

Robert Burton (1577–1640) of BNC and Christ Church has been hailed as a pioneer of psychology. In 1621 he published *The Anatomy of Melancholy, What it is With all the Kinds, Causes, Symptoms, Prognostics, and several Cures of it. In Three Main Partitions with their several Sections, Members and Subsections, Philosophically, Medicinally, Historically opened and cut up.*

At once a medical analysis of the milder modes of mental illness, it is also implicitly a satire on the futility of human learning and effort. Burton's wide-ranging erudition enabled him to make his book a treasure-trove of quotations, maxims and anecdotes. By 1676 it was in its eighth edition. Lord Byron, two centuries after its first publication, avowed it an invaluable 'mine of knowledge that, though much worked, was inexhaustible'. Milton and Lamb also were indebted to the *Anatomy*.

The antiquary, diarist and gossip Anthony Wood, though normally quite willing to be snide, held Burton, by contrast, to be 'an exact Mathematician, a curious Calculator of Nativities, a general read Scholar, a thro'-pac'd Philologist, and one that understood the surveying of Lands well'. Apart from these accomplishments Wood also credited him with 'great honesty, plain dealing and Charity' and recorded that 'the Antients' of Christ Church remembered 'his company was very merry, facete and juvenile'. But, addicted to scandal, Wood could not forebear to add that, having calculated exactly the hour of his death, Burton put 'a noose about his neck' so that he should not be proved in error. His monument in Christ Church cathedral styles him Democritus Junior, i.e. acolyte to the Greek philosopher who was renowned for laughing at the follies of mankind. Burton's recommended cure for others with depression was 'Be not solitary, be not idle.' His habitual cure for himself was to stroll down to Folly Bridge to hear the boatmen swear at each other.

Edward Pococke (1604–91), Oxford's first professor of Arabic, was born near the Angel Inn and had already made himself conversant with Arabic, Hebrew and Syriac before accepting the post of chaplain to the English 'Turkey Merchants' at Aleppo in Syria in 1630. Pococke stayed five years, perfecting his existing languages, adding Samaritan and Amharic, befriending local Muslim and Jewish scholars and amassing hundreds of precious manuscripts, in the purchase of which he was never mistaken, deceived or cheated. Stoically braving an outbreak of plague (1634), he attracted the interest of Archbishop Laud, who commissioned him to purchase further manuscripts and coins and, on his return to Oxford, in 1636 appointed him first occupant of the chair he had himself founded. In 1649 he published his *Specimen of Arab History*, a landmark in oriental studies, much broader in scope than its title implies, with lengthy asides on Arabic science and literature. The *Specimen* and a subsequent translation and commentary on a work of the Jewish sage Maimonides are additionally landmarks in typography as the first texts to issue from Oxford in Arabic and Hebrew script. Pococke also found time to publish an account (1659) of '*Kauhi*' (coffee), Oxford's newly fashionable Arabic drink. Following the Restoration, Pococke resided at Christ Church as Professor of Hebrew and a revered adornment of the university. Pococke's memory was preserved by a gigantic cedar and a fig tree, grown at Christ Church from seeds he had himself procured from the Levant.

Wider Horizons: Alumni

William Camden (1551–1623), educated at St Paul's School, Magdalen, Broadgates Hall and Christ Church, taught at Westminster School, where his pupils included Ben Jonson, who credited his influence with 'all that I am in arts, all that I know'. School holidays Camden devoted to antiquarian explorations, publishing his findings in his *Britannia: A chorographicall description of the most flourishing Kingdomes of England, Scotland and Ireland, and the Ilands adioyning, out of the depth of Antiquitie* (1586). He left his readers in little doubt about his veneration for his alma mater – 'OXFORD, I say, our most noble Athens, the Muses-seate, and one of England's staies: nay, The Sun, the Eye, and the Soule thereof, the very Source and most clere spring of good literature and wisdome: From whence, religion, civility and learning are spread most plenteouslie into all parts of the Realme. A faire and godlie Citie, whether a man respect the seemly beautie of private houses or the statelie magnificence of publicke buildings, together with the whole-some sight and pleasant prospect thereof.'

Camden's *Britannia* went through six editions by 1607 and appeared in an English version in 1610. Headmaster of Westminster from 1593 onwards, he resigned to become Clarenceux King-of-Arms at the College of Heralds, exercising jurisdiction on heraldic matters in England south of the Trent. Camden also published a history of Elizabeth's reign and established Oxford's first professorship in ancient history in 1622. As Camden's executor his close friend William Heather (?1563–1627) chorister of the Chapel Royal, became involved in the financial arrangements for this and in 1626 himself founded Oxford's first chair of music. The Camden Society was founded (1838) in Camden's honour to publish historical documents relating to the early history of the British empire.

Sir Henry Wotton (1568–1639) of Winchester-New-Queen's pedigree, a contemporary and close friend of Donne, rose via espionage for the Earl of Essex to become a roving English envoy, in which capacity he coined the classic observation that 'an Ambassador is an honest man, sent abroad to lie for the good of his country'. On returning home he published *The Elements of Architecture* (1624), drawing on his knowledge of contemporary Italian buildings and classic authorities from Virtuvius to Palladio. In 123 pages Wotton discussed the siting, foundations, features, materials and proportions of different types of buildings and the architectural use of painting and sculpture. Wotton's *Elements* was the first extended treatise in English to recognise that the architect was more than an artisan and it remained a hugely influential statement of the fundamentals of architectural taste for over a century – despite the fact that it was unillustrated. Wotton was also an accomplished poet and had wide-ranging scientific interests. He corresponded with Francis Bacon about experiments with a *camera obscura* he had seen in Kepler's house. His own experiments included distilling essences from herbs and improving the traditional water-clock. Wotton's friend, Izaak Walton, author of *The Compleat Angler*, who was to write his biography, consulted him about oils for luring fish.

ARCHBISHOP LAUD

William Laud (1573–1645) provoked his contemporaries and posterity in equal measure – 'not a bigot but a martinet', 'a great churchman but a busybody of the first order', 'a restless spirit and cannot see when things are well'.

Laud was made a Fellow of St John's at twenty and built a reputation as a forthright preacher, speaking so strongly against Calvinist tendencies in the university that he was reproved by the Vice-Chancellor as virtually a Papist. This did not prevent Laud from becoming President of St John's in 1611. His High Church stance also recommended

Archbishop Laud, a great benefactor of Oxford

him to Charles I (r.1625–49), who favoured the restoration of ritual in Anglican worship and the strengthening of hierarchy in church government. Royal favour raised Laud swiftly along an escalator of episcopal preferment – Bishop of St David's, of Bath and Wells, of London and finally, of Canterbury. Appointed Chancellor of Oxford in 1629, Laud determined to re-establish discipline and orthodoxy within the university, setting himself to become Oxford's Justinian. Just as the Byzantine emperor had rationalised the confused corpus of a thousand years of Roman law-making into a coherent and comprehensive code, so Laud oversaw the compilation of a body of statutes which served as both a constitution for the university and a code of conduct for its members. Accepted in 1636, the Laudian Code remained in force until 1854. Structurally speaking, Laud's most significant innovation was the establishment of the Hebdomadal Board (from *hebdomadalis conventus*, weekly board meeting) as the central governing body of the university. Consisting of all the college heads, it was to meet weekly on a Monday. Laud also required the Vice-Chancellor to send him a weekly report. The Laudian code, running to three fat volumes in Latin, covered in detail such matters as sermons and smoking, dress and drinking, hair-length and harlots. Fraternisation with townsfolk was banned. Laud shared Kettell's hair obsession and instituted a fine of 6s 8d. for wearing hair curled or over-long. He also demanded that academics 'abstain from that absurd and assuming practice of walking publicly in boots'. Under-eighteens caught visiting wine or tobacco shops were to be flogged. All would observe a nine o'clock curfew. Laud's style of Anglicanism hastened a national exodus which followed in the wake of the Pilgrim Fathers to that 'New England' beyond the Archbishop's reach. Some forty thousand souls joined the 'Great Migration' of the 1630s. Of Brasenose men alone there went Richard Bellingham, a future Governor of Massachusetts, Richard Mather, grandfather of the noted author and divine, Cotton Mather, and Lawrence Washington, great-great-grandfather of the first President, leaving his buttery bill unpaid. (His descendants paid off the bill a couple of centuries later.) Laud's efforts to establish a University Press proved abortive. He was particularly concerned that it should, by printing them, preserve for posterity the fragile, often irreplaceable, manuscripts at risk of rotting away in libraries throughout Oxford. His personal priority was documentation relating to the early history of the Eastern churches, much of which he had procured through Pococke and presented himself. In 1633 a Board of Delegates – the future governing body of the Press – was summoned to select a manuscript from the Bodleian for printing. Having done so, it was not to meet again for decades.

Laud's other major legacy was the building programme at his old college, financed by his acquisition of seventeen church livings. The Cook's Buildings were in a novel three-storey mode but even more innovatory was the construction of Canterbury Quad, the first classical quad in Oxford, adorned with bronze statues of Charles I and Henriette Marie, by the Huguenot master Hubert Le Sueur. In 1636 the royal couple came in person to honour the opening ceremony, which proved lavish in the extreme. Laud himself arrived with a cavalcade of fifty outriders. The attendant banquet and festivities cost £2,666.1s.7d. – equal to more than half the cost of the buildings. Apart from 153 birds and beasts of various kinds the diners also demolished an ornate pudding moulded to represent a session of the University Convocation. Laud recorded smugly in his diary that 'all things were in very good order and ... no man went out at the Gates ... but content ...'. The occasion marked the zenith of his career.

Laud subsequently paid the highest price for his autocratic style and loyalty to the king. When civil war engulfed the nation in 1642 he was impeached for high treason by Parliament and beheaded in 1645, his body being eventually re-interred at St John's in 1663. The college retains many items of Laudiana, including the cap he wore to the scaffold, his diary and the manuscript account of his trial which he wrote in the Tower.

Laud found a serviceable instrument of his reforming purposes in Brian Twyne (?1579–1644). Following his physician father to Corpus Christi, Twyne before he was thirty (1608) had published the earliest history of Oxford. Considering his age it was a fine effort, if blighted by his unyielding determination to uphold the claim that Alfred was Oxford's founder and that it therefore long predated Cambridge. A quarter of a century later Twyne became chief co-editor of Laud's statutes and was rewarded with the post of first Keeper of the university's archives. This was no less than he deserved, having already dedicated a decade to their preservation. Twyne eventually collected sixty manuscript volumes which became the fundamental resource for such later writers as the much better known Anthony Wood, who never paid the slightest acknowledgment of his debt to his predecessor.

Court, Capital and Camp

During the civil wars of the 1640s prosperous and densely populated London and East Anglia were solidly for Parliament. Equally firmly behind the Crown were the economically backward and thinly peopled regions of the South West, Wales and North West. The heart of the realm, from the south coast to Scotland, was thus contested territory, with Oxford lying at its very centre. Oxford men were prominent on both sides of the conflict. Leaders of the Parliamentary opposition included Sir John Eliot (Exeter), John Pym (Broadgates Hall), John Hampden (Magdalen) and Speaker Lenthall (St Alban Hall).

Many Oxford townsmen were sympathetic to Parliament as townsmen tended generally to be but the university rallied to the king.

Royalist troops initially occupied the city from 28 August 1642 until 8 September. Days after their departure Parliamentary troops arrived to demolish newly erected fortifications, distribute arms to local sympathizers, burn 'Popish' books and pictures and search colleges for hidden plate and weapons. University College and Christ Church lost their plate as punishment for trying to conceal it. The image of the Virgin and Child over St Mary's porch was mutilated (the angels are still headless) and at New College a gilt and alabaster likeness of the king in the Warden's lodgings was smashed. Prudent forethought protected the eight superb stained-glass windows which Abraham van Linge had made for University College chapel in 1641; they were kept in store and not finally put up until the 1660s, though quite possibly not in the order originally intended.

Following the indecisive battle of Edgehill, twenty-five miles north of Oxford, the Parliamentarians withdrew from Oxford and the Royalists withdrew to Oxford, the king entering the city on Saturday 29 October 1642. Over the next four years the university city would serve as the sovereign's court, his temporary capital and his chief military headquarters. Four major confrontations would be fought within a thirty mile radius of Oxford during this period.

Despite their protestations of loyalty the Oxford citizenry were disarmed. The king took up residence at Christ Church, installing his queen at Merton and the dashing Prince Rupert at St John's. A truncated Royalist Parliament met from June 1643 onwards – forty-four

A Charles I crown piece of 1643–4 with a view of Oxford in the background

Lords meeting in the Upper Schools, a hundred and eighteen Commoners in the Great Congregational Hall and the executive committee of the Privy Council (in effect the Cabinet) at Oriel. Even his enemies continued to treat the king with deference, sending up from London a bolt of the appropriate cloth for a suit to be run up so that His Majesty could pass the time with a game of real (i.e. royal) tennis.

Along with the monarch, his ministers and his military forces Oxford acquired many other temporary residents of varying degrees of distinction. Royal physician William Harvey (1578–1657), the discoverer of the circulation of the blood, served briefly as Warden of Merton. He spent much time visiting Ralph Bathurst of Trinity 'who had a hen to hatch eggs in his chamber, which they daily opened to discern the progress and way of generation'. Harvey concluded that every living being has its origin in an egg and later published his conclusions in *Essays on Generation in Animals* (1651). John Taylor (?1578–1653), a London ferryman by trade and versifier by avocation (hence his soubriquet of 'the Water Poet') ran a Royalist pub. Royal portraitist William Dobson (1610–46) depicted the king, Prince Rupert and other courtiers. The Ashmolean has Dobson's portraits of the plant-hunting Tradescant family, of the poet Sir John Suckling and of Dobson's own wife. Wenceslaus Hollar (1607–77), Bohemian by birth, engraver by training and royalist soldier by choice, made an important, if not entirely trustworthy, map of the city as it was in 1643. A plan of the fortifications was also made in 1644 by Bernard de Gomme, a Dutch mercenary adviser on defence works.

The militarisation of Oxford inevitably involved the sequestration of many prominent buildings for warlike purposes. The Schools of Law and Logic became granaries, as did the Laudian library at St John's. The Schools of Music and Astronomy became factories for making uniforms. Powder was stored in the cloisters and tower of New College. There was an arsenal at All Souls and an artillery park at Magdalen which, being outside the city walls, served as a virtual fortress against attack from the east. Elias Ashmole served with the guns there. Cattle were penned in Christ Church quadrangle and provisions stacked in the tower at Brasenose. Port Meadow, Gloucester Green and the Parks were used as drill grounds.

Ditches, drawbridges, earthen ramparts and wooden palisades surrounded the entire city. Remnants of earthworks can still be seen, as an
embankment on the east side of the Warden's garden at Wadham and a
garden terrace at Rhodes House. The Cherwell itself was blocked with
barriers to forestall a water-borne assault. The *enceinte* was achieved
over the summer of 1643 by the forced labour of all members of the
university aged sixteen to sixty. The required *corvée* was, though,
scarcely oppressive – one day a week and a fine of one shilling for
missing.

The mobilisation of resources reached well beyond the city walls. In
December 1643 Charles I sent out foragers to bring all surplus food
from surrounding areas into the city. Out at Osney the corn mills were
converted to manufacture gunpowder and a sword factory was established at Wolvercote. St Clements, to the east, London side of the city,
from which an approach was thought most likely, suffered particularly.
Its orchards were chopped down to make fortifications and almost an
entire street of houses was demolished to deny cover to an approaching
enemy. The Black Horse, then a newly built inn, was one of the few
survivors. Within Oxford the city's covered corn market was demolished so that the timber could be cannibalised and the lead roof melted
down into bullets. Even brass kitchenware was requisitioned to be
turned into ordnance. But the king's most urgent and unremitting need
was money.

As early as 1642 the university had given him £1,360 and on 1
January 1643 another £200. St. John's offered £800 to save its college
plate from being recycled into coinage at the royal mint established at
New Inn Hall under Thomas Bushell. The king took both. By June
1643 the king was asking for £2,000 from the university and the same
from the city. These extraordinary grants were in addition to the sums
extorted weekly in local taxes from colleges and households alike. In
the end almost a ton of gold and silver was transmuted into currency to
pay and provision the royal forces. The denominations struck ranged
from a penny to £3 – the gold 'triple unite', the highest value coin ever
produced in seventeenth century England. Examples of Oxford-min-
ted currency can be seen in the Heberden Coin Room at the Ashmolean Museum. The handsome crown piece of 1644 depicts a sword-

waving monarch with the spires and towers of Oxford visible in the background through the legs of his high-stepping steed. Many of the coins bear the royalist propaganda claim that the king was fighting for RELIG. PROT. LEG. ANG. LIBER. PAR. – the Protestant religion, the laws of England and the liberties of Parliament.

Constant depredations and disorder cannot but have disrupted and depressed the lives of Town and Gown. In addition to this a substantial part of the town was devastated by fire in 1644. By 1645 university teaching had almost completely ceased as students were cleared out of their rooms to make way for soldiers. Those students who remained were, according to Anthony Wood, 'much debauched and idle by their bearing arms and keeping company with rude soldiers'. The king and his court appear to have been largely indifferent to the descent of academia from Arcadia to anarchy, distracting their hours with plays, concerts, assignations and duels. Charles even appointed a Master of Revels.

In May 1645 Charles left Oxford with a large part of his total forces for what he trusted would be a decisive summer campaign. It was, the royalists being soundly beaten at Naseby on 14 June. By September the king was back in Oxford, alarmed that neither a sound defence nor a secure retreat seemed feasible. Meanwhile Cromwell and his best general, Fairfax, set up camp at Headington Hill. Woodstock was taken on 26 April 1646. The following day Charles I, having trimmed back his long hair and donned a false beard, fled over Magdalen bridge with a chaplain and a groom, posing as their servant. The luckless monarch's spurs can be seen in the Ashmolean Museum; the Bodleian, which famously refused to break its most cardinal rule and lend him a book, holds items of his correspondence.

Fairfax tightened his grip on the city until it was finally surrendered to him on 20 June. (A painting of the siege of Oxford by Jan de Wyck can be seen in the Museum of Oxford.) A Cambridge man, Fairfax nevertheless immediately put a guard on the Bodleian to protect it from fanatic would-be looters, declaring 'I very much desire the preservation of that place (so famous for learning) from ruin'. The royalist garrison of 3,000 left on 24 June under a safe conduct and with flags flying and drums beating. With them departed the portraitists and the pastry-

The King Escapes out of Oxford in a disguised maner

King Charles's escape from Oxford

cooks. German-born Prince Rupert, held responsible for numerous cavalier atrocities, was given ten days to leave England.

It was a quarter of a century before Anthony Wood was to write his description of the exhausted city but he had been an eyewitness to its condition and could write with feeling: 'The colleges were much out of repair by the negligence of soldiers, courtiers and others who lay in them ... Their treasure and plate was all gone, the books of some libraries embezzled, and the number of scholars few, and most indigent. The halls ... were very ruinous. Further, also, having few or none in them except their respective Principals and families, the chambers in them were, to prevent ruin and inuries of weather, rented out ... In a word, there was scarce the face of a University left, all things being out of order and disturbed.'

CLARENDON

Having suffered so much from the civil wars it was perhaps only just that in the long run Oxford should gain some profit from its ordeal. One of Charles I's most faithful advisers was Edward Hyde (1609–74),

THE
HISTORY
OF THE
REBELLION and CIVIL WARS
IN
·ENGLAND,
Begun in the Year 1641.

With the precedent Paſſages, and Actions, that contributed
thereunto, and the happy End, and Concluſion thereof
by the KING's bleſſed RESTORATION, and
RETURN upon the 29ᵗʰ of *May*, in the Year 1660.

Written by the Right Honourable

EDWARD Earl of CLARENDON,

Late Lord High Chancellour of *England*, Privy Counſellour
in the Reigns of King CHARLES the Firſt and the Second.

Κτῆμα ἰς ἀιᾶ. *Thucyd.*

Ne quid Falſi dicere audeat, ne quid Veri non audeat. Cicero.

VOLUME THE FIRST.

OXFORD,
Printed at the THEATRE, *An. Dom.* MDCCII.

Lord Clarendon's *History of the Civil War*. The profits financed the Clarendon
Building in Broad Street

whose daughter married the king's younger son, James, and whom the king created Earl of Clarendon. Clarendon, living at All Souls from October 1642 to March 1645, had been instrumental in helping to raise cash from the university for the king's cause. At the Restoration of the monarchy in 1660 he not only became chief minister to the new king, Charles II, but Chancellor of Oxford as well. When Charles tired of his loyal but schoolmasterly servant Clarendon prudently retired to compose his *True Historical Narrative of the Rebellion and Wars in England*. It eventually appeared posthumously in three volumes (1702–4) to tremendous success. Clarendon's son having presented the copyright to the university, the profits were used to help finance the construction of the handsome Clarendon Building (1710–13) built to the designs of Wren's protegé, Hawksmoor, to house the University Press. An elegant statue of Clarendon himself, by Wren's favoured sculptor, Francis Bird, can be seen in a niche at the building's western end. Clarendon's great-grandson left the loyal royalist's manuscripts to the university in hope of the belated fulfilment of a pet project sketched out in Clarendon's *Dialogue on Education* – an academy to teach the gentlemanly accomplishments of riding, fencing and dancing. The project remained a dead letter but funds originally accumulated for it were in 1868 diverted to support the establishment of the Clarendon Laboratory, the first to be built in Europe expressly for experimental instruction in Physics.

CHAPTER FOUR

Republic, Reaction and Revolution

Cromwellian Oxford

The departure of the Royalist army marked the end of Oxford's days as a substitute capital but its history and the politics of the nation would remain closely intertwined for another half century. The victorious Parliament lost no time in asserting its authority over the former royal capital. A suspensory order was issued, forbidding any elections to university or college appointments and seven Puritan divines were despatched with authority to preach wherever they chose. When not preaching they were to serve as the advance guard of a new administrative junta. Among their number was the fanatic Francis Cheynell and the trimmer Edward Reynolds who would serve as Vice-Chancellor (1648–51) and eventually trim so successfully back to the Royalist side that he ended his days as Bishop of Norwich. On May Day 1647 Parliament appointed a twenty-four man Commission to reorganise the university, rid it of 'Malignants' and correct the 'offences, abuses and disorders especially of late times committed there'. On 20 May in a flagrant gesture of defiance New College celebrated the birthday of the Prince of Wales with a bonfire on the mount in its garden.

The Parliamentary Visitors summoned the leadership of the university to appear before them on 4 June between the hours of nine and eleven in the morning. Circumstances conspired deliciously to prevent this. The Visitors, paying due obeisance to the demands of Puritan 'godliness', trooped into St Mary's for a preparatory act of worship but the sermon delivered to them as an inspiration for their labours went on so long that by the time the service ended it was already past eleven o'clock. Dr Samuel Fell, Vice-Chancellor and Dean of Christ Church (1638–47) had already adjourned Convocation, the assemblage representing the university as a whole, punctiliously at eleven and the two processions met midway but to no purpose between St Mary's and the Schools building where their confrontation had been scheduled to take place. The meeting was, therefore, rearranged for September. In the interim Dr Fell, the proctors, six heads of colleges and three canons of Christ Church were summoned to London and dismissed from office. Oxford ignored the dismissals – 'not a man stirred from his place or removed'. Early in 1648, however, Chancellor Pembroke came in person to impose the will of Parliament, replacing all but three Heads of Houses. Dr Fell was replaced by Reynolds in both his offices but Mrs Fell refused to quit the Deanery and faced out a siege designed to 'weary them out with noise, rudeness, smell of tobacco etc.' until she was finally carried out bodily in a chair by armed troopers 'and her children after her upon boards, as if they were going like so many Pyes to the Oven.'

In all over four hundred heads of houses, professors, students and servants were ejected, chiefly from Christ Church, Magdalen, All Souls, where thirty-three of the forty Fellows were ousted and New College, where seventy-nine of all ranks were expelled. A similar number submitted and stayed. Meanwhile in the wider world a second civil war was being fought and lost by the king. Protracted negotiations having foundered, the diminutive, duplicitous monarch was executed on 30 January 1649, the monarchy itself abolished and a republic declared by the name of a Commonwealth.

By May 1649 the university was judged to be sufficiently cowed for Cromwell and Fairfax to make a state visit and, apparently without a trace of self-consciousness, to receive the honorary degree of Doctor of Civil Laws, an ironic gesture towards the two men who had done most to subvert the ancient constitution and substitute rule at the point of a cavalryman's sword. The conquerors lodged at All Souls, where Anthony Wood observed derisively 'one of the new Fellows . . . spake a speech to them which, though bad, yet good enough for soldiers'. At Magdalen there was more 'good cheer and bad speeches. After dinner they played at Bowls in the College Green'. Cromwell requited the college for its hospitality by removing its organ to Hampton Court. (Charles II sent it back in 1660.) At St Mary's two sermons were preached 'for the Army and their blessed proceedings' but Cromwell went out of his way to reassure the purged ranks of the professoriate that he and his generals 'knew no Commonwealth could flourish without learning, and that they, whatsoever the world said to the contrary, meant to encourage it, and were so far from subtracting any of their means that they purposed to add more . . .' When it came to the city's military potential, however, the victors took no chances, organising a comprehensive slighting of the ancient castle fortifications.

When Lord Pembroke died in 1650 the university prudently elected Cromwell, a Cambridge man, as Chancellor in his place. Effective authority was wielded by a new Dean of Christ Church and Vice-Chancellor, Cromwell's personal chaplain, John Owen (1616–83). Owen was the son of an Oxfordshire vicar and had been educated at an Oxford school and at Queen's, quitting Oxford in 1637 rather than submit to the Laudian regime. As *de facto* ruler of the university from 1651 to 1658 Owen proved wise, tolerant and successful. He turned a judiciously blind eye to the use of the proscribed Anglican liturgy in private houses, restored discipline and revived recruitment. By 1658 the annual intake of undergraduates had recovered to 460. Even the Royalist John Evelyn, returning to visit his alma mater in 1654, felt 'satisfied with the civilities' and thoroughly enjoyed a tour of the Physic Garden guided by Bobart himself. Numerous bothersome commissions were visited upon the university throughout this period but the university rediscovered its customary talent for frustrating them by the time-honoured tactics of delay, obfuscation and masterly inactivity.

WISDOM AT WADHAM

Having appointed his chaplain to head the university, Cromwell appointed his future brother-in-law, Dr John Wilkins (1614–72) to head Wadham College. Despite the self-evident nepotism it proved an equally inspired choice. Wilkins was the son of an Oxford goldsmith who was thought to be 'a very ingenious man with a very mechanical head . . . (which) . . . ran much upon the perpetual motion'. Wilkins had evidently inherited his father's interests and already published one of the earliest examples of science fiction, *The Discovery of a World in the Moon* (1638), as well as a work on crytography (1641).

Wilkins refused to allow religious disputations in college and was himself a model of the intellectual style he aimed to cultivate – 'a close, naked, natural way of speaking; positive expressions; clear sense; a native easiness'. Appropriately, Wilkins' own preoccupations were in the field of communications. He hoped to devise an Esperanto-style universal language and aspired to develop methods of teaching deaf-mutes to communicate. He converted Wadham's garden from an orchard to a formal arrangement and adorned it with curiosities such as 'an hollow Statue which ... utter'd Words, by a long concealed pipe' and transparent glass bee-hives, designed by one of the undergraduates, Christopher Wren (1632–1723). Wilkins also installed a water-squirt for creating an artificial mist 'wherein a Person placed at a due distance ... might see an exquisite Rainbow'.

Wilkins' Wadham served as the venue, nucleus and catalyst of a group of brllliant young scientists whose informal meetings became institutionalised in London in 1662 as the Royal Society, Europe's oldest scientific association. Thomas Sprat, the Society's first historian and another of Wilkins' proteges, was unequivocal about its origins: 'It was ... in Dr Wilkins his Lodgings, in Wadham College, which was then the place of Resort for Vertuous and Learned Men, that the first meetings were made, which laid the foundations of all this that followed.' Sprat depicted Oxford as an oasis of sanity in a 'dismal Age' beset by 'passions and madness' and a welcoming refuge for 'Gentlemen of Philosophical Minds' seeking 'security and ease of retirement among Gown-men'. Sprat believed that, apart from leading to the establishment of the Royal Society, the chief importance of the meetings of this clique was to foster a cadre of intellectuals 'invincibly arm'd against all the inchantments of Enthusiasm' but he also claimed that by its influence 'the University itself, or at least any part of its Discipline and Order, was saved from ruin'.

It is a tribute to Wilkins' character that he could gain the respect and regard of even High Church Royalists like John Evelyn, who praised him as 'most obliging and universally Curious' and of Christopher Wren, even while Wren's own uncle, a bishop, was imprisoned in the

Tower of London on the orders of the Cromwellian regime. Their brilliant contemporaries included Robert Boyle (1627–91) and Robert Hooke (1635–73) (see below).

Several members of the Wadham circle were physicians. Jonathan Goddard (?1617–75) had been chief medical officer of the Parliamentary army before serving as Warden of Merton (1651–60). Tradition credits him with the suggestion that surplus sugar produced on the plantations of Barbados could be distilled to make a potable 'wine', thus winning a footnote in history as the father of Caribbean rum. Thomas Willis (1621–75), who became Sedleian Professor of Natural Philosophy (1660), published a ground-breaking anatomy of the brain and discovered the relationship between sugar and diabetes. Ralph Bathurst (1620–1704) was a former naval surgeon and a bounteous future President of Trinity College. Thomas Sydenham (1624–89) had served as a cavalry captain in the parliamentary army and actually acquired his professional training at Montpellier *after* receiving the medical degree granted him by Oxford. Mathematical interests were common to self-taught Seth Ward (1617–89), Savilian Professor of Astronomy (1649) and John Wallis (1618–73) whose skills as Parliament's code-breaker gained him the Savilian Professorship of Geometry. Wallis's *Arithmetica Infinitorum*, published at Oxford in 1655, made him famous. He also introduced the mathematical symbol for infinity.

The talents of William Petty (1623–87) embraced medicine, music, mathematics and much more besides. Educated in France and the Netherlands, he qualified as a doctor before lecturing on anatomy at Oxford and gaining overnight celebrity in 1650 by reviving the apparent corpse of Ann Greene. A local girl whose illegitimate child was stillborn, Ann had been nevertheless convicted of its murder and hanged. When her body was taken down, however, she was found to be still breathing and, thanks to Petty's administration of stimulants, was successfully revived. Petty himself appears to have been, if anything, rather miffed by his 'miracle' as he had been looking forward to using Anne's cadaver for dissection.

Oxford, however, generally hailed the incident as proof of divine intervention on behalf of the innocent and a slim volume of verses was published to mark the event, Wren himself contributing one in Latin. In the course of his subsequent career Petty pioneered the use of statistics for the study of population and taxation. A sufferer from severe myopia, he once reduced a bullying braggart to a laughing-stock when challenged to fight a duel with him. As the person challenged Petty had the choice of venue and weapons. To even the odds he opted for a cellar at midnight with tree-fellers' axes.

TWO LAW-MAKERS: BOYLE AND HOOKE

A son of the Earl of Cork and pupil of Wotton at Eton, Robert Boyle was fluent in French and Latin as a small boy and after a six-year Grand Tour added Italian. His religious convictions caused him to learn Hebrew, Greek and Syriac and to become a lifelong patron of efforts to propagate the gospel, subsidising Irish, Welsh, Turkish and Malay editions of the Bible. Boyle settled in Oxford in 1654, lodging with an apothecary whose High Street shop, next to University College, served as an occasional venue for meetings of the Wadham group. Boyle hired Robert Hooke, then a servitor at Christ Church, as his laboratory assistant. At Boyle's direction Hooke devised an effective air-pump which enabled him to conduct experiments which led to the formulation of Boyle's Law: that the volume of a confined gas varies inversely with its pressure. Boyle also investigated colours, crystallography, fluid mechanics, combustion and respiration – despite delicate health, impaired eyesight and a defective memory which often brought him to despair. In the *Sceptical Chymist* (1661) Boyle defined the chemical element as the practical limit of chemical analysis. He was also the first to distinguish between a mixture and a compound. Boyle moved to London in 1668 to devote more time to the Royal Society and the East India Company, of which he was a director.

Hooke preceded Boyle in 1662 to become first curator of experiments at the Royal Society. Now remembered for the theory of elasticity known as Hooke's Law, Hooke also invented or improved the reflecting telescope, compound microscope, marine barometer, quadrant, and universal joint, as well as making many contributions to the construction of clocks and watches and becoming City Surveyor of London after the Great Fire of 1666. Hooke also coined the modern biological usage of the word 'cell', having been the first to observe and identify one, using a microscope of his own manufacture.

'THIS MIRACLE OF YOUTH'

Wren's name is now synonymous with the terse grandiloquence of his epitaph 'builder of St Paul's etc.' – the latter comprising Hampton Court, Greenwich Observatory, Chelsea Hospital, fifty-one City of London churches, the towers of Westminster Abbey ... But until he was thirty Wren was primarily renowned as a scientist whose versatility easily matched the talents of Petty or Boyle. Hooke marvelled at his uniquely gifted combination of 'such a mechanical hand and so philosophic a mind'. Wren excelled at making scientific models, experimented with blood transfusions, devised a device for planting seeds and another for writing in raised characters for the blind to read, explained the mechanism of eclipses and pondered the problem of determining longitude at sea. It was also Wren who provided the illustrations for Dr Willis's *Anatomy of the Brain*. Initially it seemed that he might himself be drawn to a career in medicine. Appointed a Fellow of All Souls (1653), he designed its huge but highly accurate sundial and served as college bursar. In 1661 he was appointed Savilian Professor of Astronomy, still not yet thirty.

Gardens of Eden

If republican Oxford nurtured the embryo of a scientific renaissance it was also vulnerable to the millennarian tendencies of the times. The abolition of the monarchy was taken by some 'Phanaticks' as a portent of the Last Days and the Second Coming of Christ. With the machinery for licensing both press and preachers broken down prognostications and pamphleteering proliferated. Against this febrile background movements as varied as the Diggers and the Quakers emerged. In 1656 James Nayler, a Quaker, rode into Bristol on a donkey in imitation of Christ. Oxford opted for the digging mode.

Some millennarians believed that a life devoted to gardening, in imitation of Adam rather than Christ, could assist the advent of a New Eden by anticipating it in outward form. One such was Ralph Austen (d.1676) an Oxford university administrator who devoted half a century of his life to the cultivation of fruit trees and had his own nursery, estimated to sell some 20,000 plants a year. In 1653 Austen published *A Treatise on Fruit-trees, showing the manner of grafting, setting, pruning and ordering of them in all respects*, as well as a voluminous pamplet, *The Spirituall Use of an Orchard or Garden of Fruit Trees*, the title page of which bore the legend 'Profits and Pleasures'. It promised to reveal 'divers Similitudes between Naturall and Spirituall Fruit Trees : according to Scripture and Experience'. A combined edition appeared in 1657. Anthony Wood claimed that the inclusion of the theological section damaged its sales, 'which being all divinity, and nothing therein of the practice part of gardening, many refused to buy it'. Further editions appeared, however, in 1662 and 1667. Austen was also a champion of home-made cider as 'soothing to the mind'.

In 1657 William Coles of New College published *Adam in Eden: a History of Plants, fruits, Herbs and Flowers with their several names, whether Greek, Latin or English, the places they grow, their descriptions and kinds, their times of flourishing and decreasing, and also their special signatures, anatomical appropriations and particular physical virtues*. Coles's work summarised the traditional lore of 'physic gardening' and attempted to revive the ancient Doctrine of Signatures which taught that illnesses in different parts of the body were to be treated with plants that resembled them, as walnuts for brain disorders or quince fuzz for hair loss. Coles especially recommended gardening as a remedial counterpoint to studious confinement: 'if a man be wearied by over-much study ... there is no better place in the world to recreate himself than in a Garden, there being no sense but may be delighted therein ...'.

A LASTING FASHION

Oxford's inhabitants seem, however, to have opted for indoor relaxation instead. The success of the coffee-house opened by Jacob the Jew in 1650 at the Angel inspired imitators. Jobson's followed in 1654. Tillyard's, opened the following year at 90 High Street, became a favourite haunt of Wren, Boyle and Hooke. A century later a dozen coffee-houses still flourished, some with their own libraries and offering 'liquors adapted to every species of reading. Amorous tales may be

perused over Arrack ... politics over coffee, divinity over port ...
learning no longer remains a dry pursuit'. There were some twenty
coffee-houses by 1800 but soon afterwards the discriminatory tax
which made coffee unaffordable to the poor was abolished and it
rapidly lost its social cachet. The coffee-houses then disappeared
rapidly. Coffee-drinking as a social institution was revived in the 1920s,
much to the disgust of misogynistic die-hards, by female undergraduates taking a mid-morning break between lectures.

Restoration ...

When Clarendon took over as Chancellor he was obliged to admit that
'things were less bad under the Commonwealth than might have been
expected', although he gave the credit for this to a benign Deity. The
benevolence of the Almighty proved such that 'many who were
wickedly introduced applied themselves to the study of good learning
and the practice of virtue', so that when Charles II was restored to his
throne he found Oxford 'abounding in excellent learning and devoted
to duty and obedience'.

Both city and university responded to the return of the monarchy
with enthusiasm. Indeed, they can even be said to have anticipated it
because when, in September 1658, Richard Cromwell had been
proclaimed Lord Protector in succession to his father 'the Mayor,
recorder, town clerk etc. ... accompanied by troopers, were pelted
with carrot and turnip-tops by young scholars and others...'. May-
poles, banned as ungodly during the Commonwealth, were set up on
Restoration Day, 29 May 1660. The King's Head put up its sign again,
along with 'all tokens of monarchy that were lately defaced or
obscured'. Even the Puritans 'tack'd about to participate of the universal joy'.

... and Refuge

In late September 1663 Charles II (r.1660–85) made a week-long state
visit to Oxford. It was part of a larger 'progress' through the western
part of his dominions and as such an element in a public relations

strategy intended to revive popular attachment to the throne. The Oxford interlude was almost entirely given over to banquets and other junketings as Carfax Conduit ran with free claret, but it did also include a session, in Christ Church after morning service, of touching 'divers scores of people' for 'the King's Evil'. A tubercular infection, which physicians were later to label as scrofula, the King's Evil took the form of unsightly and painful swellings around the neck. It was widely believed that these symptoms could be relieved by the laying on of the sovereign's hands. Charles II seemed, however, to be an eminent rationalist and sceptic, genuinely interested in science. Only the year before he had himself enrolled as a founder-member of the Royal Society. The decision to use the university as the setting for a display of monarchical magic seems doubly perverse, given Oxford's standing as *the* contemporary centre of scientific enquiry. It also seems curious that Charles, who, in the semi-privacy of his court at least, often affected a flippant attitude to religion, should resume a tradition whose continuity had been entirely severed by England's republican episode. Oliver Cromwell may have put his head on the coinage and had himself buried in Westminster Abbey but he never pretended to thaumaturgical powers. Perhaps that was the point Charles wanted to make – his father *had* been a martyr, he was himself, by virtue of his royal blood, *special*. Whatever his motives Charles performed his part dutifully and went on to do the same many more times, touching an estimated 100,000 sufferers in the course of his reign.

Whether or not the king thought he could cure scrofula, he was in no doubt that plague was beyond the royal remit. Fleeing the capital to escape its last great outbreak in 1665, Charles and his court settled in Oxford in September and stayed until February of the following year. The king, like his father before him, ensconced himself in Christ Church and lodged his consort, the Portuguese princess, Catherine of Braganza at Merton. Lady Castlemaine, the king's current mistress, took to her bed, also in Merton, to give birth to George, Duke of Northumberland. Royal attendants, apparently following the custom of the French court, freely relieved themselves in fireplaces, coal cellars and stair-wells. Quite like old times. Along with the king came the business of government. Sir Leoline Jenkins, Master of Jesus (1661–73), transferred his other occupation, presiding over the Court of Admiralty, to Oxford and carried on business as usual. Parliament assembled to pass the vindictive Five Mile Act, which drew a *cordon sanitaire* of that radius around every city and parliamentary borough, within which clergymen and schoolmasters were forbidden to live unless they took an oath not to support any effort to alter the government of church or state. In practice the statute was so vaguely framed that it proved impossible to enforce and few prosecutions were attempted under its terms.

One significant by-product of the royal sojourn was the inaugural publication of the *Oxford Gazette* on Tuesday 14 November 1665 to satisfy news-hungry courtiers deprived of London gossip. When the court returned to the capital the publication was re-named the *London Gazette*. Pepys thought it 'very pretty, full of news and no folly in it'. The *London Gazette* still survives as the government's official news-sheet, giving notice of official appointments.

Another effect of the Merry Monarch's prolonged presence may have been further encouragement to the anti-Puritan reaction which

Anthony Wood, the opinionated author of *The History and Antiquities of the University of Oxford* in 1695

had, in the eyes of the dyspeptic Anthony Wood by 1666 turned Oxford into a veritable Sodom: 'Baudy houses and light huswifes giving divers young men the pox ... Multitudes of alehouses ... keeping dice, cards, sketells, shuffle-boards, billiard tables ... Extravigance in apparell, having their suits and hats dect with colored ribbons and long haire periwiggs ... Lying and swearing much used ... Atheism ... Disrespect to seniors ....' Needless to say 'solid and serious learning decline ... because of coffee-houses, where they spend all their time'.

Oxford by this date had reached a population of 9,000, putting it on a par with Colchester. Of its inhabitants some 2,000 were either members of the university or their servants.

LACKING PRINCIPALS

Just as the republican take-over of Oxford had been accompanied by a clear-out of the contumacious so, too, the royalist reaction took its toll. Those displaced included many worthy of less summary treatment, while those who replaced them were often less than paragons. At Merton the appointment of Thomas Clayton (1661–93) was so opposed by the Fellows that for weeks they refused to hand over the keys to the Warden's Lodgings. His rule turned out to be as pernicious as they feared. Clayton milked college funds so shamelessly for the benefit of himself and his termagant wife, that the bursar believed they must 'sit thinking how to put the college to charge, to please themselves, and no end there is to their unlimited desire'. At least the Fellows could commiserate with each other in Oxford's first common room. At Exeter under Arthur Bury (1666–90) for four years the Fellows were not on speaking terms, being violently split into two factions in a theological dispute which spilled over into duplicated elections to Fellowships. When the official Visitor, a bishop, arrived to remove Bury from his post, his supporters simply refused him entry. Inept housekeeping under Henry Savage (1651–72), compounded by a loss of London rents after the Great Fire of 1666, brought Balliol to the brink of ruin. Savage did at least respond by producing the first ever college history, *Balliofergus*, as a fund-raising device. At St John's Peter Mews (1667–73) was appointed to succeed his own father-in-law. A colourful character, scarred in battle and an adept secret agent abroad, all in the royalist cause, Mews was nominated by the king in recognition of his 'sober life' – a claim somewhat contradicted by his only publication '*An Exe-Ale-tation of Ale*', which did not prevent him becoming Bishop of Winchester. At New College standards of administrative discipline slid so badly that no less than a third of the entrants were being admitted as 'founder's kin' and almost half the senior Fellows were absentees, mostly living in London to attend profitable legal practices.

Dr Fell

There was, however, no lack of discipline at Christ Church under Dr John Fell (1625–86). The son of Samuel Fell, entered to the college by his father at eleven, he had served as an officer in the Oxford garrison and after its defeat lived humbly opposite Merton with the cantankerous Anthony Wood as his neighbour. Fell was ultimately rewarded for his loyalty with appointment as Dean of Christ Church, Vice-Chancellor (1666–9) and Bishop of Oxford (1676). At Christ Church he vigorously resumed his father's building programme, which had been stalled by the war. He was also instrumental in securing Sheldon's financial support for the building which bears his name. A connoisseur of typography and collector of type-faces, Fell also did much to improve standards at the University Press, himself master-minded a promotional publishing programme for the university and wrote or edited a dozen hefty academic works. A zealous churchman, attending four public services daily and holding two more at home, as Vice-Chancellor Fell was a merciless martinet, rigidly enforcing curfews, attendance at lectures and the academic dress code. Not only did he routinely sit in on oral examinations but, if he thought they were too undemanding, he simply took over himself. Despite his very real achievements, Fell is best remembered by an uncomplimentary squib composed in his 'honour'

> I do not love thee, Dr Fell,
> The reason why I cannot tell;
> But this I know, and know full well,
> I do not love thee, Dr Fell.

A DIARIST'S DIVERSIONS

Samuel Pepys (1633–1703) diarist, naval administrator and *bon viveur* visited Oxford for the day on Tuesday 9 June 1668. A man on the make with a keen sense of the value of money, Pepys recorded his outgoings in detail but seems to have been very open-handed and delighted with what he saw. Having set out by coach from Newport Pagnell at dawn he hired a guide on his arrival in Oxford – 'a very sweet place' – for the sum of £1 2s. 6d., then paid 2s. 6d. to be barbered and bought a book about Stonehenge for 4s. It cost another 10s. to see 'the schools and library' and 5s. more 'to him that showed us All Souls College and Chicly's pictures' and 1s. to a boy who took him to Christ Church. Dinner with service cost £1 0s. 6d. and another 1s 2d. was spent on strawberries, then in season. A visit to 'Brazen Nose College to the butteries' cost yet another 2s. tip to the butler. This was so that Pepys could inspect the celebrated impression of a seventeen-inch handprint left by the allegedly nine-foot tall Lancashire wrestler John Middleton when he visited the college in 1617. (The college still owns a life-size portrait of the giant, ironically known as ' The Child of Hale', a name given to the college boat when Brasenose dominated Oxford rowing in Victorian times.) Then there was 1s. coach fare to the Physic Garden and another 1s. to go up to 'Friar Bacons study' on Folly Bridge and finally 2s. for a bottle of sack. Somewhat surprisingly in the light of this constant haemmorhage of cash Pepys signed off with the observation 'Oxford mighty fine place: and well seated, and cheap entertainment'.

In February the following year Pepys visited the London studio of 'Mr Streeters the famous history-painter...' Wren happened to be there with 'several virtuosos looking upon the paintings which he is making for the new Theatre at Oxford' (i.e. the Sheldonian) ... 'and indeed, they look as though they would be very fine'.

Three months later Pepys, having called on Robert Hooke's London home, went to lunch at the Spanish Ambassador's to find himself seated with 'an Oxford scholar in a Doctor's of Laws gowne' who 'sat like a fool for want of French or Spanish; but only Latin, which he spoke like a Englishman'. Pepys – 'to my great content' made 'much use of my

French and Spanish' and completed his triumph by making 'the company very merry at my defending Cambridge against Oxford.'

The London Road

When Pepys visited Oxford a thrice weekly coach service to London had been going for a year. Departure from Oxford was at 4 a.m. and, after an overnight stop at Beaconsfield, the capital was reached at 4 p.m. the following day. By 1669 the university's licensed 'flying coach' was expected to make the journey in a single day of thirteen hours, at least in summer, when the roads were dry and hard. When two local entrepreneurs presumed to set up in competition the Vice-Chancellor banned all members of the University from travelling on the rival service or using it to send letters or parcels. Not for almost another century would it be possible to reach London in a single day all year round.

WREN RETURNS

Although Wren resigned his All Souls Fellowship and after the Great Fire of 1666 was largely preoccupied with the reconstruction of London, he did devote time to other projects. His first completed essay in architecture was the chapel of Pembroke College, Cambridge, commissioned by his uncle, the Bishop of Ely. His first large project, however, was at Oxford, the construction of a new theatre for the conduct of university ceremonies, previously performed in St Mary's. Commissioned by Gilbert Sheldon, Warden of All Souls and Archbishop of Canterbury at a cost of £12,200, it was modelled on an illustration Wren had seen of the Theatre of Marcellus in Rome. Wren himself never visited Italy, indeed only ever went abroad once, to Paris, thus fortuitously absenting himself from England during the plague of 1665. Unlike the Theatre of Marcellus, which is open to the sky, Wren's version, to be practical in an English climate, had to be roofed in. Wren was particularly proud of the roof, based on the calculations of his friend John Wallis, the Savilian Professor of Geometry. The ceiling, seventy feet by eighty feet, dispenses with cross-beams to spectacular effect. Streeter's painted panels depict the Triumph of Religion, Arts

The Clarendon Building and the Sheldonian Theatre

and Science over Envy, Hatred and Malice – a retrospective, triumphalist dig at the vanquished Commonwealth. Apart from complimenting the interior woodwork and the carving around the north doorway Pevsner is disparaging: 'classical ... as no previous Oxford building had been, so for Oxford it may be called revolutionary ... it is, as a young amateur's job, just a little confused'. Begun in 1663 and completed in 1669, the Sheldonian Theatre was opened, in the words of John Evelyn 'with the greatest splendour and formality that might be' in an eight hour ceremony before 'a world of strangers and other Companie ... from all parts of the Nation'. Evelyn himself was one of the first contingent to be given honorary degrees in the university's new landmark building. Whatever its status, within a few years there were dunghills up against its walls.

Wren's other Oxford projects include the north range of Garden Quad at Trinity (1665–8), now unrecognisable as his work but originally incorporating a mansard roof in the French style, Oxford's first ; probably the Williamson Building at Queen's (1671–2); chancel-screens at All Souls (1664), St John's (1670) and Merton (1671–4); and

Tom Tower (1681–2) above the front gateway at Christ Church. Of this last Wren wrote to Dr Fell to justify his choice of a Gothic, rather than classical, treatment on grounds of architectural good manners: 'I resolved it ought to be Gothic to agree with the Founder's work'. Anything other would result in an 'unhandsome medley'. An expert conservationist, Wren also performed much-needed restoration work on Duke Humfrey's Library.

OXFORD PROMOTED

Dr Fell's concern to promote the image of Oxford was pursued through the production of an informative yearbook and by subsidising the antiquarian researches of Anthony Wood and the engraving work of David Loggan. The *Oxford Almanack* was, unlike most of its genre, from the first (1674) a very up-market effort, generous in format and embellished with allegorical figures symbolising Time. In addition to the calendar for the year it gave information on tides and lists of monarchs and university officials. The *Oxford Almanack* became a regular annual production from 1676 onwards, engaging the talents of such leading academics as Henry Aldrich and George Clarke. The Almanack for 1683 shows a cluster of mathematicians paying tribute to Wren and the Royal Society, of which he had become President, against a background of the Oxford skyline, newly graced by his Tom Tower.

Fell's former neighbour and troublesome protégé Anthony Wood (1632–95) was born in a house right opposite Merton, from which he graduated (1652) after five undistinguished years. A singularly unclubbable character, Wood was embittered by his failure to gain a Fellowship, which must have rankled daily as he returned to inhabit the family home, just across the street from Merton's main gate. Living as a recluse in two garret rooms, he devoted his energies to compiling a large format, two volume survey of *The History and Antiquities of the University of Oxford*, published (1674), with the encouragement of Ralph Bathurst of Trinity and Fell's financial support. This was followed by another Fell-sponsored enterprise, a vast biographical dictionary of Oxford writers and clerics, *Athenae Oxonienses* (1691–2). In this latter work Wood repeated the story that Clarendon had taken bribes in making appointments. The late Earl's son took great umbrage and decisive action, resulting in Wood's condemnation by the Vice-Chancellor's court and the public burning of the offending parts of the book. Hearne epitomised Wood as 'a most egregious, illiterate, dull Blockhead, a conceited, impudent Coxcombe'. Wood's autobiography and diaries, the latter sometimes almost as abusive as Hearne's, eventually passed to the Bodleian. Wood asked to be buried in Merton's chapel 'as close to the wall as the place will permit, and I desire that there may be some little monument erected over my grave'. His wishes were observed.

David Loggan (1635–?1700) was born in Danzig but emigrated to England as a teenager and was living out at Nuffield by 1665. The ambivalent advantage of an introduction to university circles by Anthony Wood led to Loggan's appointment (1669) as its official engraver. Loggan's masterpiece is his *Oxonia Illustrata* (1675) which contains forty double-page plates, giving a plan and general views of Oxford, thirty-seven views of colleges and university buildings and illustrations of the varieties of academic dress. Loggan worked with painstaking accuracy and not a little imagination. At Merton games of tennis and fives are shown, at Pembroke a bowling alley and a floral sundial. Domestic items like piles of wood stacked for winter add immediacy to his scenes. There are even touches of humour, like the chained fox in Corpus Christi as an allusion to its founder. *Oxonia Illustrata* was intended as a companion to Wood's *History* because there a cross-references from its pictures to the relevant pages of Wood's text. Notable visitors to the university were often presented with copies of both works. Loggan also engraved plates for Robert Morison's *Historia Plantarum Oxoniensis* (1680).

JOHN LOCKE

John Locke (1632–1704) is now largely thought of as a political thinker, associated with the notion of government as a contract between ruler and ruled and is therefore, in an indirect way, the philosophical begetter of the constitution of the United States. He did actually draft the original constitution for the colony of Carolina. Locke had, however, interests as wide-ranging as those of Petty or Wren and an intellect as profound as Newton's. Educated at Westminster alongside Dryden, at Christ Church he followed his own inclinations, attending lectures by Wallis, Ward and Pococke. Locke was also acquainted with the Wilkins coterie, became a lifelong friend of Boyle and Sydenham and like them quit Oxford for a wider world. He was back at Christ Church at the time of the Exclusion crisis of 1681 (see below) and mystified many of his colleagues by unexplained departures for days at a time. Locke was almost certainly not privy to his patron Shaftesbury's political plotting but when Shaftesbury was accused of treason and fled abroad suspicion naturally fell on him, despite his renowned taciturnity and discretion. In 1684 Lord Sunderland, the Secretary of State, wrote to Dr Fell to demand Locke's dismissal. Fell demurred on the grounds that he had no grounds for doing so. Back came a letter direct from the king himself. Fell complied instantly, the co-signatories of Locke's expulsion including such luminaries as Pococke and Aldrich. Locke fled to Holland, where Shaftesbury had died in exile. He finally returned to England and favour with William and Mary – but not to Oxford. Later – much later – 'the House' eventually honoured Locke as 'an ornament of this society' and commissioned a full-length statue (1757) by Rysbrack for its college library.

Crisis and Confrontation

Charles II, Supreme Governor of the Church of England, was actually a would-be Catholic ('the only religion for a Gentleman') but had the political discretion to delay the announcement of his conversion until he was actually on his deathbed. His younger brother, James, Duke of York was less tactful. Converting to Catholicism around 1672, he compounded his alienation by marrying a Catholic Italian, and, refusing to take the Anglican sacrament as required by law for office-holders, resigned his position as Lord High Admiral. As anti-Catholic feeling grew in force, a movement emerged around the Earl of Shaftesbury to bar James from succeeding his brother on the throne. Charles had a dozen or more bastards but no legitimate heir, the queen being barren. The king was, however, determined to protect the hereditary principle and when an Exclusion Bill was presented in Parliament in

1679 simply dissolved the House of Commons. In 1680 a second Bill was aimed at the Duke of York, 'notoriously known to have been perverted from the Protestant to the Popish Religion'. Charles scuppered this by persuading the Lords to reject it. In 1681 he changed tactics yet again, ordering Parliament to assemble in Oxford, and thus separating the Exclusionists from calling on the support of the London mob to overawe their opponents.

Charles skilfully offered concessions, even to the point of a supervisory Regency under the Protestant William, Prince of Orange, the Duke of York's son-in-law. Shaftsbury demanded that the succession pass to the Duke of Monmouth, Charles's oldest bastard son, who was both popular and a Protestant. Only Sir Leoline Jenkins seemed willing to speak up for the king. Then the king spoke up for himself. Initially appearing to arrive without his robes of state, as though coming to hear the debates for his own amusement, he had in fact concealed his crown and robes with him in his sedan chair. Once formally attired, the king faced his antagonists. Thinking they came to witness a royal submission, they were astonished at their dismissal in a single sentence. Their sovereign, smug in the knowledge that a secret treaty with his cousin Louis XIV of France had just brought him £385,000, could do without Parliament henceforth, and did so for the rest of his reign. When Monmouth did raise a rebellion to seize the throne on his father's death Oxford showed its immediate willingness to arm and give vigorous assistance in its suppression.

A CABINET OF CURIOSITIES

Royal gardener John Tradescant (1570–?1638) collected more than plants and opened a curio show, grandly entitled the Museum Tradescantianum (aka Tradescant's Ark) at his nursery in South Lambeth. Tradescant's travels to Russia and North Africa enabled him to assemble a collection of exhibits which seems decidedly arbitrary to the modern mind but struck contemporaries as simply stunning by its extent and variety: 'fowls, fishes, serpents, worms ... pretious stones ... coins, shells, feathers ... curiosities in carving, paintings ... medalls of sundry sorts'. Charles I and Laud were both among the visitors. The king himself enlarged the collection by donating items of hunting and hawking gear which had belonged to Henry VIII. Tradescant's son, also John (1608–62) extended the collection by purchase, exchanges and donations, acquiring such items as Chinese lanterns and a stuffed dodo, the fragmentary remains of which are now in Oxford's University Museum. In 1656 Tradescant junior collaborated with the wealthy dilettante Elias Ashmole (1617–92) to produce the first museum catalogue to be printed in Britain. Ashmole had studied at Brasenose and married a wealthy old widow, thus freeing himself to indulge his interests in alchemy, astrology, antiquarianism and, above all, heraldry. In 1659 Tradescant made over his collection to Ashmole by deed of gift; but he subsequently made a will bequeathing it to his widow for her lifetime and enjoining her to arrange that at her death it should pass to Oxford or Cambridge, as she decided. Ashmole inevitably contested the will after Tradescant's demise and an unseemly wrangle ensued, with claims from Ashmole that Widow Tradescant was selling off exhibits piecemeal and counter-claims from her that he was harassing her. Eventually Ashmole's rightful ownership was recognised in court, the Earl of Clarendon presiding, and the collection was moved to his house. Tradescant's widow was later found drowned in her own garden pond.

Ashmole, who had risen to become Windsor Herald and Comptroller of the Excise, wrote to the Vice-Chancellor in 1677, offering to turn over the collection as 'some testimony of my Duty and filial Respect to my honoured mother the University of Oxford', providing that it should be housed in an appropriate, purpose-built repository. What has become 'the Old Ashmolean', now housing the Museum of the History of Science, was begun in 1678 and completed in 1683. Apart from displaying the twelve cartloads of 'Tradeskin's Curiosities' – ranging from the 'Easter Egges of the Patriarchs of Jerusalem' to a 'Turkish toothbrush' – it was also intended to provide premises for the teaching of experimental science. For this reason the basement laboratory was built with a specially strengthened vaulted roof in case of explosions. The designer is unknown but Pevsner considered the external carving, by William Bird, to be 'outstandingly fine'.

The first keeper of the Ashmolean was Robert Plot (1640–96). He had intended to become the Leland of his age but contented himself with publishing *The Natural History of Oxfordshire Being an Essay towards the Natural History of England* (1677) and later produced a similar volume on Staffordshire. Plot's book was very well received and gained its author the post of secretary to the Royal Society. When James, Duke of York visited Oxford in 1683, he was presented with a copy of Plot's work and Wood's *Antiquities*. Plot also became Professor of Chemistry and a herald and resigned his post at the Ashmolean in 1690. He was succeeded by his assistant Edward Lhuyd (1660–1709), a Welshman from Jesus College. Lhuyd made investigatory tours, in the tradition of Leland, Camden and Plot, in Wales, Scotland, Ireland, Cornwall and Brittany. Out of this came a comparative grammar and dictionary of the Welsh, Irish, Cornish and Breton languages. Out of that, in due course, evolved the idea that 'the Celts' were a single people, united in ancient times by a common culture. Lhuyd can thus be regarded as the unwitting founder of the various Celtic separatist and nationalist movements which have emerged over succeeding centuries. Or perhaps not so unwitting because in 1696 he founded the Red Herring Club to promote interest in Celtic cultures.

Edward Lhuyd, the second keeper of the Ashmolean Museum

A Meddling Monarch

For James II (r.1685–8) Oxford proved to be the anvil upon which his reign was shattered. Perhaps Fell's supine obedience in dismissing Locke at the orders of Charles II encouraged James to believe that he could overawe the University and, once having taken this bastion of Anglican orthodoxy, proceed to restore Catholicism throughout his realm. Even before James II began to intervene in university appointments his very accession was taken as a dispensation by Catholic sympathisers such as Obadiah Walker, the aged Master (1676–89) of University College who opened a private Catholic chapel for himself, where Mass was celebrated 'notwithstanding the laws to the contrary'. This was disquieting enough but then James appointed Dr Massey, a convert to Romanism, to succeed Dr Fell as Dean of Christ Church. The appointment was, however, in the gift of the Crown, so no objection could be upheld on strictly legal grounds. The Presidency of Magdalen, however, was not a matter of royal prerogative. On the death of Dr Clerke in March 1687 the king ordered the Fellows to elect in his place Anthony Farmer, a notorious, quarrelsome drunkard who had openly boasted that his supposed conversion to the Roman faith would bring him preferment. Apart from any other objections, the king's nominee had never been a Fellow of Magdalen and was therefore technically ineligible for the post of President. Refusing to entertain Farmer's candidacy the Fellows of Magdalen elected one of their own number, Dr John Hough, instead. Forced to defend their choice before a legal commission, the Fellows convinced its president, the notorious and compliant Judge Jeffries, that Farmer was, indeed, 'a very bad man'. Determined to impose his own candidate, even if it were not a Catholic, James then ordered the Fellows to choose Samuel Parker, newly elected Bishop of Oxford and an outspoken champion of absolute monarchy. In September 1687 James even came to Oxford to enforce his demand in person, summoning the Magdalen Fellows to attend on him in the Dean's Lodgings at Christ Church, where he told them 'I am king and will be obeyed'. No Oxford locksmith, however, could be found willing to open the door of the President's Lodgings at Magdalen and the king was obliged to have his own servants force it open to admit his man. James's attempt to consolidate his triumph by installing twenty-five new Fellows of his choice rebounded on him. If the statutes of one college could be overridden and its Fellows summarily deprived of tenure without cause, who was safe? The Magdalen martyrs became heroes of resistance, encouraging defiance throughout the land against other royal attempts to pack city councils, the army and the courts with Catholics. Providence itself intervened, striking Parker dead of a convulsive fit in March 1688. In October James admitted defeat and permitted the restoration of Hough and the other Fellows. 25 October was joyously celebrated throughout Oxford as a new 'Restoration Day'. By December James had fled into exile, leaving the throne to pass, by invitation, to his Protestant daughter, Mary and her husband, the Dutch *stadholder*, William III of the House of Orange.

WILLIAM OF ORANGE

William III (r.1688–1702) stayed in Oxford barely more than an hour, apparently only to insult it: 'The University was at great charge in providing a banquet for the king; but the king would not eat anything, but went out; and some rabble and townsmen that had got in seized upon the banquet in the face of the whole University'. The king, who detested ceremonial of any kind, may also have feared poisoning.

One thing the martial William did do for Oxford was stimulate a new trend in gardening, one of his less belligerent pursuits. Walter Harris of New College, one of William's personal physicians, published an account of William's Dutch residence *The Gardens of Het Loo*, in 1699. The Dutch had adapted the grandiose style of French taste to more confined settings and made it thus well suited to college surroundings. Special features included profuse planting of evergreens, intricate box hedges, topiary and potted plants to be moved around. These were already in evidence when Celia Fiennes visited Oxford about five years after William's accession. Bobart installed Yew Men at the entrance to the Physic Garden. The President's garden at St John's made a theme of evergreen obelisks. Wadham's enthusiastic adoption of topiary even extended to topiary balustrades. Trinity outdid them both with pyramids and pillars of evergreens, panels of yew along its stone walls and a clipped labyrinth 'adorned with fountains, close arbours, round stone tables and other embellishments'.

CELIA FIENNES

Between 1685 and 1710 Celia Fiennes (pronounced Fines) (1662– 1741), feisty daughter of a Cromwellian colonel, rode through every single English county, recording her impressions in an opinionated prose of eccentric spelling and punctuation. Internal evidence suggests that she passed through Oxford *c.* 1694. In approaching the city she displayed the conventional, one might almost say classic reactions: 'its scituation is fine ... pleasant and compact ... a fine Causy (causeway) ... towers and spires appear very well at a distance ... the High Street is a very noble one'. St Mary's she found 'very large and lofty but

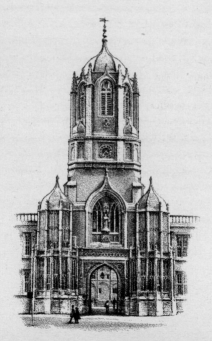

Tom Tower, Christ Church as designed by Christopher Wren

nothing very Curious in it', whereas the Sheldonian was 'a Noble Pile'. An inveterate collector of souvenirs, she eagerly visited its subterranean print-room 'where I printed my name severall tymes'. The adjacent, recently opened Ashmolean next delighted her with its 'many curiositys ... of Mettles Stones Ambers Gumms' and especially a demonstration of the magnetic power of the loadstone. Touring the colleges she thought 'Waddom Hall ... but little' but was impressed at Christ Church and especially by the 'tower new-built for to hang the Mighty Tom'. At the 'Colledge St Magdalines' she praised the 'fine ring of bells ... very large and good Cloyster' and 'gravell walk'. As there is no King's College at Oxford, she presumably meant that she visited University College, accepting the legend of its foundation by King Alfred.

As the Fiennes family had an historical connection with 'New Colledge' and Celia had relatives studying there her attitude was rather proprietorial ('New Colledge which belongs to the Fiennes's ...') and certainly very favourable, 'very neate ... the buildings good, the Chapple very fine: the Garden was new-makeing' and featured 'the Colledg Arms cutt in box ... next plott a Sun-dial cutt in box and true-lovers knotts'. Here Celia was 'very handsomly entertained by Mr Cross', one of her nephew's tutors. Dining at Corpus Christi, she enjoyed 'their very good bread and beare'. 'The Physick Garden afforded great diversion and pleasure, the variety of flowers and plants would have entertained one a week. ...' As usual she was fascinated by the novelty items, such as the 'Sensible plant' (mimosa) whose leaves curled up when squeezed and then uncurled again and the 'Humble plant' which, when struck 'falls flatt on the ground stalke and all, and after some tyme revives againe'.

Celia's cousins escorted her to St John's, where she saw 'the great Curiosity much spoken off, King Charles the Firsts Picture ... all written hand and containes the whole Comon prayer, its very small ... but where a straight line is you may read a word or two'. Another curiosity which struck her was 'a very odd custom in Queen Coll. for every new-years-day there is a certain sum laid out in Needles and Thread which was left by the Founder, and every Gentleman of that Colledge has one given him with these words: Take this and be thrifty'.

Very charming but so what? So this – which was evidently either forgotten at that time or not told to Celia – the needles and thread are less an injunction to patch your clothes than to remember the college founder Robert Eglesfield, being a pun in French (*aiguilles et fils*, needles and thread) on his name.

The date of Celia's visit can be fixed approximately by the fact that she refers to Queen's College Library (1693–4) as 'all new and a stately building' and Trinity College chapel (1692–3) 'which was not finish'd the last tyme I was at Oxford, but now is a beautifull magnifficent Structure, its lofty and curiously painted the rooffe and sides the history of Christ's ascension and very fine Carving of thin white wood just like that at Windsor, it being the same hand'. In the absence of any other documentation Celia Fiennes' testimony is the sole authority for the claim that the superb carving which is still so striking a feature of the chapel was indeed the work of the great Grinling Gibbons. Even Pevsner is impressed: 'wood carving of a quality not surpassed as an ensemble by anything in Britain'.

CHAPTER FIVE

Complacency and Corruption

Adam Smith (1723-90), who spent six years at Balliol in the 1740s, industriously polishing his Greek and French, concluded that 'the greater part of the public professors have for these many years, given up altogether even the pretence of teaching'. In his magisterial *Enquiry into the Causes of the Wealth of Nations* (1776), Smith defined an English University as 'a sanctuary in which exploded systems and obsolete prejudices find shelter and protection after they have been hunted out of every corner of the world'. Smith had no reason to regard Oxford with affection, having been cold-shouldered, like most Scots, but he could find some objective confirmation of his judgments in the fact that medical teaching there had virtually expired, as students trekked to Edinburgh and London in preference.

In terms of its student body Oxford became increasingly exclusive or rather exclusionist. During the eighteenth century less than 3 per cent came from outside England and Wales and the percentage of poor students, which had already fallen from 55 in 1557 to 27 by 1711 was down to 11 by 1800. Oxford's University Press produced only fourteen new titles between 1713 and 1755. During the course of the eighteenth century some forty-one British towns were responsible for the production of fifty or more book titles. London produced six-sevenths of the entire output. Edinburgh ranked second, accounting for three times as many titles as Oxford which was third, but third by a long way. In fairness some excellent works were produced by ex-dons in the hours left over by their undemanding duties as country parsons. James Woodforde (ex-New College) kept a diary which is often as diverting as it is informative and Gilbert White (ex-Oriel) composed in *The Natural*

History and Antiquities of Selborne (1789), a minor classic which would decades later inspire the young Charles Darwin to study living things.

The notion that this was an era of mediocrity and indolence seems confirmed by default in the list of thirty-five all-time 'Famous Oxonians' published on the website of the University's own Information Office. *Pace* the anxiously capitalised caution PLEASE NOTE THAT THIS IS NOT A COMPREHENSIVE LIST, it is significant that it includes only two figures from the period 1688–1815: Jethro Tull (1692) and Samuel Johnson (1728). Jethro Tull is famous for the invention of a seed-drill which very few farmers seem actually to have used. Johnson, of course, really did make a difference to the history of both the English language and English literature but the fact remains that he was essentially a self-educated drop-out as far as Oxford was concerned, achieving his deserved eminence after decades of exploitation and obscurity as a hack-writer in London, the true intellectual hub of eighteenth century Britain. What he left behind him was a cultural cul-de-sac, a little world of complacent ease, buttressed by dignified routines and occasionally ruffled by futile discords.

Lost Cause

Oxford's relative detachment from the mainstream of public life in the eighteenth century is illustrated by the strength of its attachment to the defunct House of Stuart. This sentiment, known as Jacobitism from the Latin name (Jacobus) of the last Stuart king, James II, found its chief supporters among Tory churchmen and country squires, to the contempt of the Whigs who dominated the government until mid-century. The accession of German-speaking George I in 1714 was challenged in 1715 by an armed uprising in Scotland on behalf of James III – the 'Old Pretender' – son and successor of James II, who had died in exile in France in 1701. The '15' was to be crushed relatively easily, to the chagrin of many in Oxford, like the curmudgeonly Thomas Hearne, who counted himself one of the 'honest people who are for King James III'; but there were anxious months to pass through first. Church bells were rung on 28 May 1715 to mark the birthday of 'the Duke of Brunswick, commonly called King George', as Hearne would

have it. On the following day, Restoration Day, the anniversary of
Charles II's return to the throne, houses throughout Oxford were
illuminated in honour of the exiled and now Catholic House of Stuart
and Quaker meeting-houses were vandalised by mobs for good measure. The government in London, thoroughly alarmed at this
demonstration, declared martial law in Oxford and despatched a force
of cavalry to maintain order. At almost the same time George I, having
recently bought the library of Bishop Moore, presented it to the
University of Cambridge as a mark of his approval for its firm adherence
to the Hanoverian succession . The contrast between these two gestures
provoked a witty verse from Dr Joseph Trapp, Oxford's first Professor
of Poetry:

> The King, observing with judicious eyes,
> The state of both his Universities,
> To one he sent a regiment. For why?
> That learned body wanted loyalty.
> To t'other he sent books, as well discerning
> How much that loyal body wanted learning.

Sir William Browne, an eccentric but scholarly physician riposted with
elegance:

> The King to Oxford sent his troop of horse,
> For Tories own no argument but force.
> With equal care to Cambridge books he sent,
> For Whigs allow no force but argument.

Tensions were, however, too serious to be defused by wit and in
Parliament a Bill was actually drafted to suspend Oxford's constitution,
vest power of appointment to all university and college offices in the
Crown and have their revenues handled by a specially appointed
commission. The defeat of the Jacobite uprising led to the proposal
being quietly dropped and it did not occur to the sovereign to omit
Oxford from the establishment of new Regius Professorships in
Modern History (1724). This was despite the fact that the university
had elected as its Vice-Chancellor (1718–22) Robert Shippen (1673–
1745), a fierce Jacobite whose younger brother William headed the
Jacobite tendency in the Commons. The elder Shippen had, according

to Hearne, been elected their Principal by the Fellows of Brasenose because they thought such an ignorant man would leave their idleness undisturbed.

A panegyric to the memory of James II continued to be delivered at Brasenose until 1734 and Jacobite sentiment smouldered on in Oxford even after the bloody suppression of the much more serious uprising of Bonnie Prince Charlie in 1745–6. Although the University presented George II with a sycophantic address of congratulation on the crushing of 'the most wicked rebellion in favour of a popish pretender', when the new Radcliffe Library was opened later that same year, the occasion was hijacked for the delivery 'amidst the greatest applause' of 'a violent Jacobite speech'. There was even further Jacobite rioting in February 1748, the ringleaders being sentenced to two years imprisonment.

A POOR IMPRESSION

The German bibliophile Zacharias Conrad von Uffenbach (1683–1734, visiting Oxford for two months in 1710, saw little to commend in 'badly built' Magdalen, Merton's 'ugly, old buildings', the 'very mediocre' gardens of New College or the hall of Christ Church reeking 'so strongly of bread and meat that one cannot remain in it'. The Mercury fountain in Tom Quad was out of order and the music at the weekly concert 'weak and poor'. None of the monuments in the Cathedral were up to those in Lubeck: 'One cannot but wonder at this, as in most things, the English are so wasteful and expensive'. The Physic Garden, 'wild and overgrown', was much less impressive than Leyden's and its curator, Bobart, was distinguished by scruffy clothes, 'a generally villainous appearance' and 'face and hands as black and coarse as those of the poorest ... farm-labourer'. Though a 'good and honest man ... in the science of botany he is the careful gardener rather than the learned expert'. The technician at the chemistry laboratory was even worse: 'not only are the finest instruments ... lying in pieces but everything is covered in filth'. Gross ignorance and vulgarity of mind seemed to von Uffenbach the singular characteristics of all those entrusted with the university's treasures. At St John's he was proudly shown the bladder-stone of a bishop of London in a gold box. At the Bodleian the Sub-Librarian, Mr Crab, passed over fine ancient codices to show off pictures embroidered in silk, of which according to von Uffenbach, he had 'even better ones worked by my own grandmother'. As for the Ashmolean, the mayor of Luneburg 'has twice as many specimens'. As for the return to London, 'God be thanked'.

THOMAS HEARNE

Thomas Hearne (1678–1735) of St Edmund Hall worked so devotedly at the Bodleian that in 1713 he was offered the Librarianship of the Royal Society but declined it rather than quit Oxford. Alas, he soon found his loyalties in conflict. Refusing to swear allegiance to the House of Hanover he thereby blocked his own academic advancement. Confined to St Edmund Hall like a pike in a pond he poured his thwarted ambition into a hundred and forty-five diary volumes of unconstrained bile. Hearne accused his colleagues of knavery, drunkenness, stinginess, puritanism and embezzlement, dismissing Dr Kennet of his own college as 'republican, Whiggish, giddy-headed and scandalous'. Not that Hearne confined his contempt to Oxford. Multi-talented Sir John Vanbrugh, dramatist and architect of Blenheim Palace was merely a 'Blockhead' and the court composer Handel and his orchestra, who played in Oxford in 1733, were scorned as 'a lousy crew of foreign fiddlers'.

EDMOND HALLEY

Astronomer's House in New College Lane bears a discreet plaque identifying it as the former residence of Edmond Halley (1656–1742), whose name is invariably linked with the comet whose recurrent appearances he was the first to predict. Educated at St Paul's, Halley left Queen's without a degree and in 1676 voyaged to the remote Atlantic island of St Helena to make the first catalogue of the stars of the southern hemisphere. Published (1679) as the *Catalogus Stellarum Australium*, this project assured him an Oxford MA at royal command and his election as FRS at twenty-two. Halley was the first to make an observation of the transit of Mercury and correctly predicted that the comet named after him would reappear in 1758, 1835, 1910 and 1986. By climbing Mount Snowdon he extended Boyle's Law to establish the relationship between barometric pressure and height above sea-level.

He also translated Arabic astronomical writings into Latin and predicted the path of the solar eclipse of 1715. Halley's other investigations ranged over meteors, monsoons, trade winds and underwater diving. To explore the problem of magnetic compass variations, he persuaded William III to put a Royal Navy ship at his disposal. Halley was also the pioneer of isometric mapping, personally paid for the publication of Newton's *Principia Mathematica* when he was himself almost bankrupt and with the publication of his *Breslau Table of Mortality* (1693) laid the actuarial foundations for the calculation of life insurance and annuities. Halley was appointed Savilian Professor of Geometry in 1703 and in 1705 successfully petitioned the university to build the observatory which survives to this day on the roof of Astronomer's House. In 1720 he succeeded John Flamsteed as Astronomer Royal of England.

Halls to Colleges

A further indication of Oxford's loss of corporate vigour was the fact that only two new colleges were founded in the eighteenth century. Both were really re-foundations and neither can be called an indisputable success.

Worcester College grew out of the ruins of Gloucester College. Left derelict after the dissolution, the former Benedictine foundation was bought in 1560 by Sir Thomas White to become Gloucester Hall, a subsidiary out-station for his new foundation, St John's College. Gloucester Hall was still fairly flourishing under Principal Degory Wheare (1626–47), Professor of Ancient History, whose students included the 'Cavalier Poet', Richard Lovelace and the naval captain, courtier and diplomat Sir Kenelm Digby. But soldiers were quartered there during the civil wars and clearly did the place no good. Tax records for 1667 reveal that by then its inhabitants had been reduced to the Principal and his family, eleven scholars and five servants with a widow and another family living in as paying guests. Loggan depicts the paths as overgrown with grass. By 1701 there were no students at all. Principal Benjamin Woodroffe (1692–1711) projected its rebirth as a theological institution for adherents of the Orthodox churches of Greece and Syria. Erecting a gimcrack block ('Woodroffe's Folly') on part of the semi-derelict Gloucester Hall site, he managed to recruit up to ten such students annually for a few years but the scheme foundered by 1707, leaving Woodroffe, or rather his rich wife, £2,000 the poorer. Expensive lawsuits completed his ruin and sent him to London's dismal Fleet prison.

Thanks to Richard Blechinden of St John's a bequest of Sir Thomas Cookes (d.1701) was released to upgrade Gloucester Hall to an independent college, on the lines of the Broadgates-Pembroke conversion of the previous century. Ironically Cookes had originally intended to leave the money for a workhouse for the poor but had been dissuaded from this by Woodroffe. Named after the county in which Cookes had his estates, Worcester College was launched with Blechinden as its first Provost (1714–36). He proved skilful in securing bequests, most notably almost all the large fortune of bachelor George Clarke (1661–1736) of All Souls, who was disgusted by the internecine feuding at his own institution. Clarke's bequest also included drawings by Inigo Jones and an important cache of civil war documents, including the papers of his father, who had held office under both Commonwealth and Restoration regimes. A silver-gilt loving cup, also presented by Clarke, bears an appropriate inscription in his honour, *tantum nos Fundator* – almost our Founder. Despite these benefactions Worcester remained a small college for the rest of the century, distinguished, if at all, only by the quality of its buildings (designed by Clarke as well) and even they were put up by fits and starts until momentum finally fizzled out in the 1790s.

Hart Hall, first mentioned in 1301, came under the control of Exeter but achieved a limited, though precarious, autonomy in the sixteenth century when the future poet and preacher John Donne was a student there. Under the Commonwealth Philip Stevens (1653–60) managed to stage a brief revival but Hart Hall then declined until Principal Richard Newton (1710–53) embarked on a grim thirty year struggle against Rector Conybeare of Exeter to release the institution from his residual control and re-found it as a college. Incorporation was finally achieved in 1740. Newton was an educationist as much as a scholar and his statutes devoted much detail to tutorial arrangements and work-schedules. Hertford's bread-and-butter intake consisted of bourgeois boys aiming for Anglican orders. Gentlemen-commoners were admitted but Newton imposed a novel ban on credit to curb their normal extravagance and excesses. This proved more popular with parents than with pupils. The Hertford man destined to achieve the greatest fame was the future radical leader Charles James Fox (1764), who devoted much of his adult life to extravagance and excesses. Fox actually seems to have worked rather hard, professed to find mathematics 'entertaining', confirmed a love of Greek literature which remained lifelong and left after a couple of years without a degree, his father, Lord Holland, being immensely rich. Had some of that wealth come Hertford's way it might have reversed a decline which proved terminal. By 1805 there were only two Fellows left and no students and Hertford needed to be rescued yet again.

HOSTILE WITNESSES

A contemporary critic, admittedly a Whig one, sneered that Oxford was noteworthy as the place where moral philosophy was taught by debauchees and astronomy by teachers who never looked soberly upon the stars. Even Gladstone, looking back from the perspective of Queen Victoria's day, for all his usually uncritical fondness for his *alma mater*, could only observe of this era that 'indolence and greed had their unrestricted reign'. Probably the most widely quoted denunciation of eighteenth century Oxford comes from Edward Gibbon (1737–94), diminutive author of the majestic *Decline and Fall of the Roman Empire*. Like Johnson's great *Dictionary*, this was a work of single-handed endeavour, produced entirely outside the purlieus of the university. Gibbon entered Magdalen shortly before he was fifteen and left fourteen months later, having proclaimed himself a convert to Catholicism, which was the sort of thing, in an age of Protestant prejudice, that teenagers did to get back at their parents but which carried with it automatic disqualification from the rigidly orthodox university. In Gibbon's case this involved no regret – indeed, he had not been physically at Magdalen for long periods even when he was theoretically a member of the college. Gibbon epitomised his Oxford interlude as 'the most idle and unprofitable of my whole life'. The tutors he regarded as 'decent, easy men, who supinely enjoyed the gifts of the founder ... From the toll of reading or thinking they had absolved their conscience.' A single and widely shared philosophical achievement yet remained the ability 'to unite the opposite extremes of bigotry and indifference'. Jeremy Bentham (1748–1832) was equally scathing about Queen's: 'mendacity and insincerity – in these I found the sure and only sure effects of an English University education'. Perhaps few institutions could have catered adequately with such a precocious twelve year old.

Magdalen and Queen's may have been bad. Wadham was, if anything, worse. Absenteeism was rife among the dons. At one point a single Fellow served simultaneously as Dean, Bursar, Librarian, Tutor and Divinity Lecturer. However, as annual admissions had fallen from over thirty to about a dozen this may not have mattered over-much. In 1739 scandal enlivened the torpor as Warden Robert Thistlethwayte fled to exile in Boulogne after being accused of homosexual assaults on the college butler, the college barber and an undergraduate.

Just as Gibbon was publishing his damning memoirs (1792), Robert Southey (1774–1843), a future Poet Laureate, was entering Balliol to be told 'You won't learn anything by my lectures, so if you have any studies of your own, you had better pursue them'. Southey dutifully took the advice, to little avail, noting years later, 'I never remember to have dreamt of Oxford – a sure proof of how little it entered unto my moral being'.

The Oxford career of Percy Bysshe Shelley (1792–1822) was brief. He came up in 1810 and was sent down in 1811. At Eton he had tried to conjure up the devil and had succeeded in destroying a willow tree with a burning-glass. His twin fascinations with science and the supernatural found no legitimate outlet at University College, where his political views seemed as outlandish as his dress and he was soon labelled by the authorities as 'the ring leader of every species of mischief in our grave walls'. Shelley's room, strewn with papers and clothes, cluttered with phials and 'philosophical instruments', stained and scorched by his experiments, looked like a sorcerer's den. What did for him, however, was his literary efforts. At a time when the by now revered monarch, George III, was about to be certified irredeemably mad, it was neither tactful nor tasteful to print a burlesque of verses supposedly composed by a deranged female who had attempted to assassinate him. Shelley compounded the annoyance by gratuitously circulating to bishops and Heads of Houses a pamphlet setting out the arguments for *The Necessity of Atheism*. Anyone who got past the title would have discovered that Shelley actually meant pantheism. But the powers that be had had enough and summoned him to account. Correctly forecasting a recalcitrant refusal to respond, they had the documents for his expulsion already signed before the futile interrogation began. Shelley departed to Soho with some vague plan of hanging around hospitals until he metamorphosed into a physician but made a disastrous marriage instead.

Shelley's celebrated memorial (1893) at University College shows the drowned poet in white marble on a substructure of bronze with the mourning Muse of Poetry. Originally intended for the Protestant Cemetery in Rome – which may explain its flamboyance – the memorial was the work of the accomplished Edward Onslow Ford (1852–1901), who usually went in for bronze busts of his arty neighbours in St John's Wood. It has evoked a range of responses: 'all extremely lush', 'has all the aura of a religious shrine', 'reminds one of a municipal art gallery in an industrial town'.

Home Improvements

If the university did less to embellish young minds than perhaps it might have, it did much to embellish itself. Indeed Pevsner observes approvingly that 'The early eighteenth century was a period of great architecture at Oxford. Here, as it had not been true since the Middle Ages, one can say that without Oxford English architecture cannot be fully understood ....'

Peckwater Quad (1705–14) at Christ Church is the work of the versatile Dean Aldrich (1647–1710), to whom several other projects are also attributed, notably All Saints church, rebuilt in the High Street after the collapse of its spire in 1700 destroyed the original, medieval structure. Aldrich, who entered Christ Church at fifteen stayed for the rest of his life. The textbook of logic he published in 1691 was last republished in 1862. He was also an expert on geometry, chemistry and heraldry and composed *Hark the bonny Christ Church bells*. As a disciplined exercise in Palladian uniformity Aldrich's Peckwater Quad represented a successful innovation not only for Oxford but for Britain, significantly predating the progenitors of the Palladian passion which are usually credited. The Grand Tour only became routine after the Peace of Utrecht (1713), Leoni's English version of Palladio's *Four Books of Architecture* and the first volume of Colen Campbell's *Vitruvius Britannicus* only appeared in 1715 and the Society of the Dilettanti was not founded until almost a generation later, in 1732. Aldrich's understanding of Vitruvius and Palladio was therefore academic in the best sense, gleaned and refined from books and engravings in his own vast collections and those of other colleges. Even von Uffenbach, so dismissive of Oxford in general, was impressed by the as yet unfinished composition when he saw it in the year of Aldrich's death: 'well and sumptuous like a royal castle'. That other hyper-critical German, Pevsner, writing over two and a half centuries later, was even more enthusiastic: 'amazingly classical ... impeccably uniform' – remarking on its striking contrast with the continuing conservatism of contemporary buildings at University College and Oriel and even with Hawksmoor's more flamboyant Baroque Clarendon Building (1711–15), which was only begun as Aldrich's work neared completion. Generations of privileged young men were to live in Peckwater Quad and return to their shires to build Palladian country houses of their own. Aldrich not merely enlarged the accommodation of a college but reoriented the taste of a century.

Several other colleges undertook substantial building programmes. The Garden Quad of New College (1700–7) may also be by Aldrich. The Fellows' Building and Quad at Corpus dates from 1701–12, its Gentlemen Commoners' Building from 1737. The Warden's Lodgings at All Souls are from 1704–6. Queen's was almost totally rebuilt between 1709 and 1734, its front quadrangle hailed by Pevsner as 'the grandest piece of classical architecture in Oxford'. Balliol's Bristol Buildings dates from 1714. The Library at Christ Church was begun in 1717 and to it were later added an Anatomy school (1766–7) and Canterbury Quad (1773). Oriel's Robinson Quad dates from 1719–29. Magdalen added its New Buildings range in 1733. Handsome wrought iron work was a special feature of the period. The years 1710–15 alone witnessed the installation of communion rails in the chapels of Queen's and Brasenose, and gates in the hall of Queen's, on the Clarendon Building and St Mary's and the gardens of New College and Trinity.

The changes which accompanied the building boom of the early eighteenth century are evident in the illustrations of William Williams *Oxonia Depicta* (1733). In the lifetime since Loggan, garden layouts had become more subtle and the handsome new accommodation blocks emphasised by their grandeur the desire of gentlemen commoners to share the comforts enjoyed by the Fellows. A visitor observed in 1721 that 'Oxford daily increases in fine clothes and fine buildings, never were bricklayers, carpenters, tailors and periwig makers better encouraged there'. Other luxury trades such as gunsmiths, jewellers and watchmakers prospered from local affluence. By the later eighteenth century it became normal for each undergraduate to have his own room or even 'set' of rooms, guarded by a stout door to ensure silence for the studious and privacy for the idle and drunk. A reconstruction of an undergraduate's room at Christ Church in the 1770s can be seen in the Museum of Oxford.

JOHNSON AT OXFORD

Samuel Johnson's father was a book-seller in Lichfield and Johnson's voracious appetite for books was first whetted by what he found on the shelves of his father's shop. Passing from the local grammar school to Pembroke College in 1728, Johnson was compelled to leave, after just fourteen months, without a degree. By his own admission he was notoriously idle. A bishop told Johnson's biographer, James Boswell, that Johnson 'was generally seen lounging at the College gate, with a circle of young students round him, whom he was encouraging with wit, and keeping from their studies'. Johnson himself once insouciantly informed his tutor that he had failed to turn up for instruction because he had been sliding on the ice in Christ Church meadow. What drove Johnson from Oxford, however, was not academic inefficiency but sheer poverty. When his shoes became so worn that his feet were visible through them 'he was too proud to accept of money and somebody having set a pair of new shoes at his door, he threw them away with indignation'. Johnson departed for an uncertain future, initially as a schoolmaster and, lacking a degree, an underpaid one at that. The death of his father shortly afterwards plunged him into a deep melancholia which was to burden him recurrently throughout life.

Johnson finally returned to Pembroke, a quarter of a century later, in 1754, in the company of the poet Thomas Warton the Younger. Although the Master 'received him very coldly' and did not invite him to dine, he was delighted to be recognised by old college servants. The appearance of his historic *Dictionary* the following year brought him both fame and financial security. Dublin honoured him with the Doctorate invariably attached to his name and Oxford finally made amends and honoured him similarly in 1775. By then he was a welcome guest at High Table, where he held his own, despatching three bottles of port in an evening with satisfaction and apparently without any adverse effects.

For all that he loved it, Johnson had few illusions about Oxford's shortcomings and when asked by King George III what conditions were like in the university tactfully replied that although 'he could not much commend their diligence', he thought the Press was improving. On another occasion he defended its failings with engaging casuistry: 'That the rules are sometimes ill observed, may be true; but it is nothing against the system. The members of a University may, for a season, be unmindful of their duty. I am arguing for the excellency of the institution.' Despite the wretchedness which blighted Johnson's own undergraduate days he remained warmly attached to Pembroke, referring to it as 'a nest of singing birds'. He delighted particularly in playing the guide. Shortly before his death he accompanied the bluestocking Hannah More on a visit, pointing out his old room and 'all the rooms of the poets who had been of his college'. She was herself pleased to see that the common room was dominated by 'a fine large print' of her host.

Benefactors and Buildings

John Radcliffe (1652–1714) was barely in his teens when he entered University College and became a Fellow of Lincoln College at eighteen. Taking a subsequent degree in medicine, Radcliffe set up as a physician and gained a reputation as a brilliant diagnostician, more, apparently, on the basis of instinct than of technique. Moving to London in 1684, he was soon making twenty guineas a day and became physician to King William III, whom he treated with kingly candour ('I would not have Your Majesty's two legs for his three kingdoms.') By 1707 Radcliffe was worth £80,000, most of which he left to the university and University College. £40,000 went to the building of the Radcliffe Camera as a library, to the designs of James Gibbs. This was quite a professional coup in the context of Oxford because Gibbs was a Catholic and a Scot into the bargain.

In 1758 £4,000 was released from the residue of Radcliffe's estate towards the founding of the Radcliffe Infirmary as a hospital for the city of Oxford. Another grant made possible the building of the Radcliffe Observatory, completed eighty years after the donor's death. Designed

The Radcliffe Camera

by James Wyatt, this unusual building was modelled on the ancient Tower of the Winds in Athens and as such was a very early foreunner of the Greek Revival in architecture. Adorned with sculptures by the eminent John Bacon and artificial 'Coade stone' panels by J.F. Rossi, it is now home to postgraduate Green College.

Radcliffe's generosity, even though largely funded by the mutually satisfactory interaction of quackery and hypochondria, is also commemorated in the name of Radcliffe Square, 'the heart of Oxford', which Pevsner has hailed somewhat ambiguously as 'unique in the world ... or if that seems a hazardous statement, it is certainly unparalleled at Cambridge'. Radcliffe Quad (1716–19) at University College was also built with £5,000 of the physician's money.

As imperial expansion enriched Britain as a whole Oxford shared in the bounty. Christopher Codrington (1688–1710) was the son of the Governor-General of the Leeward Islands, a substantial owner of slave-worked plantations. Codrington junior, a gentleman-commoner at Christ Church, went on to combine a Fellowship at All Souls with intermittent campaigning in Flanders and the West Indies. Succeeding to his father's estates and office in 1699, he withdrew from public life after failing to take the sugar-rich island of Guadeloupe from the French in 1703. Bibilophilia filled his remaining years and at his death he left All Souls 12,000 volumes and £10,000 towards a new library, handsomely built (1716–20) to the designs of Hawksmoor, with bookcases by Gibbs (1740). The great jurist Sir William Blackstone (1723–80) built up its impressive legal component. History became another special strength. Among its treasures are three hundred and fifty *incunabula* and four hundred and fifty drawings from the office of Sir Christopher Wren. The Codrington Library is remarkable not only for being a Classical building in Gothic dress but also for being the first Oxford college library not to have been built at first floor level for fear of damp and rats.

Methodists

Oxford did produce one distinctive minority who, contrary to Gibbon's charge, were neither bigoted nor idle nor indifferent. They came

John Wesley

to be called – among other things – 'Methodists', on account of the
regularity of their devotions and the orderliness of their observances in
fasting and good works. It was not meant as a compliment. John
Wesley (1703–91) entered Christ Church in 1720, was ordained in the
cathedral there in 1725 and became a Fellow of Lincoln College in
1726. In 1729 he and three others formed a 'Holy Club' whose
members held prayer meetings, visited prisoners in Oxford castle gaol
and went among the sick dispensing hope and charity. Braving ridicule,
Wesley and his tiny band persevered until his departure to minister to
the reluctant residents of the new penal colony of Georgia in 1734. The
founder of Georgia, General George Oglethorpe (1696–1785), had
been at Corpus Christi before entering the army and was, by the
standards of the Hanoverian army, an intellectual. In his wake Wesley
left behind a disciple in cross-eyed, leather-lunged George Whitefield
of Pembroke College, destined to follow him across the Atlantic to

become a future catalyst of the 'Great Awakening' of the American frontier.

In 1768 six Methodists of St Edmund Hall were arraigned before the Vice-Chancellor for failing to uphold the Thirty-Nine Articles, subscription to which was still technically binding on all members of the University. All were expelled. Samuel Johnson thought this 'extremely just and proper'. Boswell objected that they had the repute of 'good beings', provoking a rebuke of characteristic Johnsonian robustness, that 'a cow is a very good animal in a field but we turn her out of a garden'.

In 'founding' Methodism Wesley had never intended to establish a new church. Indeed, the real spiritual turning-point of his life came only after his return from Georgia, as a result of contact there with Moravian refugees from Germany. Their fervour inspired in him that 'enthusiasm' which Wesley's Oxford regarded with suspicion or contempt. Wesley's mission was mission – to revitalise somnolent Anglicanism from within and to take it outdoors to the people. Methodism in its wider manifestation has been credited with major historical reverberations – averting social revolution and inspiring the Sunday School movement, mass education, missionary enterprise in Asia and Africa, the abolition of slavery and the re-moralisation of the brutal realm of the Hanoverians to become the respectable, law-abiding society of the Victorians. Perhaps – but in Oxford its impact was pretty limited. Although he did preach the prestigious University Sermon seven times Wesley was barred from St Mary's after 1744, when he took advantage of his pulpit to lambast his former colleagues for their idleness, drunkenness and corruption. A plaque now marks the site of Oxford's first Methodist church at 32–4 New Inn Hall Street, which Wesley described in 1783 as 'a lightsome, cheerful place and well filled with rich and poor, scholars as well as townsmen'. Oxford's oldest (1835) extant Methodist church is at Rose Hill, Iffley and, unusually, has a graveyard. The one time Westminster College at North Hinksey derived from the Wesleyan Training College established in 1851 in Horseferry Road, Westminster. It moved to its present site in 1959 and became part of Oxford Brookes University in 2000 as the Westminster Institute of Education. It retains a specialist centre which offers short courses and an MA in Methodist Studies.

PROFESSORS AND PRIZES

For an institution allegedly slumped in intellectual torpor Oxford continued to attract a perhaps surprising number of benefactions. Shrewd, shrewish Queen Caroline, consort of boorish George II (r.1727–60), was said to have 'conversation as unrefined as her spelling was incorrect' but she did wangle Halley a fictitious naval appointment so that he could pay an assistant and she did contribute £2,000 to the building fund at Queen's, which acknowledged her gift by placing a statue of her over its front entrance.

The Professorship of Poetry was established in 1708 with funds bequeathed by Henry Birkhead (?1617–96), a lawyer, Latin poet and sometime Fellow of All Souls. Unlike most chairs it carried only a nominal stipend, was tenable for ten (now five) years only and its occupants were to be chosen by the votes of Convocation – i.e. all Oxford MAs who bother to turn up. Thomas Warton, an early holder of the chair, went on to become Poet Laureate (1785–90). Other Professors of Poetry would include John Keble, Matthew Arnold, C. Day-Lewis also a Laureate, W.H. Auden and Nobel Prize-winner Seamus Heaney. In 1728 £3,000 was left by William Sherrard (1659–1728) to re-endow the Professorship of Botany. Sherrard, a Fellow of St John's, had been granted three five-year leaves of absence to go plant-hunting but by being away twenty years finally provoked even indulgent St John's into depriving him of his Fellowship. Sherrard financed his peregrinations by tutoring young aristocrats and then representing the Turkey Company in Smyrna. He only ever published one book but was highly regarded by other botanists and had several plants named *Sherardia* in his honour. Sherrard's German assistant John Jacob Dillennius (1687–1747) was nominated by him as first occupant of the chair and produced the *Historia Muscorum* (1741), a ground-breaking study of mosses.

The Professorship of Anglo-Saxon was founded under the will of the eccentric Dr Richard Rawlinson (1690–1755), a reclusive Jacobite, educated at St Paul's and St John's, who lived a life of self-imposed poverty but spent prodigally on amassing historical materials of all kinds. Apart from the chair he endowed, he provided a salary for the keeper of the Ashmolean and left 5,700 manuscripts to the Bodleian and his heart (in an urn) to St John's. The auction of his collections took sixty-eight days, the printed books alone running to 9,405 lots. Among his many publications were '*A full and Impartial Account*' of the Oxford Jacobite demonstrations of 1715 and exculpatory memoirs of Anthony Wood, Elias Ashmole and Thomas Hearne.

The origins of the Professorship of Experimental Philosophy (1749) are even more bizarre. Arch-careerist Nathaniel Crew (1633–1721), successively Proctor, Rector of Lincoln College and Bishop of Oxford obliged the future James II by marrying him to his Catholic second wife and was rewarded with promotion to the wealthy see of Durham. Under James II, Crew served as a sycophantic tool against the church of which he was a senior bishop. The king's flight saw Crew try, quite literally, to buy his way back into favour at the new court of William and Mary but he was ultimately obliged to make his amends with posterity instead, leaving his fortune to charitable purposes of which the scientific chair was one. His name is perpetuated in one of the most prestigious of Oxford ceremonies, the Creweian Oration, pronounced in alternate years by the Professor of Poetry and the university's Public Orator at the *Encaenia* which marks the high-point of Oxford's academic ceremonial. Named for a thoroughly discreditable character, the Oration is, ironically, a review of the excellences of the university year. Until 1972, when Roy Fuller as Professor of Poetry ended the tradition, the speech was given in Latin. The occasion was customarily preceded by the consumption of champagne and strawberries by senior members of the university – also funded out of the Creweian Benefaction.

Examinations in eighteenth century Oxford became cursory and formulaic to the point of farce. According to John Scott, subsequently first Earl of Eldon and a ferociously reactionary Lord Chancellor, his examination for the Bachelor's degree in 1770 consisted solely of the following exchange:

Ex.   What is the Hebrew for the place of a skull?
S.   Golgotha
E.   Who founded University College?
S.   King Alfred
E.   Very well, sir, you are competent for your degree.

In such circumstances competition for prizes and scholarships offered an alternative field of endeavour for ambitious young men to display intellectual prowess and mark themselves out for future distinction, either within the university, or, more usually, outside it. John Ruskin joked that his father expected him to 'take all the prizes every year' as a prelude to becoming Archbishop of Canterbury. Thomas Gaisford, Dean of Christ Church (1831–55) famously observed in concluding a sermon that 'the study of Greek literature not only elevates above the vulgar herd but leads not infrequently to positions of considerable emolument'. Gaisford's convictions led him to found and fund the Gaisford Prizes for Greek Verse and Prose in 1856. In doing so he was maintaining a tradition already a century old. The Vinerian Law Scholarships were established in 1758 and in 1768 came the Chancellor's Prizes for Latin Verse, Latin Prose and an English essay. In 1806 the award best known outside Oxford was founded, the Newdigate Prize for English Verse, which Ruskin did win. The establishment of prizes or scholarships was also a far easier, less expensive and more certain means of encouraging particular talents or interests than any wholesale attempt to reform the examination system as such.

Scholarship and Statesmanship

The name of Sir William Blackstone (1723–80) might be linked with that of Locke as a begetter of the US constitution, though in the case of Blackstone the influence was more immediate. Orphaned but favoured by the notice of the Prime Minister, Sir Robert Walpole, he entered Pembroke as a classical scholar in 1738 and enrolled in the Middle Temple to study law, which he found easy. His other interests included architecture, Shakespeare and composing verse, though it has been observed that 'nothing has been lost to English literature by Blackstone's seeking in poetry only a relaxation'. Elected a Fellow of All Souls at twenty-one, he proved a zealously methodical bursar and archivist, setting the accounting system to rights and attempting to limit the grosser abuses of the founder's kin tradition. Blackstone's managerial skills soon had him elected (1755) to the Board of Delegates of the University Press, which he likewise did much to rescue from 'languishing in lazy obscurity'. On the advice of the Solicitor-General, the future Lord Mansfield, Blackstone began to lecture on English law, which he did to such effect that Mr Viner, a legal author, left £12,000 to found a chair in English law. Blackstone became the first Vinerian Professor in 1758, lecturing until 1766 and drawing on his lectures to compose the magisterial *Commentaries on the Laws of England*, which were published in four volumes between 1765 and 1769. The author's death before the age of sixty was attributed to drinking port and a total disinclination to physical exercise.

For America's Founding Fathers Blackstone's *Commentaries* were to serve as the standard work of reference on the constitutional tradition which they sought at once to reject, amend and perpetuate. Blackstone's statue in the great hall of the Royal Courts of Justice in London was the gift of the American Bar Association. The *Commentaries* went through eight editions before their author's death and were last reprinted as though still a current text in 1844. In the United States the work was still being republished forty years after that. Thomas Jefferson when President condemned the *Commentaries* on the grounds that first it was inappropriate for an independent country to revere an alien authority on such a fundamental matter as its own laws and secondly students thought that if they quoted Blackstone that was all they needed to know about the law.

Contemporaries were in awe of Sir William Jones (1746–94) and rightly so as 'the first European to open the treasures of Oriental learning, the poetry and wisdom of our Indian empire'. If Oxford taught him little directly it enabled him to learn much. A chess prodigy as a child, a star pupil at Harrow, at nineteen Jones was appointed tutor to the seven year old brother of Georgiana Spencer, Duchess of Devonshire. This was a tactful way for the Spencer family (ancestors of the late Diana, Princess of Wales) to finance his passage through University College, where he became a Fellow at twenty. It also helped to pay for riding and fencing lessons from Domenico Angelo, the finest teacher of the gentlemanly accomplishments of the age. Jones's first work, a translation of a Persian biography into French, appeared when he was twenty-four and the following year it was followed by a Persian grammar which remained a standard text for the next half century.

Elected FRS, a member of Johnson's Literary Club and knighted, Jones spent the last decade of his life as a judge in Calcutta, where he began, but did not live to complete, a systematic codification of Hindu and Islamic law. Jones also became the first Englishman to master Sanskrit, the classical language of Hindu culture and, by recognising its similarity to Greek, invented comparative philology as a field of scholarship. In founding the Asiatic Society of Bengal he established the first learned society devoted to the study of Asian cultures. In compliment to Jones's extraordinary endeavours India's emblematic asoka tree is known to botanists as *Jonesia asoka*. The East India Company paid for a statue by John Bacon to stand in St Paul's Cathedral; Jones clutches a volume of the laws of Manu and stares across at his friends Dr Johnson and Sir Joshua Reynolds, who painted his portrait for Earl Spencer. In the antechapel of University College is an impressive monument (1794) by Flaxman, depicting Jones at work on his Hindu digest, assisted by Indian *pandits*.

A TRANSATLANTIC GESTURE: JAMES SMITHSON

'The best blood of England flows in my veins. On my father's side I am a Northumberland, on my mother's I am related to kings; but this avails me not. My name shall live in the memory of man when the titles of the Northumberlands and the Percys are extinct and forgotten.' It was an accurate prediction. You have heard of the Smithsonian Institution; the words were those of its founder. The illegitimate James Smithson (1765–1829) entered Pembroke College as a gentleman commoner in 1782 under the marital surname of his mother, Macie, rather than of his father, Sir Hugh Smithson Percy, first Duke of Northumberland. Macie changed his name to Smithson following the death of his mother in 1791.

The best chemist of his year, with a special interest in mineralogy, Smithson was elected FRS in 1787. Although never a scientist of the first rank, he published twenty-seven papers and was respected by those who were, numbering Cavendish, Davy, Banks and Ampere among his friends. Zinc carbonate was named Smithsonite after him. Although he lived like a gentleman, he was not rich and would never become so through his own efforts, being a compulsive gambler. His fortune came by inheritance from a half-brother and was bequeathed by him to the United States as an anti-monarchist gesture. Congress initially moved to reject his gift but John Quincy Adams ensured the acceptance of the £104,960 which made possible the opening of the Smithsonian in 1846. A fire at the Institution in 1865 destroyed all Smithson's papers except one volume, as well as his collection of 10,000 mineral specimens.

UP, UP AND AWAY

A thoughtful visitor to Oxford must eventually be struck by the fact that, for a city steeped in its own past, it has very few plaques honouring famous persons and events, perhaps because there are potentially so many that almost every building would be overwhelmed and disfigured by them. So plaques in Oxford gain an added significance by their relative rarity. One is on the long, bare wall overlooking Merton Field to the south, beside Deadman's Walk. The plaque was unveiled in 1984 and reads as follows – *James Sadler 1753–1828 First English Aeronaut who*

The first aerial ascent in a hot-air balloon from Merton Field on 7 July 1810 by James Sadler, son of an Oxford pastry cook

in a fire balloon made a sucessful ascent from near this place – 4 October 1784 to land near Woodeaton. Sadler was a lab technician in the University's chemistry department and had already experimented with unmanned hydrogen-filled balloons, one of which, launched in Oxford in February 1784 'before a great concourse of people', came down in Kent. The very first manned balloon flight was made in France in 1783. On 27 August 1784 the Scot, James Tytler, editor of the *Encyclopaedia Britannica*, made a solo *ascent* of 350 feet at Edinburgh. On 15 September 1784 the Italian Vincenzo Lunardi made a balloon *flight* from London to Ware. Sadler's flight the following month was much shorter, about six miles.

In November 1784 Sadler, ascending this time from the Physic Garden in a hydrogen balloon, landed near Aylesbury after a fourteen mile flight of twenty minutes. He made six more flights in 1785, one with William Windham MP, Dr Johnson's friend and pall-bearer. After an interval of a quarter of a century he made another ascent from Merton Field in 1810 to mark the installation of Lord Grenville as Chancellor. Sadler had spent the intervening years experimenting with steamboats for the Royal Navy and at Portsmouth had installed the first steam-engine ever to be used in a navy dockyard. These ventures ended badly, however, leaving Sadler in severe financial difficulties. Ballooning offered a way out and Sadler, though nearly sixty, turned professional, making forty more flights over the next five years. His son Windham William Sadler ballooned successfully across the Irish Sea but was killed (1824) on his thirty-first flight when his balloon hit a factory chimney at Blackburn. James Sadler is buried in the churchyard of the former church of St Peter-in-the-East, which now serves as the library of St Edmund Hall.

Changing Oxford: the University

Discontent with prevailing academic attitudes was expressed in 1773 by John Napleton (?1738–1817) of Brasenose in his (anonymous!) *Considerations on the Public Exercises for the First and Second Degrees in the University of Oxford.* Dismissed as a martinet by colleagues, Napleton left Oxford in 1778 for a career in the Church which proved more rewarding in every sense. After this false start the campaign for better teaching and meaningful examinations was taken up by the heads of three colleges. John Eveleigh, Provost of Oriel (1781–1814) placed elections to college Fellowships entirely on the basis of academic merit. Cyril Jackson, Dean of Christ Church (1783–1819) tutored the tiresome offspring of George III and perhaps as a result of this unpalatable experience was said to have developed 'a wonderful tact in managing that most unmanageable class of Undergraduates, Noblemen'. If Jackson had charm for the exalted, he reserved his enthusiasm for the talented, exhorting such brilliant pupils as the future Prime Ministers, Canning and Peel, to throw themselves into their work like tigers. John Parsons, Master of Balliol (1798–1819), likewise followed the Oriel model of the career open to talents. Together these three badgered the university into passing a New Examination Statute in 1800, establishing rigorous *written* Pass and Honours examinations in Mathematics and *Literae Humaniores* (aka 'Greats') (i.e. Greek and Latin and their associated Literatures, History and Philosophy). Jackson was doubtless thrilled when Peel responded to him by becoming the first Oxford man to gain a 'Double First'. Not until 1853, however, were the next subjects – Natural Science, Law and Modern History – to be added to the list of examined topics. That wise and witty churchman, Sidney Smith, who deplored the 'infinite quantity of talent ... annually destroyed in the Universities of England' saw that so much remained to be done and urgently done but would not be done. 'A set of lectures upon political economy would be discouraged in Oxford, probably despised, probably not permitted. To discuss the enclosure of commons and to dwell upon imports and exports, to come so near to common life, would seem undignified and contemptible.'

If Oxford's need for academic reform seems absurdly self-evident in retrospect, it must be remembered that demand for any type of institutional change at the turning of the eighteenth century would have to be made against the background of fear and repression induced by the horrors of the French Revolution and the threat of foreign invasion. Political reform in Britain was put on hold for a generation. Oxford was safe in its slumbers for a while.

Changing Oxford: the City

The industrial innovations transforming the cities of Britain in the eighteenth century bypassed Oxford. Despite discernible enhancements to its daily life, Oxford's unhurried pace of change made its urban tone and rhythms increasingly anachronistic in the world's first industrial nation – which is just how many Oxonians wanted Oxford to remain, 'whispering from her towers the last enchantments of the Middle Age'.

Although Oxford could not but share in the benefits of overall commercial expansion, it did so only incrementally. By 1740 there was a post courier service to the capital every day except Saturday; as there was no business done on the Sabbath deliveries on that day would have been superfluous. The coaching business flourished with over a hundred coaches passing through Oxford daily. Turnpike trusts, formed between 1719 and 1797, greatly improved road construction and surfacing, making possible the development of services timetabled to the minute by the end of the century. But the bulk of the food, fodder and fuel brought in from the countryside continued to come by lumbering wagons or river barges, both of which varied in reliability with the seasons. The canal linking Oxford with industrial Coventry ninety miles away, begun in 1769, was not completed until 1790. The last section, from Banbury, less than twenty-eight miles in length, required the construction of a lock for every mile, plus forty-one stone or brick bridges and thirty-eight wooden ones. The total cost was £307,000, enough to build about sixty churches at current prices. The canal's main benefit was to bring coal far more cheaply direct from the Midlands than 'sea-coal' from Tyneside, which had to make a three hundred mile voyage to London and then be carried up the Thames in barges. The canal, like the river, could still freeze solid but its value to the town was sufficiently self-evident to justify major expenditures between 1829 and 1834. These straightened and shortened it by thirteen and a half miles, just in time for the advent of the railways to render it obsolete.

A new amenity was the construction (1742–8) of the Holywell Music Room, reputedly the oldest surviving purpose-built concert hall

The masthead of Jackson's *Oxford Journal*

in Europe. Another sign of a quickening civic spirit was the appearance of local newspapers. The *Oxford Flying Weekly and Cirencester Gazette* only lasted from 1746 to 1748 but *Jackson's Oxford Journal*, dating, under various names, from 1753 achieved a continuous existence until 1909 and was Oxford's only paper until 1806, when it was joined by the *Oxford University and City Herald*.

A major step towards the removal of much medieval urban clutter was the establishment in 1771 of a Paving Commission, composed of both academics and citizens, which remained in existence until 1865. Much like a modern development corporation it effectively by-passed the existing structure of local government in the interests of dynamism and efficiency, Oxford's city corporation having become notoriously corrupt, even by the venal standards of the eighteenth century. Magdalen bridge, restored in 1723, was completely rebuilt in 1772–82 to the designs of John Gwynn, surveyor to the Commissioners and architect of the city's new covered market (1774), which housed no less than forty butchers and game-dealers. A symbolic and practical break with the past came with the demolition of the ancient city gates, long redundant for purposes of defence and security and now merely an obstruction to traffic. The wholesale street clearance programme of 1771 met the wholehearted approval of the Reverend Edward

Tatham, a future Rector of Lincoln College: 'Our forefathers seem to have consulted petty Convenience and monastic exclusiveness, while they neglected that Uniformity of design, which is indispensable to Magnificence, and that Elegance of Approach, which adds half the Delight.'

By 1801, when the first national census revealed that London was heading to pass the million mark in population, Oxford still had only 11,694 inhabitants, plus 3,000 residents of the university, many of whom were absent for the vacations which made up half the year. The population structure was also atypical of the nation as a whole. The concentration of male students, taught by dons whose terms of election required most to remain unmarried, both waited on by college servants who were overwhelmingly male, meant that Oxford was one of the few places in the whole country where males outnumbered females. As late as 1851 Oxford still had 27 per cent of its local labour force in domestic service, twice the national average.

Royalist and Reactionary

Not until the accession of George III (r.1760–1820), a thoroughly English and English-speaking monarch, was Tory Oxford finally reconciled to the prevailing political order. His visit in 1786 was, indeed, a signal success. In the years of revolutionary peril which followed soon after, Oxford proved reliably reactionary and patriotic. The colleges collected £1,000 for the relief of refugees from the French Terror in 1792. In 1793 Tom Paine was burned in effigy at Carfax – in vacation, which marked the incident as the work of townsmen, rather than students. The magistrates 'in consideration of the right feeling thus roughly displayed wisely connived at the tumultuous and somewhat riotous expression of it'. A Volunteer Corps was raised in 1798 against the possibility of invasion, with Town and Gown for once standing together in the ranks. During the brief truce of 1802 Nelson was honoured with a Doctorate of Civil Laws in recognition of his very uncivil treatment of the French navy. In June 1814, when the Allies prematurely thought Napoleon beaten, the Prince Regent squired the Tsar, the King of Prussia, General Blucher, Prince Metternich et al. to a tumultuous reception in the Sheldonian. Meanwhile sky-high wartime agricultural prices fattened the rent rolls of the colleges satisfyingly.

UNCHANGING OXFORD

Generations of undergraduates and alumni have adorned the walls of their rooms with prints of Oxford first published by Rudolph Ackermann (1764–1834) on the very eve of the city's transformation by the railways and the first intrusions of modern industry. As such Ackermann's prints represent a collective portrait of 'ancient Oxford' which through endless reproduction has achieved an iconic timelessness. A Saxon by birth and coach-builder by trade, Ackermann took to publishing prints in his thirties. His shop at 101 Strand became a London institution. A man of many talents, he was responsible for designing Nelson's funeral car, ran a drawing-school, set up a factory at Chelsea to produce waterproof paper and cloth and sold a profitable range of fancy goods made by French emigrés. He also pioneered gaslighting and introduced fine-art lithography to Britain.

Ackermann's *History of the University of Oxford: Its Colleges, Halls and Public Buildings* appeared in two quarto volumes in 1814, with text by William Combe. Combe's immediate acquaintance with his subject must have been considerably limited by the fact of his permanent confinement to the environs of King's Bench prison in Southwark, as a lifelong debtor. The sixty-nine coloured aquatint plates were the work of such talents as A. C. Pugin, a French emigré and father of the illustrious architect. Thirty-two of the plates were devoted to 'founders' and another seventeen to illustrating the niceties of academic dress. Caricaturist Thomas Rowlandson (1756–1827) portrayed university life at the same period in an altogether racier manner. In 1832–6 James Ingram published a three volume survey of the *Memorials of Oxford*, illustrated with wood engravings by Orlando Jewitt (1799–1869) of Headington, then home to a coterie of engravers. Jewitt also illustrated an 1842 *Guide to the Architectural Antiquities in the Neighbourhood of Oxford*.

England's greatest painter, Joseph William Mallord Turner (1775–1851), made several paintings of Oxford scenes. But Oxford also had its own Turner in his namesake and near contemporary, Oxfordshire-born William Turner (1789–1862). An early pupil of the eminent London watercolourist John Varley, in 1811 Turner returned to settle in Oxford where he could make a good living by teaching.

Proficiency in watercolour painting was considered a social and cultural asset in an era suffused with romantic notions of the sublime and picturesque in nature. In an age before photography it was also considered a highly desirable skill for any profession or field of study requiring visual records, i.e. doctors, botanists, cartographers, surveyors, engineers and military men. Turner, who lived in St John's Street and died there at No. 16, described himself in the census as an 'Artist and Teacher of Landscape Painting'. Like the painters of East Anglia, Gainsborough and Constable, he skilfully exploited clouds and other atmospheric effects to give grandeur to scenes of countryside lacking spectacular mountains and gorges. Examples of Turner's work can be seen in the Ashmolean and Museum of Oxford. Others are in the possession of Worcester College and Exeter College.

CHAPTER SIX

Railways, Religion and Reform

Seductive Still

In that politically disturbed interval between the defeat of Napoleon and the advent of the railways, Oxford's calm continued to charm those who were not of its chosen number – mostly. Critic and essayist, William Hazlitt, not a university man, asserted that 'we could pass our lives at Oxford without having or wanting any other idea – that of the place is enough. We imbibe the air of thought ... Let him then who is fond of indulging in dreamlike existence go to Oxford and stay there.'

The artist and diarist Benjamin Haydon was less enchanted than bemused by his donnish encounters: 'Everybody showed you Latin and Greek books to explain any question, as if they had been English. It seemed never to enter their conception that there were people in the World who knew nothing of the one or the other.' The formidably opinionated William Cobbett, a self-appointed enemy of privilege in all its forms, was unlikely to be predisposed in favour of Oxford. Passing through on one of his celebrated *Rural Rides*, he was neither enchanted nor bemused, and let rip with customary vituperation: 'Upon beholding the masses of buildings at Oxford, devoted to what they call "learning", I could not help reflecting on the drones that they contain and the wasps they send forth! However, malignant as some are, the great and prevalent characteristic is *folly*; emptiness of head, want of talent: and one half of the fellows who are what they call *educated* here are unfit to be clerks in a grocer's ....' One wonders how Cobbett would have reacted had he known that one day his own life and writings would be judged a suitable subject of study for Oxford undergraduates in the schools of both History and English.

Oxford was still working its magic on Americans a generation later when to many of its inhabitants it had been spoiled by the railway and the doubling of its population. Nathaniel Hawthorne, enchanted by the thought as much as by the sight of 'grassy quadrangles, where cloistered walks have echoed to the quiet footsteps of twenty genera-tions', declared in 1856 that 'the world, surely, has not another place like Oxford: it is a despair to see such a place and ever to leave it'. Herman Melville, a year later, was similarly moved: 'Most interesting spot I have seen in England ... here I first confessed with gratitude my mother land and hailed her with pride... Lands for centuries never molested by labour... sacred to beauty and tranquility ... The pic-turesque never goes beyond this – I know nothing more fitted by mild and beautiful rebuke to chastise the presumptuous ranting of Yankees.' Coming from a land of endless horizons and brand new buildings, Americans were charmed by Oxford's pervasive atmosphere of antique closure, a single theme repeated with subtle variation in ivy-clad by-ways and collegiate gardens for which the word 'bower' might have been invented.

A RACE APART

As *The Times* itself remarked in 1870: 'Truth is stranger than fiction even in a subject which has so much exercised the invention of novelists as University life.' Indeed. The dons of unreformed Oxford were free to combine the cloistered life of a learned cleric with the tastes and interests of a country squire. It was an environment in which eccentricity could flourish, usually unremarked and certainly unrebuked.

William Buckland (1784–1856), Reader in Mineralogy and Canon of Christ Church, kept a menagerie in his lodgings on the corner of Peckwater Quad and at his table served up such oddities as crocodile, mice in batter and chops cut from a panther which had been dead and buried for two days before he heard that it was available for his delectation. On being asked what was the worst thing he had eaten Buckland could not choose for certain between a mole and blue-bottle flies.

Dr Routh, President of Magdalen (1791–1854), who died in office at a hundred, still wore shoe-buckles and a wig half a century after Pitt's war-financing wig-powder tax had driven wigs out of fashion. When the Fellows of Magdalen determined to enforce the rule against keeping dogs Routh blithely referred to his own dogs henceforth as cats, which were not proscribed.

The historian J.R. Green (1837–83) summarised these dons' cloistered outlook on life: 'Oxford was their world and beyond Oxford lay only wide wastes of shallowness and inaccuracy... Their delight was to take a "progressive idea" and roast it over the common room fire ... most of them had a great dream-work on hand, of which not a chapter was ever written ... their real love of learning was mingled with a pedantry of mind and of life and a feminine rigour over the little observances of society and discipline.'

Age of Steam

Oxford for once could count itself in the vanguard of modernity when gas lighting first illuminated the High Street in 1819. From 1835 onwards it became generally available throughout the town. An expanding volume of traffic prompted the reconstruction of Folly Bridge between 1824 and 1827. By 1829 the largest coaching operator was running thirteen daily services to London. By the 1840s almost three hundred wagons were entering Oxford daily with produce from the surrounding countryside. Then came the railway.

Oxford's reaction was less reluctant than resistant. The town corporation feared the loss of tolls on Folly Bridge. The Oxford Canal Company feared the competition. The university feared the threat to undergraduate morals – and underground drainage. Low-lying Oxford has always been prone to flooding. Railway construction, it was thought, would create dangerous disturbance to subterranean watercourses.

The university used its parliamentary connections to block Bills authorising construction of a railway to Oxford in 1837 and 1838 and again in 1840. When the enabling legislation was finally passed in 1843 it contained extraordinary provisions granting university authorities special rights of access to railway property and personnel and the power to demand refusal of transport to undergraduates should their travel plans be deemed undesirable – i.e. to Ascot race-meeting in particular and London in general. The university also ensured that the railway station should be located well out of town, to the west, and not by Magdalen Bridge as its promoters had originally intended. The connection to Didcot opened in 1844. The cheapest fare to London was then six shillings, compared to five shillings by stagecoach. At first the trains took seven hours to reach London, compared with six hours by coach but within a few years the railway journey time was down to two hours and twenty minutes. The connection to Banbury was opened in 1850, its track ballast being dug from what became Hinksey Lake, subsequently bought to serve Oxford as a reservoir. By 1851 a link to Bletchley opened up communication to Birmingham and Cambridge.

As anticipated, the railway killed the long-distance coaching business. By 1854 the service was down to three a week. The impact on local carriers was more muted. Whatever shortfall there was in hauling goods from surrounding villages was more than made up by what was to be taken to or from the railway station. The hostility which had relegated the station to the edge of town created a predictable, timetabled demand for the carriage of passengers and baggage to and from the Randolph Hotel (1864), a new amenity which offered distinctly more sophisticated accommodations for such visitors as the young Henry James than could be found at the more traditional inns.

In 1865 the Great Western Railway proposed to establish a major carriage works in Oxford. The prospect of 'Industry' in all its raw nakedness implied to many the transformation of the town into a community of such size, mobility and anonymity that undergraduates might in the words of Goldwin Smith, Regius Professor of Modern History, have 'unrestrained access to the population'. 'Everyone knows the character of the students of Paris', he snorted, as though that settled the argument. Apparently it did and the GWR set up its works at Swindon instead. This may have satisfied the opponents of industry but deprived those for whom it would have provided work. Underemployment remained a chronic problem in Victorian Oxford thanks to the mass-migration of consumers during university vacations. The

An illustration from *College Life* 1850, showing a ferocious fight between 'Town and Gown'

city's last bread riot occurred as late as 1867. In 1890 local MP A.W. Hall, himself a leading brewer, asserted that 'the great need of Oxford is some large industry'. All it got, in 1900, was a factory in Park End Street to meet the demand for Frank Cooper's eponymous marmalade.

Jericho

Oxford's first industrial suburb, Jericho, took its name from an inn of that name and from Jericho Gardens, west of the Radcliffe Infirmary. To generations of wags the name signified a remoteness of biblical antiquity, with an associated echo of jerrybuilding. In 1825 the association of the name and the area was confirmed by the establishment of William Carter's Jericho Iron and Brass Foundry, almost immediately joined by the imposing new Walton Street building for Oxford University Press (1826–32), which was soon to become the area's most substantial employer. Cheap terraced housing rapidly extended on a grid-pattern of surrounding streets. Flooding and poor sanitation exposed the area to repeated devastation by cholera in the national epidemics of 1832, 1849 and 1854. While some migrated gladly out to Wolvercote, those who stayed eventually benefited from the generosity of an OUP senior manager, Thomas Combe, who built local schools and in 1869 the splendid church of St Barnabas. An Anglo-Catholic and an early patron of the Pre-Raphaelites – he gave his collection to the Ashmolean – Combe chose (Sir) Arthur Blomfield, a son of the Bishop of London, as his architect. Blomfield obliged with a striking exercise in Romanesque, complemented by a Venetian campanile. In *Jude the Obscure* Thomas Hardy, for five years Blomfield's assistant, calls the church St Silas and Jericho Beersheba. Boldly simple outside, St Barnabas was boldly rich inside and became renowned for its paraphernalia of crosses, cassocks, chasubles and birettas. Aesthetically and liturgically it constituted a deliberately dramatic statement – overstatement? – in a dreary district. Diarist Francis Kilvert, himself a clergyman and an Oxford graduate, observed of its Ascension Day service in 1876 that 'the poor humble Roman Church hard by is quite plain, simple and Low Church in its ritual compared with St. Barnabas in its festal dress. . .'. Just why this should be so becomes apparent from the following . . .

The 'Oxford Movement'

Timorous and introspective, John Henry Newman (1801–90) recoiled in horror from the hard-drinking hearties he initially encountered at Trinity in 1817. Self-defined as an outsider – 'I am not noticed at all except by being silently stared at' – Newman was also self-evidently a shrimp, if not a wimp. When rowdies invaded his room because he was 'reading too much' he ordered them out – 'One then said he would knock me down, if I were not too contemptible a fellow.' Yet it was Newman, rather than the muscular knuckleheads, who was to shake Oxford like an earthquake over the succeeding three decades.

Finding, not untypically for the time, that he had 'as little tutorial assistance or guidance as it is easy to conceive', Newman set himself a punishing schedule, aiming at a solid twelve hours of study a day. Diligence went unrewarded – 'I got a common pass, but of honours nothing'. He found consolation in the violin and the friendship of

John Henry Newman, one of the leaders of the Oxford Movement

Edward Pusey (1800–82), who was renowned for his 'exceeding slovenliness of person' and disarming sweetness of smile.

Despite Newman's apparent academic mediocrity, by 1827 he was a Fellow of Oriel and had also served as curate of St Clement's when that parish was still an impoverished and filthy satellite of Oxford, rather than part of the city proper. Newman's curacy had been brief (1824–6) but significant. A burgeoning population had rendered the medieval parish church too small and in 1824 land was given to build a new one, the first to be built on a new site in Oxford since the Reformation. Newman's appointment during the transition from the one to the other was taken as 'a kind of guarantee to the subscribers that every exertion shall be made, when the church is built, to recover the parish from meeting-houses and on the other hand ale-houses, into which (people) have been drawn for want of convenient Sunday worship'. Newman, in other words, was being punted as an ecclesiastical superstar in orthodoxy's battle against the twin evils of drink and dissent. While a new parsonage was being built the charismatic curate stayed at Littlemore in a cottage which has become the George Inn.

Ironically, no sooner was the new St Clement's finished (1826) than Newman's curacy ended. In 1828 he was instituted vicar of the University Church of St Mary the Virgin. He drew 'almost every man of note in the University, old or young' to hear his 'most entrancing of voices'. A contemporary averred that 'the influence he had gained, apparently without setting himself to seek it, was something altogether unlike anything else in our time. A mysterious veneration had by degrees gathered round him ... light-hearted undergraduates would drop their voices and whisper "There's Newman".' As for his sermons – 'high poems they rather were, as of an inspired singer, or the out-pourings of a prophet, rapt yet self-possessed.'

The major thrust of Newman's 'outpourings' was the urgency of a spiritual revival in the dormant, unthinking, unfeeling Church of England, which should rather be inspired by a clear recognition of its direct succession from the apostolic church. For its proponents this affiliation implied a greater sympathy towards Rome and a greater ritualisation of worship. In an academic community explicitly defined as a bastion of Anglican orthodoxy this stance could not but prove profoundly divisive. The arguments propagated by Newman and his sympathisers were set forth in tracts and thus their campaign became known as Tractarianism and later simply as 'the Oxford Movement'.

Writer Richard Ford, a Trinity man, returning to Oxford after some twenty years, was staggered by the change in the atmosphere he encountered in 1842, especially as it affected undergraduates, who struck him as being 'of a priggish, macerated look'. In contrast to the roaring boys who had once terrorised Newman, they were now inclined to 'drink toast and water and fast on Wednesdays and Satur-days' to the perplexity of their tutors and the heads of colleges. Ford blamed Newman's lieutenant, Canon Pusey of Christ Church, whom he saw as a crypto-Jesuit.

The construction of the Martyr's Memorial in 1841, ostensibly to mark the tercentenary of the circulation of an officially approved Bible in English, represented a scarcely covert assertion of Protestant reaction to Tractarianism's apparent desire for a rapprochement with Rome. The architect, George Gilbert Scott, influenced by the recently founded Oxford Architectural and Historical Society, aimed at a sup-posed archaeological accuracy which was to characterise his later work. The moving spirit behind the project was the Reverend C.P. Golightly

(1807–85), curate of St Andrew's, Headington and a former Oriel colleague of Newman – with whom he had quarrelled bitterly. Golightly's entire literary output was to be devoted to attacks on Newman and his disciples.

In 1841 Newman's Tract XC provoked a breaking-point when it proposed that the central doctrines of Catholicism were fundamentally compatible with Anglicanism. Convocation, the collective assembly of all the university's MAs gathered in the Sheldonian to consider a proposal that this tract should be publicly condemned, the atmosphere of the meeting being heightened and dramatised by a tremendous snowstorm outside. Although the proctors used the powers of their office to veto the proposal in an attempt to head off an outright confrontation the occasion forced Newman to realise that his position was untenable. Resigning as vicar of St Mary's, he withdrew to a religious community at Littlemore and on 9 October 1845, while an autumnal gale howled reproachfully, was received into the Roman church by the (Blessed) Father Dominic Barberi.

Newman left Oxford forever on 23 February 1846. In 1864 he noted in his famous third person autobiography *Apologia Pro Vita Sua*, 'I have never seen Oxford since, excepting its spires, as they are seen from the railway'. Newman, whose compositions include the novel *Loss and Gain*, *The Dream of Gerontius* and the much-loved hymn *Lead, Kindly Light* went on to play a leading role in the revival of Catholicism in Victorian England and was elevated to the rank of Cardinal in 1879.

A decade after Newman's departure Pusey, by then Regius Professor of Hebrew, was less identified with religious controversy than with rearguard opposition to academic reform. Pusey House was to be founded in his memory in 1884 to house his theological library and serve as a centre of 'sacred learning' and ministry in the Anglo-Catholic tradition. Its main buildings in St Giles date from 1912–26.

Mark Pattison (1813—84), Rector of Lincoln College, looking back on the religious controversies of the 1830s and 1840s from the perspective of the 1880s concluded that Oxford academia had been collectively bewitched into damaging distraction from its proper business, the need for further reform in the interests of excellence.

KEBLE

Newman himself regarded John Keble (1792–1866) as the 'true and primary' author of the Oxford Movement and its actual birth as dating from 14 July 1833 when Keble used the occasion of the Assize Sermon in St Mary's to preach on 'National Apostasy' and to lambast the newly elected Whig government's dispossession of ten Irish bishops as an unwarranted interference by the state in the affairs of the Church. Keble's father had been a clergyman and Fellow of Corpus, where Keble himself gained a Double First in 1811. Elected a Fellow at Oriel he had served it as singularly inept finance officer, achieving consistent inaccuracies of plus or minus £1,800 in a variety of accounts by adding in or subtracting the date. In 1827 Keble produced a volume of sacred verse, *The Christian Year*, which was to run through ninety editions. In 1831 he was appointed Professor of Poetry but in 1836 left Oxford to become vicar of Hursley near Winchester, serving as a conscientious country pastor from then until his death. Despite his detachment from Oxford, Keble remained involved in the scriptural labours of the Oxford Movement and himself wrote several of the *Tracts for the Times*. When he died it was resolved by his admirers that he should be commemorated by the foundation of a new college which would offer a High Church setting for the education of young men of moderate means – a double blow at the old incubus of aristocratic exclusiveness and the new succubus of secularism. The project moved with remarkable speed, the foundation stone of Keble College being laid on the second anniversary of Keble's death. It was the first foundation of an entirely new Oxford college since Wadham in 1612, Pembroke, Worcester and Hertford being technically re-foundations.

The architect chosen for the project, William Butterfield (1814–1900), himself a committed follower of the Oxford Movement, made the new foundation look as unlike any existing college as possible. His 'determination to be singular' was expressed not only in the exuberant polychromy of his brickwork but also in such structural innovations as the abandonment of staircases for corridors as the standard mode of arranging students' rooms. This model was to become general for the women's colleges which were shortly to emerge. Keble's imposing entrance gateway and tower was paid for by Pusey out of his own pocket. One of the most celebrated paintings of the century, *The Light of the World*, by the Pre-Raphaelite William Holman Hunt, was donated to the chapel by Thomas Combe's widow. Keble's architecture has continued to provoke comment. Writing in the 1930s Christopher Hobhouse excoriated it as 'violently offensive to all the senses ... colours and proportions can only be described as obscene ... choice of materials is unspeakable ... But his scale is superb .. Only a crank could like his work but it is a mistake not to admire it.'

To the ire of the Bishop of Oxford the lordly chapel was, and remains, unconsecrated. Appropriately in the light of its affiliation in 1933 the college received the outstanding Brooke collection of medieval illuminated manuscripts. In keeping with its self-imposed austerity, its anti-aristocratic ethos and its desire to deny meddling politicians scope for intervention Keble was, and remains, unendowed. Thanks to its first warden, Edward Talbot, a daring appointment in his mid-twenties, Keble set out, however, to pursue academic breadth and excellence rather than theological particularity and exclusiveness. Within a generation it had become Oxford's fourth biggest college.

Another protégé of Pusey, Richard Meux Benson (1824–1915), appointed vicar of Cowley, was inspired by one of Keble's sermons to establish (1865) an order, the Society of St John the Evangelist, the first stable men's religious community to be established within the Church of England since the Reformation. Benson had originally intended that the 'Cowley Fathers' should be missionaries overseas but was persuaded by the Bishop of Oxford that the transformation of Cowley from a village to a suburb created a more urgent need nearer home. G.F. Bodley designed the striking conventual church of St John the Evangelist, next to the mission buildings in Marston Road. Benson did go on to establish separate congregations in the USA and Canada and branch houses in South Africa and India. His particular contribution was the promotion of spiritual retreats. The Cowley Fathers left Oxford for Westminster in 1980 and their premises were taken over by St Stephen's House, an Anglo-Catholic seminary, founded (1876) by Oxford's Professor of Pastoral Theology, Edward King.

A SUCCESSFUL SPOOF

The Adventures of Mr Verdant Green, purportedly an insider's view of undergraduate life, was actually the work of the Reverend Edward Bradley, a graduate of University College, Durham, who spent a year in Oxford, though not as a member of the university. To those on the

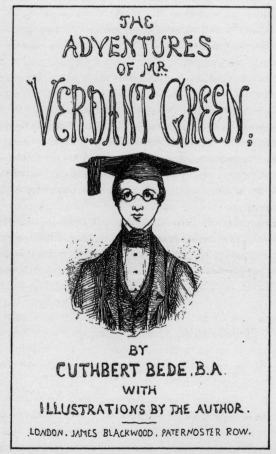

The Adventures of Mr Verdant Green, a novel of university life

alert the author's name, Cuthbert Bede, should have been a give-away, Cuthbert and Bede being the patron saints of Durham Cathedral. Cuthbert Bede chooses to study in Oxford, having dismissed Durham on account of its 'infancy' and lack of prestige and Cambridge because his father believed that nothing but mathematics was taught there and he 'remembered that the great Newton was horsed during the time that he was a Cambridge undergraduate and he had a hazy idea that the same indignities were still practised there'.

On arrival in Oxford, Green, an archetypal Pickwickian innocent, hires a guide who 'could do the alls, collidges and principal hedifices in a nour and naff' and who introduces him to 'Dr Portman', the 'master of Brazenface', a scarcely veiled caricature of Frederic Plumptre, Master of University College and Vice-Chancellor (1848–52). Green is then required as a condition of entering his course of studies to swear allegiance to the queen, reject the pretensions of the Pope, subscribe to the Thirty-Nine Articles of the Church of England and promise to obey the Laudian Statutes, a copy of which, in Latin, was placed in his uncomprehending grasp. *Verdant Green*, first published in parts in 1853-6, sold 170,000 copies over the next thirty years and a further 80,000 in the half century after that. It was reprinted as a paperback in 1982 with an introduction by the novelist Anthony Powell. Hippolyte Taine, preparing the section of university life for his *Notes sur l'Angleterre*, drew freely on *Verdant Green*, together with Thackeray's *Pendennis* and Hughes's *Tom Brown at Oxford*. Bradley made only £350 from the book and never wrote anything half as good again.

A Wind of Change

'... the fact that so few books of profound research emanate from the University of Oxford materially impairs its character as a seat of learning'.
Royal Commission 1850

Like Ackermann's prints, *Verdant Green* presented a timely snapshot of an Oxford that was about to disappear. Many of the inanities it lampooned would be swept away with the Laudian Statues as a result of the enquiries and recommendations of the Royal Commission of 1850. To

outsiders Oxford's faults were glaring and the success of the newly
established universities of London and Durham, not to mention the
ancient Scottish universities, afforded standards for comparison against
which Oxford appeared smug, stagnant, unproductive, expensive and
exclusive. It scorned whole realms of scholarly enquiry. Consumed by
religious controversy, it still denied access to Catholics, Dissenters and
Jews. Most Fellows still owed their posts to family connections and did
so little teaching that an undergraduate anxious for a good degree had
to pay for private tuition.

The Royal Commission was established in the teeth of instinctive
opposition. The Hebdomadal Board refused outright to co-operate.
No matter. The University Reform Act of 1854 replaced it with a
Hebdomadal Council in which the dominance of the Heads of Houses
was diluted by limiting their number to six and including six professors
and six members of Convocation. The number of Fellowships open to
laymen was enlarged and restrictions on non-residence increased.
Measures were set in hand for further revision of college statutes and
university examinations. Not until the 1871 Universities Test Act,
however, was Oxford to be opened to non-Anglicans. A knowledge of
Greek remained a compulsory requirement for undergraduate entrance
until 1919, of Latin for half a century after that. A further Royal
Commission in 1871 led to the University Reform Act of 1877 which
upgraded research and teaching standards, established new laboratories
and created a Common University Fund to extort resources from the
richer colleges for the benefit of the University as a whole.

A ROYAL INTERLUDE

In 1859 Prince Albert's relentless, and ultimately counter-productive,
concern for the education of his eldest son led to the enrolment at
Christ Church of the first Prince of Wales in history to study at Oxford.
An eminently sociable and by no means unintelligent youth, Edward
was strictly segregated from ordinary undergraduates and immured in
sixteenth century Frewen Hall, with a colonel for a minder. Goldwin
Smith, who was almost as learned as he was dry, was selected to give the
prince a private course of history lectures in the dining room of New
Inn Hall across the street. Henry Acland (1815–1900), the Regius

Professor of Medicine, was deputed to watch over his medical condition and the Professor of Ecclesiastical History over his spiritual state. Another tutor, H.W. Fisher, father of H.A.L. Fisher was appointed to enlighten him in constitutional law. It says much for the prince's amiability that he became friendly with all, endured the history and law with good grace and later even appointed Fisher as his own private secretary. Forbidden to smoke, he managed to do so on the sly. His only permitted indulgence was riding to hounds with the South Oxfordshire. At the end of the year the prince undertook a hugely successful tour of North America, returning to Oxford for the Michaelmas term. Then he left for Cambridge – where he was even further removed from temptation by being immured out at Madingley, miles from the city itself.

LEWIS CARROLL

Lewis Carroll is known world-wide as the author of those timeless fantasies *Alice's Adventure in Wonderland* (1865) and *Through the Looking-Glass and What Alice Found There* (1871). His real name was Charles Lutwidge Dodgson (1832–98). The derivation of 'Lewis Carroll' was itself typical of the Alice genre in its reflection of Oxford's pre-occupation with puzzles, paradoxes and peculiarities of language, Lewis being the English of Lutwidge (i.e. German Ludwig) and Carroll from the Latin Carolus for Charles. A product of Arnold's Rugby, Dodgson taught mathematics at Christ Church, which was his home from his undergraduate days until his death. A reclusive bachelor, he obscured his excursions into children's literature behind his pseudonym and became almost paranoid about avoiding personal publicity. Letters bearing his authorial name were simply returned to their senders unread.

The original story about Alice was literally born on the river as an amusement for Alice Liddell, the daughter of the Dean of Christ Church. Alice and two of her little friends clamoured for a story as they drifted along in a punt down to Godstow one hot July afternoon and Dodgson capitulated and improvised one, as rich in eccentricity as the university itself.

In 1863 the Prince of Wales, newly married to the beautiful Princess

Alexandra of Denmark, returned to Oxford for a celebratory visit, staying in the Deanery at Christ Church. The bonfire, banquets and fireworks which marked this occasion all occur as motifs in *Looking-Glass*.

At Ruskin's suggestion 'Alice' was visually immortalised in the drawings of Sir John Tenniel, at the time a noted illustrator for *Punch* magazine. Dodgson himself inspired the characterisation of the White Knight. The book was eventually to be translated into over fifty languages, translated to the stage and transferred onto a range of biscuit boxes. There was a nursery edition, a birthday book and even a photographic facsimile edition of the original manuscript. The success of 'Alice' brought Dodgson a comfortable income which he distributed generously among his numerous sisters and their offspring. His legacy is perpetuated by Carroll societies in Britain and North America. In 1932 Columbia University conferred an honorary degree on eighty year old Alice Liddell for the delight she had brought to generations of children by teasing an Oxford don into writing down the playful fancyings of his fantastical imagination.

Painfully shy and inhibited by a stammer, Dodgson maintained a wide circle of friendship through a correspondence which included leading actress Ellen Terry, Millais, Rossetti, Tennyson and Prime Minister Lord Salisbury. He systematically listed every letter he sent and received and briefly summarised the contents of each. Over 100,000 are recorded in his 'register'. Thousands were written to children, many including comic verses, anagrams, acrostics and marginal drawings. Some were written back to front, so that they had to be read in a mirror, others backwards, with the words in reverse order, starting at the bottom right of a page and working upwards to end at the top left. Dodgson's penchant for paper friendships led him to invent the 'Wonderland Postage-Stamp Case' with twelve separate pockets for stamps of different values. He accompanied this with a pamphlet on *Eight or Nine Wise Words about Letter-Writing*. Both were available from Emberlin and Son, Stationers of 4 Magdalen Street. He also kept the local printers busy, composing some two hundred pamphlets on subjects as varied as vivisection, prostitution, London fire precautions and Tristan da Cunha.

Dodgson kept students at arms length, although he famously defended them during the outcry occasioned by the riotous burning of some venerable statues. He found *female* children, by contrast, unthreatening and made many of them into nude photographic subjects, an avocation which a less innocent age might consider as open to malicious construction. Certainly his letters reveal an obsessive persistence in soliciting subjects to draw or photograph in various stages of undress.

AN OXFORD GIANT: GLADSTONE

It was said of William Gladstone (1809–98) that he thought that to be called 'a characteristically Oxford man' was to have been paid 'the highest compliment that could be paid to a human being'. Gladstone, who was to serve four terms as prime minister and become the 'Grand Old Man' of British politics, came up to Christ Church under Gaisford and as a contemporary of Liddell and Acland. His first floor rooms in the north-east corner of Canterbury Quad were said to be the most fashionable available and his father made him a handsome annual allowance of £250, as well as paying for his horse and private tutoring. (Oxford's famed one-to-one tutorials originated outside the university among the 'crammers' who remedied its manifest pedagogical deficiencies – for a price.) Even so, Gladstone complained he could not manage, a disarming confession for a future Chancellor of Exchequer renowned for his rigour with the nation's finances.

It is difficult to see where the money went. He was moderate with wine, walked as his only exercise, studied hard and found recreation in an essay-writing club, named after his initials, as its founder, The Weg. As his lifelong political rival Disraeli was to observe of Gladstone, he had 'not a single redeeming defect'. In 1864, when his own son Stephen was at Oxford, Gladstone allowed him £300 all in, on the grounds that 'at the present day, money goes much further in three important items – books, clothes and journeys' – a tribute to the impact of industrialisation, railways and Gladstone's own tax-cutting budgets when he served as Chancellor of the Exchequer.

Conspicuously religious himself, Gladstone as an undergraduate pronounced the spiritual state of Oxford in general 'the most painful spectacle it ever fell to my lot to behold' – the sort of absolute statement which was to be characteristic of his rhetoric in the House of Commons. What he could offer in the line of oratory swiftly became clear in the meetings of the recently founded (1825) Oxford Union debating society, of which he became President in 1830. Despite the qualms he confided to his diary Gladstone achieved a double first in classics and maths, each involving a week of examinations. Tradition has it that during the course of a *viva* when a satisfied examiner signalled that they should move on to the next topic Gladstone baldly demanded to finish his exposition before doing so.

From Oxford Gladstone moved immediately into the Commons and between 1847 and 1859 was elected as Burgess (MP) for the university four times. Believing that Oxford 'inculcated a reverence for what is ancient and free and great' (i.e. itself), he initially opposed the proposal for a royal commission in 1850. Its findings changed his mind and, assisted by Jowett, Gladstone himself drafted the Bill for its reform, writing some three hundred and fifty letters personally in this connection. Rejecting radical proposals to overthrow the entire collegiate structure in favour of a faculty system, he opted for 'working with the materials which we possess . . . and giving to reform in cases where there is a choice the character of return and restoration'. The aim he thought should be 'to permit regeneration rather than to impose novelty, to work from within a set of historic institutions rather than from an *a priori* plan.' Gladstone's efforts on behalf of the university were recognised by the award of an honorary DCL (1857) and an Honorary Fellowship at All Souls (1858). But the rearguard had its revenge by voting him out as University Burgess in 1865. Gladstone's involvement in university reform led seamlessly to his next crusade – to reform the institution Oxford was expected to feed with able graduates eager to serve the public good, the civil service.

In 1890 the 'GOM' returned to All Souls for an extended visit. The ten days he passed there were, he claimed, the happiest of his life, though he, the radical in politics, deplored many of the changes that he saw: the abolition of gold-tasselled caps to mark out members of the nobility and 'the spectacle of men in boating costume . . . in the High Street'. In his day, he recalled, men 'kept a supply of breeches which they only wore for that purpose and in which they never sat down lest any creases should appear'. (So, that's where the money went.) Above all he disliked the advent of female 'undergraduettes', even though they were still not actually allowed to take degrees and one of his own daughters was to be Principal of Newnham College, Cambridge. Gladstone, gowned on all occasions, nevertheless deigned to address the Union on a subject of his choice: what, if anything, Homer knew about Babylonian religion. A special commemorative volume was published to mark his visit. The ostensible purpose of the foray had been to check certain references for articles he was drafting about the Old Testament. His hidden agenda was to assess the youth of his day in preparation for a forthcoming fourth term as Prime Minister, in his eighties. He returned again in 1892 to deliver '*An Academic Sketch*', the first ever in the Romanes Lecture series, which was destined to become Oxford's most prestigious public platform. When Gladstone died in Eights Week 1898 the Union cancelled the customary frivolous end-of-term subject it had scheduled and debated its adjournment as a mark of respect. The President closed its proceedings by quoting Gladstone's own deathbed tribute to Oxford: 'My most earnest prayers are hers to the uttermost and the last'.

AN OXFORD GENIUS

William Morris (1834–96) and Sir Edward Burne-Jones (1833–98) met as freshmen at Exeter in 1853 and became lifelong friends, artistic collaborators and business partners. Expelled from Marlborough for his part in a school rebellion, Morris was already in love with the Middle Ages, thanks to the novels of Sir Walter Scott and his own explorations of the glorious 'wool churches' of the Cotswolds. Oxford – 'a vision of greyroofed houses, a long street and the sound of many bells' – delighted him as an environment but bored him as a centre of learning. 'I took very ill to the studies of the place but fell to very vigorously on history and especially medieval history' – Froissart's *Chronicles* of the Hundred Years War, Malory's *Morte d'Arthur* and the marvellous manuscript collections of the Bodleian. Morris and Burne-Jones vowed to establish a brotherhood dedicated to 'a crusade and holy war against the age', specifically the crass materialism and uncritical technophilia epitomised by the Great Exhibition of 1851. Morris also discovered a talent for composing poetry with great facility. Comfortably cushioned by a £900 annuity from his late father, he subsidised and wrote for the *Oxford and Cambridge Magazine*, which lasted for a year and was 'very *young* indeed'.

Uncertain of his future direction, but having 'made up my mind to take up art in some form', Morris initially articled himself to the Oxford architect G.E. Street, then practising in Beaumont Street. A former assistant to George Gilbert Scott, Street had as his assistant Philip Webb, who had been born in Beaumont Street and was himself to be succeeded by Richard Norman Shaw, future architect of New Scotland Yard. Street himself designed the large new parish church of St Philip and St James (1860–66) in North Oxford. His other Oxford work in the 1850s and 1860s consisted of schools in Paradise Square and Great Clarendon Street and restorations at St Ebbe's, St Michael's, St James at Cowley and the chapel of Jesus College. Street's masterpiece was to be the Royal Courts of Justice in London. While Morris was with him Street would have been working on the two books he published in 1855: *Brick and Marble in the Middle Ages* and *The Architecture of North Italy*. Morris stayed with Street for less than a year but imbibed a profound respect for 'truth to materials' and an awareness of the significance of church decoration which he was to turn to entrepreneurial advantage.

Another legacy of Morris's Oxford undergraduate years was aesthetic anger, kindled by Exeter's decision to demolish its authentic medieval chapel and replace it (1854–60), at a cost of £17,000, with a reproduction of the Sainte-Chapelle in Paris in miniature from the drawing-board of George Gilbert Scott. Morris detested the substitution of the fake, however accomplished, for the genuine article. A quarter of a century later Morris and Webb would found the Society for the Protection of Ancient Buildings – privately known to himself as 'Anti-Scrape' – specifically to preserve them from the depredations of Scott and other restorationists of his ilk. (Ironically the chapel of Exeter was to be adorned in 1890 by a tapestry of the *Adoration of the Magi*, sombre in tone, rich in detail, designed by Burne-Jones and manufactured by Morris's own firm.)

Through Burne-Jones Morris was introduced to Dante Gabriel Rossetti, the suave, compelling figure at the heart of a semi-secret artistic coterie who styled themselves Pre-Raphaelites on the grounds that only art predating the Renaissance possessed artistic value and moral validity. Rossetti was a friend of Benjamin Woodward, who was then (1857) building a new home for the Oxford Union. Thanks to this contact Morris and Burne-Jones returned to Oxford as members of a team commissioned to decorate the ceiling of the Union's Debating Room (now the Old Library) with ten scenes from Malory. Unfortunately the result was more fiasco than fresco. Technical ignorance of the techniques of tempera painting condemned their efforts to fading into oblivion. Morris returned in 1875 to repaint the subsidiary decoration.

In 1861 Morris put up the money to found Morris, Marshall, Faulkner & Co. Fine Art Workmen in Painting, Carving Furniture and the Metals. Webb became one of the most active creative members of 'The Firm'. C.J. Faulkner, an Oxford maths don, kept the books. Initially The Firm focused on ecclesiastical furnishings because their avant-garde designs were unacceptable and too expensive for regular trade outlets. The business, reorganised under tighter direction by Morris in the 1870s, eventually accomplished a mass-market, middle-class revolution in English interior design through its furniture, wallpapers, carpets and textiles. In designing and manufacturing stained-glass windows, the mainstay of The Firm's cash-flow in the 1860s, Morris and Burne-Jones discovered a metier which they made their own. Outstanding Oxford examples can be seen in Christ Church Cathedral and the chapels of St Edmund Hall and Manchester College.

Morris, who declined the Professorship of Poetry at Oxford in favour of lecturing to working men, devoted his later years to the socialist movement and reviving the art of printing fine books. His tomb, by Webb, is at Kelmscott, the Oxfordshire village where he had lived in the stone Tudor Manor House. Morris Cottages (1902) were built there in his memory to Webb's designs. Burne-Jones found late fame as a painter and was honoured by Oxford with a DCL, by Exeter with an honorary Fellowship and by the Queen, on the advice of Gladstone, with a baronetcy.

THE ARNOLD DYNASTY

Thomas Arnold (1795–1842) came up to Christ Church at sixteen, became a Fellow of Oriel at twenty and headmaster of Rugby School at thirty-three. In a decade he reinvented the English public school system of education and thus England's future social and political elite. Had Oxford done nothing else for nineteenth century Britain the effects of the Arnoldian revolution would alone have measured its significance. Arnold's ideal was the Christian gentleman and he put the chapel, literally and symbolically at the heart of school life. Although himself a winner of the Chancellor's Prize for Latin Prose, Arnold believed that the traditional curriculum of Latin and Greek should be broadened to include history and modern languages. He died suddenly of angina only a year after appointment as Regius Professor of Modern History at Oxford. Arnold strides like a demi-god through the pages of Thomas Hughes' hugely influential novel of schoolboy life at the reformed Rugby, *Tom Brown's Schooldays*. The author wrote from first-hand experience of Rugby, was a contemporary of Arnold's son, Matthew, at Oxford and followed his minor masterpiece with a sequel, *Tom Brown at Oxford* (1861).

Thomas Arnold's eldest son, Matthew Arnold (1822–88) won the Newdigate prize for a poem on Cromwell in 1843. Despite a reputation for indolence, affectation and malicious practical jokes, he followed his father into a Fellowship at Oriel and in 1857 was elected Professor of Poetry. His interest in Celtic literature was instrumental in causing Oxford to found a chair of Celtic Studies. Matthew Arnold is also responsible for two of the most celebrated descriptions of Oxford as the 'home of lost causes' (*Essays in Criticism* 1865) and the city of 'dreaming spires' (*Thyrsis in New Poems* 1867). His most anthologised poem is probably the profound and melancholy existential meditation *Dover Beach* (1867).

Arnold was also responsible for giving new currency to the legend of the 'Scholar Gypsy', first noted by Joseph Glanvill in 1661. According to Glanvill a brilliant scholar, forced from his studies by poverty, quits Oxford, falls in with a band of gypsies and masters their secret lore so 'as to be able to outdo his Instructors'. Meeting by chance two former

Matthew Arnold

fellow-scholars, he rebuffs their condemnation of his lifestyle by claiming a knowledge which transcends all their learning and demonstrates it by leaving them alone in a tavern room and returning to repeat in detail their entire conversation in his absence – claiming to have himself predetermined it by his own powers of mind. Matthew Arnold retold the legend in verse as *The Scholar Gypsy* (1853).

Believing that beauty could replace belief and poetry stand in for scripture in a world increasingly riddled by doubt, Arnold spent fifteen years of his intellectual prime as a schools inspector, attempting, in terms of standards and motivation, to do for the English many what his father had done for the English few – to place within their grasp an awareness of 'the best that has been thought and said in the world'.

After University College Thomas Arnold's second son, Thomas (1823–1900) failed as a farmer in New Zealand then succeeded as a schools inspector in Tasmania. Conversion to Catholicism brought him to the notice of Newman, who persuaded him to Ireland as a teacher of English literature. Apostasising from Romanism, Arnold returned to Oxford, built the house which is now Wycliffe Hall and took private pupils. Reconversion to Rome cost him the chair of Anglo-Saxon. He entitled his embittered autobiography *Passages from a Wandering Life*.

Thomas Arnold's eldest daughter, Mary Augusta (1851–1920) has been better known by her married, authorial name, Mrs Humphrey Ward. Mary lived in her father's Oxford home from sixteen and married Ward, a Fellow of BNC in 1872, moving to 5 (now 17) Bradmore Road and becoming the first secretary of Somerville College in 1879. When her husband became a regular contributor to *The Times* newspaper, she moved to London (1881). Her most successful novel, *Robert Elsmere* (1888) is set against the religious ferment of the Oxford she knew. Tracing her clergyman hero's struggle in London's slums, the book argues that true Christians should give priority to the social message of the Gospel, rather than to disputes over liturgical niceties. The inspirational philosophy don, T.H. Green of Balliol appears in the novel, thinly disguised as Henry Gray. Gladstone, reviewing the book as *Robert Elsmere and the Battle of Belief* for the May 1888 edition of *The Nineteenth Century*, interpreted it as an attack on Christianity as such. Mrs Ward, having returned to 2 Bradmore Road to nurse her dying mother, met Gladstone twice at the Warden's Lodgings at Keble to defend her views. Despite her social activism, in 1908 Mrs Ward became first president of the Anti-Suffrage League, believing that women's influence was best exerted through the home. In later life she also pioneered education for disabled children. Her memoir *A Writer's Recollections* (1918) draws a vivid picture of Oxford life, from its portrait of Jowett to its estimate of the domestic impact of William Morris and Liberty prints.

JOHN RUSKIN: AN OXFORD PROPHET

John Ruskin (1819–1900) was a quintessentially bourgeois figure who saw the virtues of the feudal age as the remedy for the failings of his own. His father was 'the head of the sherry trade', a South London wine merchant so wealthy he could buy the house next door to accommodate the overflow of his son's collections. Privately educated, reclusive and delicate, Ruskin became a gentleman commoner at Christ Church with rooms in Peckwater Quad in 1837. His mother took rooms at 90 High Street and he visited her daily for tea and usually after dinner as well. Father, who bridled at the word 'commoner' even in junction with 'gentleman', came up at weekends. In 1839, at his

third attempt, Ruskin won the Newdigate Prize. Illness then interrupted his studies, forcing recuperation abroad. He finally graduated in
1842 with an honorary double fourth.

Despite these somewhat hesitant academic beginnings Ruskin
developed into the most influential art critic of his age and from his art
criticism branched out into social theory. His reputation was established
by the multi-volume *Modern Painters* (1843–60) and his spirited defence
of the young artistic clique who styled themselves Pre-Raphaelites. It
was confirmed by *The Stones of Venice* (1851–2) whose seminal chapter
'*On the Nature of Gothic*' hit the youthful William Morris like a
bombshell and thus, indirectly, 'caused' the Arts and Crafts movement
which dominated English creative life in the 1870s and 1880s. Its basic
argument was that medieval art and craft were inseparable and that both
were grounded in spiritual and aesthetic values rather than the pursuit
of profit, resulting in creations which were sublime, authentic and
socially just.

Ruskin achieved his social and cultural eminence outside Oxford.
Renewed involvement in the life of the university began when Acland,
a close friend since undergraduate days, enlisted Ruskin's support for
the project to build a university museum in Parks Road. Ruskin's
participation helped to ensure that the building would be constructed
in a dramatic Venetian Gothic idiom with domestic asides, the chemical laboratory being a pastiche of the Abbot's kitchen at Glastonbury.
Ruskin also contributed some highly distinctive touches to the managerial style of the project in its construction phase; a temporary mess
and reading-room were erected for the comfort of the workmen and
each day's labour began, in what Ruskin conceived as a medieval spirit
of dedication, with morning prayers administered by a rota of university clergy, reaching up to the Vice-Chancellor himself.

In 1870 Ruskin was appointed Slade Professor of Fine Art and in
1871 the Ruskin School of Drawing and Fine Art was opened. Ruskin
presented it with works from his own rich collections and taught there
in person, his platform manner reminding one onlooker of 'an elderly
macaw picking grapes'. Initially Ruskin banned women ('the bonnets')
from his lectures on the grounds that they were 'of no use to the female
mind and they would occupy the seats in mere disappointed puzzle-

ment'. This was doubly presumptuous. Ruskin's personal life betrayed his own singular incapacity to penetrate the female mind – or, indeed, body.

In 1876, in pursuance of his theories on the dignity and social duty of labour, Ruskin inspired a group of undergraduates to undertake the upgrading and beautification of a stretch of road running through North Hinksey. Oscar Wilde was one who responded to this call to arms. A competent surveyor subsequently reported to the concerned local landowner that the young gentlemen's efforts had resulted in no discernible damage. Ruskin's appointment was discontinued in 1879 owing to a breakdown in his mental health and renewed briefly in 1883–4 before being again terminated for the same reason.

North Oxford

For many, Ruskin's enduring Oxford legacy is the University Museum. For others it is leafy North Oxford, whose domestic architecture embodies the Gothicisms he so enthusiastically espoused. In cultural terms North Oxford became synonymous with the literary tastes and liberal values supposedly epitomised by Hampstead in London. Oxford's most residentially desirable suburb was built up on land mostly purchased by St John's College three centuries earlier with the bequest of its founder's widow. The first residents were mostly wealthy merchants. Thomas Mallam, twice Mayor of Oxford, had 72 Woodstock Road built for him in 1840. The Park Town estate was laid out in 1853–5 and like Park Villas of the same period was still Italianate, rather than Gothic. Following the abolition of the celibacy rule for Fellowships in 1877, North Oxford thickened out as 'married quarters' for academics. Much was the work of prolific local architect William Wilkinson (1819–91), who designed the Randolph Hotel (1864–6) and laid out the Norham Manor estate from 1860 onwards. 1, 5, 7, 11 and 13 Norham Gardens are by Wilkinson himself . No. 60 Banbury Road is the only intact survivor of four North Oxford villas he published in his *English Country Houses* (1875). The building regulations strictly forbade roughcast exteriors, imposed high standards of sanitation and workmanship and provided for spacious gardens. Ruskin

A house built on the Banbury Road for a prosperous tradesman in 1875

himself approved the development though others dismissed it as 'interminable streets of villadom'. Since 1945 family houses have been largely converted to flats, college rooms and b & bs. A 1962 threat to demolish North Oxford wholesale for 'development' as the 99 year leases of 1855 ran out, was defeated by a campaign headed by John Betjeman. In 1968 designation as a conservation area at last brought a measure of protection.

Beyond North Oxford lies Summertown. Dotted with Regency villas and cottages from the 1820s, it was substantially developed from 1889 when it was incorporated into Oxford proper. In the twentieth century it became the home of Oliver and Gurden's 'Famous Oxford Cakes', Radio Oxford, the Delegacy of Local Examinations and the international headquarters of Oxfam.

Apes versus Angels

The condition of science at Oxford remained dismal until after mid-century. The efforts of the ordained geologist William Buckland to reconcile the fossil record with the literalism of Genesis proved so unavailing that a colleague observed contemptuously:

> Some doubts were once expressed about the Flood,
> Buckland arose, and all was clear as – mud.

When the British Medical Association met in Oxford in 1835 Buckland showed off a selection of fossils, after which the assembly trooped off to the Town Hall, specially borrowed for the occasion, to watch a demonstration of a new procedure for crushing a stone in the bladder. After their AGM in the Radcliffe they heard a paper on 'Autumnal Fever and Epidemic Scarlatina'. That was it. Between 1840 and 1854 the *total* number of Oxford graduates in medicine was fourteen. In 1858 it was reckoned that there were less than forty living Oxford medical graduates in the entire world.

Another indication of the paucity of scientific talent available in mid-Victorian Oxford is the fact that Charles Daubeny, an Edinburgh-trained physician whose first publication was on volcanoes, held the chairs of chemistry, botany and rural economy simultaneously. On three occasions Daubeny, acting as examiner in medicine, was unable to award any candidate any class of degree at all. Science at Oxford suffered to a considerable extent from what it was not: a body of knowledge to be gleaned from a half shelf of canonical books. The wife of one eminent classicist opined that any scholar of her husband's calibre could 'get up' science in a fortnight. It was a not untypical attitude. Science, moreover, appeared to have no intellectual tradition or any use for intuition. Perceived as mechanistic, it was dismissed as worthy only of mechanicals. Between 1830 and 1900 not one single head of an Oxford college came from a scientific background.

Oxford's rebirth as a centre of medical education began with the appointment of Henry Acland as Lecturer in Anatomy in 1845. He soon became a physician at the Radcliffe Infirmary and in 1857 Regius Professor of Medicine, a post he was to hold for thirty-seven years. The nursing home he founded became the Acland Hospital on Banbury Road but a far more important legacy arose from his initiative in founding the University Museum to provide a new impetus to the modernisation of science at Oxford.

In 1860, as part of this strategy, the newly opened museum hosted the annual meeting of the British Association for the Advancement of Science. The most dramatic episode was a set-piece debate on Darwin's theory of evolution as advanced in his recently published *Origin of Species* (1859). The fundamentalist case was advanced by the oleagenous Bishop of Oxford, 'Soapy Sam' Wilberforce (1805–73), once a youthful star of the Union and still an active debater in the House of Lords. Wilberforce sneeringly enquired of his opponent, the eminent T.H. Huxley, inventor of the very term 'biology', what he felt about having an ape for a grandfather? The rebuke from the man who had appointed himself 'Darwin's bulldog' was majestic in its directness, that he would be ashamed only to be aware of any connection with a man who used his great intellectual gifts to obscure the truth. In fact, Huxley on this occasion rather mumbled his riposte and it was left to another disciple of Darwin, J.D. Hooker, to put the rhetorical boot in. Huxley left with a new determination to upgrade his skills at public speaking and did so, eventually to great effect.

A chair in zoology having been established in 1854, another, in entomology, was created in 1861. In 1868 the Clarendon Laboratory for physics was opened. A chair in physiology was founded in 1877 but engineering had to wait another twenty years. In remedying its manifest deficiencies, moreover, science at Oxford relied significantly on external talents or training. Acland himself had been trained at Edinburgh. Charles Pritchard (1808–93), a Cambridge man who had pursued astronomy as a side-line to being a country vicar, was appointed Savilian Professor of Astronomy in 1870 and by 1875 had designed and erected a new observatory in the University Parks. R.B. Clifton (1836–1921) the first Professor of Experimental Physics listed work as his recreation in *Who's Who* and was elected FRS, but achieved very little else, which is scarcely surprising from a man who observed that 'the wish to do research betrays a certain restlessness of spirit'.

THE PURSUIT OF EXCELLENCE

> First come I. My name is Jowett
> There's no knowledge but I know it.
> I am Master of this College
> What I don't know isn't knowledge.

As Master of Balliol from 1870 until his death Benjamin Jowett (1817–93) was perhaps the single most influential don, if not in Oxford, then certainly in England. His aim was to make Balliol a powerhouse of excellence, an excellence which would energise the nation. A multiple university prize-winner, Jowett was elected a Fellow while still an undergraduate. In 1848 he organised the first summer reading-party, an innovation which was to become a marked feature of Oxford life for most of the following century. With terms so full of social and sporting engagements as to preclude serious reading the dedicated scholar was advised to make use of what were perhaps misleadingly called 'vacations'. Well into the twentieth century it was seriously maintained that undergraduates who had to work to support themselves during vacations should therefore be denied entry to the university.

Denied the Mastership of Balliol in 1855, Jowett became Regius Professor of Greek and, in 1882, Vice-Chancellor. As a Balliol tutor he nurtured able young men of limited means and as Master promoted a

Benjamin Jowett, Vice-Chancellor of the University 1882–86, Master of Balliol and Regius Professor of Greek

major building programme to house his expanding army of protégés, readily confessing to 'a general prejudice against all persons who do not succeed in the world'. Jowett was routinely ruthless with the second rate and would not hesitate to crush an overawed undergraduate with the contemptuous dismissal of a failed conversational gambit as 'singularly commonplace'. Jowett defended his unashamed partiality for 'young men of rank or wealth', as well as those of ability, on grounds which were both pragmatic and high-minded: 'one must remember how important it is to influence towards good those who are going to have an influence over hundreds of thousands of other lives'. Jowett understood this quite literally and his conviction was borne out by the facts. By the late 1890s more than forty Balliol men were to be found in the House of Commons. Between 1878 and 1914 over two hundred entered the Indian Civil Service, where they exercised power over not hundreds or thousands of lives but millions. Jowett numbered among his regular correspondents the reformers Florence Nightingale and Josephine Butler and among his acolytes the poets Swinburne, Clough, Belloc and G.M. Hopkins, Archbishops Lang and Temple and Cardinal Manning and the future statesmen Curzon, Grey and Milner. It was another of Jowett's Balliol disciples, the future Prime Minister H.H. Asquith, who coined the immortal tag that Balliol men were characterised by 'effortless superiority'.

An expert on Plato and Hegel, Jowett was neither overly austere nor puritanical in his cultural tastes, instituting Sunday concerts at Balliol and supporting the Oxford University Dramatic Society. Regarded as something of an oracle, he was given to pithy pronouncements, epitomised by his advice to a young lady assailed by religious doubts: 'You must believe in God, my dear, despite what the clergymen say'.

Jowett's concern for teaching was matched by the concern of his near contemporary Mark Pattison for research. Pattison, who 'lived wholly for study' believed that 'education among us has sunk into a trade' and was a passionate admirer of the research-oriented German universities, which were being taken as a model by cutting-edge American institutions like Johns Hopkins. A common admiration for Teutonic intellectuality may have proved helpful when Pattison met the famously aloof George Eliot in the course of her visit to Oxford in

1870. Pattison may even have been the inspiration for the dessicated scholar Casaubon in her masterpiece, *Middlemarch*, which appeared in 1871–2. He was certainly Roger Wendover in Mrs Humphry Ward's *Robert Elsmere*.

HEARTIES...

Recruitment to late Victorian Oxford was dominated by less than a dozen major public schools – Eton and its traditional rival Harrow, Winchester, Arnold's reformed Rugby and its imitator Marlborough, and the London quartet of Westminster, Charterhouse, Merchant Taylors' and St Paul's. Sharing a common pre-university education undergraduates thus shared a common culture, which was centred on the cult of sport, a cult which was elaborated and continued at university level. The roots of this cult lay in the need to find some outlet for the physical energies of youths confined to all-male institutions, the emergence of a new style of 'muscular Christianity' and the stimulus that the advent of cheap and reliable railway services gave to the possibility of competition between teams drawn from schools previously isolated from one another by sheer distance. At times and in some colleges it seemed that the 'athlocracy' might overwhelm the scholarly altogether. Lionel Hedges, who played cricket for Kent at county level even before he arrived, once brusquely dismissed 'a seedy, middle-aged gentleman', whom he took to be a bothersome newspaper reporter, only to discover later that he was the personal tutor assigned to him, with whom he had yet to acquaint himself.

Brasenose in particular became renowned as a stronghold of 'hearties', boasting among its members 'Squire' Osbaldeston, who once won a thousand guineas by riding two hundred miles in less than ten hours, William Webb Ellis, the supposed inventor of rugby football, and W.B. Woodgate, author of the classic *Oars and Sculls and How to Use Them*. Woodgate also founded Vincent's Club, which took its name from its first (1863) meeting-place, above the premises of a High Street printer of that name. Its membership, limited to a hundred, then a hundred and fifty, then two hundred and fifty, was by invitation only and was dominated by sporting heroes. Vincent's became the traditional meeting-place for the committee which awarded 'Blues' to athletes who had represented Oxford at an approved sport in a 'varsity' match against Cambridge. Vincent's own governing committee can also claim the distinction of having invented the multi-crested tie which soon became the identifying marker of the gentle-manly, rather than professional, sporting fraternity. Complemented by blazers in a variety of vivid stripes, these became the elements of an arcane and complex heraldry of sporting prowess quite baffling to the uninitiated. When Mr. Gladstone saw men in boating-dress on the High Street, what he misinterpreted as mere sartorial sloppiness was in fact partisan pride in riparian prowess. The institutionalisation of uni-versity sport reached its climax in the last third of the century with the establishment of clubs or inter-varsity competitions in athletics (1860), cricket (1862), rugby (1869), soccer (1871), cycling (1873), golf (1875), polo (1878), cross country (1880), lawn tennis (1881), yacht-ing (1884), hockey (1890), swimming (1892) and boxing and fencing (1897).

Oxford added little to sport that was new as such – apart from the piquancy of beating Cambridge. (At the time of writing there are seventy-seven regular inter-varsity fixtures.) No new sport was invented at Oxford. 'Chair-tilting', a mode of sedentary combat in which the occupants of wheeled armchairs propelled themselves backwards at each other at full tilt across paved quadrangles, flourished briefly in the 1860s but failed to institutionalise itself. The ancient 'sport' of 'Town vs Gown' skirmishing, however, continued with undiminished vigour, especially on Guy Fawkes' Night.

In many careers a good sporting record at Oxford came to count as much as, if not more than, academic distinction. Recruiters for the colonial service in particular took it as proof of a sound constitution, able to withstand the enervating effects of a tropical climate, and evi-dence of the sort of 'can do' determination required of a man in his early twenties expected to rule half a million people single-handed. The Sudan Civil Service was to set special store by this criterion. Of three hundred and ninety-three men it recruited, no less than seventy-one had represented either Oxford or Cambridge at university level, prompting the observation that the Sudan was 'a land of Blacks ruled by Blues'.

The epitome of the Corinthian spirit was Charles Burgess Fry (1872–1956), for whom the over-used soubriquet 'legendary' for once seems scarcely adequate. In 1891 he played soccer for England against a visiting Canadian side. In 1893 he equalled the world long jump record. In 1894 he was Oxford University Captain of Cricket and Soccer and Athletics. A classicist of note, he also won the top scholarship to Wadham, ahead of a future Lord Chancellor, F.E. Smith, Lord Birkenhead – and, it is rumoured, Fry also turned down the offer of the throne of Albania.

... AND ARTIES

> 'Untruthful! My nephew Algernon? Impossible! He is an Oxonian!'
> Lady Bracknell, *The Importance of Being Earnest*

In the prevalently sporty atmosphere of late Victorian Oxford many aesthetes were permanently on the defensive or at least the evasive. One famously was said to have affected a permanent limp on the grounds that even the most thuggish sportsman would hesitate to beat up a *crippled* lover of art and poetry. Oscar Fingal O'Flahertie Wills Wilde (1854–1900) felt no need to be defensive. He was an aesthete with the physique of an athlete, and a very tall, powerfully built one at that. When four hearties tried to vandalise his rooms in Magdalen he booted the first down the stairs, doubled up the second with a punch in the stomach, threw the third on top of the other two and carried the fourth out bodily. Wilde was also anything but evasive. He was his own invention and Oxford was where he invented himself. Wilde annihilated all traces of an Irish accent, transformed himself into a dandy and won the Newdigate Prize. He decorated his room with Japanese ceramics and served his guests a lethal punch of gin and whisky. He became a Freemason of the suitably named Apollo Lodge, dined lavishly at the Mitre and as 'O'Flighty' swiftly became a university 'character' and the model for the Duke of Dorset in Beerbohm's *Zuleika Dobson*. Wilde's quip that on some days he found it 'difficult to live up to his blue china' became the subject of a reproving sermon at St Mary's. True to pseudo-aristocratic type he also defaulted on his debts to local tradesmen.

An excellent classicist, Wilde already had a degree from Trinity College, Dublin and held the view that 'in examinations the foolish ask questions that the wise cannot answer'. In his oral examinations on the *Odyssey* and Aeschylus, he charmed the examiners into chatting about dogs and Walt Whitman. In another, devoted to the New Testament, the examiner sought to humiliate him by requiring a translation from the Greek of *Acts* 27, describing St Paul's shipwreck and containing several obscure nautical terms. Wilde sailed into the passage with ease and when bidden to halt by his defeated antagonist replied 'Please may I go on? I want to see what happened . . . .'

Despite being kicked out for a term for coming back a month late from a visit to Greece, despite not being offered a Fellowship – which he naturally affected to scorn – Wilde retained his affection for 'Magdalen's tall tower tipped with tremulous gold' and for Oxford itself – 'inspite of the roaring of the young lions at the Union and the screaming of rabbits in the home of the vivisector, in spite of Keble college and the tramways and the sporting punts, Oxford still remains the most beautiful thing in England and nowhere else are life and art so exquisitely blended, so perfectly made into one'. Wilde's affection for his *alma mater* proved perhaps unfortunate in one respect. It was when revisiting Oxford that he first encountered Lord Alfred Douglas.

Wilde was attracted particularly to the 'refined and comely decadence' and overwrought prose style of Walter Pater (1839–94) of Brasenose. A would-be successor to Ruskin as the Svengali of the *virtuosi*, Pater had gained national repute with his *Studies in the History of the Renaissance* (1873). John Buchan chose Brasenose specifically out of admiration for Pater. Gerard Manley Hopkins was another acolyte. Unlike the hirsute and ascetic-looking Ruskin, however, Pater, fleshy, bald and with a ferocious moustache, resembled a Belgian butcher rather than a Florentine grandee. A friend of Swinburne and the Pre-Raphaelites, Pater lived at 2 Bradmore Road in the house formerly occupied by Mrs Humphrey Ward. His real home, his rooms in college, would doubtless also have appealed to Wilde, being painted a delicate yellow and entered through doors with 'pretty and fantastic iron-work, brought by him from Brittany'. In opposition to prevailing popular taste he eschewed ornament for austerity, a bowl of dried rose-petals and a few engravings his chosen adornments. Unusually for a connoisseur he had little desire for valuable items and was as delighted to possess a tray of copies of ancient Greek coins as the *cognoscenti* would the real thing.

If Pater had a successor in the following generation it was perhaps Balliol's Francis Urquhart (pronounced Ercart) (1868–1934), universally known as 'Sligger' ('the sleek one'), the first post-Reformation Catholic to become a Fellow. He was like Pater in his attractiveness to students, though they were perhaps more drawn to his personality than his intellect. Like Jowett he was interested only in those who possessed social standing or unusual ability, inviting them to reading parties at his chalet near Chamonix over a period of forty years, from 1891 to 1931. His pupils included Herbert Asquith, Roger Casement, Ronald Knox, Harold Macmillan, Cyril Connolly, Quintin Hogg, Dick Crossman and Compton Mackenzie (1883–1972). The latter's semi-auto-biographical *Sinister Street* (1913–14) drew on his Oxford experiences to win praise from Ford Madox Ford and F. Scott Fitzgerald.

Symphonies in Stone

There was very little building in the period of the French Wars. The armed forces drained men from the labour market and the government drained money from the economy. From the 1820s onwards, however, Oxford, like most cities, experienced a resumption of building activity which, while it fluctuated, never again experienced such a hiatus. Behind this lay an expansion of student numbers, from two hundred and twenty-five matriculants a year in 1820 to three hundred and eighty by 1820 to six hundred and ninety-five by 1875 to eight hundred and forty by 1900. The city itself expanded in population, to 28,000 by mid-century and 50,000 by 1901. The abandonment of the 'nightwatchman state' in favour of the provision of public services created demands for schools, hospitals, libraries and improvements in infrastructure to serve them. At the same time the advent of the canal and the railway greatly diminished the cost of transporting building materials.

The colleges were initially concerned, however, with restoration rather than expansion. In the 1820s Lincoln, Pembroke, All Souls, Exeter and Merton all undertook extensive refacing projects, which left them in William Morris's view, 'ruined by fakement various'. Perhaps, but the work was doubtless timely and went on piecemeal throughout the century. Almost half a century later Nathaniel Hawthorne noted that the local Headington stone crumbled swiftly when exposed to the elements 'so that twenty years do the work of a hundred, so far as appearances go ... The effect of this is very picturesque ...'. He also recorded that whenever it became necessary to replace it 'they use a more durable material', which thanks to the railway could be brought economically from farther afield. But Hawthorne also thought that the result 'does not well assort with the antiquity into which it is intruded'. Hardy's Jude was moved to a more philosophical observation: 'It seemed impossible that modern thought could house itself in such decrepit and superseded chambers'.

Between 1841 and 1845 a major new complex to the designs of C.R. Cockerell, Professor of Architecture at the Royal Academy Schools, was erected on Beaumont Street and St Giles Street to accommodate the much enlarged collections of the Ashmolean and to house a new institute for the teaching of modern languages. The former was financed by Sir Roger Newdigate and the Reverend Francis Randolph, honoured in the name of the hotel opposite. The latter was the gift of the architect Sir Robert Taylor (1714–88), whose bequest was successfully blocked by his son until Sir Robert's death in 1834. College initiatives belong largely to mid-century. New Building (1842) at University College was by Sir Charles Barry, then working on the new Houses of Parliament. Salvin's Buildings (1852–3) at Balliol are named for their designer, the restorer of the Tower of London. Butterfield supplied the chapel (1856–7) and Sir Alfred Waterhouse, designer of London's Natural History Museum, the Broad Street range. As well as a new chapel George Gilbert Scott was also responsible for the Library, Rector's Lodgings and Broad Street range at Exeter. He also restored the chapels at All Souls, New and University College, the hall at Merton, library at University College and Founder's Tower at Magdalen.

All these are names of major significance in the profession of architecture. But the greatest architectural impact on Oxford, at least in terms of sheer output, was made by a purely local man, Sir Thomas Graham Jackson (1835–1924), a pupil of Scott and non-resident Fellow of Wadham. Betjeman was to describe him as 'a man of great culture who wrote better than he practised'. Jackson established his reputation with the University Examination Schools, an exuberant confection once pungently summarised as 'cross-pollinated'. In this it reflects an eclecticism which led critics to dub his work as 'Anglo-Jackson'. Most of Hertford College, including its flamboyant Loire chateau staircase and the much-photographed Bridge of Sighs, is Jackson's. New Quad at Brasenose is his, as are the President's Lodgings and adjoining range at Trinity. His many restoration, extension and alteration projects included the Bodleian, the spire of St Mary's, the Radcliffe Observatory and Carfax tower. Jackson also built the High Schools in George Street and Banbury Road and the University Parks cricket pavilion. Jackson additionally pioneered the use of a yellowish limestone from Clipsham in Rutland, which proved highly successful to resisting pollution and has been employed repeatedly as a replacement for decayed Headington ashlar.

The Examination Schools building by the architect T.G. Jackson. Exams were first held there in 1882

'YOU WILL LEAVE BY THE TOWN DRAIN'

The Reverend W.A. Spooner (1844–1930) was remarkable for a supposedly unwitting trick of speech which gave his name to the language as the begetter of the 'Spoonerism', though many must surely have been the invention of generations of undergraduates. 'You have hissed all my mystery lectures' sounds credible but surely some inner editorial mechanism would have prevented a Victorian clergyman from interrogating his domestic servants over a failure to despatch a letter on time by asking 'Which of you has pissed the most?'.

A myopic albino, Spooner as a young man became the first undergraduate in the entire history of New College not to have come up from Winchester. Forty-one years later he was unanimously elected Warden. A first-rate teacher, examiner and speech-maker, he supported the unpopular causes of science and women's education and involved himself in philanthropic projects in Oxford and Bethnal Green. His affability was legendary, if occasionally qualified by absent-mindedness, as in welcoming a colleague: 'Do come to dinner tonight. We have the new Fellow, Casson, coming'. 'But, Warden, I am Casson.' 'Oh, well. Never mind. Come anyway.' On another occasion he is said to have hailed a familiar face: 'Now, let me see. Was it you or your brother who was killed in the war?'

Oxford retro – the Bridge of Sighs

CHAPTER SEVEN

Opening Up, Reaching Out

Though nineteenth century Oxford may have seemed preoccupied with self-generated controversy and reluctant to engage with a larger world of rapid change it could not but redefine its relationships with that larger world if it was to sustain its claim to an integral role in national life. In addition to sustaining its prime function as the intellectual powerhouse of a ruling élite Oxford also became increasingly aware of its potential to enlarge the horizons and uplift the condition of the ruled.

Enter Dissent

Anglicanism in eighteenth century Oxford managed to achieve a spiteful edge of bigotry in dealing with Nonconformity, reducing Quakers and Baptists to marginality by violent harassment. As a greater toleration emerged nationally Oxford's local Anglo-Catholic revival imposed a new barrier to their acceptance within the university. When proposals for relaxing the subscription to the Thirty-Nine Articles were put forward in 1834, with the support of the instinctively conservative but essentially pragmatic Duke of Wellington as Chancellor, a fierce opposition was raised successfully by Newman, Pusey and the Regius and Lady Margaret Professors of Divinity. Cambridge was already admitting Dissenters without incurring the wrath of Heaven. University College, London had no religious tests whatever – hence rapidly becoming known as the 'Godless college on Gower Street'. Not for another twenty years, however, was further progress made in Oxford and then it was by the House of Commons taking advantage of the passage of the 1854 Oxford University Bill to decree the abolition of subscription for matriculation and first degrees. The 1871 University Tests Act abolished Anglicanism as a requirement for anything except theological degrees and professorships. After 1877 the only requirement to be in Holy Orders was for chaplains. Teaching for the university at Oxford was no longer a short-term rite of passage to be endured by a young clergyman while waiting for a college appointment to a pleasant country vicarage to fall vacant. It could now become in its own right a serious profession for the professional scholar. Modern don is Victorian dissenter made anew.

Training institutions for Nonconformist ministers originally established elsewhere relocated to Oxford as Mansfield College and Manchester College. Mansfield, formerly Spring Hill, a Congregationalist foundation of 1838, came from Birmingham in 1886, eventually moving into its own buildings, designed by Basil Champneys. In 1890 its 'settlement' in London's East End pioneered a 'poor man's lawyer' scheme from which modern legal aid has evolved. The fine college organ was to be played by Dr Albert Schweitzer when he was a special lecturer there. Its first female student, Constance Todd, admitted in 1913, became the first female to be ordained as a Christian minister. Mansfield finally became a full college of the University in 1995. Nowadays only about a fifth of its students follow theological courses. Its sectarian origins have fostered the development of a strong link with North America.

Manchester, now known as Harris Manchester, traces its origins to Warrington Academy, where the Unitarian minister Joseph Priestley, discoverer of oxygen, taught. During its peripatetic existence since 1786 its faculty has included Quaker chemist John Dalton, the early formulator of atomic theory, the socially engaged novelist Elizabeth Gaskell and, quixotically, Cardinal Newman's brother, Francis. Manchester's meanderings from Lancashire to York to Manchester to London – gallantly justified by its current website as evidence of its adaptability – finally ended in Oxford in 1899 next door to Wadham. Manchester College came to develop strong links with the WEA and retains a significant bias towards mature students. The college still trains ministers of the General Assembly but is broadly a liberal arts college with a significant US student intake.

HERTFORD REBORN

In 1820 Magdalen Hall, the adjunct to the college proper, burned down after a particularly lively student party and its inhabitants were relocated to defunct Hertford College. In 1868 Dr Michell, newly appointed as Vice-Principal of this Magdalen out-station determined to revive the institution as a fully renascent Hertford with the financial backing of a member of the Baring banking family. The long tenure (1877–1922) of Michell's successor, Dr Boyd, enabled him to secure the success of the enterprise while his personal preferences brought it strength in classics and golf. The need for extensive reconstruction of the college buildings gave architect Thomas Jackson opportunities of which he took unrestrained advantage.

OUTREACH

The idea of providing some sort of advanced education for 'the masses' was originally embodied in the Mechanics' Institutes established by George Birkbeck in Britain's industrial cities in the 1820s. Their purpose was chiefly to instruct working men in the theoretical principles which underlay their practical skills. The notion that universities might play a part in this sort of activity can be traced back to King's College, London whose staff began to offer extra-mural courses for women in 1847. The Reverend William Sewell of Exeter College suggested a similar initiative from Oxford in 1850 but nothing came it. The success of a self-started North of England Council for Promoting the Higher Education of Women some twenty years later encouraged Cambridge to enter the field in 1873, sending lecturers out as far as Derby, Nottingham and Leicester. In 1876 London established a Society for the Extension of University Teaching. Oxford joined the 'extension movement' in 1878. Initial leadership was given by the ubiquitous Acland but the real dynamo was Michael Sadler (1861–1943) of Christ Church, a former President of the Union. When Sadler took over in 1885 there were twenty-seven courses running. By 1890 enrolments had risen to over 20,000. By 1893 the sub-committee of the Examinations Delegacy which supervised extension activity had been promoted to an independent delegacy in its own right and four hundred courses were being offered.

Sadler pioneered innovations which were soon copied elsewhere, such as travelling libraries to support lecturers. Even more valuable was his initiative in importing from the United States the idea of the summer school, bringing external students into the university during the Long Vacation to take advantage of its under-utilised facilities and to imbibe something of its atmosphere. Sadler became convinced that access to the extension movement was hampered by the absence of adequate provision for secondary education, the gap between elementary and extension levels being too great for many to leap. He persuaded the university to organise a conference in 1893 to discuss the matter. This made so great an impression on the university that it wrote formally to Prime Minister Gladstone, calling for a Royal Commission. This was duly appointed, with Sadler as a member, and its recommendations were embodied in the landmark Education Act of 1902. Sadler went on to become one of the first professional 'educationists', pioneering the comparative study of educational systems and transforming the local college in Leeds into a great civic university. Returning to Oxford as Master of University College, Sadler founded the Friends of the Bodleian library and was uniquely honoured for an academic by being granted the freedom of the city. He refused the mayoralty of Oxford on grounds of age.

Degrees by Degrees: Women's Education

'Inferior to us God made you and inferior to the end of time you will remain.'

Dean Burgon, sermon in New College 1873

In 1866 women, mostly the wives and sisters of Oxford faculty were granted permission to attend university lectures. In 1873 the permission was extended to college lectures. In the same year a committee was established to organise classes and lectures specifically for women. The leading lights in this group were Mrs Humphrey Ward and the wives of the philosophy don T.H. Green and of Bishop Mandell Creighton, the founding editor of the *English Historical Review*. In 1875 female students were permitted to sit for a limited range of university examinations.

1878 was to prove the decisive year in the cause of women's higher education. On 4 June another committee was convened 'to attempt the establishment in Oxford of a small hall or hostel in connexion with the Church of England, for the reception of women desirous of availing themselves of the special advantages which Oxford offers for higher education'. The outcome of their efforts was the foundation of Lady Margaret Hall. A breakaway group established Somerville on a non-denominational basis. Both colleges received their first students in October 1879.

On 22 June 1878 another meeting constituted itself as an Association for the Higher Education of Women in Oxford. Its tireless Honorary Secretary, from 1894 until its dissolution in 1920 was Annie Rogers (1856–1937), daughter of the Oxford historian of price movements, Thorold Rogers. The new Halls of residence initially remained just that. Responsibility for academic matters was vested in the Association, which also had responsibility for home students, i.e. those not from outside Oxford, who lived with their families.

Lady Margaret Hall was named in honour of medieval benefactress Lady Margaret Beaufort. Its first Principal (1878–1909), Elizabeth Wordsworth (1840–1932), a great-niece of the poet, evidently thought

Students from Lady Margaret Hall with their college in the background in the 1870s

the mother of Henry VII was a worthy role-model for her charges: 'She was a gentlewoman, a scholar and a saint: and after being married three times she took a vow of celibacy: what more could be expected of any woman?' The first intake, of nine students, gathered as a group to be escorted to lectures by a chaperone. The first, purpose-built accommodation was erected to the designs of Basil Champneys in two stages in 1881 and 1884. At the insistence of St John's College, the ground landlord, they were to be convertible to private houses if the Hall failed as a venture. By 1892, however, LMH had forty-one students and had ceased to be purely residential, providing its own tuition. One of the earliest students was Gertrude Bell, admitted at sixteen. The first woman to achieve a first in modern history, Bell made the Middle East her special field of expertise and became noted as a traveller, writer, archaeologist and political analyst. Later graduates have included the historical writers Dame Veronica Wedgwood and Lady Antonia Fraser and Benazir Bhutto, twice Prime Minister of Pakistan. Despite her own accomplishments Elizabeth Wordsworth was more the saint than the scholar and cared little for learning for its own sake. It was entirely characteristic of her personal priorities that she should found the Lady Margaret Hall Settlement for social service in Lambeth in 1897. On the fiftieth anniversary of the foundation of Lady Margaret Hall she was honoured by the university with a DCL and by the Crown with appointment as DBE.

Somerville was named for self-taught Scottish science writer Mary Somerville (1780–1872). She was fifty-one before she published her first book but won a European reputation for her lucid expositions of complex scientific ideas. Somerville's first intake of twelve students found themselves under the direction of Madeleine Shaw Lefevre who accomplished the challenging task of making a (purely Platonic) conquest of John Ruskin. Incorporated as a non-profit joint-stock company, Somerville in 1882 led the way among women's societies in Oxford by becoming the first to employ its own tutors. In 1894 it became the first to style itself a college because it was felt that this 'would not only improve the educational status of Somerville in the eyes of the public but would be understood as implying the desire of the Governing body to raise it above the level of a Hall of Residence'.

As further evidence of its commitment to academic excellence in 1903 Somerville became the first women's institution to offer the possibility of research. In 1904 a college library was opened in the presence of the Vice-Chancellor. Students marked the occasion by performing a masque specially written for the occasion by the poet Robert Bridges. Shortly afterwards the college was enriched by the gift of the library of the philosopher John Stuart Mill, presented by his step-daughter Harriet Taylor. Early students of Somerville included Cornelia Sorabji, pioneering Indian campaigner for women's rights and Eleanor Rathbone, the first woman graduate to be elected as a Member of Parliament. Later Somervillians were to include Indira Gandhi and Margaret Thatcher.

St Hugh's College originated in 1886 in rented housing on the Norham estate, taken by Elizabeth Wordsworth to accommodate girls too poor to attend Lady Margaret Hall. It was named for St Hugh, the medieval bishop of Lincoln, Miss Wordsworth's own father having held that bishopric which, until the Reformation, included Oxford. Successors to the first four impoverished students have included the formidable Labour politician Barbara Castle and the novelists Mary Renault and Brigid Brophy. A member of the council of St Hugh's College for forty-two years, Annie Rogers, creator of the college garden, is remembered by a commemorative sundial. Knocked down by a lorry at the age of eighty-one, she left a personal account of the struggle for female access to higher education which appeared post-humously as *Degrees by Degrees* (1938).

St Hilda's was established in 1893 by Dorothea Beale, Principal of Cheltenham Ladies College to enable her brightest girls to proceed to higher education. Opened in the presence of Bishop Stubbs, it became appropriately adept in producing outstanding medieval historians, as well as novelist Barbara Pym and Dame Helen Gardner, Merton Professor of English Literature. From 1901 to 1920 St Hilda's was incorporated with the Teacher Training College which Miss Beale had also established in Cheltenham. It was named after the seventh century abbess who made Whitby into a great centre of learning.

For a flavour of the early days of the women's colleges a contributory chapter to *Oxford and Oxford Life* (1892) by Miss K.M. Gent of Lady

Margaret Hall is revealing. She conveys the atmosphere of a slightly claustrophobic Arcadia. Girls were not forced to chapel but 'a sceptical tone about religion' would be 'considered the height of bad breeding'. Far from finding 'long rows of pale, heavy-eyed girls bending over books on a lovely summer afternoon' the casual visitor would be more likely to find 'the greater number playing "Prisoner's Base" on the lawn' or, in bad weather, scampering through the corridors in 'a game of hide-and-seek all over the house, with the blinds pulled down'. Hockey, however, was considered 'too rough', although the gymnasium was normally – a curious phrase – 'the scene of great festivity'. Given that 'the "masculine" or fast girl has been so rare that it would be almost impossible to allude to her at all', the inmates of LMH seem to have accepted a genteel regime of gender apartheid as the norm – 'intercourse with male members of the university is not extensive'. Although girls were permitted to visit men in their rooms if they were accompanied by 'a chaperone approved by the Principal' they were only allowed to offer tea in their own rooms to 'lady friends'. Even brothers had to be 'entertained in state in the drawing-room'. Despite the fact that dances were banned outright Miss Gent reported confidently that most girls knew that 'such a delightful period of comparative liberty will never come to them again'. A century later the university's chaperones would be replaced by 'sexual harassment advisers' – a central, supervisory panel of seven, two for each of ninety-three academic departments and others for every identifiable body from the University Parks and Archives to the Transport Studies Unit.

Women were permitted to sit the Oxford Honours examinations from 1894 onwards but although their papers were classified they were still not permitted to receive degrees. An attempt to challenge this in 1895-6 was decisively defeated. As in riposte to this snub, in 1899 ten women were placed in the First Class in English – and no men. In 1910 the establishment of a University Delegacy for the Supervision of Women Students signalled their acceptance as a permanent presence. Such recognition was, perhaps more institutional than social. Harold Macmillan, who went up to Balliol in 1912, was to reminisce that 'We knew, of course, that there were women's colleges with women students. But we were not conscious of either. Their colleges were situated on the suburban periphery . . . They were not members of the Union. They joined no political societies. . . For practical purposes they did not exist.'

In 1920 women were finally admitted to full membership of the university, including the award of degrees, with scarcely a murmur. Crime writer and Dante translator Dorothy L. Sayers of Somerville was among the first group of graduands. Her *Gaudy Night* (1936) gave a controversial picture of life in a women's college. Her most famous creation, suave, aristocratic Lord Peter Wimsey was naturally an Oxford man.

MISSION: ARNOLD TOYNBEE

Few brief lives can have been led to greater effect than that of Arnold Toynbee (1852–83). A disciple of T.H. Green, a labourer on Ruskin's abortive Hinksey Road project and a protégé of Jowett, Toynbee specialised in the new field of economic history in an attempt to throw light on the social problems caused by industrialisation. An activist in church reform, trade unionism and the co-operative movement, he also lectured to large audiences of working men in Bradford, Bolton, Newcastle, Leicester and London, as well as teaching economics at Balliol to aspirants for the Indian Civil Service. Overwork killed him at thirty. A selection of Toynbee's lectures, with a memoir by Jowett, was published posthumously under the title *The Industrial Revolution*, a now fundamental – if contested – historical concept. It went through four editions in ten years. In 1889 a biography of Toynbee became one of the earliest volumes in the Johns Hopkins Historical Series.

Toynbee Hall, in the poorest part of London's East End, was founded in 1884 by Toynbee's admirers as the first ever 'university settlement'. Oxford graduates served there, in collegiate-style build-ings, thus recognising their privileged position in society by 'putting something back'. Canon Samuel Barnett (1844–1913), a Wadham graduate and first director of Toynbee Hall defined its aims as being to 'educate citizens in the knowledge of one another, to provide teaching for those willing to learn and recreation to those who are weary'. In 1885 Barnett started a series of vacation courses in Oxford for London elementary school teachers on the principle that 'culture spreads by contact'. This initiative led in 1892 to the establishment by the university of a Day Training College at which students reading for a degree could gain a government teacher's certificate by part-time study. An examination in the history, theory and practice of education was instituted from 1896. In the first two years fifty-one men and twenty-one women took the diploma. By 1903 the number was three hundred and twenty. A Delegacy for the Training of Secondary Teachers was established in 1902.

In London Toynbee Hall's activities in due course helped to give birth to the Workers' Educational Association, the Workers' Travel Association and the Youth Hostels Association. Sir William Beveridge (Balliol), architect of Britain's welfare state, influential socialist historian R.H. Tawney (Balliol) and future Prime Minister Clement Attlee (University College) all served an apprenticeship in grappling with social realities at Toynbee Hall. Other settlements were soon set up by individual Oxford and Cambridge colleges and many public schools. After a spell at Toynbee Hall American Jane Addams established Hull House in Chicago on similar lines. The Toynbee ideal also inspired initiatives closer to home as colleges ran boys' clubs in Oxford's poorer districts, Balliol in St. Ebbe's and Worcester in St. Clements.

JUDE THE EXCLUDED

Thomas Hardy's *Jude the Obscure* was published in book form in 1895, having previously appeared in instalments under the perhaps more revealing title of *Hearts Insurgent*. Set a generation in the past, it is primarily, in the author's words, a story of 'a deadly war waged between flesh and spirit' but much of the action is set in 'Christminster' (i.e. Oxford), which also serves as an ideal of the values to which Jude aspires. The eponymous hero is a stonemason (like Hardy's own father) who holds a romantic, illusory view of Oxford as 'a castle manned by scholarship and religion' which serves a noble purpose as 'the intellectual and spiritual granary of this country' for Jude it is also the doorway to golden opportunities. At another level Christminster represents a parallel to the marital ideal Jude is fated never to attain, despite his gentleness and struggle against drink and despair. Jude's cousin and lover, Sue Bridehead, shares no such illusions about this 'nest of common schoolmasters' and reminds Jude that 'you are one of the very men Christminster was intended for when the colleges were founded; a man with a passion for learning but no money or opportunities or friends'. The social exclusiveness and inner worthlessness of the university are exposed by Hardy in powerful metaphors – everywhere the outsider runs up against high walls, decaying walls. Diligent and bright, Jude slaves to master Greek but his attempt to enter the university is curtly rebuffed in a cursory note from the head of a college who bids him accept his station in life and perfect his mastery of the stonemason's craft. Rejected, beaten and broken by the appalling tragedy of his childrens' deaths, Jude still elects to die in Christminster, expiring to the sound of 'Remembrance Day' celebrations to mark the conferring of an honorary degree on a nobleman entirely indifferent to the accolade.

Jude the Obscure was burned by the Bishop of Wakefield and savaged by critics as 'dirt, drivel and damnation'. Hardy never wrote another novel. Given the foundation of Keble, the flowering of extension classes and the emergence of women's colleges, the strictures levelled against Oxford in *Jude the Obscure* may seem a trifle redundant or at least past their time. Oxford itself seemed unperturbed, honouring Hardy with a D. Litt.

Ruskin College

> We're all working class students
> we come from the great unwashed
> Full of reforming fervour
> but now that's all been squashed.
>
> For we're at Ruskin College
> away from the common herd.
> We believe in the English method
> and Marx is a dirty word.
>
> (To the tune of the Eton Boating Song)

The college that bears Ruskin's name was founded in his memory in 1899 by two wealthy American admirers, Walter Vrooman and twenty-five year old Charles Beard (1874–1948). Their aim was to provide residential education for working men (from 1919 women also). Both soon returned to the USA, Vrooman to establish a base for 'labor education' in Trenton, Missouri and Beard to outrage the historical establishment by his iconclastic interpretations of the American Revolutionary period.

Ruskin College has been of inestimable importance in the history of Britain's trade union and co-operative movements and of the Labour Party, although George Bernard Shaw refused to lecture there on the grounds that any working man should have an instinctive aversion to Oxford. Another sceptic of the 1960s interpreted its very existence as self-evident proof of the British Establishment's genius for disarming potential enemies by embracing them. Maybe so, but Ruskin College did give birth to the History Workshop which, under the inspiration of Raphael Samuel, pioneered 'history from below' and in 1970 hosted Britain's first national conference on 'Women's liberation' – an occurrence curiously omitted from the college's official history. The 1945 Labour landslide saw thirteen Ruskin graduates elected to the Commons. In 1976 Prime Minister James Callaghan chose Ruskin as the venue for a landmark speech calling for a national debate on the nature and purposes of education. At the time of writing Ruskin's most famous 'old boy' is Deputy Prime Minister John Prescott.

Ruskin students can nowadays opt to study Creative Writing or Employment Studies, take Diploma courses in Social work or Social Change or Master's degree courses in Women's Studies or Popular Memory and Public History. Ruskin's current students range in age from twenty-two to seventy-four and have an average age of thirty-five. Over half have been workless and there is a positive bias in recruitment towards the disadvantaged, dyslexic and disabled. On the occasion of its centenary, alumni congratulations were e-mailed from Poland, Tanzania and Australia, from a professor at UCLA and from 'Hermann the German'. Ruskin's outreach benefit has been matched by the stimulus it gave within the university itself to the study of practical and contemporary politics. Although Oxford faculty, such as the Fabian socialist historian G.D.H. Cole (1889–1958), have played a prominent part in the life of Ruskin College, as supporters and teachers, it is not technically a part of the university.

SCHOOLS FOR SCHOOLCHILDREN

Once dons began to become married men with children of their own to educate they began to take an interest in the provision of pre-university education in Oxford itself.

Nixon's Free Grammar School had been opened in 1659 from the largesse of a former mayor. Perhaps the timing implies a now forgotten political agenda; Nixon was a prominent leader of the Parliamentary faction in Oxford. The school had experienced fluctuating fortunes and was intended to cater for the offspring of townsmen. It was not the sort of establishment academics were looking for and in any case was closed down in 1894 following adverse reports by government inspectors. Nixon's was replaced by the Oxford Municipal Secondary School in 1895. Public provision was further extended by the opening of the Oxford Selective Central School for Boys in 1900. The very names of these establishments betray their limited aspirations. They were not what parents with ambitions for their children were looking for either.

For a modest fee girls could go to a school which moved among a variety of locations – Tubb's Tenement on Gloucester Green, Penson's Gardens (now under the Westgate Centre), the old Wesleyan chapel in New Inn Hall Street – and underwent even more name changes: Oxford United Charity and Sunday School for Girls, Oxford Girls' British School, Penson's Gardens Girls' British School and finally Central School for Girls, as which it was taken over by Oxford School Board in 1898. Also at Gloucester Green were St Mary Magdalen Boys' School (1841) and from 1871, the Oxford Boys' Central School, whose building now serves as the Tourist Information Centre.

Magdalen College School, founded in 1480 to provide Magdalen College with choristers, had become an ordinary and by no means unsuccessful grammar school by Tudor times, with such illustrious names as the philosopher Thomas Hobbes and Edward Hyde, Earl of Clarendon among its pupils. But it had decayed badly in the eighteenth century, both educationally and physically. Revival began in 1846 under twenty-three year old J.E. Millard, himself a former Magdalen chorister. New buildings were acquired in 1851 at the corner of Longwall and High Street and by the end of the century the roll was up to a hundred boys. In 1894 another new building, designed by Sir Arthur Blomfield, was erected at the junction of Iffley Road and Cowley Place. Old boys who became locally influential included historian J.R. Green, Austin Lane Poole, Arabist and President of St John's and bookseller Sir Basil Blackwell.

St Edward's School, established in 1863, was an off-shoot of the Oxford Movement and therefore most acceptable to those of the Tractarian tendency. Its permanent premises were designed by local architect William Wilkinson. Warden (i.e. headmaster) W.H. Ferguson was an old boy of Magdalen College School. Early pupils included Kenneth Grahame, author of *The Wind in the Willows* and Sir Geoffrey de Havilland, the aviation pioneer. Later came actor Laurence Olivier and World War Two air aces Douglas Bader and Guy Gibson, VC, leader of the 'Dam Busters' raid. None of these went on to university at Oxford.

Oxford High School for Girls was founded in 1875 as the eighth under the Girls Public Day School Trust scheme. By 1880 it was able to move into premises at Banbury Road, purpose-built to the designs of Sir Thomas Jackson. By 1888 the roll had risen from an initial twenty-nine to two hundred and forty. Old girls of the school include writer Rose Macaulay, historian Eileen Power, poet Elizabeth Jennings and actress Dame Maggie Smith. The original buildings are now occupied by the university Department of Metallurgy.

The City of Oxford High school, designed inevitably by Jackson, opened in George Street in 1881 with forty-seven pupils and the mildly threatening motto *Nemo repente sapit* – No one becomes wise suddenly. The chief promoter of the enterprise was the philosopher T.H. Green, the first university member to serve on Oxford's city council. A tablet at the school acknowledged his role in 'completing the City's "Ladder of Learning" from Elementary School to University – a project dearest to his heart. Thus were united town and gown in common cause.'

The school's most famous old boy was T.E. Lawrence (1888–1935) – 'Lawrence of Arabia' – who was there from the age of eight until he went on to Jesus. Whatever local provision might be available at secondary level, of course, most dons would wish their sons, at least, to progress to one of the public schools. For this reason the really crucial need was for a preparatory school which would take boys up to the Common Entrance examination.

Summer Fields School, founded in 1864, had as its slogan *Mens sana in Corpore sano* – a healthy mind in a healthy body. This was less a pretentious cliché than a marketing pitch. The school's founder, Archibald Maclaren, had been responsible for gymnastic training in the British army and set up Oxford University's own gymnasium. His wife was the daughter of an Oxford bookseller of radical sympathies. By 1904 Summer Fields had one hundred and twenty-five boys on its roll. Ronald Knox went to Summer Fields. So did future Prime Minister Harold Macmillan, whose obituarist described his years there as unhappy, characterising the school as 'a rather bleak factory programmed to produce scholars for the leading public schools'. If it was, it at least delivered what it promised. Of 3,318 boys who passed through between 1964 and 1984 1,296 went to Eton and over two hundred each to Harrow, Winchester and Radley.

What became known as the Dragon School originated in a meeting held in 1877 by thirty anxious graduates, including four Heads of Houses and seven professors. The leadership was entrusted to Dean Liddell of Christ Church. Established as the Oxford Preparatory School it became known as the Dragon after the boys themselves adopted this as their own emblem, although the name was not formally changed until 1921. The school's distinctive ethos was the creation of Charles Cotterill Lynam, known as 'the Skipper', who was headmaster for thirty-four years. He allowed pupils bicycles, permitted sport on Sundays and discarded traditional Eton-type uniforms in favour of flannel shorts and open-necked shirts. Despite the relaxed atmosphere academic standards were kept high. Half of the pupils were boarders, half day boys. A very small percentage of girls was also always present. 'Dragons' soon developed the sort of alumni networking which is normally associated with public schools and universities. Distinguished ex-pupils included the scientist J.B.S. Haldane, novelists Naomi Mitchison (Haldane's sister), Nevile Shute and John Mortimer, Labour leader Hugh Gaitskell, Leonard Cheshire VC and the poet John Betjeman.

Oxford's other service to school education was to prove very much more pervasive, the development from 1873 onwards, in collaboration with Cambridge, of a massive apparatus of school-level certificated examinations, whose requirements shaped what was taught in English classrooms and whose outcomes provided the benchmarks for employer and university selection for the best part of a century. Initially established in response to meet the needs of the public schools, in 1905 the Joint Board instituted its School Certificate for general application, adding a Higher Certificate in 1918.

IMAGES OF OXFORD

The perfection of plausible photographic images by the 1850s created a new hobby and a new industry. A commercial photographer, Edward Bracher, was already in business at 26 High St in that decade. By 1864 there were at least ten photographers in Oxford. Every annual intake created a fresh demand for college, team and club photographs. There was also scope for individual portraiture and the production of souvenir views of colleges, chapels and ceremonial occasions for sale to visitors.

By 1900 the number of photographers had risen to nearly twenty, the largest being Hills and Saunders in Cornmarket St. The most celebrated individual photographer was Henry Taunt (1842–1922), an apprentice of Bracher's, who set up for himself in 1868, producing a shilling series of picturesque views. In 1871 Taunt was appointed official photographer to the Oxford Architectural and Historical Society.

Among amateur photographers the most notable was Sir William Herschel, who had pioneered the use of fingerprints to identify criminals while serving in India. On his return he settled in Oxford, became semi-attached to the university as a lecturer in divinity and served as town councillor. As President of the Oxford Camera Club he presided over a major photographic convention held in Oxford in 1901 and experimented with techniques of colour photography. Herschel was also a close friend of Sarah Acland, daughter of the Regius Professor of Medicine, who became Oxford's first major female photographer in the 1890s.

A World of Words: OUP

'Being published by the Oxford University Press is rather like being
married to a duchess: the honour is almost greater than the pleasure.'

G.M. Young 1956

It was only in the second half of the nineteenth century that Oxford
University Press finally emerged as a major force in publishing, both
commercially and editorially. The legacy of its slothful past was not
easily eroded. Not until 1907 did it manage to dispose of the last
remaining copy of a run of five hundred Coptic New Testaments
printed in 1716. Recovery was an indirect by-product of the religious
revival of the early nineteenth century which created a massive demand
for Bibles and prayer-books. Bible profits alone in 1850 yielded
£60,000, which was earmarked to fund the construction of the University Museum. An ever bigger market opened up as the advent of
free, compulsory schooling created a need for textbooks on an
unprecedented scale. The experienced Scottish publisher Alexander
Macmillan was head-hunted to manage commercial operations in
London. This association soon paid off for the tribe of Macmillan,
whose family firm published the first of the *Alice* books in 1865. The
driving-force at the Oxford end was the Reverend Bartholomew Price,
Sedleian Professor of Natural Philosophy and future Master of Pembroke, a mathematician who turned out to be a financial whizz.
Between them they created a new, prestigious academic imprint, the
Clarendon Press. In 1896 OUP opened a New York office, from
which it was to grow into a major US publisher. Other branches followed in Canada (1904), Australia (1908) and India (1912). Charles
Cannan, Price's successor, correctly foresaw that declining religious
observance would lead to declining revenue from Bibles and also
realised that Oxford's ongoing great Dictionary project could be
exploited to yield spin-off dictionaries which would provide a com-
pensating flow of revenue. In the triumphant words of his own
daughter: 'The Press which for too long had published too many books
on religious polemics bound in chocolate brown, needed him, so he
went on to make it the most learned and the greatest Publishing House
in the world.' In 1900 Cannan published the *Oxford Book of English*

Verse, edited by Arthur Quiller-Couch. It was the first of a whole genre of *Oxford books of* and had sold half a million copies by the time of its editor's death in 1944. *A New Oxford Book of English Verse* was subsequently edited by Dame Helen Gardner. Under Cannan's successor, Humphrey Milford, OUP extended its range to become a market leader in medical, music and children's publishing and inaugurated the highly successful *Oxford Dictionary of Quotations*.

While OUP was going global a local press of significance to Oxford itself was developing. The Alden Press established by Henry Alden in 1832 produced the weekly *Oxford Chronicle*, two local monthlies and a local almanac and specialised in publishing books by local authors and on local subjects. Under Edward Alden the firm met the need for local maps and guides created by the advent of that by-product of the railway, the day-tripper. *Alden's Oxford Guide* became the standard *vademecum* from its first appearance in 1874.

THE BIBLE OF THE ENGLISH LANGUAGE

> The vast volume and range of the English language can be perhaps best appreciated by turning over a sequence of the 15,000 quarto pages of the Oxford English Dictionary.'
>
> *The Character of England* (1950)

Whereas France has the Académie Francaise to pronounce authoritatively on matters of language, Britain has the Oxford English Dictionary. Its origin can be pinpointed to a paper delivered to the Philological Society in 1857 by Dr R.C. Trench *On some Deficiencies in our English Dictionaries*. This prompted a decision the following year to compile an entirely new dictionary from scratch, organised on 'historical' lines, i.e. giving for every word not only its meaning and pronunciation but also its etymology, changes in its meaning over time and examples of its usage illustrated by quotation. For twenty years the tireless F.J. Furnivall, founder of separate societies dedicated to the appreciation of Chaucer, Wyclife, Shakespeare, Shelley and Browning, laboured to collect materials. But not until 1878 was an actual start made on the compilation of *A New English Dictionary on Historical Principles*. The editor selected, James Murray (1837–1915), was a self-

Dr J.H. Murray, the editor of the *New English Dictionary*, in the 'Scriptorium', the iron shed on the Banbury Road that was his workshop

educated former teacher and bank clerk. Murray worked in a corrugated-iron shed in the back garden of his home, Sunnyside, in the Banbury Road. Some idea of the scale of the enterprise can be judged from the fact that the slips of paper on which quotations were written out eventually weighed three tons. The first volume, covering A–Ant-, appeared in 1884. Murray thought the rest could be completed in twelve years but by the time he died only the letter 'T' had been reached. Murray's heroic endeavour was recognised by the award of nine honorary degrees, including one from Oxford in 1914. He was also knighted and in 1900 invited to give the Romanes Lecture. Murray was assisted in his labours not only by a professional team but also by several of his eleven children.

Completion of the OED was finally achieved in 1928 – 414,825 words and 1,827,306 quotations. Work immediately began on producing a *Supplement* to catch up with changes in the language. It appeared in 867 pages in 1933, from which time the term *Oxford English Dictionary* came into general use. Murray's successors as editor were H. Bradley, who had settled in Oxford in 1896 and was elected to a Fellowship at Magdalen, W.A. Craigie, Professor of Anglo-Saxon and an expert on Frisian and Icelandic, and C.T. Onions, who also settled in Oxford to devote himself entirely to the task. In 1957 a new Supplement was begun under New Zealander Robert Burchfield. A *Second Edition* was completed in 1989.

WHO WAS WHO

The *Dictionary of National Biography* did not become a product of Oxford University Press until 1917, but Oxford in its larger meaning was involved from the outset in the sense that hundreds of Oxford graduates were responsible for contributing entries. The project was established in 1882 by George Smith of Smith, Elder and Co, with Sir Leslie Stephen, father of Virginia Woolf, being appointed editor. The first volume appeared in 1885, the 63rd and last in 1900. Editors of the decennial supplements which have appeared ever since have included such eminent Oxford scholars as H.W.C. Davis, Regius Professor of Modern History, J.R.H. Weaver, President of Trinity and Lord Blake, President of Queen's. The DNB as a CD-Rom carries over 30,000 biographies and 37,000,000 words. A completely rewritten version, expanded to 50,000 entries is scheduled for 2004.

'No politics and fewer principles'

The editorial line proclaimed in the first issue of *Isis* (1892) committed it to being 'humorous without being ill-humoured, critical without being captious, militant without being malevolent' and promised to support neither party 'should we last until the General Election'. And in doing just the latter lay its first great triumph. What made *Isis* remarkable among student magazines was not its contents – the usual melange of reports of Union debates, sporting events and theatrical productions, interspersed with facetious witticisms and (very) light verse – but the fact that it continued to exist. Student magazines at Oxford had invariably foundered when the enthusiasm or funds which had brought them into being dried up. *Isis* was different. The fact that it could double its price in 1893, from 3d. to 6d., meant that people were willing to pay for it when a daily paper was just 1d. One reason may have been a new feature of that year, the weekly appearance of an *Isis*

Idol, usually a sporting hero, or possibly a Union wag or a member of the Oxford University Dramatic Society. The first ever Idol was the captain of Rugby. C.B. Fry was an inevitable Idol. The other reason why people bought *Isis* was that it attracted such genuinely talented undergraduate writers as Max Beerbohm, Hilaire Belloc and John Buchan.

A decade later, in 1903, the first women's student magazine appeared under the title *Fritillary*. The editorial style of *Fritillary* was frumpy rather than fatuous and it sported an uninviting cover of municipal grey. It survived nonetheless for the next three decades.

WRITERS FOR READERS

While *Isis* was essentially a house magazine, relentlessly inward-looking, late Victorian Oxford nurtured much literary talent whose writings had a wide cultural impact. *The Short History of the English People* (1874) by Oxford-born Jesus historian J.R. Green (1837–83), with its strong emphasis on everyday life, won an unexpectedly large readership. Green's enduring local legacy was the Oxford Historical Society (1884), which began the serious investigation of the history of both the city and the university. W.W. Fowler, Lincoln's expert on the Roman republic, found a cult following for his books on bird-watching. Australian-born Gilbert Murray (1866–1957), Regius Professor of Greek from 1908, demystified many of its major literary texts for the lay reader through his fresh translations. As a keen supporter of women's education at Oxford and an ardent chairman of the League of Nation's Union, Murray was the model for Adolphus Cusins in Shaw's *Major Barbara*.

Far more, of course, was produced through the agency of Oxford's graduates. Typical of thousands was T.W.Webb, a conscientious country parson in Herefordshire, whose *Celestial Objects for Common Telescopes* (1859) went through five editions by 1899 to do more to popularise astronomy than any other single work. Francis Palgrave of Balliol spent most of his life as an official of the government's education department but in compiling *The Golden Treasury of best songs and Lyrical poems in the English language* (1861) created a common canon which did more to shape the literary taste of the succeeding century of English schooling than any amount of government directives. Appropriately, Palgrave returned to Oxford as Professor of Poetry (1885–95).

Dozens of major writers passed through Oxford in this period as undergraduates. Poet Gerard Manley Hopkins and *belle lettriste* Hilaire Belloc, both in their very different ways important Catholic writers, were Balliol men, as was Anthony Hope, author of *The Prisoner of Zenda*, the James Bond of its day. John Buchan, author of Zenda's successor of the next generation, *The Thirty-Nine Steps*, was already a published author before he even entered Brasenose and wrote a history of his college while still an undergraduate.

BOOKS FOR SCHOLARS

Benjamin Henry Blackwell opened his bookshop at 50 Broad Street in 1879. Its original stock consisted almost entirely of secondhand books. Loggan's *Oxonia Illustrata* of 1675 was listed in the first catalogue at £5. In 1883 Blackwell bought the freehold and moved in to live above the shop, later expanding into adjacent premises. Bishop Stubbs commended what rapidly became an Oxford institution as the 'the literary man's public house'. In 1889 Basil Henry Blackwell (1889–1984) was born at the Broad Street premises. After being educated at Magdalen College School and Merton, Basil worked for OUP in London, returning in 1913 to develop a publishing arm to the family business, with that doyenne of crime writers and Dante scholars, Dorothy L. Sayers, as his first editorial assistant. Basil – 'the Gaffer' – was to be knighted in 1956 and honoured by both city and university. Richard Blackwell (1918–80) went from the Dragon School to Winchester to New College, a First and then on to the chairmanship of what was still a family business but under his leadership became an international one. A Vice-President of the company, Henry Schollick, had the distinction of inventing book tokens.

The Proper Study of Mankind: Pitt-Rivers

Oxford's broadening cultural impact beyond its own boundaries was matched by a broadening or redefinition of academic concerns within them, albeit many initiatives were to be external in origin.

Blackwell's, the Broad Street bookshop

Augustus Henry Lane-Fox Pitt-Rivers (1827–1900) was a professional soldier whose career had been built on his crusade to improve standards of musketry. His interest in the evolution of the rifle inspired him in two directions. First to apply to artefacts in general Darwinian notions of evolution by marginal, often chance, adaptations and secondly to collect such artefacts and arrange them in 'development series' until his home resembled an ethnographic museum. In 1874 the government agreed to house his collection, initially in the South

Kensington Museum's out-station at Bethnal Green, and then in the main museum itself. In 1880 Pitt-Rivers inherited a Wiltshire estate of 29,000 acres. He was now immensely rich and when living alone in his London home was waited on by no less than eleven servants. His estate, mostly deer forest until the beginning of the nineteenth century, also proved to be immensely rich in antiquities, ranging across the prehistoric, Roman and Saxon periods. Pitt-Rivers ardently undertook the excavation of barrows, cemeteries, military camps and even whole villages scattered across his lands. In an age of enthusiastic amateurs, many driven by the motives and employing the methods of mere treasure-hunters, Pitt-Rivers evolved disciplined and systematic procedures which set new standards of meticulous recording and prompt publication for the benefit of the archaeological community. In 1882 the 'father of British archaeology' was appropriately appointed as the nation's first official inspector of ancient monuments.

As the South Kensington Museum in turn experienced its own space problems in 1883 Pitt-Rivers offered to relocate his artefact collection, now totalling some 14,000 exhibits, to Oxford, providing the university was prepared to fund a building to accommodate it and a lecturer to utilise it for teaching purposes. The Pitt-Rivers Museum was duly built as an adjunct to the University Museum and the relevant ethnographic items from the Ashmolean added to it in 1886, along with natural history collections, such as Buckland's fossils. Edward Burnett Tylor (1832–1917) was appointed as Britain's first lecturer in anthropology. On Tylor's advice an Oxford zoology graduate, Henry Balfour, was appointed curator of the collection in 1891, holding the position until his death in 1939. Anthropology became available at Oxford as a formal diploma course from 1907 onwards.

UPDATING THE ASHMOLEAN

The University Museum, having moved into its new premises in 1845, was repeatedly enriched by munificent donations. The creation of the Pitt-Rivers represented a timely opportunity for the Ashmolean to unload superfluous clutter and refocus itself under its dynamic new keeper, Arthur Evans (1851–1941). After a first in history at Brasenose, Evans had written an eye-witness account of an insurrection in Bosnia, lived for six years in Dubrovnik and then returned to marry the daughter of historian E.A. Freeman. From youth Evans used his acute myopia to advantage to uncover minute details on ancient coins and gems, one of his several fields of expertise. At the Ashmolean – a name at last acquired formally in 1899 – Evans' keepership (1884–1908) resulted in its reorganisation by University Statute into two main branches of Antiquities and Fine Arts. Outside Oxford Evans would become famous as the excavator of the palace complex at Knossos on Crete and the inventor of the term 'Minoan civilization'. He continued excavating at Knossos until 1935, restoring large sections of the royal palace to some resemblance of its original appearance. He also founded the British School at Athens. From 1893 onwards he lived in some style at the Youlbury estate – 'an earthly paradise' – on Boar's Hill.

TAKING HISTORY SERIOUSLY

In his inaugural lectures of 1848 the new Regius Professor of History H.H. Vaughan set out the case for research as a major duty for the historian, although his much praised eloquence was not subsequently matched by much research activity on his own behalf. Ancient history had always been a respected study at Oxford but not until 1862 was a chair of Modern History established and to many at the time the Civil Wars still seemed dangerously modern, the memory of Oxford's own ordeals doubtless revived daily as High Tables viewed their post-Restoration plate. History and Law, which originally formed a combined school were separated in 1872, though Oxford remained particularly attached to constitutional history. It also remained chary of modernity. Half a century after the outbreak of the Great War its course of study still ended at 1914.

Oxford's first great historian, in the modern sense of being a master of primary sources, was William Stubbs (1825–91). A poor widow's son, he worked his way through Christ Church as a part-time college servant – which consequently barred him from being offered a teaching post there, though Trinity took him on briefly. Twice passed over for professorships, he was finally (1866) appointed to the Regius chair, where he amply justified his selection by rigorously editing a mountain of primary source materials and producing a magisterial *Constitutional*

History of England (1873–8). He was appointed Bishop of Oxford in 1888.

Stubb's successor as Regius Professor was E.A. Freeman (1823–92), whose hefty histories of the Norman Conquest (5 vols), the reign of William Rufus (2 vols) and the kingdom of Sicily (4 vols unfinished) were far less securely grounded in primary materials. A vindictive critic, Freeman was renowned as an eccentric, much given to reciting poetry to himself and jumping into the air at the onset of a particularly pleasing passage. For all his love of poetry, however, he was deeply sceptical of the introduction of English as a degree subject, fearing that it might be little more than 'mere chatter about Shelley'.

> Ladling out the butter
> From alternate tubs:
> Stubbs butters Freeman, ·
> And Freeman butters Stubbs.

J.A. Froude (1818–94) was a Fellow of Exeter. Disenchanted with religion by his chosen mentor Newman's defection to Rome, Froude daringly published a soul-searching novel, *The Nemesis of Faith* (1849), which was vilified by Archbishop Whateley and publicly burned in college by a colleague. Froude quit Oxford to live by journalism in London and still managed to write a definitive twelve volume history of England from the fall of Wolsey (1529) to the Armada (1588), which put Freeman to shame. In 1892 he had the last laugh, being appointed Freeman's successor to the Regius chair, in which he proved himself as outstanding a lecturer as he was a prose stylist.

The long career of Sir Charles Oman (1860–1946) represented the maturing of the historical profession. Establishing his reputation with *The Art of War in the Middle Ages*, he consolidated it with a seven volume *History of the Peninsular War*. Strikingly handsome and dignified, the 'uncrowned king of Oxford' was Chichele Professor of Modern History from 1905, represented Oxford in the Commons (1919–35) and, merely as a hobby, was an eminent numismatist. His daughter, Carola Oman, wrote a charming memoir of her Oxford childhood.

A first class classicist, H.A.L. Fisher (1865–1940) took to modern history because he thought there was little worthwhile left to attempt in ancient history. Study in Paris brought him under the stimulating influence of French historical techniques and led him to develop an expertise on Napoleon applauded by the French themselves, while he also wrote respectably on medieval European and Tudor history. Fisher left New College to serve as a dynamic Vice-Chancellor of Sheffield University, then became minister of education in Lloyd George's wartime government. In this post he passed a landmark Education Act, which doubled the salaries of elementary school teachers, created state scholarships to open up university to children from poor families and made the School Certificate a universal qualification in place of fifty-five separate ones. Returning to Oxford as Warden of New College, Fisher also served in the British delegation to the League of Nations and as President of the British Academy and wrote a three volume history of Europe which long remained a standard text. Fisher was awarded the Order of Merit but treasured even more his admission to the elite ranks of the Massachusetts Historical Society.

Given such the presence – or admittedly not infrequent absence – of such *eminenti* it is remarkable to read in the *Official Handbook to the University of Oxford* as late as the 1951 edition that with the largest intake of arts graduates the Honour School of Modern History, being 'free from severe linguistic tests' (i.e. only French and Latin were required) 'attracts some students of poor quality... As a discipline it is in some ways, by the very nature of the subject, inferior to those schools which require the exercise of accurate study of other languages or exacting logical and theoretical inquiries.' But, if history still wasn't taken seriously at Oxford, it had at least become clear that Oxford historians were taken seriously outside it.

Law Unto Themselves

Splitting from history in 1872 enabled Oxford's academic lawyers to establish an Honour School of Jurisprudence under the leadership of Sir William Anson (1843–1914), the first lay Warden of All Souls and author of standard works on the constitution and the law of contract, the latter running to sixteen editions over the course of half a century.

At All Souls Anson redefined the opportunities afforded by its privileged freedom from the routines of teaching to make it much more of a 'think tank'. Though doubtless all of Oxford would have shuddered at the barbarism of such a term, Anson sought to attract 'men of the world' to enter into the life of the college, to stimulate its own internal life and to prepare or refresh themselves for the tasks they undertook in the public sphere. Among his early 'catches' were Curzon, future Archbishop of Canterbury Cosmo Gordon Lang and two successive editors of *The Times*. Through Anson's colleagues A.V. Dicey and Sir Frederick Pollock (1845–1937), founding editor of the *Law Quarterly Review* and a friend of Oliver Wendell Holmes for sixty years, strong academic links were developed between Oxford lawyers and the United States, especially Harvard. Pollock's successor in the chair of Jurisprudence was the Russian medievalist Sir Paul Vinogradoff (1854–1925), who was the first to introduce the seminar to Oxford as a method of teaching.

The development of anthropology as a recognised discipline was part of a larger process in which broadening access to the university was matched by a broadening of its studies. Chairs were created for International Law and Diplomacy (1859), Chinese (1875), Celtic Studies (1876) and English Language (1885). Unsurprisingly many initiatives aroused opposition and derision. When Modern Languages gained formal approval in 1903 its field of study was sneeringly dismissed as 'the Honour School for intending schoolmistresses'. The thought that there might be nothing wrong in that was, of course, unthinkable. In the decade leading up to the Great War new chairs came into being for English Literature (1904), the history of the British Commonwealth (1905), the history of war (1909), Romance Languages (1909) and Government and Public Administration (1912). A School of Geography was established in 1898, of Forestry in 1907 and an Institute of Agricultural Economics opened in 1913.

Imported Talents

For all its tendency to involution Oxford deserves credit for its willingness to recognise and embrace intellectual talent from far beyond its own frontiers. Tylor's appointment in anthropology is a case in point. Too sickly to work in his Quaker family's foundry, he travelled as a teenager to recover his health and as a result of a chance meeting on a horse-bus in Havana, went on an ethnographic expedition to Mexico and wrote a book about it. His *Primitive Culture* (1871) was recognised as a classic and won him an Oxford DCL in 1875. So he was well known to the university when the Pitt-Rivers opportunity arose. In 1896 Tylor was appointed Oxford's first Professor of Anthropology and in 1912 he was knighted.

When Tylor's Oxford life was just beginning the hugely productive career of Friedrich Max-Muller (1823–1900) was already thirty years old. At Leipzig University he attended ten different courses per term but was persuaded to focus on Sanskrit, was awarded his doctorate in his teens and at twenty published a volume of Sanskrit fables in translation. At Berlin he absorbed comparative philology and in Paris began preparing a definitive edition of the Brahman scripture *Rigveda*. Fearing for his precious manuscripts during the revolution of 1848, he fled to London. As the first volume of his *Rigveda* was to be published by OUP, Max-Muller settled in Oxford in May 1848. His extraordinary intellectual powers were gradually recognised throughout the university. In 1850 he was appointed Deputy Taylorian Professor of modern European languages. He was appointed curator of the Bodleian and elected a life Fellow of All Souls. Marriage made him a brother-in-law of historian J.A. Froude. In 1860 the chair of Sanskrit became vacant and in a hotly fought election Max-Muller, the foreigner, was defeated by the vote of country clergy who turned out in droves to vote him down. The winner, Sir Monier Monier-Williams, was able in due course to display his gratitude by building the university an Indian Institute (now the History faculty offices). Opened in 1875 to train probationers for the Indian Civil Service, the Institute's activities led to the development of academic interest in Indian history and forestry and to an accumulation of Indian art and artefacts which became the core of the Ashmolean's current Oriental collections.

Thwarted, Max-Muller turned his prodigious industry towards comparative philology and in 1868 a new chair in that field was established for him. From this he branched into the comparative study of mythology and religion. In 1875 he began a fifty-one volume series of *Sacred Books of the East* for OUP. Although debarred by the debacle of 1860 from representing Sanskrit officially at Oxford scholars came from then remote Japan to attach themselves to him as a master. Max-Muller was known personally to the monarchs of Prussia, Sweden, Rumania and Turkey as well as Queen Victoria, who appointed him of the Privy Council. He was awarded the French *Légion d'Honneur*, the Prussian *Pour Le Mérite* and five other national decorations, seven honorary doctorates and membership of thirty-four academies and learned societies. Oxford established a fund named after him to support research on Indian cultures and received immediate contributions from Edward VII, Kaiser Wilhelm II and numerous Indian princes. In Tokyo a Society for Oriental research was founded to commemorate him.

Unlike Max-Muller, who came as a virtual supplicant, in the case of William Osler (1849–1919) it was the university which did the asking, inviting him to become Regius Professor of Medicine in 1904. Head-hunted from McGill University in his native Canada by the University of Pennsylvania, Osler had moved on to create at Johns Hopkins the first integrated unit for clinical medicine in any English-speaking country, with teaching, treatment, research and laboratory facilities in close co-operation. Osler and his American wife lived for their first year in the house of Mrs Max-Muller and then bought 13 Norham Gardens which had been built for University Orator Thomas Dallin. To it they added such North American comforts as additional bathrooms and central heating and established a tradition of transatlantic hospitality, keeping open house to compatriots and colleagues alike. Appropriately the Oslers' former house is now home to the Oxford University Newcomers Club, which exists to help newly arrived partners of members of the university settle in and meet people. As head of Oxford's medical school Osler established the Sir William Dunn School of Pathology and persuaded OUP to enter medical publishing. His own textbook *The Principles and Practice of Medicine* went through nine editions between 1891 and 1920 and was translated into French, German, Spanish and Chinese. Election to Christ Church delighted him by linking him with his intellectual heroes, John Locke and Robert Burton. His own broad culture brought him the presidencies of the

Bibliographical Society and the Classical Association, his lifetime achievements a baronetcy and a portrait by John Singer Sargent.

Joseph Wright (1858–1940), who was brought to Oxford on the recommendation of Max-Muller, had been sent out to work at six. The educational ladder which eventually brought to him to succeed to his sponsor's professorial chair consisted of the factory school at a woollen mill, the Mechanics' Institute in Bradford, three months self-tuition in Heidelberg and part-time study at the Yorkshire College of Science in Leeds while supporting himself as a full-time schoolmaster. Initially a mathematician, Wright switched to comparative philology while undertaking a self-financed doctorate at Heidelberg. He came to Oxford initially to teach Gothic, Old English and Old German for the Association for the Higher Education of Women but was soon head-hunted by the Taylorian Institution. His magnum opus was an *English Dialect Dictionary* in six volumes, into which he poured his entire personal savings. The finished work covered 100,000 words, illustrated by 500,000 quotations. In 1901 Wright was elected to succeed to Max-Muller's chair.

CECIL RHODES

Oxford's acquisition of off-beat or overseas talents was a haphazard process. One of its least academic offspring was to put it on a more systematic basis, at least at the student level.

Cecil Rhodes (1853–1902) was a sickly youth obsessed with manliness. Despatched to Natal for his health, he succeeded in growing cotton where neighbours told him it was impossible. As speculating in South African diamonds then made him a millionaire by the time he was twenty Rhodes could possibly be forgiven for believing that very little was impossible – except apparently getting into and through Oxford. University College rejected him. Oriel accepted him grudgingly – 'All the colleges send me their failures', carped its Provost. A bout of rowing so enervated Rhodes that a doctor told him he had only six months to live. For the rest of his life Rhodes was in a hurry. Alternating between South Africa and Oriel enabled him to conserve his health and further his business interests but meant that he was twenty-eight before he finally achieved his degree. Despite his wealth

Rhodes lived modestly enough in lodgings at 18 and 116 High Street and 6 King Edward Street. In South Africa, by contrast he could spread himself and did – financing the armed annexation of an area more than twice the size of France which he named after himself, Rhodesia.

Rhodes was an unashamed Imperialist but perhaps nowadays might be called a globaliser, driven by a sense that great historical forces were making the world one as never before. Rhodes believed that to be born British was to have drawn first prize in the lottery of life, that the British were the best people in the world and that the more of it they ruled the better. Rhodes believed that the planet would eventually be dominated by the English-speaking peoples and that the interests of rulers and ruled would best be served by selecting the future élite and providing it with the world's finest education – Oxford – though the favoured few were most emphatically not to be 'merely bookworms'.

To fulfil his vision Rhodes left the bulk of his fortune to endow the scholarships which bear his name. (Oriel got £100,000.) Rhodes' will sets out at length the four criteria for selecting candidates and includes his preferred weighting for each:

i) 'literary and scholastic attainments' (3/10)
ii) 'fondness of and success in many outdoor sports' (2/10)
iii) 'qualities of manhood, truth, courage, devotion to duty, sympathy for the protection of the weak, kindliness, unselfishness and fellowship' (3/10)
iv) 'moral force of character and . . . instincts to lead' (2/10)

Privately Rhodes used a different terminology and weighting: 'smug' (scholarship) (4/10); 'brutality' (sport) (2/10); 'tact and leadership' (2/10); and 'unctuous rectitude' (2/10). While it doubtless never occurred to Rhodes that women might figure in his scheme – he had a marked personal preference for the companionship of hardy younger men – he did explicitly declare that 'No student shall be qualified or disqualified . . . on account of race or religious opinions'.

The Oxford Union passed a motion regretting Rhodes's scheme. The first Rhodes scholars arrived nonetheless in 1903. An enlightened duke in *Zuleika Dobson* held that while 'Americans have a perfect right to exist . . . he did often find himself wishing Mr Rhodes had not enabled them to exercise that right at Oxford'. Some sporty types, however, shrewdly recognised that the selective importation of 'gigantic colonials' might enable the university to achieve the nirvana of competitive ambition and 'wipe out Cambridge altogether!'.

Over the years the territorial distribution of Rhodes Scholarships has varied and been enlarged to include women. German students were also originally included in the scheme, by a codicil in Rhodes' will, reflecting his belief that this might help to 'make war impossible'. The German scholarships were suspended in 1916, resumed 1929–39 and resumed again since 1969.

The roll-call of former Rhodes Scholars includes Norman Manley (Jesus 1914–15, 1919–20), Prime Minister of Jamaica; Nobel Laureate Howard Florey (Magdalen 1922–4); James Fulbright (Pembroke 1925–8), founder of the Fulbright Scholarship scheme; Robert Penn Warren (Christ Church 1928–31) double Pulitzer Prize winner and first US Poet Laureate; his fellow critic and collaborator Cleanth Brooks (Exeter); Dean Rusk (St John's 1931–4) US Secretary of State; Dom Mintoff (Hertford 1939–41) Prime Minister of Malta; Kris Kristofferson (Merton 1958–60) actor; and William Jefferson Clinton (University College 1968) President of the United States. Given the dissolution of the imperial mission in half a century it is clear that the Rhodes Scholarships did much more for Oxford than they did for the Empire.

Rhodes House in South Parks Road was built as a memorial to Rhodes, as a centre of scholarship and as the headquarters of the Rhodes Trust which administers the scholarships. An H-plan Cotswold manor house, it was constructed (1926–9) to the designs of Sir Herbert Baker, a suitably imperial architect (New Delhi, South Africa House). For a modern building it is rich in symbolism, incorporating representations of the British lion, the American eagle, the Zimbabwe bird, the Matopo mountains (Rhodes' burial place) and quotations from Aristotle and Horace (*Non Omnis Moriar*, I shall not wholly die). The comprehensive library includes not only Rhodes's own papers but also those of the Anti-Slavery Society and those of the Brooke family, the hereditary 'white Rajahs' of Sarawak. A statue of Rhodes can be seen on Oriel's building on the High Street.

Hour of the Viceroy: Curzon

Fifteen of the Viceroys of India were Oxford men and none was more viceregal than George Nathaniel Curzon (1859–1925). The winner of seventeen prizes at Eton, at Balliol under Jowett he devoted much time to political debating and became President of the Union but was mortified to receive a second class in his final degree examinations, vowing 'Now I shall devote the rest of my life to showing the examiners that they have made a mistake'. The award of the Lothian and Arnold History Essay prizes and a Fellowship at All Souls scarcely compensated for the blot on a curriculum vitae of previously unqualified triumphs. After Oxford the direction of Curzon's restless ambition was shaped by two forces: a deep fascination with the cultures of Asia and the possibilities of empire and a life lived in constant pain. The onset of a curvature of the spine began in his undergraduate years, forcing Curzon to wear a steel corset whose rigidity reinforced the impression of aloofness conveyed by an already haughty manner. Max Beerbohm dubbed him 'Britannia's butler'. Scorning the limitation of his disability, Curzon entered the Commons, travelled adventurously, wrote three books on Asian affairs and married a wealthy American heiress. When he became Viceroy of India at thirty-nine her fortune sustained a life-style which outshone that of the king-emperor himself. Whenever Curzon and his adoring vicereine dined *in private* they did so to the strains of a forty piece orchestra. Curzon's wife had been told that the Indian climate would kill her and it did, at the age of thirty-four. Returning to England shortly after the election of a Liberal government bent on reforming everything, the grief-stricken Curzon heard rumours that the ancient universities were included in the firing line. Oxford's existing Chancellor, the elderly Viscount Goschen, a vastly experienced administrator, had already begun to take pre-emptive action, collecting data from colleges and faculty to show that much was happening at Oxford and much of what was happening was good. That there were still abuses, however, was undeniable. One Professor of Ancient History, scheduled to give a weekly lecture in one term – scarcely an onerous teaching load – routinely gave all eight in a single week and retired to London for the rest of the year.

Goschen's death in 1907 precipitated a fiercely contested election for the succession from which Curzon emerged victorious. Oxford would fill the emptiness of his bereavement. In May Curzon was installed in office at the Sheldonian with a public splendour not seen since 1715. The *Encaenia* of that year was a particularly brilliant occasion, with honorary degrees being conferred on Auguste Rodin, Camille Saint-Saëns, Mark Twain and Rudyard Kipling.

The bombshell was thrown, with acute timing, in July, on the eve of the Long Vacation, when the Bishop of Birmingham rose in the House of Lords to denounce Oxford and Cambridge as playgrounds of the 'idle rich' and to call for a Royal Commission to investigate their manifest abuses. Curzon countered as swiftly as possible in October by announcing the university's recognition of the valuable work being done by the newly founded Workers' Educational Association and pledging to give it active support. In 1908 an official report appeared on *Oxford and the Working Classes*. Committees were formed. Meetings were held. Consultations were made. The result, published in 1909, was a *Red Book* of recommendations, substantial in scale and elegant in composition which made an impressive case for Oxford as 'a focus of culture, a school of character and a nursery of thought'. Critics dubbed it the *Scarlet Letter* but even the progressive minority within the university registered approval. More to the point, no more was heard of a Royal Commission.

Freedom of the City

In 1825 the university finally renounced its right to extort a public penitential pledge of good behaviour on the anniversary of St Scholastica's Day. The Municipal Corporations Act of 1835 set the city's government on a less corrupt and more coherent basis. In 1889 Oxford achieved county borough status and marked its new dignity and Queen Victoria's Diamond Jubilee with the construction of an ostentatious new Town Hall (1897), opened by the Prince of Wales, who obviously bore no grudge at the memory of his youthful mortifications. At the accession of the Prince as Edward VII in 1901 the formal proclamation to the university was made from the steps of St Mary's – and a separate proclamation was made elsewhere to 'the town' as though its inhabitants still constituted a separate order of humanity.

One development that brought Town and Gown to rub shoulders was the advent of horse-drawn trams in 1881. Carfax was the nodal point of a system of radiating lines along any one of which a flat-rate penny fare would convey a passenger to the terminal point. Moreover, on the heels of the horse-tram, to mangle a metaphor, came the 'safety bicycle' of the 1880s, equipped for the first time with pneumatic tyres. The bicycle would henceforth become a permanent presence on Oxford's streets.

An electric tram service was mooted in 1906. The university pronounced the idea of overhead power lines unthinkable, a view which seems to have commanded general agreement. The expensive subsurface alternative proved expensively abortive. Taking advantage of the resulting impasse in 1913 the young proprietor of a local motor business approached the council for a licence to run a motor bus service. No licence was forthcoming. So he started the service anyway. As it would have been illegal to take fares on his buses passengers paid by buying coupons in local shops. In their first four days of operation the new service carried 17,000 passengers. Oxford had taken its first decisive step towards becoming what John Betjeman was to call 'Motopolis'.

'A COVETED TROPHY': THE PRINCE OF WALES

In 1912 the Prince of Wales, the future Edward VIII, took up residence at Magdalen, a college chosen by George V on the grounds that he had been advised that Christ Church was overrun with *nouveaux riches*. The Master of Magdalen. T.H. Warren, was an ardent snob who, in the words of the prince, treated his new student as 'a coveted trophy' and irritated him by constant reference to the fact that his own father-in-law was a baronet. Warren's most prestigious previous social scalp had been the enrolment of Prince Chichibu of Japan. On being told that the prince's name meant 'Son of God' Warren is said to have replied blithely 'you will find that we have the sons of many other distinguished men in this college'. The Prince of Wales was less segregated from ordinary undergraduates than his grandfather had been, though having a motor car at his disposal made him conspicuous in the town. He was also allowed to smoke freely. Though far from bookish, the heir to the throne was already completely fluent in French and German but no attempt was made to exploit his linguistic talent academically. The outbreak of the Great War curtailed a sojourn of two years passed to little advantage. Warren was doubtless delighted by his elevation to the ranks of knighthood as Knight Commander of the Victorian Order.

Zuleika Dobson

Max Beerbohm (1872–1956) left Merton without a degree but with a genius for refined self-promotion which left him indelibly labelled as 'the incomparable Max'. George Bernard Shaw, whom he succeeded as drama critic of the *Saturday Review*, first gave him that accolade, but the fact that it stuck was a tribute to Beerbohm's own versatile talents as essayist, parodist, critic and caricaturist. It was not a judgment universally shared. Vita Sackville-West dismissed him as 'a shallow,

Max Beerbohm author of *Zuleika Dobson*, 1911

affected, self-conscious fribble'. Lytton Strachey hailed his 'remarkable and seductive genius ... the smallest in the world'. Evelyn Waugh found him, at seventy-five, 'a delicious little old dandy ...' but confessed that 'Much of what he said would have been commonplace but for his exquisite delivery'. In his own self-defence Beerbohm remarked with characteristic self-deprecation 'I was a modest, good-humoured boy. It is Oxford that has made me insufferable.'

Beerbohm's masterpiece, and only completed novel, *Zuleika Dobson* (1911) is quite simply the funniest ever written about Oxford. The premise is elementary to the point of fatuousness. Zuleika arrives in Oxford during Eights Week to visit her uncle, the Warden of St Judas College. She is so stunning that instantly 'a hundred eyes were fixed on her and half as many hearts lost to her'. As 'one of those born to make chaos cosmic' she cuts a literally lethal swathe through the hapless population of the innocently unsuspecting university, for Zuleika possesses a deadly instinct for Oxford's Achilles' heel. 'You will think me lamentably crude,' she murmurs artfully, 'my experience of life has been drawn from life itself.' The prose sparkles with gems of pithy observation: 'Beauty and the lust for learning have yet to be allied.'; 'Women who love the same man have a kind of bitter freemasonry.' Beerbohm's gifts for metaphor and simile anticipate P.G. Wodehouse: 'she was hardly more affable than a cameo'; he 'regarded himself very seriously, very sternly, from various angles, like a man invited to paint his own portrait for the Uffizi'; the man struck him as 'looking like nothing so much as a gargoyle hewn by a drunken stonemason for the adornment of a Methodist Chapel in one of the vilest suburbs of Leeds...'. Zuleika's 'library', we are told, consisted of two jewel-encrusted volumes – Bradshaw and the ABC Guide – railway time-tables. The novel closes with the entire undergraduate body hurling themselves *en masse* into the Isis like lemmings – except for the hapless Noaks who trips over on the way. Meanwhile Zuleika requests her maid to look up the next convenient train for Cambridge ...

CHAPTER EIGHT

War and Waugh

Lost Generation

According to the Oxford University Roll of Service the number of Oxford graduates and undergraduates 'sent down by the Kaiser' to serve in the armed forces amounted to 14,561. Of the Oxford cohort 2,708 were to be killed in action and sixteen were to win the Victoria Cross, four of them from Merton, three from Christ Church. Eight former Presidents of the Union were killed.

The call to arms was heard far beyond Britain itself. William A. Fleet, Magdalen's first Rhodes scholar, died in action in 1918 commanding a company of Grenadier Guards. He is commemorated by the Fleet Fellowships. Many eager volunteers who rushed to the colours in the autumn of 1914 had already been in the Officer Cadet Training Units established in public schools as a result of the manifest shortcomings in military organisation and standards revealed by the South African War of 1899–1902. Others had acquired the rudiments of fieldcraft and map-reading in the recently established Boy Scout movement. Assumed from their social class and education to be automatic 'officer material', Oxford undergraduates would suffer disproportionately as the junior commanders who were expected to lead by example and from the front. This assumption was epitomised in the death of Raymond Asquith of All Souls, eldest son of Prime Minister Herbert Asquith, killed in 1916. Clement Attlee (1883–1967), a graduate of University College and former lecturer at Ruskin College, rose to the rank of major and survived two serious injuries to return safely and eventually become Churchill's deputy in World War Two and to succeed him as Prime Minister (1945–51).

The loss occasioned by the Great War to the intellectual capital of the university and the nation can only be imagined. Physicist H.G.J. – 'Harry' – Moseley (1887–1915), a Trinity graduate and son of Oxford's Linacre Professor of Anatomy, under the direction of Sir Ernest Rutherford at Manchester University, was pioneering the use of the new technology of X-rays to investigate the structure of the atom. Predicted as a future Nobel laureate, he was killed at Gallipoli. The memorial panels at Christ Church read like a roll-call of England's élite, bearing such names as Gladstone, Cecil, Goschen, Heathcoat Amory, Leveson Gower, Leigh Pemberton, Harmsworth and Vansittart and recording the deaths of three earls, a viscount, two lords, four baronets and half a dozen 'Honourables'. A Victoria Cross and DSO were won by thirty-seven year old Christ Church graduate Lt.Col. J.S. Collings-Wells of the Bedfordshire Regiment, killed leading a counter-attack in March 1918 to safeguard the withdrawal of his battalion, then reeling from six days of rearguard actions against the German spring offensive.

Some recruits, like the poet Robert Graves, were glad to defer university, imagining it to be a marginally less restrictive but still dreary version of school, whereas war beckoned as a shining adventure. John Fox Russell of Magdalen College School was to join Graves's regiment, the Royal Welch Fusiliers, as a medical officer and win a posthumous VC. Vera Brittain (1893–1970), who came up to Somerville in 1914 found university life insupportable and enrolled as a VAD (Voluntary Aid Detachment) nursing auxiliary, serving in France and Malta before resuming her place at Somerville at the end of hostilities, having lost both her fiancé and a beloved brother. Her account of the war years, *Testament of Youth* (1933), made her famous as the first woman writer to express the tragedy she had both witnessed and suffered.

The war produced much poetry and killed many poets. Edward Thomas (1878–1917) of Lincoln College had successfully supported his young family with his biographical and topographical writing, including a book on Oxford, before a meeting with Robert Frost in 1913 turned him to poetry. Thomas was killed at Arras, only a few of his pieces having appeared in his lifetime under the pseudonym Edward Eastway. Julian Grenfell (1888–1915) had already been published before entering Balliol, where he boxed for the university. Unlike many of his contemporaries Grenfell was a regular officer, having joined the army in 1910. He won the DSO in November 1914 'for a daring feat of individual reconaissance' and was killed at the First Battle of Ypres in May 1915. His celebrated poem *Into Battle*, much anthologised subsequently, appeared in *The Times* on the day his death was announced. Grenfell's younger brother Gerald, who had followed him to Balliol and won the Craven scholarship and a tennis blue, was killed in action two months later. Other Balliol dead included Ronald Poulton, captain of the undefeated England rugby XV of 1914 and G.N. Walford and J.A. Liddell, who were both awarded posthumous VCs. Walford, a thirty-two year old Captain of artillery, was killed in the moment of victory leading an infantry assault on the Old Fort at Suvla Bay, Gallipoli in April 1915. That same year Liddell, with the Royal Flying Corps, though severely wounded on a reconnaissance flight between Ostend and Bruges, managed to land his badly damaged craft, saving the life of his observer – there were no parachutes then.

Both the Chavasse twins were to be decorated. Born at 36 New Inn Hall Street, Oxford, when their father was Principal of Wycliffe Hall, they grew up in Liverpool when he became the Anglican bishop there. Both ran in the 400 yards for Britain at the 1908 Olympics. Both entered Trinity. Noel trained as a surgeon and joined the Royal Army Medical Corps. Christopher followed his father into the Church. Ironically it was Christopher who was first in France as a chaplain at No. 10 General Hospital at St Nazaire. Noel, as medical officer of the 10th Battalion (Liverpool Scottish) of the King's (Liverpool) Regiment, was awarded the Victoria Cross for carrying twenty casualties to safety under fire during the battle of the Somme in July 1916. He had already been awarded the Military Cross. A year later, at Passchendale, despite his own multiple wounds, Noel Chavasse again risked his life in the same way and endured two days under fire treating the injured until himself being disembowelled by an artillery shell which destroyed his forward aid post. For this action he was awarded a bar to his VC, making him the only man in the Great War to receive this highest award twice and only one in three ever to do so.

Christopher Chavasse was awarded the MC, Croix de Guerre and OBE (Military Division) for his acts of gallantry. Returning to Oxford in 1922 as Rector of St Aldate's he set himself to fulfil his father's vision and establish what has been called 'the low Church answer to Keble'. Chavasse presided over the first decade in the life of St Peter's College as its Master (1929–39), securing its finances through his friendship with Lord Nuffield. He went on to become Bishop of Rochester. St Peter's was finally recognised as a full college of the University in 1961, a year before Chavasse died in retirement at Garsington. Its buildings are arranged along New Inn Hall Street, on which Chavasse was born. The oldest, Linton House, was built in 1797 as headquarters of the Oxford Canal Company.

The guerrilla exploits of T.E. Lawrence (1888–1935) with the rebel forces of Prince Faysal, future King of Iraq, were to win him world-wide fame as 'Lawrence of Arabia'. Lawrence had passed his teenage years at 2 Polstead Road, Oxford. A precociously learned child, by twelve he was recouping his tuition fees at Oxford High School with scholarships. Having been born at Tremadoc, Lawrence qualified for a Welsh exhibition at Jesus but, apart from a term in room V4, preferred to live at home where a back garden shed was converted into a bungalow for him. Ignoring college life and attending few lectures, he wrote a thesis on the influence of the Crusades on European military architecture and used a vacation to walk from Palestine through Syria to Turkey and, on the side, indulge in a little freelance archaeology and espionage, observing Ottoman railway construction. Lawrence had already demonstrated his daring spirit by exploring the full length of an Oxford subterranean Saxon sewer by canoe, entering it at Hythe Bridge and emerging in what was to become Christ Church Memorial Gardens.

Graduating with a first in History, Lawrence was awarded a four year travel demyship by Magdalen and until the outbreak of war worked on a British Museum archaeological expedition in Syria led by Sir Leonard Woolley, a New College graduate and former assistant to Sir Arthur Evans at the Ashmolean, which now displays the Hittite seals Lawrence collected during this period. This experience enabled Lawrence to improve his Arabic and encouraged him to adopt Arab modes of dress and diet. Even more to the point it enabled him to collaborate with Woolley on gathering topographical information of military value, which was the underlying but unstated purpose of the enterprise. When war broke out, being at 5 ft 5 inches under the minimum height for combat service, Lawrence was confined to a desk job in intelligence in Cairo until 1916 when he was seconded to liaise with what became 'the Arab revolt'.

Exhausted by his exertions in the field and depressed by his failure to secure Arab interests in the post-war diplomatic settlement, Lawrence gratefully accepted a research fellowship at All Souls, where he began drafting an account of his exploits. He also arranged for the republication in 1921, with an admirable introduction by himself, of C.M. Doughty's *Travels in Arabia Deserta* of 1888. Its finely wrought prose style was the model for Lawrence's own. The Doughty project was to prove the sole immediate outcome of Lawrence's sojourn at All Souls because he lost the original manuscript of his desert deeds on Reading station and set himself to rewrite it entirely, not once but twice. The completed version was finally published in 1926 in a luxurious and loss-making limited edition, only reaching a wider public the following year as the much-abridged *The Revolt in the Desert*. A full text of *The Seven Pillars of Wisdom* finally appeared in the year of his death. All Souls possesses a pastel portrait of Lawrence by his friend Eric Kennington, who had been his art editor on *Seven Pillars*. The Museum of the History of Science has a camera Lawrence used for his archaeological work and the Bodleian has one of the eight copies of the first draft of *The Seven Pillars of Wisdom* which Lawrence had printed by *The Oxford Times* to show to such friends as Robert Graves for their opinions.

Scarcely less remarkable in purely military terms, though far less well known, were the exploits of (Sir) Adrian Carton de Wiart (1880–1963) who had as an undergraduate absconded from Balliol to fight the Boers. In 1914 he lost an eye and gained the DSO fighting the 'Mad Mullah' in Somaliland. On the Western Front he was severely wounded eight times, lost his left hand and won the VC at the Somme.

Charles Morgan (1894–1958), having quit the Royal Navy as a result of harsh treatment (which supplied the material for his first novel *The Gunroom*) then quit BNC to rejoin when war broke out. His participation in the disastrous Naval Brigade expedition to hold Antwerp led to a lucky escape into neutral Holland where, as the guest of the aristocratic de Pallandt family of Rosendaal castle, he acquired a first-rate education in European culture and wrote the first version of *The Gunroom*, losing the manuscript when the ship taking him home hit a mine. Morgan, however, returned safely to Oxford to complete his degree and become President of OUDS and, a decade later, winner of the Hawthornden Prize for *The Fountain*, a best-seller on both sides of the Atlantic. Morgan's books were translated into nineteen languages and brought him the presidency of International PEN. A passionate Francophile, he was awarded the Legion of Honour, became Oxford's Zaharoff Lecturer in French Studies in 1948 and became only the second English writer after Kipling to be made a member of the Institute of France.

The city as well as the university, of course, supplied its share of recruits for the forces. The local regiment, the Oxfordshire and Buckinghamshire Light Infantry, was expanded from its normal peacetime strength of two battalions to twelve and fought on the Somme and at Passchendaele as well as in Italy and Macedonia. In 1916 most of the first (i.e. pre-war, professional) battalion was taken prisoner after the fall of the besieged city of Kut-el-Amara in Mesopotamia. In 1917 C.S.M. Edward Brooks (1883–1944) of the Oxfordshire and Buckinghamshire Light Infantry darted forward from his position in the second rank of an offensive on the Western Front to seize a German machine-gun single-handed and turn it on the enemy. For this he was awarded the VC. Brooks, a Headington man, returned safely to become a worker in the Morris car factory. G.F. J. Cumberlege (1891–1979) a recent Worcester College graduate, served with the same regiment, was awarded the MC and DSO and Croce de Guerra, mentioned in despatches three times and returned to head OUP's operations in India and New York before being appointed as its chief. His many publishing achievements included T.E. Lawrence's translation of the *Odyssey*, Morison and Comager's *The Growth of the American Republic* and, in collaboration with Cambridge University Press, the *New English Bible*.

THOSE ALSO SERVE . . .

Although still relatively weak in science the university supplied its quota of 'backroom boys'. The physiologist J.S. Haldane (1860–1936) devised a portable oxygen apparatus for the treatment of gas poisoning and with the assistance of Bertram Lambert, a chemistry graduate of Merton, invented what became the standard issue gas mask, thus saving incalculable numbers of lives. To the novel dimension of aerial warfare particularly significant contributions were made. Port Meadow served as an aerodrome, with the Royal Flying Corps accommodated in huts in the Parks. An Oxford school of aeronautics was established. The work done by Danish Professor of Pathology Georges Dreyer (1873–1934) on the oxygen supply problems of flying at height gained him a CBE and election to the Royal Society. The future Professor Sir Henry Tizard (1885–1959), then a junior science don, qualified to become his own test pilot and made valuable improvements to bomb-sights and aviation fuel. Even more hazardous were the experiments conducted by Frederick Lindemann (1886–1957), a former fellow student with Tizard in Berlin. In the summer of 1917 Lindemann repeatedly risked his life flying solo to validate his explanation of how a plane often found itself at the mercy of a potentially fatal 'spin' and to test his theory of how a pilot could extricate himself from it. In 1919, thanks largely to Tizard's support, Lindemann was rewarded with the chair of Experimental Philosophy (i.e. physics). A Committee of Advanced Studies was established to attract neutral Americans to undertake postgraduate scientific studies at Oxford, rather than at German universities. A new qualification, the D. Phil., was introduced in 1917. Inadvertently this somewhat improvised initiative paved the way for a major strengthening of science at Oxford in the inter-war period.

Non-scientific members of the academic community served as opportunities offered. Many were transferred to the greatly expanded Whitehall bureaucracy. H.W. Garrod (1878–1960), a Merton classics don, impressed his superiors as 'of quite exceptional ability' and was created CBE for his handling of 'the general economic problems created by a world shortage of capital, supply, tonnage etc.'

An Oxfordshire Volunteer company was spontaneously raised to serve as a sort of 'Home Guard', despite official discouragement, under A.D. Godley (1856–1925), Ulsterman, Alpinist and satirist, a Magdalen classics don, editor of the *Oxford Magazine* and of the *Classical Review* and public orator of the university. 'Godley's Army' attracted into its ranks the Poet Laureate Robert Bridges, classicist Gilbert Murray and Sir Walter Raleigh, Professor of English Literature. May Cannan, daughter of the Secretary of the University Press, mobilised volunteers and sponsors to establish and equip a sixty bed convalescent hospital in a wing of Magdalen College School, then went to work, unpaid, at OUP. The Press itself used its own special skills to undertake top secret printing for the Admiralty's Naval Intelligence Department. Throughout the city families took in refugees from Serbia and the sacked Belgian university city of Louvain. Many were initially accommodated at Ruskin until they could be allocated more permanent lodgings. It was the plight of the Belgians which caused Gilbert Murray to reverse his attitude to the hostilities, having initially subscribed to a public plea for British neutrality. His agonised reappraisal, set out as *How Can War Ever be Right?* argued that for all its inevitable suffering war cannot be reduced to a balance sheet of life versus death and concluded that 'in some causes it is better to fight and be broken than to yield peacefully'. Shortly afterwards the Central Committee of National Patriotic Organizations, chaired by Prime Minister Asquith (ex-Balliol) secured from six Oxford history dons a publication setting out *Why We Are At War: Great Britain's Case*. This was followed by almost a hundred 'Oxford Pamphlets', several of which proved more noteworthy for their patriotism than their objectivity. In 1917 Lloyd George appointed John Buchan to cordinate British propaganda as head of a new centralised Department of Information.

As elsewhere the civilian population of Oxford suffered from shortages of food and fuel. Merton Field was turned into allotments for growing vegetables and women replaced absent men in unaccustomed roles. The large number of convalescing soldiers promised good prospects for prostitutes from far afield and in March 1917 Oxford appointed its first female police constable to combat this threat to public virtue. Women ticket collectors manned the barrier at the station, postwomen delivered the mail and conductresses took fares on the buses.

For a second time in its history Oxford became dominated by military activity. The University Examination Schools became the headquarters of the Third Southern General Hospital, which soon took over the Town Hall and the workhouse in Cowley Road. Somerville

College became a branch hospital where Robert Graves, perforated by multiple fragments of a tombstone, was amongst its convalescents; its students were taken in by Oriel. A tented hospital for convalescents was set up in New College garden. Merton housed nurses. C.R.L. Fletcher, a Magdalen history don, wrote *A Handy Guide to Oxford* for the benefit of convalescents well enough to build up their strength by a little exploration. It remained a standard guide-book for the next thirty years.

From 1916 onwards many college rooms were given over to battalions of officer cadets. These were young rankers who had so distinguished themselves as to be thought worthy of three months release from the trenches to fit them for commissions. The dining hall of Wycliffe Hall served as temporary accommodation for refugees from Serbia and from St Hugh's successively before being fitted up as a dummy aeroplane.

Oxford's industrial facilities were also mobilised. The Oxfordshire Steam Ploughing Company at Cowley switched to making bomb cases. WRM Motors Ltd which local entrepreneur William Morris had established in the former Oxford Military College buildings in 1912 continued to make cars, but for war purposes, and also produced grenades and mines.

SOLDIERING ON

In 1913–14 Oxford's undergraduate population had numbered 1,400. By 1915 it was down to five hundred and fifty, mostly female or foreign or unfit for service. In 1916 Balliol had just thirty undergraduates, all 'oddities of one kind or another' in the words of one of their number, Aldous Huxley. Magdalen had only twenty. By 1917 there were only four hundred and sixty students still in residence, of whom thirty were medical students and a hundred and twenty were members of the Officers Training Corps awaiting admission to Cadet battalions. By 1918 the overall figure had fallen to three hundred and sixty-nine.

American divinity student J. Brett Langstaff entered Magdalen just as, what was from his viewpoint 'the European war', broke out. Langstaff's early days were clouded by that preliminary skirmishing over paperwork which appears to have aggravated Anglo-American educational exchanges ever since their beginnings. Until he was able to take up residence in college the bemused newcomer at least had the consolation of sharing lodgings with the brilliant and kindly Spanish-American philosopher-poet George Santayana (1863–1952). Santayana had astonished Harvard colleagues by resigning his professorship in 1912, at the seeming peak of his career and reputation. He was to settle in Oxford for the duration of the war. Santayana once described his intellectual vocation as being 'to say in English as many un-English things as possible'. If so, his Oxford years were an aberration for he wrote a number of popular essays celebrating the English character and countryside and serious studies of *Egotism in German Philosophy* (1916) and *Philosophical Opinion in America* (1918), which demonstrated his firm adherence to the Allied cause. At the end of the war Christ Church offered him life membership but he declined and eventually settled in Rome.

Langstaff's encounter with Santayana appears to have been a happy chance but the apparently naïve Yankee subsequently revealed himself to be an assiduous collector of impressive social contacts. Having a room opposite Prince George of Teck helped Langstaff's networking. Langstaff himself sang to convalescent officers billeted in the great houses of the surrounding Oxford countryside, including Blenheim and Nuneham Courtney, where he became a regular guest of Lord Harcourt's family. As an American Langstaff also found a warm welcome at the Oslers' in Norham Gardens. During one Long Vacation he was even assigned a room in the medieval almshouse at Ewelme, which had become a perquisite of the Regius Professorship of Medicine. Robert Bridges proved to be an uncomfortable conquest, however, as dismissive of American culture as he was contemptuous of American neutrality.

Langstaff set himself to investigate the development of the liturgy of the Anglican Communion service, from its medieval origins through to its variant forms in Scotland and North America. In the matter of research Oxford's *laisser-faire* attitude ('approach' would be far too pro-active a word) left Langstaff initially floundering after the intensively structured regime of the American seminary from which he had graduated. Doggedness, self-discipline and mounting intellectual excitement brought their own reward in time – 'at Oxford I was being given the liberty of working out my own ideas with the aid of tutors, original source material and, above all, I was given time. I was learning to be patient with myself as long as I was persevering.' He also found time to put on plays in Oscar Wilde's old room. The outcome of Langstaff's endeavours was a dissertation fit for recycling as a publishable book. Half a century later he was able to recycle his letters home as a memoir, *Oxford – 1914*. Langstaff subsequently enlisted in the Artist's Rifles as a chaplain but was soon invalided out.

POETRY AND PROSE

As Langstaff was coming up to Magdalen, a young Harvard philosopher, T.S. Eliot was entering Merton to complete his doctorate on F.H. Bradley, himself a Merton Fellow. Eliot was rapidly disenchanted – 'I do not think anyone would come to Oxford to seek for anything very original or subtle in philosophy' – so he played tennis, rowed and honed his prose style but made little progress with his thesis, turning instead to poetry. He made his reading debut with a rendition of *The Love Song of Alfred J. Prufrock*, given to a literary clique appropriately known as the Coterie. Such diversions proved inadequate. Eliot eventually concluded that being at Oxford was too much like a foretaste of what it would be like to be dead. Seduced by the pull of the metropolis and the enthusiastic patronage of fellow exile Ezra Pound, he abandoned Oxford and his Harvard scholarship to plunge impulsively into a disastrous marriage.

Of those few British nationals still pursuing undergraduate studies Aldous Huxley (1894–1963) would have been disbarred from military service by his sight, already severely damaged by a traumatic eye infection, which at one stage forced him to use braille. Huxley, a grandson of T.H. Huxley and great-grandson of Dr Thomas Arnold, triumphed over his disability to gain a first in English Literature in 1916, won the Stanhope Prize, played jazz, wrote poetry and was drawn into the pacifist, avant-garde set hosted by Lady Ottoline Morrell at Garsington Manor, where he served out the rest of the war as an agricultural labourer and met his future wife, Maria Nys. Huxley rewarded Lady Ottoline's patronage and hospitality by caricaturing her cruelly in his first novel *Crome Yellow* (1921).

Novelist L.P. Hartley (1895–1972) entered Balliol in 1915 to read history but volunteered in April 1916 and served with the Norfolk Regiment until invalided out in September 1918. Unable to resume his studies until April 1919, it took until 1921 for him to finish his degree. The interruption proved extremely worthwhile in the sense that it enabled him to participate in the social and literary life of a brilliant post-war generation which he otherwise would have missed. By the time he left Oxford he had already had some stories published in *Oxford Outlook* and by entering Lady Ottoline's circle made the acquaintance of the Sitwells and Asquiths who were to become lifelong friends and supporters of his career.

The Oxford sojourn of W.B. Yeats (1865–1939) was, by contrast, passed largely outside the circles of the literary glitterati, although he was invited to speak at the Union. In 1917, aged fifty-two, he married a young English girl, Georgie Hyde-Lees, settling opposite Balliol at 4 Broad Street (since demolished). They stayed until 1921, when they had to let the house to save money. *The Wild Swans at Coole* appeared in 1919 and *Michael Robartes and the Dancer* in 1921 but, with Georgie as his psychic muse, Yeats was primarily preoccupied with the preternatural influences and supernatural symbolism which ultimately issued in *A Vision* (1925). By the time that had appeared Yeats's life had been transformed by his appointment as a Senator of the newly independent Irish Free State and the award of the Nobel Prize for Literature. Yeats's old home was transformed by being absorbed into The Shamrock Tea Rooms ('dainty and inexpensive Catering ... Music is *not* provided'), his former dining-room being elevated to the dignity of the Yeats Room, with his poems and prints by his artist brother, Jack, on display.

A few hundred yards away from Yeats, at 66 High Street, between 1915 and 1919 lodged Ronald Firbank (1886–1926). At Cambridge, which he left without a degree, he had befriended Vyvyan Holland, Oscar Wilde's son, and he continued to ape what he took to be the manner of his icon with calculated eccentricities of gesture and appearance. Oxford offered Firbank a refuge from bombing in London and an isolation which he used to compose three novels on stacks of blue postcards. When the war ended he left, thus ensuring that he never came into personal contact with the post-war Oxford generation of Waugh, Auden and Powell, all intense admirers of his work.

Of the female undergraduates of the period few would have greater influence than (Dame) Margery Perham (1895–1982). After a first in Modern History and a fellowship at St Hugh's she would, thanks to a timely grant from the Rhodes trustees, become a peripatetic student of 'native affairs' and the doyenne of Africanists of her generation, powerfully influencing government policy and training successive cadres of colonial administrators.

REMEMBRANCE

> Clad in beauty of dreams begotten,
> Strange old city for ever young,
> Keep the dreams that we have forgotten,
> Keep the songs we have never sung.
> So shall we hear your music calling,
> So from a land where songs are few,
> When the shadows of life are falling,
> Mother, your sons come back to you.
> Christ Church undergraduate 1915

At the *Encaenia* in 1919 Oxford saluted the victors with honorary degrees. The line-up was impressive. Beside Admirals Beatty, Hall and Wemyss and Field Marshals Wilson and Haig – the latter a Brasenose man – were ranked the American General Pershing, Australian General Monash and French General Joffre, trade union leader J.R. Clynes, Belgian historian Henri Pirenne and future US President, Herbert Hoover, who had distinguished himself in organising relief for refugees.

Christ Church commemorated its fallen with a Garden of Remembrance, leading from St Aldate's through to Christ Church Meadow. Of Christ Church men two hundred and twenty-five did not return. From Balliol the figure was a hundred and ninety-three, from Magdalen the losses amounted to a hundred and eighty-six, from University College a hundred and seventy-three, from Keble a hundred and sixty-three, even Worcester, a small college, lost eighty-two. The highest loss, two hundred and fifty-seven, was at New College. Controversially at the time the college, at the explicit urging of Warden

Spooner, erected in its chapel a memorial to its German Rhodes scholars:

> In memory of the men of this College who coming from a
> Foreign Land entered into the inheritance of this place and
> Returning fought and died for their country in the war 1914–19

BACK FROM THE TRENCHES

Maurice Bowra (1898–1971), too young to serve when war broke out, visited his parents in China in 1916 and passed through revolutionary Petrograd on his way back, thus kindling a lifelong interest in Russian literature. After serving with the artillery at Passchendaele, he took up his deferred New College scholarship, became a star pupil of Gilbert Murray and in 1922 became a Fellow of Wadham, his home for the rest of his life. Bowra served as Master from 1938 to 1970 and published thirty volumes of literary criticism and classical scholarship. Professor of Poetry (1946–51), Vice-Chancellor (1951–4) and President of the British Academy (1958–62), Bowra was renowned for his sybaritic hospitality and wit, both bawdy and catty, and for being 'the best company in the world'. His memorial in the cloister garden at Wadham matches his extraordinary personality, the head and body seeming to emanate from and evaporate into an empty chair, like a jovial host suspended in permanent limbo at an eternal luncheon party.

Edmund Blunden (1896–1974) won the MC with the Royal Sussex Regiment and later recalled his ordeal poetically in *Third Ypres* and *Report on Experience*, expressing the self-blame of many survivors. He stayed long enough at Queen's to rescue the work of John Clare from obscurity but quit to take up literary journalism and then a chair at Tokyo Imperial University, where he made a lasting impression on Japanese literary studies in only three years. As a Fellow of Merton in the 1930s Blunden numbered the ill-fated Keith Douglas among his pupils. Blunden served as Professor of Poetry in 1966–8.

Ulsterman C.S. Lewis (1893–1963) trained with the Oxford Officer Training Corps and was wounded so badly at Arras in April 1918 that he was still convalescing when the war ended. After winning the Chancellor's English Essay Prize and taking a double First, he was

C.S. Lewis, Fellow of Magdalen College

elected a Fellow of Magdalen, where his pupil John Betjeman described him as 'breezy, tweedy, beer-drinking and jolly'. Lewis was also a deeply serious Christian. Although his first published work was poetry and he also wrote science fiction, he was to win fame as a religious broadcaster and as the author of *The Screwtape Letters* (1940), a supposed correspondence between Satan and a trainee devil in which the former expertly instructs the latter on the weaknesses of humanity. In later life Lewis won an even wider reputation with his seven volume children's classic of Christian symbolism, the *Chronicles of Narnia*. His late and unexpected marriage to an American poet became the subject of the film *Shadowlands*, in which he was played with characteristic intensity by Sir Anthony Hopkins. Lewis lived for most of his Oxford years at The Kilns, Headington Quarry and is buried at Holy Trinity, Headington.

The Magdalen rooms occupied by C.S. Lewis – and the bar of the Eagle and Child in St Giles – were regular venues for the meetings of the Inklings, a clubby clique consisting of Lewis himself, fellow English dons J.R.R. Tolkien (1892–1973) and Nevill Coghill (1899–1980) and Charles Williams of the Oxford University Press.

Born in South Africa of German descent, Tolkien had contracted trench fever during the catastrophic campaign on the Somme. Like Lewis he was determined to inject rigour into the teaching of English through the intensive study of philology, dialect and pre-modern – very pre-modern – texts. Tolkien became Professor of Anglo-Saxon in 1925 and with Lewis's encouragement published *The Hobbit* in 1937. It was Lewis also who encouraged him to persevere with the *Lord of the Rings* trilogy which finally appeared in 1954–5. Tolkien's motivation was to provide the English with a replacement for the mythology they had somehow mislaid over the centuries but the trilogy received its most enthusiastic reception in the United States. Its campus cult status brought so many unsought pilgrims to Tolkien's door that he was forced to quit Oxford for a reclusive exile in Bournemouth.

The son of an Irish baronet, Nevill Coghill had served with the artillery in Salonika and Bulgaria before switching from History to English at Exeter College. Coghill became known to generations of school pupils through his modern verse translation of Chaucer's *Canterbury Tales* (1951), which eventually became the basis of a successful stage musical. At Oxford Coghill was to make something of a speciality of outdoor theatrical productions, including a 1949 version of *The Tempest* with a magical *coup de théâtre* in which Ariel appeared to skip across the lake of Worcester College gardens (in fact supported by a barely submerged gangway). Coghill also memorably directed his former pupil Richard Burton in Marlowe's *Doctor Faustus* at the Oxford Playhouse and subsequently co-directed a film version of it with Burton.

Charles Williams served not in the forces but with Oxford University Press, while maintaining a volume of literary output – anthologies, reviews, biography, theology, cricism, 'supernatural thrillers' and thirty volumes of verse – which put most dons to shame. An expert on Arthurian legends, he was awarded an honorary MA in 1943 in recognition of his brilliant courses of public lectures.

Some came back from the trenches but not to Oxford. Lord Robert Cecil left Christ Church for the Grenadier Guards, won the *Croix de Guerre* but turned to the City and politics rather than complete his degree. Future Prime Minister Harold Macmillan (1894–1986), severely wounded while serving with the Grenadiers, chose not to return to Balliol: 'I could not face it. To me it was a city of ghosts. Of our eight scholars and exhibitioners who came up in 1912, H.S. and I alone were alive. It was too much.' Macmillan did eventually return – as Chancellor of the University.

Waugh Stories

Oxford's undergraduate population rose from 1,357 in February 1919 to 2,659 by October to 5,689 by 1920. The immediate post-war undergraduate generation thought itself particularly brilliant, socially, if not academically. Its members were often self-consciously gay in both senses of the word. Politics were of little interest, except during the General Strike of 1926 when many undergraduates thought it might be fun to volunteer as a blackleg driver of a bus or train. For future Labour party leader Hugh Gaitskell (1906–63), then at New College, the event was an epiphany, turning him to socialism and an initial career as a WEA lecturer in economics in the Nottinghamshire coalfield. Presidents of the Union in the 1920s included ten future MPs and two future Lord Chancellors. For the most part, however, the preoccupations of the most noteworthy undergraduates revolved around self-display and self-indulgence.

Handsome, suave Beverley Nichols (1898–1983) had already sampled a term at Balliol in 1917 before serving as an Army propagandist in America, where he skilfully exploited an entirely unmerited status as a war hero in uniforms of his own devising and completed his first novel. Returning to Balliol in 1919 he determined to maintain the momentum of his celebrity, revitalised *Isis*, launched the leftish *Oxford Outlook*, founded a new Liberal club, served a term as President of the Union and scraped a history degree. By the time he went down he was already notorious and had published a second novel, *Patchwork*, set in Oxford.

At Christ Church future Labour peer, but then Communist activist, Tom Driberg (1905–76) wrote poetry and joined the editorial board of *Cherwell* before being sent down without a degree for a homosexual indiscretion. His subsequent career embraced periods as a pavement artist, gossip columnist, MI5 agent, war correspondent and MP. His posthumous autobiography was justly titled *Ruling Passions*.

Evelyn Waugh (1903–66) found his own college, Hertford, dull and his tutors even duller. He found compensation in the company of future novelists Anthony Powell and Graham Greene, Balliol contemporaries. Greene's habitual drunkenness probably did not offend, though his Communism might have – and his attempts to ward off boredom by playing Russian roulette and doing freelance undercover work for the German embassy he kept to himself. Waugh also devoted much effort to associating himself with the grandees of Magdalen and Christ Church, most notably Harold Acton, whom he met at a talk given by G.K. Chesterton. Acton (1904–94), who is credited by some with the invention of 'Oxford Bags', was like the dandified Max Beerbohm a generation before him, an arch poseur whose posturing veiled a very genuine talent. Mid-way through his very long life he would publish a volume of autobiography appropriately entitled *Memoirs of an Aesthete* (1948) but his first volume of verse had already been published while he was still at Oxford. Later he would live in China, then settle in Florence and write about Chinese literature and Italian history.

Waugh, unsurprisingly in view of his own attitudes to study, took a third, had a wretched time schoolmastering and then turned his Oxford years to comic effect in his first novel *Decline and Fall* (1928). Waugh's *Brideshead Revisited* (1945) revisited the Oxford of his youth, taking Harold Acton as the prototype for Anthony Blanche. The book was to have a profound effect on the image and self-image of the university's inhabitants when it was televised in 1981. Waugh converted to Catholicism in 1930 and in 1935 wrote a biography of the Oxford martyr Edmund Campion, which won the Hawthornden Prize. His last publications returned to Oxford themes: a biography of his friend and spiritual mentor, Ronald Knox and a volume of autobiography wryly entitled *A Little Learning* (1964).

The Very Reverend Monsignor Ronald Arbuthnot Knox (1888–1957) became a dominant Oxford figure of the inter-war years. The son and grandson of Anglican bishops, he was educated at Summer Fields, Eton, where he was Captain of School, and Balliol, where he became President of the Union and won the Hertford, Ireland and Craven Scholarships and the Gaisford and Chancellor's Prizes for Greek and Latin Verse respectively. A Fellow of Trinity and an Anglican priest by the age of twenty-four, he left Oxford in 1914, converting to Catholicism in 1917. *A Spiritual Aeneid* (1918) described his conversion. In 1926 Knox returned to Oxford as Catholic chaplain to the university. Apart from his powerful spiritual influence on undergraduates, Knox is chiefly remembered for his widely used re-translation of the Bible. He also wrote detective stories and *Let Dons Delight* (1939) a brilliant exposition of the disintegration of a common culture through a series of Senior Common Room conversations at fifty year intervals from the reign of Elizabeth I down to 1938.

John Betjeman (1906–84) revelled in his 'beautiful panelled eighteenth century rooms on the second floor of New Buildings' at Magdalen and plunged into the social whirl with relish, editing *Cherwell* and attending Anglo-Catholic sherry parties. A product of the Dragon School, Betjeman already knew and loved Oxford well and was devastated to leave without a degree, having failed the compulsory Divinity examination ('Divvers') – a supremely cruel irony for an ardent Anglican devotee of ecclesiastical architecture, as he himself noted – 'Failed in Divinity! O, towers and spires!' Betjeman characteristically bounced back with the publication of an affectionate and witty tribute-cum-guidebook, *An Oxford Treasure Chest* (1938), inventing such splendid spoof figures as a Professor of Medieval Icthyology and commenting knowledgeably and acerbically on college architecture. Betjeman was even more acerbic on the transformation of the city which had occurred in the short time since his ignominious departure. Oxford, he observed, was not one city but three. The collegiate core was still recognisable as Jude's Christminster, around and beyond it was the city inhabited by 'ordinary people' whose very existence was invisible to visitors except during the annual junketings of St Giles Fair. Both were now threatened by the pervasive impact of a new Oxford – 'Motopolis' – an unsought by-product of the new Morris motor car factory at Cowley on the city's eastern fringe.

In literary terms Betjeman returned to the scenes of childhood in

New Bats in Old Belfries, celebrating North Oxford, '*where once there grazed the cows, Emancipated children swing on old apple boughs*'. In 1960 he returned again with *Summoned by Bells*, a two-thousand-line blank verse account of his earliest days, from exploring the side-streets of North Oxford by bike to the period of schoolmastering which followed his departure from Magdalen and preceded his self-reinventions as architectural critic, film critic, war-time propagandist, broadcaster, pioneer conservationist of things Victorian and all-round National Treasure. Appointed Poet Laureate in 1972, Betjeman became the most popular poet since Kipling and Housman. Magdalen made him an Honorary Fellow and, very appropriately in the light of his architectural enthusiams, so did Keble.

Academically speaking the undergraduate career of W.H. Auden (1907–73) was scarcely more distinguished than Betjeman's. He went down with a third, though this was by no means exceptional. During the 1920s over a third of degrees awarded were thirds or fourths. Auden had, however, already confessed to his tutor at Christ Church, Nevill Coghill that he intended to be not just a poet but a great poet. Ironically in view of T.S. Eliot's Oxford experiences, it was his recently published *The Waste Land* (1922), which exerted the most decisive influence on Auden's early poetic development. Auden finally returned to Oxford in 1956 as Professor of Poetry and made himself a fixture in the Cadena cafe in Cornmarket, where he would advise undergraduate versifiers on poetic technique. In 1972 he returned yet again to live in a 'grace and favour' cottage in the grounds of Christ Church. As an adoptive New Yorker he was appalled to find that he had to return to his *alma mater* to be mugged. He also claimed that the traffic noise was worse. His High Table colleagues thought him a drunken bore. The experience was not a success.

Auden's undergraduate friends included poets Stephen Spender (1909–95) at University College and Louis MacNeice (1907–63) at Merton. MacNeice took a double first, read much philosophy, published his first volume of verse, *Blind Fireworks*, and co-edited *Oxford Poetry* with Spender. Critic Cyril Connolly, who was to co-edit *Horizon* with Spender during World War Two was another member of this literary generation.

The View from Elysium

Oxford in the inter-war period was encircled by *literati*, such as Edmund Blunden and Gilbert Murray, who were both part of it and others who were apart from it. Archaeologist Sir Arthur Evans (1851–1941) had led the way, his Youlbury estate at Boar's Hill being admired as 'an earthly paradise'. Evans could trace a direct ancestral line of descent from Georg Dionysius Ehret (1710–70), the German-born botanic artist who was briefly head gardener of Oxford's Botanic Gardens in 1750–51 and at Boar's Hill Evans made a much-admired garden with a lake, plantations of conifers and a profusion of Mediterranean plants, brought home from his travels, including pines whose seeds he claimed to have gathered in a wood once known to Dante and Byron. Such romantic attachments did not inhibit him from allowing the local Boy Scout troop to use Youlbury for training and camping. After the war from which so many of those boys did not return he erected an inscribed sundial in their memory – 'They fell before their Time. But, wherever they now lie, Here they are never far away.' In 1928 Evans successfully persuaded the newly-founded Oxford Preservation Trust to buy up the area described in Matthew Arnold's *Thyrsis* to save at least some of it from speculative house-building. He also paid for the erection of the fifty foot Jarn Mound to preserve the immemorial view over the treetops towards Islip, where Edward the Confessor had been born.

Robert Bridges (1844–1930), as an undergraduate at Corpus, had befriended Gerard Manley Hopkins but had kept his own poetic ambitions to himself. After his gruelling London medical career was cut short by illness, Bridges married the daughter of Sir Alfred Waterhouse, architect of the Natural History Museum and of the Oxford Union's Debating Hall and Balliol's Broad Street frontage. In 1907 Bridges and his wife settled at Chilswell House, Boar's Hill. Appointed Poet Laureate in 1913, Bridges declined to stand for the Oxford Professorship of Poetry. In 1918 he arranged for the publication of G.M. Hopkins's complete verse and for the remainder of his life served Oxford University Press as an adviser on style, phonetics and typography. He also devoted much effort to hymn-writing and an attempted reform of English spelling.

Bridges' successor as Poet Laureate was his Boar's Hill neighbour, John Masefield (1878–1967), then at the height of his popularity thanks to the success of his *Collected Poems* (1923), novels and children's books. In 1935 Masefield was honoured with the Order of Merit.

In a cottage in Masefield's garden lived ex-lieutenant Robert Graves (1895–1985), who had been severely wounded and twice mentioned in dispatches while serving with the Royal Welch Fusiliers. Graves had taken up his deferred place at St John's but was unable to adjust to college life and dropped out, although he did eventually produce a thesis which gained him a B. Litt. In the interim he tried running a village shop (badly) before turning to writing full-time to support his young family. He also made the acquaintance of that other dislocated ex-serviceman, T.E. Lawrence, in whose rooms at All Souls Graves was introduced to Ezra Pound. Graves spent most of the rest of his life in Majorca but did return periodically to Oxford as Professor of Poetry (1961–6).

John Buchan (1875–1940), best remembered as the author of *The Thirty-Nine Steps*, won the Newdigate and the Stanhope Historical Essay Prizes, was President of the Union and took a first. After twenty years as a barrister, publisher, colonial administrator and prolific author, Buchan settled at Elsfield Manor in 1919. There he wrote an account of war poet Julian Grenfell, a history of the Royal Scots Fusiliers and two novels which linked Elsfield Manor itself with Dr Johnson (*Midwinter*, 1923) and Henry VIII (*The Blanket of the Dark* 1931). Buchan, an assiduous elder of St Columba's church, crowded his last decade with service: MP for the Scottish universities, Lord High Commissioner to the General Assembly of the Church of Scotland and Governor-General of Canada.

Boar's Hill was also the chosen retirement home of the great orientalist David Margoliouth (1858–1940) whose forty-eight year tenure of the Laudian professorship enabled him to establish the sort of international reputation enjoyed by its first holder, Pococke. Initially schooled at Hackney Collegiate School, he was said to have been the brightest boy ever to get a scholarship to Winchester. As an under-graduate he managed to win no less than eight scholarships. Mono-syllabic in English, he was loquacious in Arabic or Turkish. His published work showed equal facility for translating Greek or Syriac into English and Arabic into Latin. His treatment of religious controversies, biblical or Islamic, often infuriated the orthodox but, like his friend Gilbert Murray, he was a tireless campaigner for the oppressed and the persecuted, Assyrian, Armenian or Jewish.

Down in the city Alfred Edgar Coppard (1878–1957) took a perilous plunge into literature. Obliged to leave school at nine by his father's death and the utter penury of his family, by the age of twenty Coppard had become a clerk in the Eagle Ironworks and a good enough athlete to use his prize money to indulge his enthusiasm for Hardy, James and Chekhov. In 1919, with £50 saved up, Coppard became a full-time writer, specialising in short stories, many dealing with the plight of the misfit and the underdog. '*The Poor Man*' is based on his own arrest for alleged poaching while exercising his whippets. '*The Quiet Woman*' and '*Arabesque*' are both set in his fourth-floor flat in the Cornmarket. Encouraged by Ford Madox Ford, Coppard produced a volume of stories or verse almost annually for thirty years. Admirers ranked the deceptive simplicity of his style and mastery of technique with Katherine Mansfield's. When he reached seventy-five, Oxford undergraduates, led by Sir Maurice Bowra, celebrated Coppard's birthday.

An Atlantic Angle: Samuel Eliot Morison

In 1922 Bostonian Samuel Eliot Morison (1887–1976) was appointed to Oxford's first chair of American History, funded by the newspaper tycoon Lord Harmsworth. Morison's three year tenure gave him an abiding affection for Oxford's 'dream of grey walls and green fields' and admiring wonderment for its ordered chaos – 'at once so hospitable and so indifferent to new individuals, disciplines and subjects'. He concluded that any would-be reformer would be seduced into impotence by college hospitality and that in any case 'no sensible man who knows Oxford would wish greatly to change it'. The very real freedom of the university, of the colleges and of individuals he saw as essentially interrelated and guaranteed by the labyrinthine complexity of the boards and committees charged with governing them, which, as a bonus, also harmlessly diverted academic busybodies and drones.

Decentralisation enabled anomalous institutions like Ruskin or Manchester or the then separate women's colleges 'to share the benefits of a great University without losing their individuality' to an extent unimaginable in the far more centralised US campus universities. Equally welcome to him was Oxford's freedom from 'the unreasoning and malicious criticism that every American university has to bear from Press and public', which left Oxford 'free to serve the nation' on its own terms. 'A professor need never fear, as in America, lest one day's classroom witticism appear the following day in a screaming headline. Nobody outside Oxford knows, and nobody within Oxford cares, if a certain professor be Communist or Fascist....'

Morison was the embodiment of his Puritan heritage in terms of its work ethic and would go on to write a fifteen volume history of US naval operations in World War Two and win two Pulitzer prizes. A diligent and prolific scholar, he was impressed by the scope Oxford afforded but distinctly unimpressed by what his colleagues did with their freedom. The tutorial system seemed to him to put a premium on style at the expense of substance, fostering a trained ability to 'make less knowledge go further'. The result was often academic in-breeding which enervated real intellectual distinction, resulting in 'too many college fellows who took a first, won a prize essay and have done nothing since'. Compared with their American counterparts Oxford fellows he thought to be 'underpaid but not overworked', teaching only twenty-four weeks a year instead of thirty or thirty-five, being paid extra for examining and 'dining' instead of merely eating. Professors were too often isolated from teaching. Post-graduate research was 'wholly unorganized and lamentably guided', with no seminars or training in research methods. It is noteworthy, in support of Morison's criticism, that the new national Institute of Historical Research, had been established in 1921 in London, not in Oxford.

Morison likewise found Oxford's libraries 'hopelessly uncoordinated and so decentralized that it requires years to learn what books on one's own subject may be found there'. As for funding, the university was failing miserably: 'in view of the many wealthy men among Oxford graduates, it seems to an American scandalous that the British taxpayer should be called upon ...'. And yet, and yet ... on returning to the

USA Morison confessed 'I shall regret ... the conversation and the company of the most humane and intelligent group of people I have ever known. My days of wine and roses are over.'

A PACIFIC PERSPECTIVE

To another perceptive visitor what was new and changing about Oxford in the 1930s was far less apparent than what was old and unchanging. Haruko Ichikawa, author of *A Japanese Lady in Europe* (1937) recorded her own reactions of thoughtful wonderment: 'When going round these gloomy chapels and halls it was necessary to say to yourself about once every thirty minutes "This is a school. We are not visiting a temple or an historic place but we are seeing a school. This is a factory where the future is brewed."' Coming from a society itself but lately feudal, she observed the feudal spirit extant in Oxford. Remarking to a landlady that it was creditable that milk-bottles could be left on door-steps and not stolen, she was taken aback by the explanation: '"the poor people in this place do have thieving minds, but they know what they are ... The slums are placed in the east of Town ...". Her proud tone of explanation seemed as if she meant that the pride of the town was the dishonest people who knew their social standing, rather than honest people.'

This sort of snobbery found literally concrete (or rather brick) expression in the notorious erection of the 'Cutteslowe walls', put up in a new Oxford suburb to segregate the inhabitants of a new development of private housing from those of an adjacent council estate. They both symbolised a social cancer at the heart of English society and also inflicted very real inconvenience on the residents of the council estate. Nevertheless they were not to be demolished until 1959.

New Fields to Conquer

Notwithstanding the justified strictures of thoughtful outsiders and a pace of change 'scarcely distinguishable from immobility', Oxford did introduce significant changes in teaching and research in the inter-war period. Compulsory Greek was dropped as an entrance requirement. A new undergraduate degree in Politics, Philosophy and Economics was established. PPE soon became a prestigious course, referred to as 'Modern Greats' and valued as a useful preparation for a career in public life. In history Maurice Powicke broadened the traditionally institutional approach to the medieval period by capitalising on Oxford's own wealth of manuscript resources. A chair in Economic History was also established. In 1930 a chair in International Relations was funded by Montague Burton, who had brought modish dress to the masculine masses as 'the Fifty Shilling Tailor'. The first holder of the chair, Alfred Zimmern, strongly endorsed the view that Oxford should be a 'nursery of statesmen' but his hope of developing 'a graduate school of government' failed to materialise. In 1935, however, an Institute of Economics and Statistics was created.

Science, in particular, expanded, with a doubling of undergraduate numbers over the inter-war period. This adjustment was long overdue in terms of national needs and the university's own interest in attracting the best intellectual talent. By 1922 half the undergraduates at Cambridge were enrolled in science or technology courses. The Canadian humourist Stephen Leacock, visiting Oxford that year, thought it had less expertise in applied science than might be found in the average theological college. The fact that Oxford has a Science Area but never felt the need to develop a specifically designated Arts Area says it all.

In large part Oxford's riposte to Cambridge's lead was thanks to the single-handed efforts of Professor Lindemann who combined organisational drive with a gift for hustling money out of industrial sponsors. He also took imaginative advantage of the flight of scientific talent out of Nazi Germany. Einstein resided at Christ Church in the summers of 1931 and 1932, dividing his hours between mathematics and the violin, but could not be persuaded to stay. Lindemann's own particular research interests led to Oxford becoming a leading centre in the fields of low temperature physics and high resolution spectroscopy. The Rockefeller Foundation gave generously to enable the university to develop special strengths in experimental psychology and clinical medicine.

The expansion of science was by no means universally applauded. Laboratories and equipment which had to be continually up-dated cost far more than libraries whose treasures had accumulated piecemeal over centuries. This necessarily increased dependence on outside, particularly government funds, undermining centuries of proud financial autonomy. Science teaching, moreover, required regular attendance at university-controlled facilities, taking undergraduates out of college and thereby eroding centuries of intellectual autonomy and allegedly threatening their social cohesion. Perhaps the jeremiahs could take comfort in the fact that on the eve of World War Two undergraduate enrolment in science and technology was still only 18.2 per cent and annual expenditures on science were still less than £100,000 a year.

THE LOOK OF THINGS: NEW BUILDINGS

It would be more accurate to speak of new buildings than new architecture. Much remained self-consciously conservative. The economic depression of the 1920s deprived colleges of the means for major projects. Trinity added a new library, Lincoln a new Rector's house, St Peter's a residential hall, all quiet essays in neo-Georgian. Balliol and All Souls commissioned modernistic projects but neither got off the drawing board. Out at Holywell Manor Balliol built a graduate hostel in rubble, to complement the medieval church of St Cross hard by. The most spectacular buildings, at least in terms of sheer bulk, were Rhodes House and the extension to the Bodleian Library (1937–40) by Sir Giles Gilbert Scott, grandson of the architect of the Martyrs' Memorial. The 'New Bod', financed largely by the Rockefeller Foundation, was essentially a warehouse surrounding an eleven-deck steel-framed bookstack housing five million volumes. Scott's combination of massive forms and miniature stone blocks was scarcely rescued by an eclectic mixture of Art Deco and Classical motifs. Other significant buildings of the 1930s were Lutyens's triumphantly syncretic Campion Hall, blending Mughal elements with an Arts and Crafts tradition, and an extension to the Radcliffe Science Library by his pupil, Sir Hubert Worthington. Its doors, by Eric Gill, depict distinguished Oxford men of science. Worthington also designed new premises for St Catherine's in St Aldate's, a residential block for Merton in Rose Lane and a new library for New College. The expansion in the number of female undergraduates led to the building of a new Front Quadrangle at Somerville and a virtual doubling in the size of Lady Margaret Hall to

The Deneke Building of Lady Margaret Hall of 1931–2 was designed by Giles
Gilbert Scott

the designs of G.G. Scott, mostly stripped-down neo-Georgian but
including a Byzantine-Romanesque chapel to rival Lutyens's creation.
Scott also designed what was to become the core of St Anne's College,
opposite the Radcliffe Infirmary.

In 1928 the city's boundaries were doubled in area. In the 1930s
Oxford's permanent population grew by a third to pass the hundred
thousand mark. Cowley, Headington, Marston and Iffley became
absorbed into the city as suburbs. Over five thousand new houses were
built. This rapid expansion, unmatched almost anywhere else in
England, was caused by the success of one man . . .

The Other William Morris

Lord Nuffield (1877–1963) was Britain's Henry Ford. He brought
motoring to the millions and then gave away the millions that
motoring had brought to him. Born William Morris, he went to the
village school at Headington. One of seven children, he was thwarted
in his dream of becoming a surgeon by the ill-health of his father and
instead went to work at fifteen. At sixteen he opened his own bicycle
repair shop, from which he had progressed by 1896 to 48 High Street,
assembling bikes and motor-bikes, running taxis and selling cars. He
began assembling a 'Morris Oxford' light car with bought-in parts in

1913 and sold a thousand at £175 each from 'Morris Garages' at 100 Holywell Street. In the depressed post-war market of 1921 he confronted a cash crisis that might have broken him by making bold price cuts, a kill or cure strategy which sent sales soaring. By 1926 he was Britain's largest volume vehicle producer, had begun to buy up his component suppliers and in that year established the Pressed Steel Company to make car bodies.

Additional plants were established in Coventry and Birmingham. In 1927 he bought up the Wolseley brand, then in 1937 Rover, meanwhile launching his own sports marque, the MG (from Morris Garages). Morris was created Viscount Nuffield in 1938 and elected FRS in 1939.

Perhaps surprisingly, Nuffield's gifts to the university were not initially in the fields of engineering or business, which had made him a rich man. In 1926 he gave £10,000 towards establishing a chair of Spanish Studies, surprised to find that few British businessmen spoke such a major world language. In 1931 he gave £70,000 to enlarge and modernise the Wingfield Hospital at Headington, which specialised in treating children crippled by heredity, accident or infectious diseases. (In 1950 it was renamed the Nuffield Orthopaedic hospital.) In 1936 Nuffield gave £2,000,000 to the university to establish the Nuffield Institute for Medical Research, a munificent gesture which coincided

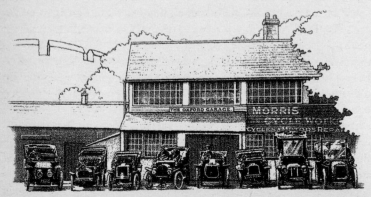

The garage in Longwall Street where William Morris built his first car in 1912

with Oxford hosting the annual meeting of the British Medical Association. Other Nuffield donations included gifts to poorer colleges such as Pembroke, Worcester and St Peter's Hall, £100,000 to the Bodleian and the same towards a new Physical Chemistry laboratory in South Parks Road.

In 1937 Nuffield offered to establish a new college on the site of the Oxford Canal wharf and basin which he had recently bought. His initial idea, apart from tidying up the western approach to the city, was a college specialising in engineering and accountancy but he was persuaded that the university's more pressing need was for a graduate college devoted to the social sciences – perhaps a vindication of Stephen Potter's angry denunciation of 'Oxford's instinctive hatred of any branch of education which is directly useful, superficially easy, or attractive'.

Nuffield not only provided the site but added £900,000 for construction and endowment. The college's, at the time unique, mission statement included a commitment to co-operation between academics and non-academics on problem-oriented projects. Provision was made for the appointment of Visiting Fellows drawn from government and business and for the admission of both male and female post-graduates.

War imposed inevitable delays in the realisation of Nuffield College. The first intake of 1945–6 had to cope in temporary accommodation as construction continued until 1949. Nuffield himself was further irked by the initial proposals for the design of the college and the hesitant progress of its academic work. When its activities did begin to bear fruit he thought the harvest more socialist than social and privately referred to his creation as 'that bloody Kremlin'. By the time he died, however, he was sufficiently convinced of its worth to bequeath it most of his remaining fortune, as well as his home, Nuffield Place – the venue for a popular college bonfire party on Guy Fawkes' Night.

Nuffield College has since become synonymous with the definitive, on-going series of general election studies, directed by the doyen of British psephologists, David Butler. It also claims to be the birthplace of an 'Oxford School' of industrial relations and to have pioneered the application of cost-benefit analysis to the problems of developing countries. Recent Nuffield projects have included investigating problems of large-scale data analysis, creating an archive dedicated to the 1966 Aberfan landslip disaster and reviewing unemployment policies across Europe. Specialised areas of expertise range from medical sociology to social statistics. In the summer of 2001 Visiting Fellows included *very* senior people drawn from the BBC, the *Financial Times*, the Court of Appeal, the Health and Safety Commission, the Government Statistical Service and the Consumers' Association. Nuffield College is physically dominated by the first tower to be built in Oxford for two centuries. In accord with its chosen policy, it has been enriched by the works of contemporary artists including John Piper, Ivon Hitchens and David Hockney.

Lord Nuffield's enduring influence has continued to stretch far beyond Oxford. His statue is to be seen at Guy's Hospital, London, of which he was a generous benefactor. The Nuffield Foundation, established with an endowment of £10,000,000 in 1943, has financed many projects which fundamentally influenced the curriculum of British schools in the teaching of science, mathematics, languages and technology; it has also extended its concerns to problems of disability, ageing and 'Bioethics'. The Nuffield Trust, founded in 1940 to co-ordinate provincial hospital co-operation in conditions of wartime emergency, now supports specialised research in the field of health policy. Nuffield funds also provide grants for hospices and recreational facilities for the armed services and baled out Manchester University's Jodrell Bank radio telescope when it ran into deficit – a generosity which reached quite literally to the stars. Nuffield's ashes are buried in Holy Trinity churchyard at Nuffield. There is no public memorial to him in the city, no statue, not even a plaque – perhaps because he qualified for the epitaph which Sir Christopher Wren's son composed for him – *Si monumentum requiris, circumspice*, if you seek his monument, look all around you.

Motopolis

John Betjeman certainly did not underestimate Nuffield's impact on Oxford: 'If ever the victory between town and gown has been decided, it has been decided now. And the victory is with Motopolis... The college buildings are endangered by motor traffic; main streets are as congested as the Strand ... buses have supplanted horse trams, the pale-faced mechanics in Oxford bags and tweed coats, walk down the Cornmarket; the farmers and labourers have disappeared; views are interrupted by motor cars; open spaces occupied by car parks ...' Betjeman did not hold Nuffield himself accountable, noting sarcastically that he had at least paid for hospitals to patch up the people his cars knocked down. Betjeman blamed the university, 'you would suppose this little Athens of European civilization ... would know something of the principles upon which a town is built... They could have planned an industrial town, with all their learning, which would have been worthy of the University City beside it. ... Morris Cowley could have been a model for the rest of England. ...'

There was, of course, another side to all this. As the Cambridge historian Peter Clarke has observed, Oxford may have been 'yanked out of the Middle Ages into a Fordist brave new world (the reverse of what an earlier William Morris had hoped for) ... but the perspective of a car worker's family ... was somewhat different. In 1934 Oxford had 5 per cent unemployment, Abertillery 50 per cent.' In 1936 the three most prosperous towns in England were Luton, Coventry and Oxford, all devoted to the manufacture of motor cars. Oxford in the inter-war years acquired eight thousand new houses and in 1938, for the first time in the history of the city, the population east of the Cherwell exceeded that to the west.

It was, indeed, all very sudden. Writing of the early 1920s Evelyn Waugh could still describe an Oxford where 'hansom cabs and open victorias were for hire ... and clergymen on bicycles were, with the cattle coming to market, the only hazards of traffic ... Correspondence was on crested cards delivered by college messengers on bicycles.'

YEARS APART, WORLDS APART

The author of *A Portrait of Oxford* (1931) recommended the following essentials for 'success' at Oxford 'plus fours; a repertoire of pornographic stories; some skill, legendary or otherwise, at golf; a Morris car; a sneer ... and an exhaustless capacity for suppurating self-conceit.' Such advice was soon to prove as worthless and dated as most 'up-to-date' advice invariably does. In contrast with the apolitical frivolity of the twenties, the thirties was to be a decade of avant-garde opinions and political commitment.

At University College the poet Stephen Spender had anticipated the trend by wearing a red tie and declaring himself a Socialist, pacifist and genius. Philip Toynbee (1916–81), great-nephew of Arnold Toynbee and grandson of Gilbert Murray, became the first Communist to be elected President of the Union. Other 1930s undergraduates included such future Labour heavyweights as Denis Healey, Michael Foot, Anthony Greenwood, Christopher Mayhew, Barbara Castle and Roy Jenkins, now the university's Chancellor. Future Labour Prime Minister Harold Wilson (1916–95) was already a junior don, while future Tory premier Edward Heath (1916–) was President of the Union in 1939.

In 1935 Nigel Nicolson (1917–) followed in the footsteps of his father, the distinguished diplomat and author Harold Nicolson (1886–1968), but was greatly initimidated by his paternal admonitions: 'Balliol does not care overmuch for the extent of a man's knowledge; it cares dreadfully for his state of mind ... what they want to find out is whether you are intelligent, not whether you are learned. They judge intelligence by the extent to which you avoid saying something stupid, rather than by the extent to which you manage to say something bright.' Nicolson drew the evident, self-protective conclusion: 'So anxious was I not to say anything stupid, that I hardly said anything at all.' His reticence was more than compensated by acquaintance with the assured John and James Pope-Hennessy; the latter's gaudy ties provoked a delegation which came to complain that he was giving the college a bad name. Within a decade James Pope-Hennessy would become the National Trust's one-man crusade for the salvation of the English country house. In old age he would also be hailed as one of the century's great diarists. Nicolson's other friends included Healey and Heath and he also managed to acquire a presentation copy of *Zuleika Dobson* from the author himself. Nigel's artist brother Ben, meanwhile, lodged at 7 Beaumont Street with Stuart Hampshire, who would go on to a brilliant career as a philosopher and become Warden of Wadham in succession to Bowra, and Jo Grimond, future leader of the Liberal

Party. Nigel Nicolson became the co-founder of the publishing firm of Weidenfeld and Nicolson and an accomplished biographer.

Other literary undergraduates of the 1930s included Canadian novelist Robertson Davies (1913–95) (Balliol), the dramatist (Sir) Terence Rattigan (1911–77), Nobel Laureate (Sir) William Golding (1911–93) (BNC); and Booker Prize winner (Dame) Iris Murdoch (1919–99), who was to become a philosophy tutor at her own college, St Anne's. In 1926 the Oxford Union had debated and voted in favour of levelling all women's colleges. (It did not admit women to membership until 1964.) The motion and result were emblematic of a carefree decade. In 1933, by contrast, the Union famously debated and voted (two hundred and seventy-five to a hundred and fifty-three) that it would not 'fight for King and Country' in the event of a future conflict. Newspapers dismissed the gesture as perverse or juvenile but it did not pass unnoticed in Nazi Germany. Nevertheless when war did come Oxford responded as before. Of the Trinity boat crew which won the Eights Week races in 1939 only two were to survive the conflict.

CHAPTER NINE

Pillar of the Establishment

Evacuees and Refugees

In 1914 Oxford had taken in the Belgians; in 1940, when the Blitz began in earnest it took in city children, ten to fifteen thousand in October alone. Sir William Beveridge personally welcomed a contingent to temporary accommodation in University College but hundreds more were consigned to scandalous squalor in a disused cinema. Like any other forced population movement evacuation involved an element of cultural encounter. One pair of kindly but prim Oxford ladies were singularly startled when their Cockney waif breezily informed them that he would put himself to bed 'so you two old geezers can get off to the boozer'. The female students of London's Slade School of Art represented a more comely enhancement of the Oxford scene.

No one, of course, then *knew* that Oxford would be entirely spared from bombing, although it certainly seemed a less certain target than London or Birmingham. Ambulance depots were established at Norham Mews and Cowley Place and a specially designed fire-fighting vessel, *Abel*, launched on the river. The owner of a local taxi service trained thirty volunteer drivers how to handle a taxi with a makeshift trailer for carrying stretcher-cases. Oxford's ARP detachment included such luminaries as the Regius Professor of Civil Law, Francis de Zulueta, who also busied himself with succouring Polish and Jewish refugees. Allegedly Oxford's total exemption from bombing came about because Hitler had scheduled it as the new capital of a Nazi-occupied Britain, qualified for the role by its central location and concentration of fine architecture.

The evacuees came, by schools, because they were told to. So were many Whitehall bureaucrats, who came by departments. The Ministry of Food, a war-time creation, took over St John's College. Regent's Park College, which began as a Particular Baptist seminary in Stepney in 1810 and had established an Oxford foothold in Mansfield College in 1927, severed its connection with its London base when the Admiralty requisitioned its Regent's Park premises.

Individual adults came of choice. Croatian-born sculptor Oscar Nemon (1906–85) fled Brussels, where he had trained and roomed with Magritte, just before the outbreak of the war and settled at Boar's Hill, where he built a studio-residence, gratefully dubbed Pleasant Land. Sir Max Beerbohm taught him English, Nemon eventually reciprocating by casting a bust now in the possession of Merton College. Another friend was Sir Karl Parker of the Ashmolean, which likewise possesses a portrait bust of Parker by Nemon. Perhaps an element of gratitude or reciprocation is embodied in the works for which Nemon is best known, his monumental portrayals of Churchill which adorn Windsor Castle and the Guildhall in the City of London. Other Oxford examples of Nemon's work include busts of Queen Elizabeth II in the hall at Christ Church and Harold Macmillan in the Oxford Union. Nemon remained in Oxford for the remainder of his life, dying in the Radcliffe and leaving uncompleted a projected depiction of Diana, Princess of Wales.

Another European refugee was the Phaidon Press, which specialised in high-quality books on art. Founded by Dr Bela Horvitz in Vienna in 1923, its proprietors fled the Nazi Anschluss to settle at 14 St Giles. Relocating to London after the war Phaidon returned for a while in 1975. Its most famous publication was Sir Ernst Gombrich's magisterial best-seller *The Story of Art*.

Having been bombed out of his London lodgings during the first phase of the Blitz, the Chinese author-artist Chiang Yee settled with the Keene family in Southmoor Road for the following two years, in an Oxford of coal-rationing and Dig for Victory allotments. Acquaintance with some Chinese undergraduates and a few literary-minded dons gave him tangential access to college life. The varied life of an exile had brought him some distinguished acquaintances – Gilbert

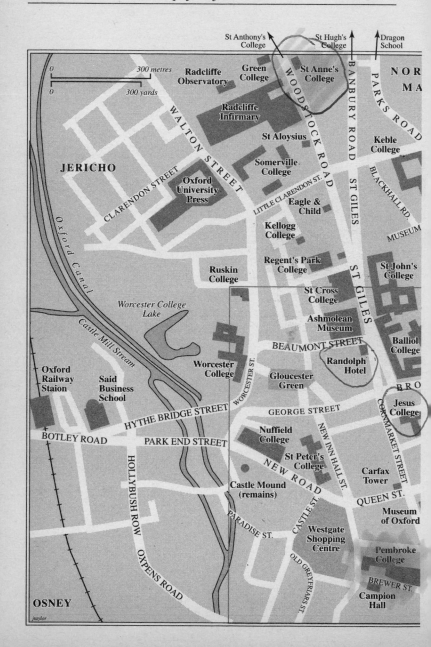

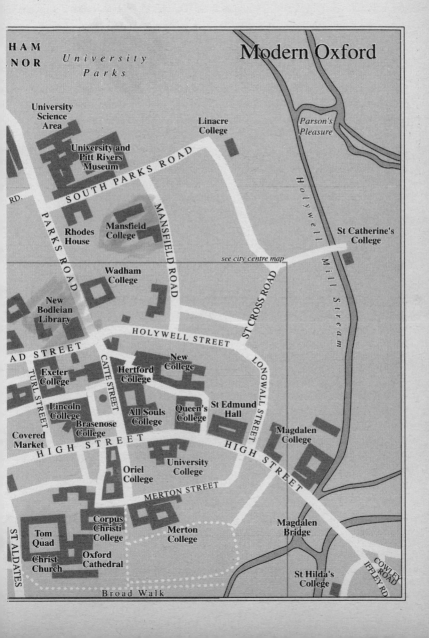

HAM
NOR

University Parks

Modern Oxford

University Science Area

Linacre College

Parson's Pleasure

University and Pitt Rivers Museum

SOUTH PARKS ROAD

RD.

PARKS ROAD

Rhodes House

Mansfield College

MANSFIELD ROAD

Holywell

St Catherine's College

see city centre map

Wadham College

New Bodleian Library

ST CROSS ROAD

Mill Stream

HOLYWELL STREET

AD STREET

CATTE STREET

New College

Exeter College

TURL STREET

Hertford College

LONGWALL STREET

Lincoln College

All Souls College

Queen's College

St Edmund Hall

Brasenose College

Magdalen College

Covered Market

HIGH STREET

Oriel College

University College

HIGH STREET

MERTON STREET

ST ALDATES

Tom Quad

Corpus Christi College

Merton College

Magdalen Bridge

Christ Church

Oxford Cathedral

St Hilda's College

COWLEY ROAD

IFFLEY RD

Broad Walk

Murray, Robert Helpmann, Sir William Beveridge – but for the most part, he continued in the solitary mode which had provided the material for his *Silent Traveller* books. These were reflective accounts of Lakeland, the Yorkshire Dales and London, punctuated with whimsical poems and delicate paintings in an idiosyncratic style which blended the traditions of a Chinese classical education with a sophisticated understanding of European culture. Chiang was typically inspired by the interplay of man and nature, the slurred crunch of a late pedestrian's hurrying footsteps on a snowy night, the puttering sound of an invisible canal boat on a misty morning, the seeming indifference of pre-occupied passers-by to the brief, blossoming glory of 'the three little cherry-trees standing negligently in the left corner by the wall of Meadow Building' at Christ Church. In *The Silent Traveller in Oxford* he takes Shelley's monument as 'a testimony to the admirable English capacity for correcting their faults' because it 'was erected in the college from which he was expelled'. Circling the pond around the statue of Mercury in Tom Quad, he notes the contentment of its inhabitants and is reminded of a disputation between sages so apposite as to imply that he had somehow become subliminally attuned to Oxford philosophers' preoccupation with language without ever actually meeting any of them. Thus:

> '... our great philosopher Chuang Tzu ... with his friend Hui Tzu, was crossing the bridge over the river Hao when he exclaimed how happy the fish seemed ... "You are not a fish," remarked Hui Tzu. "How do you know?" "You are not me," Chuang Tzu retorted. "How do you know that I do not know?" "Very well, I am not you," Hui Tzu replied. "But still you are not a fish, so it is obvious you do not know." "Let us return to our original point," Chuang Tzu pursued. "You asked me *how* I know that fish are happy: that means that *you already knew that I knew* fish are happy when you asked me." '

Very Oxford.

Perhaps it was as well that Mr Chiang's acquaintance with academia was so limited, as even his restricted awareness of donnish foibles inspired him to uncharacteristically acerbic observations, such as the advice that the casual visitor should not ask 'a don to show you the sights, because each has his own pet Oxford . . . and you will not see the real Oxford'.

Heroes

Reasonableness does not win wars and so is at something of a discount in wartime. Arrogance, obsession and daring come to the fore. And so did Oxonians, possessed of those qualities in abundance, to provide the full range of heroes – conventional, bravura and downright eccentric.

Highlander Brigadier Lorne Campbell of Airds (1902–91), a distinguished Merton sportsman, was awarded the DSO at Dunkirk, a bar to it at El Alamein and a VC in Tunisia. Oliver Philpot (1913–93) of Worcester College had learned to fly with the University Air Squadron. In 1943 he became one of the three POWs whose escape from Stalag Luft III in Silesia inspired the post-war film *The Wooden Horse*. Ingeniously adapting the legendary ruse which had deceived the Trojans, Philpot and his companions used a vaulting horse to conceal tunnelling operations while fellow-prisoners distracted camp guards with daily routines of gymnastic exercises. All three escapees scored a 'home run', reaching neutral Sweden and safety. Philpot's contemporary, Lt. Col. Alan Palmer (1913–90) of Exeter College and the Huntley & Palmer biscuit-making dynasty, fought alongside Albanian Communist partisans to become head of the Special Operations Executive in Tirana and a close comrade of the post-war dictator, Enver Hoxha.

Australian-born Spitfire pilot Richard Hillary (1919–43), a product of Oxford University's Air Squadron, was shot down for a second time and hideously burned at the height of the Battle of Britain. He had himself in the space of six days accounted for five 'kills' and been credited with a further two 'probables'. Hillary recounted his experiences and his ordeal of reconstructive plastic surgery in *The Last Enemy*, which made him nationally famous and was reprinted continuously throughout the war. Hillary insisted on returning to active duty and was killed, in unknown circumstances, at the controls of a Bristol Blenheim on a night operation. Another literary talent lost in combat was Keith Douglas (1920–44), a pupil of Edmund Blunden at Merton.

His *Selected Poems*, reflecting on Cairo, combat and corpses, appeared in 1943. He was killed in Normandy the following year. His experimental narrative of desert warfare, *Alamein to Zem Zem*, appeared in 1946. Sidney Keyes (1922–43) editor of *Cherwell* and of *Eight Oxford Poets*, published a first volume of brooding verse, *The Iron Laurel*, before being killed in Tunisia after just a fortnight in action. A posthumous collection, *The Cruel Solstice*, won the Hawthornden Prize.

Robert Runcie (1921–2000) served in the Scots Guards as a tank commander and was awarded the MC for wiping out a German gun emplacement under heavy fire, a feat which caused him occasional embarrassment when he became Archbishop of Canterbury as he would rather have been given it for the previous day's act of gallantry, pulling out a crewman out of a blazing tank under fire. He returned to BNC to take a first in Greats.

For many Oxonians the war came as a second turn around. After reading Law at Christ Church Col. Frank 'Monocle' Morgan (1893–1992) had served in the Camel Corps against the Turks in World War I and became a leading Signals boffin in World War Two. Group Captain Fred Winterbotham (1897–1990), another Christ Church man, having served as a pilot and a POW in the Great War managed to inveigle himself into membership of the Luftwaffe Club in the 1930s and subsequently headed the 'Ultra' team which deciphered German air force communications traffic from its supposedly unbreakable Enigma code. Ex-rugby star General Sir Philip Christison (1893–1993) of University College (of which he later became an honorary Fellow), having been awarded the MC at Loos in 1915 and a bar to it at Arras the following year, was awarded a DSO in World War Two for his command in Burma against the Japanese. A noted ornithologist, Christison also possessed a flair for languages which enabled him to stiffen a wavering line of compatriots with a Gaelic ballad in the Great War and to harangue his Indian troops in Urdu thirty years later.

Carton de Wiart briefly commanded the Midlands Territorial of the 61st Division, headquartered in Oxford before skilfully extricating a doomed expeditionary unit from Norway, being shot down and captured by the Italians and ending the war as Churchill's personal representative to Chiang Kai-Shek. An elegantly piratical-looking figure, he was memorably described as the Max Beerbohm of the world of danger. J.C. Masterman (1899–1971), caught and interned in Germany during the Great War, during World War Two master-minded the turning of German agents through the 'double-cross' procedure which took its name from the twenty person (hence XX, double cross) committee which supervised it. Its greatest achievement was to convince the Germans that the D-Day landings would be in Pas-de-Calais, not Normandy. The multi-talented Masterman, a novelist and dramatist, who had once played tennis and hockey for England and toured Canada with the MCC, returned to serve as Provost of Worcester and Vice-Chancellor and to found the Oxford Historic Buildings Fund.

The city as well as the university contributed its quota of leaders. On D-day Major John Howard, a former policeman serving with the 2nd Battalion Oxfordshire and Buckinghamshire Light Infantry, led a glider-borne task force to seize two vital bridges at Ranville and Bénouville in Normandy. Bookseller Richard Blackwell (1918–80), a lieutenant in the RNVR, served on the Arctic convoys and was awarded the DSC while serving in the Mediterranean.

WAR EFFORTS

As during the Great War the Examination Schools once again became a military hospital, St Hugh's became a nurses' home. The Radcliffe Infirmary was greatly expanded. The city of Oxford's interwar industrial growth enabled it to make a significant contribution to the output of war materiel. The Morris factory at Cowley produced over six hundred and fifty tanks. At Pressed Steel, where cartridge cases were a major line, the number of female workers increased more than tenfold, from two hundred and eighteen in 1938 to 2,435 by 1942. Oxford was also home to an Inter-Service Topographical Department which could draw on local printing skills. Two specialist compositors were detached from OUP to join a secret printing unit at Woburn Abbey, turning out German language propaganda leaflets. Members of the university were recruited to turn out the propaganda.

Socialist enfant terrible R.H.S. – 'Dick' – Crossman (1907–74), a former New College don and leader of the Labour Group on Oxford

City Council was drafted into the Ministry of Economic Warfare to direct British propaganda against Germany, where he had lived for a 'gap' year before taking up his fellowship. In 1932 Latvian-born Isaiah Berlin (1907–97) became the first Jew ever to be elected to All Souls; during the war he was seconded to the British embassies in Moscow and Washington, composing reports which Churchill found so impressive that he famously invited the composer Irving Berlin to lunch, erroneously believing them to be the same person. Churchill, knowing the All Souls philosopher had written brilliantly on Tolstoy and Machiavelli, asked his guest what he thought his best composition and was bemused by the reply *White Christmas.* Isaiah Berlin returned in due course to gain a knighthood and the Order of Merit and become first President of Wolfson College.

The strengthening of the university's science base likewise enlarged its capacity to support the nation's struggle for survival. An Air Ministry committee chaired by Tizard had already ensured that radar had come to its timely fruition. Lindemann, a friend of Churchill since 1921, became his chief scientific adviser – 'the Prof' – first at the Admiralty, then at No. 10, writing some 2,000 minutes for him in the course of the war. In 1941 the Prime Minister created him Baron Cherwell of Oxford. In the opinion of Lord Blake, Master of Queen's College, who contributed the entry on Cherwell to the *Dictionary of National Biography*, through his relationship with Churchill, the Prof exercised more influence on public life than any previous scientist in British history.

Zoologist Solly Zuckerman (1904–93) turned to examining the effects of bomb blast and Wadham's R.V. Jones, himself the son of an army sergeant, devised counter-measures against German bomber guidance systems and became chief scientific adviser to MI6; but in applying the physical sciences to techniques of warfare it must be admitted that the overwhelming input of high-level academic talent was provided by Cambridge.

Although Oxford sent its share of talent to the great code-breaking factory which was assembled at Bletchley Park, its most important single achievement was the transformation of penicillin from an anomalous curiosity, first noted by Alexander Fleming in 1928, to a usable drug, the first antibiotic. The breakthrough was achieved by former Rhodes scholar Howard Florey (1898–1968) and Ernst Chain (1906–79), a German biochemist and refugee from Nazi Germany. Florey, the son of an Oxfordshire shoemaker who had emigrated to Australia, had been offered the chair of pathology in his thirties. In 1945 he would share the Nobel Prize for Medicine with Chain and Fleming. Later he would become Provost of Queen's and Baron Florey of Adelaide and be honoured in the naming of the Florey Building and with a memorial in Westminster Abbey. Penicillin was first used experimentally on an Oxford policeman brought to death's door by an infection contracted while pruning roses. With no feasible alternative treatment there was nothing to lose by treating him as a guinea-pig. The effect of the penicillin was instantaneous and almost visibly 'miraculous' as the patient regained strength – until supplies ran out. Desperately the doctors recycled what they could recover from the patient's urine but lost the battle to save him after a month. The overstretched capacities of war-time Britain were unequal to the challenge of mass-producing the new 'wonder drug' but the industrial muscle of the United States brought supplies on-stream in time for the Allied counter-offensives which rolled back the Axis conquests. A small garden by the entrance to the Botanic Gardens honours the achievement of Florey's team.

Another life-saving Oxford achievement was the establishment of the Oxford Committee for Famine Relief – Oxfam from 1965 – at a meeting in the university church of St Mary the Virgin in 1942. Gilbert Murray was a founder member but Oxford businessman Cecil Jackson-Cole (1901–79), a former student of G.D.H. Cole, served as honorary secretary from then until his death, bringing to the role an inspirational blend of Christian conviction and business acumen. Initially concerned with preventing famine in German-occupied Europe, especially Greece and then the Netherlands, after the war Oxfam focused its efforts on defeated Germany and then, persuaded by Jackson-Cole's dynamism and vision, broadened its scope to reach out to Palestine, India, Korea and Hungary. Autonomous Oxfams were created in Canada, Quebec, the USA, Belgium and Germany. Oxfam's first permanent shop, opened at 17 Broad Street in 1948, is still there but is now one of a thousand. A purpose-built headquarters was opened in

Summertown in 1962. By 1985 Oxfam's annual income was exceeding £50,000,000, making it one of Britain's largest charities. Jackson-Cole, who was also responsible for founding Help the Aged and Action Aid, refused all civic and national honours.

THOSE ALSO SERVE ...

The normal routines of undergraduate life were disrupted rather than virtually annihilated as they had been a generation previously. Many undergraduates came up at seventeen and joined up after a year. A two year 'war degree' was introduced and those who could only manage a third or a fourth class in the examinations en route to achieving it were summarily sent down and into the forces. In recognition of their potential value for the war effort medical, dentistry, science and engineering students were usually allowed to complete their full courses. Varsity cricket and rugby matches were still held and so was the Boat Race but at college level some teams had to rely on college servants to make up their numbers, a seeming concession to the prevailing democratic ethos of a People's War that did not outlast it. The production of academic gowns was halted by war-time rationing and the scarcity of mortar boards meant that it was no longer *de rigueur* to wear them on formal occasions. In this respect the university fell into line with the rest of the respectable classes, the Church of England having patriotically decreed that female members of congregations would not necessarily be expected to wear a hat to church. The Senior Common Room at St John's was at one point reduced to serving sausages and mash for lunch.

Against a background of privation and inconvenience teaching carried on. The undergraduate body included many figures of future literary distinction, including Kingsley Amis, John Mortimer and Philip Larkin, whose first novel, *Jill*, is set against a background of wartime Oxford. Margaret Thatcher, then Margaret Roberts, read chemistry at Somerville and went on to do postgraduate research. Not only would she become Britain's first woman Prime Minister but also the first premier ever to have been trained as a scientist. Actor Richard Burton (1925–84) had six months reading English at Exeter College while training for the RAF and fell under the spell of Nevill Coghill, who reciprocated, cast him as Angelo in his OUDS production of *Measure for*

Measure and proclaimed him a 'genius'. He was to return in 1966 to appear in a fund-raiser. St Peter's gave him an honorary fellowship in 1973 but his self-confessed yearnings for academia proved short-lived.

WILLIAM BEVERIDGE

William Beveridge (1879–1963) had a brilliant undergraduate career at Balliol, where he was a contemporary of his future brother-in-law, socialist historian R.H. Tawney. Beveridge then walked away from an equally brilliant legal career to serve as sub-warden at Toynbee Hall, then assist Churchill in establishing labour exchanges and the nation's first system of National Insurance and then become director of the London School of Economics, which he transformed into a world class centre for social sciences. He returned to Oxford in 1937 as Master of University College and in 1941 was commissioned to make recommendations for the rationalisation of the social services which had proliferated untidily in response to the exigencies of the inter-war depression. Beveridge, however, went far beyond his brief to outline a visionary 'cradle to grave' scheme of post-war welfare provision. The 1942 'Beveridge Report' achieved the unusual distinction for a government publication of becoming a best-seller and its projected programme – the abolition of the five evil giants of Idleness, Ignorance, Disease, Squalor and Want – became an agenda for a New Jerusalem, warmly greeted by a British public eager for a war aim related to their needs and interests. Churchill, all too aware that even victory would leave the nation economically exhausted, was furious – how was it all to be paid for ? In the event it was not to be his problem. The post-war Labour administration of Clement Attlee – coincidentally a graduate of University College and Toynbee Hall – took the Beveridge Report and his non-official 1944 report on *Full Employment in a Free Society* as the blueprint for the welfare state, ennobling their author in 1946. Beveridge retired to Oxford in 1954, devoting much time to a history of price movements for which he believed he would be chiefly remembered.

NEW JERUSALEM

The post-war Oxford generation of the 1940s was to prove as talented as the post-war generation of the 1920s thought it was. Tony Crosland was President of the Union in 1946, Tony Benn in 1947 and Robin Day in 1950. The membership of the Oxford University Dramatic Society numbered a galaxy of future talents: actors Nigel Davenport and Robert Hardy; directors Lindsay Anderson, John Schlesinger, Tony Richardson, Kenneth Tynan and Sandy Wilson; stalwarts of *The Archers* Jack May and Norman Painting; not to mention industrialist (Sir) Peter Parker, broadcaster Robert Robinson, novelists John Fowles and John Cornwell (John Le Carré) and Labour Cabinet minister Shirley Williams (daughter of Vera Brittain). The following generation of 'New Elizabethans' graduating in the optimistic early 1950s included broadcaster Magnus Magnusson, TV producer Jeremy Isaacs, author Lady Antonia Fraser and media mogul Rupert Murdoch who edited *Cherwell* and would later give Oxford a chair in English.

The linkage has remained strong between Oxford and the 'creative' sector which assumed growing importance culturally and economically in Britain from the 'Swinging Sixties' onwards. Oxford contributed Richard Ingrams to *Private Eye*, Alan Bennett and Dudley Moore to *Beyond the Fringe*, and Michael Palin and Terry Jones to *Monty Python's Flying Circus*. A subsequent generation of broadcast humour is represented by Angus Deayton and Rowan Atkinson. David Dimbleby and Melvyn Bragg became broadcast heavyweights, John Birt a controversial Director-General of the BBC and Dennis Potter a controversial playwright. Female broadcasters of distinction include Esther Rantzen, Kate Adie, Libby Purves, Zeinab Badawi and Sister Wendy Becket. Novelists include Julian Barnes, Martin Amis, Timothy Mo, Vikram Seth and Penelope Lively. Among noted critics and cultural gatekeepers are Anthony Thwaite, Tom Paulin, A.N. Wilson, Marina Warner and Humphrey Carpenter, author of biographies of Tolkien and Auden and studies of The Inklings and the 'Brideshead Generation'.

Internationalisation

The global scope of World War Two gave a new urgency to the study of modern languages and recent history which was sustained by the uncertainties of the emerging Cold War. The partition of the Raj, the evacuation of Palestine and the withdrawal of Burma and Ireland from the Commonwealth all emphasised the extent to which Britain had to try harder to comprehend a world it could no longer command. As for Britain, so for the forcing-house of its élite. Oxford's potential for internationalisation has, however, traditionally been limited by its organisational and procedural peculiarities, which have inhibited transfers from North American and European university systems. Internationalisation has therefore often taken the form of creating distinct institutions or programmes, offering Oxford on Oxford's own terms.

Backed by the French Government and the Sorbonne, the Maison Française was founded in 1945 to strengthen Anglo-French relations by building up a specialist library, stocking current periodicals, organising lectures, colloquia and cultural activities and providing a base for researchers. It acquired a permanent home in Norham Road in 1967 in a building designed by Jacques Laurent and opened by André Malraux.

In 1946 an Institute for Colonial Studies was established as an academic base for what would come to be known as 'development studies'. Essentially the creation of Margery Perham, the first official, and first woman, Fellow of Nuffield College, it revealed in its very title how far Oxford and Britain had yet to adjust to the realities of a decolonising world. Ironically one its major achievements was the rescue from possible destruction of overseas records charting that very process.

St Antony's, Oxford's most cosmopolitan college, now drawing its postgraduate students from over forty countries and with former students living in over one hundred and twenty, is appropriately dedicated to international relations and area studies. Its founder was M. Antonin Besse (1877–1951), a Levantine businessman based in Aden who had made a fortune from shipping. Evelyn Waugh allegedly used him as the model for the character of Youkoumian in *Black Mischief*. Culturally French but with a Scottish wife, in 1948 Besse donated £1,500,000 which was used to convert the former Anglican Holy Trinity convent in St Giles built in 1866–8 to the designs of local architect Charles Buckeridge. Since then striking new buildings have been added thanks to the generosity of the Ford, Volkswagen and Gulbenkian foundations. The first Warden, Sir William Deakin, brought to the post an international outlook honed by his hazardous war-time experiences among Yugoslav partisans. In 1962 St Antony's became the first Oxford college to admit men and women on equal terms.

New Oxford

The long delayed formal opening to Sir Giles Gilbert Scott's New Bodleian building in 1946 was blighted by a moment of bathos when the ceremonial key to its main entrance snapped off in the hands of King George VI. In 1948 town planner Thomas Sharp revived a proposal to relieve the city centre's traffic congestion by driving a new road across Christ Church meadow. The resulting brouhaha made conservation issues a permanent feature of Oxford politics thenceforth. In 1956 Oxford became the first city outside London to legislate for a Green Belt to protect it from haphazard development. An Oxford Historic Buildings Fund, established in 1957, paid for an ongoing programme of cleaning and restoration.

Local industry continued to thrive as the Morris Minor (dismissed by Nuffield as looking like a poached egg) found favour with the motoring public and Pressed Steel's subsidiary, Prestcold, profited from the growth in commercial and domestic demand for refrigeration. In 1952 Morris merged with Austin to create the British Motor Corporation which spawned another winner with the launch of the 'Mini' car in 1959. It was fitting that such an icon of sixties 'liberation' should be launched in the year in which the notorious Cutteslowe walls were finally demolished. The city's economic buoyancy continued to stimulate immigration which included bus conductors from the West Indies and forced migrants from East Africa. In the 1960s much of the former population of St Ebbe's, comprehensively demolished in that decade, was relocated to the new Blackbird Leys housing estate, built south of the city from 1957 onwards.

The troubled history of Britain's motor industry from the 1970s took its toll at Cowley where the former Morris empire was to be completely expunged to make way for the Oxford Business Park. The workforce shrank correspondingly, from a peak of 28,000 to 6,000. In 1988 Cowley celebrated the production of the 100,000th Rover 800 but in 1996 control of the plant passed to BMW, which launched a new version of the celebrated 'Mini' in 2001. Unipart, producing automotive parts and accessories, remains another major local employer. Socially the consequences of these changes was a 'Midlandisation' of Oxford east of Magdalen bridge, a process already noted by Betjeman back in 1938 as marked by the advent of 'multiple stores, arcades, cinemas, neon lights. . .', which reduced the city centre to the status of 'the Latin Quarter of Cowley'. Industrialised, suburbanised and intermittently gentrified, Cowley also acquired a distinctly multicultural character as a place where curry and kebabs had displaced scones and Earl Grey tea as standard student fare. For many undergraduates from 'normal' social backgrounds the area was embraced as more welcoming and workable than the arcane and often still antiquated environment of a college quad. Writing in 1970 the quintessentially donnish Dacre Balsdon recorded with some puzzlement undergraduates' 'enormous fascination for flat-dwelling'.

In the city centre the readjustment of the local economy was symbolised by the opening of the Westgate and Clarendon shopping centres and the closure of the Oxpens Cattle Market. A refurbished Oxford Playhouse reopened in 1996 and historic Oxford Castle ceased to be a prison that same year. The continuing expansion of tourism and higher education in the locality helped to offset the economic damage caused by the contraction of the labour force in manufacturing. Indirectly at least the university has reasserted its traditional influence on local employment as Oxford has become Britain's biggest publishing centre outside London and one of the largest medical research complexes in Europe. Future directions are indicated by the construction of an Islamic Centre in Marston Road and a new Business School near the railway station, the £20,000,000 gift of Syrian entrepreneur Wafic Said. In 2001 a *Financial Times* survey nominated the latter's one year MBA course the best in Britain.

SHIFTING TO SCIENCE

The indisputable contribution of science to victory in World War Two testified, in Correlli Barnett's striking phrase, that 'the white coat could rank with the khaki and the blue as a garb of national salvation'. In peacetime it was increasingly seen as the key to economic salvation and therefore worthy of generous financial backing from the government. During the 1950s and 1960s the physical space occupied by science-related activities at Oxford doubled. By 1961 31 per cent of undergraduates were following science and technology courses and by 1964 annual expenditure on science exceeded £4,000,000. On a collegiate basis the percentage of science dons averaged 32.8 per cent but there were wide variations between the leaders of change – St Catherine's (56 per cent), Balliol (41 per cent) Merton and Wadham (40 per cent) – and the laggards, Queen's and Keble (23 per cent) and Christ Church (22 per cent).

Existing fields of excellence like clinical medicine and engineering expanded and new areas of study, such as metallurgy and computing, were established. New buildings went up to house such specialisms as nuclear physics, zoology and psychology. The chemistry department grew to become the biggest in Europe. Between 1945 and 1973 Oxford scientists were awarded six Nobel Prizes – against seven for the whole of France. By 1974 43 per cent of dons were in science and technology – a higher proportion than at Harvard or Yale – as against 38 per cent in the arts and 19 per cent in social sciences.

Roger Bannister breaks the four-minute mile at the University Athletic Ground in Iffley Road on 6 May 1954. Then a medical student, he was later Master of Pembroke College

Despite these dramatic developments Oxford somehow continued to retain the image of an 'arts' university in the eyes of journalists and politicians and to a very great extent within the ranks of the university itself. Science dons were in danger of becoming second class citizens – 'nondons' – because most held university appointments, rather than college fellowships. Four out of five in such fields as pharmacology, botany, anatomy and zoology had no college connection. In 1962 Oxford's five hundred and sixty fellows not only still out-numbered its four hundred and twenty-six nondons but also effectively shut them out of the university's machinery of government. Of three hundred and eighteen significantly powerful positions college fellows held two hundred and sixty-six, with a majority coming from just half a dozen colleges. Between 1962 and 1973 no less than six committees were formed to tackle the issue of what to do about the nondons. As a result five of the wealthiest colleges agreed to fund the establishment in 1965 of two new colleges to be designated St Cross and Iffley, the latter becoming Wolfson College. St Cross, initially located in a former schoolhouse on St Cross Road, far to the east of the city centre, in 1981 was able to acquire a nine hundred and ninety-nine year lease on Pusey House, thanks to the generosity of local publishing magnate Richard Blackwell, after whom its main quadrangle is named. It has remained small but accepts graduate students in all subjects, a fact well attested by the range of academic interests of its fellows: Fungal Genetics, Spanish Linguistics, Optoelectronic Engineering, Islamic Numismatics and Carpet Studies. Wolfson, blessed with an exceptional site beside the Cherwell, was housed in striking new (1968–74) buildings by the prestigious architectural partnership of Powell and Moya, grouped around the former home of J.B.S. Haldane and funded by grants from the Wolfson and Ford foundations ably solicited by its first President, Sir Isaiah Berlin. It soon became the largest graduate institution in Britain, taking pride in its informality – no High Table, no chapel and gowns only on very special occasions.

'CATS'

If New College epitomised Oxford's relationship with the medieval church and Balliol its relationship with the Victorian empire, St

Catherine's epitomised its evolving relationship to post-war British society. 'Oxford's annex for underprivileged boys' was differentiated by its orientation towards science and the predominance of working-class recruits and state school pupils among its intake. Technically founded in 1962 'Cats' can trace its origins back for almost a century before that. In 1850 the status of Nobleman was abolished as part of the university reforms of that year – but so also was that of Servitor, making it difficult for poor men to gain entry. In 1868 a society was founded to matriculate men who did not belong to any college or hall but would become subject to the discipline of a Delegacy of Non-Collegiate Students, aka 'unattached'. Over the course of the next half century it acquired various paraphernalia of collegiate existence: debating, musical and historical societies, a barge, a sportsground, college colours and a magazine. From 1931 this society was known as St Catherine's to commemorate an early club room believed (wrongly) to stand on the site of a chapel dedicated to that saint. Alumni who achieved graduation via St Catherine's have included Eric Williams, Prime Minister of Trinidad; Sir Grantley Adams, Premier of Barbados; Nobel Laureates Sir John Cornforth and Dr John Vane; Olympic gold medalist David Hemery; and industrialist J. Paul Getty.

St Catherine's was among the first men's colleges to admit women and was at the forefront in developing links with business. In all these respects it thus foreshadowed changes other colleges would eventually embrace. Much credit was owed to the dynamic leadership of its first Master, historian Alan (Lord) Bullock (1914–), a former researcher for Churchill, who raised £3,000,000 in funds from Courtaulds, Guinness, Shell and other British well-wishers and the Wolfson, Sunley, Ford and Rockefeller foundations, and to the generosity of American Dr Rudolph Light, a St Catherine's alumnus, who donated 20,000 shares in Upjohn Pharmaceuticals.

St Catherine's has had a nomadic existence. Initially headquartered in the Old Clarendon building, it moved in 1888 to larger premises designed by T.G. Jackson, adjoining his new Examination Schools and in 1936 to new buildings in St Aldate's. The college finally found its permanent home in Holywell Great Meadow, between two arms of the Cherwell, in handsome buildings by Danish architect Arne

Jacobsen (1902–71) who designed every detail down to the cutlery and chairs used in the dining hall (given by Esso Petroleum), which is the largest in Oxford – or Cambridge.

When St Catherine's vacated its St Aldate's premises they became the home of Linacre House, a society for graduate students, named in honour of the Tudor medical pioneer. In 1978 Linacre moved to St Cross Road, taking over Cherwell Edge, former home of the historian J.A. Froude, which had subsequently been a Catholic convent and part of St Anne's College. Linacre, up-graded to the status of a college, is multi-disciplinary in its intake but has a special commitment to environmental studies, reflected in both the prestigious annual Linacre Lectures series, a specialised MSc programme and a concern to manage the college itself in conformity with best standards of environmental practice.

Green College, founded in 1977, was originally to be called after Dr Radcliffe, being housed in the Radcliffe Observatory and intended for graduate students in clinical medicine. Its name reflects the generosity of its founder, Cecil Green, founder of Texas Instruments but born a Mancunian, whose parents emigrated to Canada. The college coat of arms incorporates the 'lone star' of Texas.

POSTGRADUATE EXPANSION

In 1938 Oxford had just five hundred and thirty-six postgraduates, representing 11 per cent of its student body. By 1956 the figure had risen to 1,110, more than doubling to 2,609 a decade later. By 1986 there were 3,530 postgraduates, representing some 27 per cent of the total student body. Oxford now comes second only to the much larger University of London in terms of both the absolute numbers and the percentage of its student population represented by postgraduates.

Alongside the growth in postgraduate numbers came a proliferation in specialised study centres and research units, illustrating the ever-broadening range of the university's intellectual realm. The 1960s saw the establishment of a Centre for Criminological Research Unit and a Religious Experience Research Unit. In 1972 came a Transport Studies Unit, the Wellcome Unit for the History of Medicine, a Centre

A.J. Ayer, Wykeham Professor of Logic between 1959 and 1978

for Sociol-Legal Studies and a Centre for Postgraduate Hebrew Studies. The Nissan Institute of Japanese Studies, housed at St Antony's, opened in 1981 and an Institute for Energy Studies in 1982. Since then have been added Britain's largest Humanities Computing Unit, a Centre for Galician studies (1991), a Centre for the Study of Ancient Documents (1995), a Centre for Brazilian Studies (1997), a Research Archive for Greek and Roman Sculpture (1998), a collaborative (with Warwick) Centre on Skills, Knowledge and Organizational Performance (1998) – among many others.

THE OTHER OTHER PLACE

Oxford Brookes University can trace its origin to the Oxford School of Art established in a single room of the Taylorian Institution in 1865. In 1870 a School of Science was added and in 1888 a chemistry laboratory. In 1891 Oxford City Council's Technical Instruction Committee took over control and in 1894 the institution re-opened on a new site in St Ebbe's, teaching mainly via evening classes. Within five years the rapid expansion of the school showed that there was a great demand for its offerings and that further site expansion was needed. Instead there was proliferation. When John Brookes was appointed Vice-Principal in 1928 classes were being held on nineteen different sites. A year later architecture was added to the range of offerings; guest lecturers included such luminaries as Kenneth Clark and Clough Williams-Ellis. In 1934 John Brookes was appointed Principal of a new single institution, created by merging the former Technical School and School of Art. In 1949, when catering courses were added, a new twenty-five acre site at Headington was purchased and in 1954 Lord Nuffield laid the foundation stone for what was now the College of Technology, Art and Commerce. John Brookes retired in 1956, having overseen the move to Headington. Thereafter degree level work developed rapidly, with less advanced courses being transferred to the new Oxford College of Further Education. In 1970 the college became Oxford Polytechnic, absorbing the Lady Spencer-Churchill teacher training college at Wheatley in 1977 and the Oxford School of Nursing in 1988. Fully autonomous at last in 1989, the 'Poly' was upgraded to university status in 1992, the year in which it also absorbed Dorset House School of Occupational Therapy. In 1993 the new Oxford Brookes University acquired Headington Hill Hall, the former home of media tycoon Robert Maxwell. In 1994 it established its first joint venture with Oxford University, the Oxford Institute of Legal Practice. In 1995 a new Centre for Sport was opened. Basketball, rowing, rugby, climbing and hockey are reckoned as particular strengths. In 1999 *The Times* judged Brookes the top new university for the fourth year running. In 2001 Oxford Brookes history department was rated 5★ in the nationwide Research Assessment Exercise, as opposed to a 5 rating for the history department of Oxford University. Brookes, which has a particular strength in the history of medicine, was gracious in its hour of triumph, conceding that strict equivalence between its own department of twelve and Oxford's massed ranks of a hundred and thirty history dons was not really feasible. Brookes offers a wide range of courses, from hotel management to history of art. Ironically it has been criticised for the exclusivity of its intake, attracting only two-thirds from the state sector and a disproportionate one third from independent education.

Learning and Earning

Oxford Glycosciences, established in 1988 to pioneer the development of new drugs, had a market value of £748,000,000 by 2001. Isis Innovation, Oxford's technology transfer company, by that year had some three hundred ongoing projects and was filing on average one new patent a week – while the university was spending a million pounds a year to defend them. Isis Angels Network had managed to attract some £19,000,000 in venture capital, content to mark time for investment opportunities in university research. Between 1992 and 2001 Oxford as a whole 'spun out' thirty-five companies, creating 4,000 jobs and, allegedly, thirty millionaires. Oxford Asymmetry plc was launched with a £100,000,000 price tag to create new molecules for the pharmaceutical industry. Oxford Molecular plc uses computer software to design new drugs. Opsys Ltd makes chemicals for use in mobile phones and laptop displays. Oxford Biosensors Ltd makes medical testing devices which can be used in ambulances, such as strips which give instant diagnoses from a drop of blood. Mindweavers develops computer games to help deaf children. Oxford's chemistry department in 2001 was one of only two in the UK to win a 5★ rating in the universities' research assessment exercise. It created its first spin-off company in 2001, having gained the backing of IP2IPO ('intellectual property to initial public offering') for its project to establish a new £60,000,000 chemistry building. In the same year Oxford was named as Britain's most innovative university in the Launchit 2001 competition, sponsored by Brainspark and Cross Atlantic Capital Partners. In 2001 a collaboration between Intel and Oxford University's Department of Education launched Kar2ouche, CD-roms of *Hamlet*, *Macbeth*, *Romeo and Juliet* and *A Midsummer Night's Dream*, which enable schoolchildren to create their own interpretations of Shakespeare's classics by manipulating on-screen variations of their backgrounds, props and effects and the gestures, facial expressions etc. of the characters.

ELITISM AND EXCELLENCE

Oxford University is proud to claim that it has more academic staff working in world-class research departments, rated 5★ or 5, than any other UK university and has the largest research income of any UK university. It has joined Yale and Stanford to create an Alliance for Lifelong Learning offering on-line courses, initially aimed at their half million alumni. It also has formal links with the universities of Leiden, Kyoto, Tokyo, Peking, National Taiwan University, Seoul National University, Australian National University and Jagiellonian University, Krakow. At the time of writing Oxford could also boast among its alumni the Prime Minister, the Chief Rabbi, the Poet Laureate, the King of Jordan, the conductor of the Berlin Philharmonic, the leader of the Burmese democratic opposition and Nobel Peace Laureate, Aung San Suu Kyi, Nobel Literature Laureate Sir V.S. Naipaul and arguably the world's most famous scientist, Stephen Hawking. A novel category of 'celeb' faculty also seems to be emerging, with the appointment of Israeli novelist Amos Oz as Weidenfeld Visiting Professor in European Comparative Literature and Dame Diana Rigg as a Professor of Theatre Studies. David Elstein, former CEO of Channel Five was appointed to the News International Chair of Media Studies and Richard Dawkins, author of *The Selfish Gene*, is Professor of the Public Understanding of Science.

Oxford is desperately concerned to destroy the *Brideshead* image of dissolution and exclusiveness and to enlarge its intakes from the state sector and from ethnic minorities. To further these aims it is now claimed that staff make nearly four thousand visits to schools and colleges annually in an effort to encourage applications. The introduction of new entrance examination procedures in 1985 enabled the proportion recruited from public schools to fall below 50 per cent for the first time.

BRIDESHEAD REJECTED?

The Oxford Myth, a slim volume published in 1988, was a supposed exposé written by current or recent undergraduates including Boris Johnson, future editor of *The Spectator* and MP for South Oxfordshire, and the Hon. Toby Young, future contributing editor to *Vanity Fair*. The latter observed with mild alarm that 'looking back on what I have written, Oxford emerges as a rather unpleasant place to have spent three years'. The contributors' major obsession appears to have been with cliques – the smart set/socialites, the God Squad – and the classification of their fellows into stains (nerds, who actually study); hacks (aspirant Presidents of JCRs, political clubs and the Union); 'faux proletarians'; 'young fogeys'; and – archetype and legacy of Oxford's belated 1950s modernisation – 'Northern chemists'. What was conspicuously absent from the book was any account of new movements among the student body or, indeed, any mention of ideas as such. Repeatedly denying that Oxford was anything like its depiction in the 1981 TV version of *Brideshead Revisited*, the authors of *The Oxford Myth* still managed to mention it thirteen times, a number only equalled by mentions of its author – plus five mentions of the chief characters Ryder and Flyte. Other conspicuously retrospective references included eight to Max Beerbohm or *Zuleika Dobson*, five each to Spooner, three each to C.S. Lewis and to Bertie Wooster and his creator, and two each to *The Waste Land, Decline and Fall* and *Gaudy Night*. All very retro – and not a single mention of science.

For vituperation rather than nostalgia and navel-gazing the reader is referred to Rose Ehrenreich's *A Garden of Paper Flowers*. Ms Ehrenreich, an American postgraduate, experienced an Oxford distinguished mainly by administrative inefficiency, inadequately resourced libraries, sub-standard teaching and fatuous snobberies. In the same year appeared a parallel British critique, though written very much from an outsider rather than an insider perspective– Walter Ellis's *The Oxbridge Conspiracy: How the Ancient Universities Have Kept Their Stranglehold on the Establishment*. Ellis's diatribe contrasts with Ehrenreich's in the sustained depth of its documentation but endorses her conclusion that Oxbridge is a major cause of whatever is wrong with modern Britain.

At the time of writing Oxford's current academic community alone includes the Director of the Royal Institution, the President of the Royal Society, the Chief Scientist at the Ministry of Defence, the Chairmen of the British Association for the Advancement of Science, the Food Standards Agency, the Human Fertilisation and Embryology Authority and the National Radiological Protection Board, the Chief Executives of the Medical Research Council and of the Economic and Social Research Council, the Director General of the Office of Fair Trading and the President of the National Institute of Continuing Education. You might think that Mr Ellis had a point.

Museums

The Ashmolean (Free. Open 10–5 Tuesday–Saturday 2–5 Sunday)
The Ashmolean claims to be Britain's oldest (1683) free public museum and the first to occupy purpose-built premises (now the Museum of the History of Science). The original core collection included such curiosities as Guy Fawkes' Lantern and the hat worn at the trial of Charles I by Judge Bradshaw, who had a concealed iron rim put inside it as a precaution against assassination. To these have been added mummified Egyptian cats, a Stradivarius violin and 'Powhatan's mantle', which may or may not have belonged to Pocohontas's father but is certainly three centuries old. Z.C. von Uffenbach, predictably, disapproved of the fact that it was open to 'ordinary folk' who 'impetuously handle everything in the usual English fashion . . . even the women are allowed up . . . for sixpence; they run here and there, grabbing at everything'. In 1718 the Museum acquired the fabulous Alfred Jewel, bearing the inscription '*Aelfred mec heht Gewyrcan*' (Alfred had me made), which was miraculously found in a Somerset marsh in 1693, eight centuries after it was lost there. Ethnographic materials, like those collected on Captain Cook's circumnavigation of 1772–5, were eventually passed over to the Pitt Rivers Museum. Notable Victorian acquisitions included Sir Thomas Lawrence's portfolio of Raphael and

The Alfred Jewel

Michelangelo drawings, Ruskin's gift of thirty-six Turner watercolours, the Fortnum collection of bronzes and maiolica and the Fox-Strangways gift of forty early Italian paintings including Paulo Uccello's 'The Hunt'. The Ashmolean was substantially revitalised by archaeologist Sir Arthur Evans during whose regime the rate of acquisition rose past 2,000 items per year.

The museum's major collections are divided into Antiquities, Eastern Art, Western Art, a Cast Gallery and the Heberden Coin Room. Areas of particular strength include Islamic and Greek Ceramics, Porcelain and Delftware, Indian Paintings, Miniatures, Brass Rubbings, Ruskin Drawings, and Early Twentieth Century Art. There are also works by Giotto, Holbein, Titian, Dürer, Rubens, Rembrandt, Poussin, Blake, Constable, Degas and Picasso. A visit to the Cast Gallery can introduce the viewer to reproductions of originals otherwise accessible only far away, such as the Laocoon (Vatican) or Artemesion Zeus (Athens). Other resources include the Allen Air Photographic Archive of archaeological sites, the Beazley Archive, featuring the world's largest collection of photographs of Athenian vases, and the Griffith Institute specialising in Egyptology and the ancient Near East.

The Ashmolean provides an extensive education service and gallery talks and sells souvenir reproductions and publications (e.g. Jaromir Malek, *ABC of Egyptian Hieroglyphs* [for children], Jon Whiteley, *Oxford and the Pre-Raphaelites*). The excellent website (www.ashmol.ox.ac.uk) includes artwork produced by children of the once-notorious Blackbird Leys estate under the guidance of Jamaican-born resident Teddy Dan and a children's hand-painted map of East Oxford leading on to websites covering the Cowley Road, local schools, a print workshop, cafe, arts centre and the history of a single house.

The University Museum (of Natural History) (Free. Open daily 12–5.)
The origins of the museum can be found on pages 190–91. The major collections are now grouped as Zoological, Entomological, Mineralogical and Geological (including Buckland's famous fossils), housed in what the Museum itself claims to be 'the finest neo-Gothic building in Oxford and indeed one of the most perfect in the country'. The website (www.oum.ox.ac) includes excellent features on the Wilberforce-Huxley debate, Ruskin, dodos, dinosaurs and Oxfordshire minerals.

The Pitt Rivers Museum (Free. Open 12–4.30 Monday–Saturday 2–4.30 Sunday)
Approached through the University Museum, this major collection of over half a million ethnographic objects includes Hawaiian feather cloaks, Benin bronzes, Noh masks, shrunken heads and a wide range of textiles, tools, baskets and boats and other items reflecting every human activity from warfare to magic. Particular strengths include collections of Japanese items, musical instruments, clothing and photographs of Native Americans. Unlike the Ashmolean this museum has

no restaurant and only a small shop and retains its uncompromising Victorian modes of 'typological' presentation (with correspondingly styled website, www.prm.ac.uk), but there are Saturday activity sessions for families. For the origins of this museum see pages 223–5. To some the Pitt Rivers is a trophy cabinet of imperialism, to others an Aladdin's Cave, to Sir David Attenborough a celebration of 'the multitudinous ways that once existed of being human'.

The Museum of the History of Science (Free. Open 12–4 Tuesday–Saturday)
This institution owes its inauguration in 1935 to its founding curator, the Magdalen zoologist R.W. T. Gunther (1869–1940), whose real passion for the history of science sometimes ran ahead of his expertise, as his fourteen volumes devoted to *Early Science in Oxford* (1920–45) sometimes reveal. The collections of over 10,000 scientific, mathematical and optical instruments have recently undergone major rearrangement. The website (www.mhs.ox.ac.uk) features outstanding on-line in-depth exhibitions on such themes as Cameras; Tyco Brahe; Scientific Instruments of Medieval and Renaissance Europe (520 catalogued items from Britain, Italy and the Netherlands); The Geometry of War 1500–1750 (on the application of mathematics to battle and fortification); and the Oxford Virtual Science Walk. The construction of a browsable database of the collections is ongoing and there is an on-line image library and newsletter. The shop sells an Einstein's Blackboard Mouse Mat.

The Bate Collection of Musical Instruments (Free. Open 2–5 Monday–Friday)
Housed in the Faculty of Music buildings next to Christ Church. The shop sells detailed plans of musical instruments, penny whistles, kazoos, musical boxes, musically themed jewellery and gifts as well as CDs.

The Museum of Oxford (Free to Oxford residents. 10–4 Tuesday–Friday 10–5 Saturday 12–4 Sunday)
Covers the history of Oxford as a city through items such as the town's ancient charter of 1192 and room settings of an Elizabethan inn, an eighteenth century college room, a Victorian kitchen in Jericho and a 1930s living room. Special features include an interactive gallery trail themed around food and cooking, educational workshops for children (Medieval Rubbish, the Civil War, Victorian Life) and school packs in French and German for visiting language students. A video is on sale telling the story of Oxford and its people.

Other Oxford museums include the Cathedral Treasury and Picture Gallery at Christ Church, the Oxford University Press Museum (by appointment only) in Great Clarendon Street, the Museum of Modern Art in Pembroke Street and the Telecom Museum in Speedwell Street.

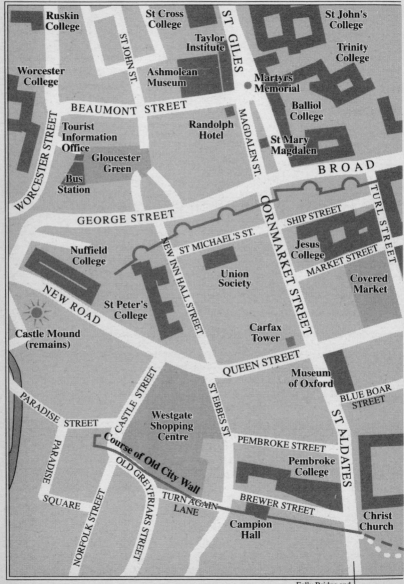

Ruskin College

St Cross College

ST GILES

St John's College

Taylor Institute

Trinity College

ST JOHN ST

Worcester College

Ashmolean Museum

Martyrs Memorial

BEAUMONT STREET

Balliol College

WORCESTER STREET

Tourist Information Office

Randolph Hotel

MAGDALEN ST.

St Mary Magdalen

Gloucester Green

BROAD

Bus Station

GEORGE STREET

CORNMARKET STREET

SHIP STREET

TURL STREET

Nuffield College

NEW INN HALL STREET

ST MICHAEL'S ST.

Jesus College

MARKET STREET

Covered Market

Union Society

St Peter's College

NEW ROAD

Castle Mound (remains)

Carfax Tower

QUEEN STREET

Museum of Oxford

BLUE BOAR STREET

CASTLE STREET

PARADISE STREET

ST EBBES ST

Westgate Shopping Centre

PEMBROKE STREET

ST ALDATES

PARADISE

Course of Old City Wall

Pembroke College

OLD GREYFRIARS STREET

NORFOLK STREET

SQUARE

TURN AGAIN LANE

BREWER STREET

Christ Church

Campion Hall

Folly Bridge and River Thames

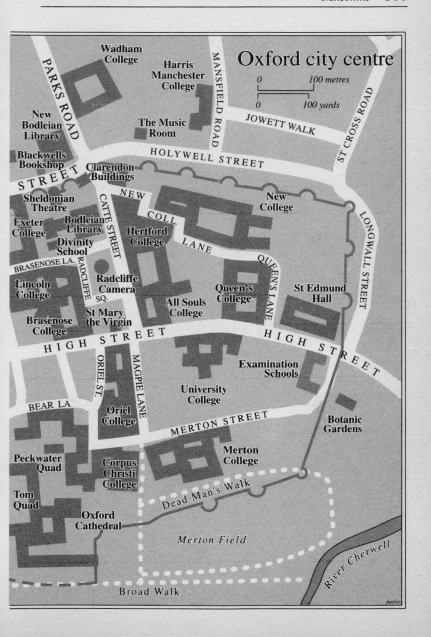

Oxford city centre

Walking Tours of Oxford

'. . . dragged through numerous dismal chapels, dusty libraries and greasy halls. I never was but once in Oxford in my life and I am sure I never wish to go there again.'

Jane Austen

To find detailed information on references highlighted in **bold** use the index. (£ denotes admission charge).

Classic Oxford Compressed

This is a short walk for those with limited time, taking in the major highlights and about half of all the colleges, including most of the oldest ones. Start from **Carfax**, where the tower (£) of the former St Martin's church still gives outstanding views over the city. Go south along **St Aldate's**, passing the **Oxford Museum** (£) and **Christ Church** to turn left into **Christ Church Memorial Gardens** a hundred yards beyond **Tom Tower**. The entrance to Christ Church (£) and **Oxford Cathedral** is on the left. Ahead and to the right is Christ Church Meadow with the River Thames in the distance. Keeping Christ Church on your left follow the path until it turns left. In the distance to your right note the tower of **Magdalen College** and to the right of that and nearer you, the **Botanic Gardens**. A plaque on the wall in the distance marks the site of Oxford's first **balloon ascent**. At the end of this section of path, where it bends right to become **Dead Man's Walk**, pass through an iron gate, which has been ingeniously constructed to frustrate the passage of bicycles, to enter a path running between **Corpus Christi** on your left and **Merton College** on your right. Through the trees on your right you should have a good view of Merton Tower. Enter Merton Street to turn left past Corpus and a rear entrance to Christ Church and its **picture gallery** (£) to turn right into **Oriel Square**. Follow the left-hand exit along King Edward Street to come into the High Street. Cross and turn right into Turl Street to pass olde-worlde shops selling books, prints and stylish traditional clothes. On your right is

Lincoln College. Take the first right, pausing to notice **Jesus College** on your left just before you turn to pass between **Exeter College** on your left and **Brasenose College** (£) on your right. You will emerge into **Radcliffe Square**. Go right to pass the **Radcliffe Camera** and reach the **University Church of St Mary the Virgin** (£) which also has a tower giving fine views. Walk along the High Street, passing **All Souls**, **University College** (on the opposite side of the road) and **Queen's College**, turn left into Queen's Lane to pass **St Edmund Hall** and **St Peter in the East** and follow the curving route (noting gargoyles high up on the building to your right) to pass the entrance to **New College** (£) with its statue of **William of Wykeham**. Continuing along this winding street will take you past the house of **Edmund Halley** and under the **Bridge of Sighs** to come out into Catte Street. Turn left past **Hertford College** and cross to pass through the archway into the courtyard of the Old **Bodleian Library**. Once there turn back to admire the Tower of Five Orders (of architecture), surmounted by a statue of **James I**. Beyond the statue of the **Earl of Pembroke** is the entrance to the **Divinity School**. Go inside to admire its airy lightness and stunning ceiling. As you come out again leave the courtyard by the left, north exit to pass between the **Clarendon Building** and the **Sheldonian Theatre** (£) and enter Broad Street. Cross to **Blackwell's** bookshop and walk west to pass **Trinity College** (£) and **Balliol** (£), opposite which the **Oxford Martyrs** were executed. At the church of St Mary Magdalene turn right into St Giles to reach the **Martyrs' Memorial**. Cross to the **Randolph Hotel** to glance down **Beaumont Street** to the **Ashmolean Museum** opposite but turn back left to pass the church of **St Michael**. Go down **Cornmarket Street** and left into Market Street to pass through the **Covered Market**. Exit onto High Street to turn right and return to Carfax.

An Oxford English Walk

Start from Carfax. Go south along St Aldate's and take the second right into Pembroke Square to find Pembroke College, alma mater of **William Camden**, **Dr Samuel Johnson** and **Sir William Blackstone**. **Tolkien** wrote *The Hobbit* while a Fellow here. Opposite this turning is Christ Church, where **Lewis Carroll** wrote *Alice in Wonderland*. Other literary alumni of 'The House' include **Thomas Linacre**, **Richard Hakluyt**, **Sir Philip Sidney**, **Robert Burton**, **John Locke**, **John Ruskin** and **W.H. Auden**. Go through Christ Church Memorial Gardens and follow the college wall on your left until you come to the right hand turn right into Dead Man's Walk. Go through the gate to reach Merton Street and turn left to reach Corpus Christi College which is associated with **Richard Hooker**, **Robert Bridges** and **Sir Isaiah Berlin**. On the other side of the road is Oriel College (entrance round the corner to the right in Oriel Square). Oriel men include **Sir Walter Raleigh**, who was a poet as well as a pirate, **Gilbert White**, **Thomas Hughes** and **J.A. Froude**. **John Taylor** lived in college during the plague of 1625 and again during the civil wars. Retrace your steps to proceed down Merton Street, which was home to **Anthony Wood**, and pass Merton, where he and **Sir Thomas Bodley** both have memorials in the ante-chapel and **T.S. Eliot** felt he might as well have. **Max Beerbohm**, despite his lack of a degree, is honoured with a room in Mob Quad especially dedicated to his memory. Other Merton men include **Edmund Blunden** and **Louis MacNeice**. At the end of Merton Street pass the Eastgate Hotel, where **C.S. Lewis** first met his unexpected American wife. On the opposite side of the road is Magdalen College, whose numerous luminaries include **John Colet**, **John Foxe**, **Joseph Addison**, **Edward Gibbon**, **Oscar Wilde**, **John Betjeman** as well as **C.S. Lewis**. Turn back along the High Street to pass University College where you may wish to see the **Shelley** monument. Its other literary alumni include **Stephen Spender**, Nobel Laureate **Sir V.S. Naipaul** and **Richard Ingrams**, former editor of the satirical magazine *Private Eye*. On the opposite side of the road is All Souls, where **T.E. Lawrence** drafted *The Seven Pillars of Wisdom*. Cross the road past the University Church of St Mary the Virgin, where **Thomas Cranmer**, author of the incomparable prose of the Anglican Book of Common Prayer, received his final humiliation. Pass Brasenose College, home to such diverse talents as **Walter Pater**, **John Buchan**, Nobel Laureate **William Golding** and best-selling pulp fiction writer **Jeffrey Archer**, and cross Radcliffe Square to Hertford College whose past members include Bible translator **William Tyndale**, poet-preacher **John Donne** and **Evelyn Waugh**. Cross Catte Street to pause in the courtyard of the Bodleian Library and exit through the south side, back onto Radcliffe Square, to turn right into Brasenose Lane. At the junction with Turl Street a left turn will take you to Lincoln College, whose alumni include **John Wesley**, **Edward Thomas**, children's writer **Dr Seuss** and spy-writer **John Le Carré**. Retrace your steps to the junction with Brasenose Lane to go north along Turl Street where Jesus College and Exeter College face each other. The former boasts **J.R. Green** and **T.E. Lawrence** amongst its former undergraduates but the latter trumps the trick with **William Morris**, **Richard Burton**, **J.R.R. Tolkien** and **Alan Bennett**. Turn right into Broad Street to reach the Clarendon Building which once housed Oxford University Press. Cross the road to pass the New Bodleian building and Blackwell's bookshop. Pause beside the handsome gates of Trinity College to recollect its formidable literary line-up of **William Stubbs**, **Sir Arthur Quiller-Couch**, **James Bryce**, **Ronald Knox** (as a Fellow), and **Terence Rattigan**. Traditional rival Balliol next door rivals this galaxy with **John Wyclif**, **John Evelyn**, **Adam Smith**, **Robert Southey**, **Matthew Arnold**, **Arnold Toynbee**, **Gerard Manley Hopkins**, **Anthony Hope** (Hawkins), **Hilaire Belloc**, **Ronald Knox** (as an undergraduate), **Julian Grenfell**, **L.P. Hartley**, **Aldous Huxley**, **Cyril Connolly** and political biographer **Roy Jenkins**, the current Chancellor of the University. At the end of Broad Street turn right to find the entrance to St John's College whose alumni include **A.E. Houseman**, **Robert Graves**, **Kingsley Amis**, **Philip Larkin** and novelist **John Wain**. Cross St Giles to walk down Beaumont Street to reach Worcester College, whose varied talents have included **Thomas de Quincey**, **Sir J.C. Masterman**, **Richard Adams**, author of *Watership Down*, media mogul **Rupert Murdoch** and prolific historian Lord **Asa Briggs**. Further along Walton Street on the same side is **Oxford University Press**, home of the *Oxford English Dictionary*. The Oxford University Press bookshop can be found at 116 High Street.

Medieval Oxford

Starting from **Carfax** turn left up Cornmarket Street. The Laura Ashley shop was built in 1386 as the New Inn. Just beyond it is the tower of the church of **St Michael** at the Northgate, Oxford's oldest extant structure, dating from the mid-eleventh century. Inside the church thirteenth century stained-glass windows depict St Edmund and the Virgin and Child. Continue north to pass the church of St Mary Magdalene, which was heavily restored in the nineteenth century but has a south chapel dating from 1320. Turn left into Beaumont Street, the site of the royal palace built by **Henry I**. On the opposite side of the road the Ashmolean Museum contains many medieval items, such as the **Alfred Jewel** and Crondall Hoard of Anglo-Saxon gold coins. At the end of Beaumont Street is Worcester College which still has a row of medieval cottages which once formed part of **Gloucester College**. Walk down Worcester Street to New Road to view the remains of the **Castle** Mound and St George's tower. Return along Queen Street to Carfax and turn right into St Aldate's, site of Oxford's medieval **Jewish community**, noting the wall plaque which marks the starting-point of the **St Scholastica's Day** riots. At Christ Church Tom Quad, the Hall and Cathedral remain as a prideful memorial to the last great prince of the medieval church, **Thomas Wolsey**. Turn left through the Memorial Gardens and follow the path, keeping Christ Church to your left to pass through the gate to enter the passage between Corpus Christi and **Merton College** to turn right into Merton Street. Beam Hall opposite Merton's Chapel is a fifteenth century **academic hall**. Follow Merton Street to its end, turn left into the High Street and then right into Queen's Lane to pass **St Edmund Hall**, **St Peter-in-the-East** and **New College**, whose garden is bounded by the medieval **city walls**. At the end of New College Lane turn left to pass **All Souls** to reach the university church of **St Mary the Virgin**.

AN OXFORD PILGRIMAGE

Appropriately we start at the **Martyrs' Memorial** and go north along St Giles to pass St John's College, whose handsome Canterbury Quad was built by

Archbishop Laud. Continue north, noting on the opposite side of the road the Eagle and Child, where Christian apologist **C.S. Lewis** and myth-maker **J.R.R. Tolkien** used to drink, and enter the Banbury Road. Turn right into Keble Road and right into Parks Road to find the entrance to **Keble College**, where **Mrs Humphrey Ward** defended her novel *Robert Elsmere* against the criticisms of **Gladstone**. Opposite stands the University Museum, an architectural embodiment of **Ruskin**'s ethics and the venue for the celebrated confrontation between **T.H. Huxley** and **Bishop Wilberforce** over Darwinism. Turn left into South Parks Road and right into Mansfield Road to reach **Mansfield College**. At the end of the road go right into Holywell Street and then left into Catte Street and left again into New College Lane to reach **New College**, whose gateway is surmounted by a statue of its founder, **William of Wykeham**. The fine T-shaped college chapel contains a striking statue of Lazarus by Sir Jacob Epstein and a moving inscription to German college dead of the World War I. Continue down the lane to **St Edmund Hall**, where you may be interested to see the crypt under St Peter-in-the-East. At the end turn left onto the High Street to pass Magdalen College where **C.S. Lewis** taught English. Cross into Rose Lane to reach Dead Man's Walk, passing the Botanic Gardens. on the site of the medieval **Jewish cemetery**. Follow the path round to reach **Christ Church** whose college chapel doubles as Oxford's cathedral and contains the shrine of **St Frideswide**. Passing through the gates to Christ Church Memorial Garden note their cardinal's hat motif in memory of **Thomas Wolsey**. Turn right and right again to go through Blue Boar Street and Bear Lane to reach Oriel, the college which through **Keble**, **Pusey** and **Newman**, gave birth to the **Oxford Movement** and through **Thomas Arnold** wrought a religious revolution in England's public schools. Go up Oriel Street to cross the High Street and reach the university church of **St Mary the Virgin**, dramatically linked with both **Cranmer** and **Newman**. Pass Brasenose College, where Archbishop **Runcie** was an undergraduate, and cross Radcliffe Square to enter the courtyard of the Bodleian Library and go into the **Divinity School**. Exit on the north side to pass leftwards onto Broad Street and turn left into Turl Street where you may wish to visit the chapel of Exeter College with its William Morris tapestry and Lincoln College, where **John Wesley**'s Holy Club gave birth to Methodism.

A Treasures Trail

This is a relatively short walk for art-lovers and well-suited to a rainy day as it is essentially a linked series of visits to galleries. Starting from the Martyrs' Memorial cross into Beaumont Street to visit the **Ashmolean**, whose art treasures include sculptures and medallions as well as paintings. From the Ashmolean pass into Gloucester Street, cross George Street and go down New

Inn Hall Street and St Ebbe's Street to turn left into Pembroke Street to reach the **Museum of Modern Art**. Leave Pembroke Street to cross St Aldate's and walk downhill to turn left to visit **Christ Church**, which has not only its cathedral and picture gallery but also numerous portraits in its dining hall. Exit into Oriel Square and pass through King Edward Street to cross the High Street into Turl Street. You may wish to see the **William Morris** tapestry in the chapel of Exeter College and the Grinling Gibbons carving in **Trinity College**.

Liquid History: A Pub Walk

Drink courses, like its rivers, through Oxford's story. Brewing, collegiate and commercial, has been a major activity for over half a millennium. The **castle** had its own brewery, as did the various religious houses. A **guild** of brewers was formed in 1571 and Oxford's mayors were frequently drawn from its ranks. By 1840 over a dozen breweries were in operation, the largest being **Hall**'s and **Morrell**'s. A heavy consumption of wine, especially port, was a hallmark of Oxford life from the eighteenth century onwards. In the 1730s undergraduate Richard Graves initially fell in with a West Country set of ale-drinkers but was 'rescued' by gentlemen-commoners who 'treated me with port-wine and arrack-punch and ... would conclude with a bottle or two of claret'. J. Campbell's *Hints for Oxford* (1825) asserted that 'hard drinking ... has of itself very much decayed in the University ... the decreasing consumption of wine promises increasing security to patent glass and the peace of the inhabitants'. The practice of **sconcing**, however, continued unabated. Oxford's central location in Lowland England made it of major importance as a stop-over on the national network of long-distance **coaching**-routes and thus provided much passing trade to the large inns which lined the major thoroughfares. The decline of coaching posed no fatal threat as 'day-trippers' by rail made up at least some of the shortfall. The Drink Map prepared in 1883 by the Oxford Band of Hope and Temperance Union revealed that the town still boasted three hundred and twelve licensed houses – one for every twenty-two adult inhabitants. In university circles the 1930s vogue for proletarian causes reintroduced bottled beer as socially acceptable, at least among the socially unacceptable. A 1982 survey of student drinking by Oxford's Department of Community Medicine found that 19 per cent of males and 4 per cent of females could be classified as 'heavy drinkers', having consumed in excess of ten pints of beer or the equivalent over a four day period. Excessive drinking appeared to be most commonly associated with groups of five or more drinking together. 21 per cent of students surveyed admitted that the effects of excess alcohol had interfered with their academic work.

Starting from Carfax walk down St Aldate's to note on the right a plaque marking the site of the Swindelstock tavern where the bloody events of **St Scholastica's Day** began. On the opposite side of the road a reconstruction of an inn-parlour of Shakespeare's day can be seen in the **Museum of Oxford**. The dramatist William Davenant, Shakespeare's godson – and some allege his real son – was born to an Oxford publican. As you continue down the hill to pass Christ Church remember the words of **Dean Aldrich**

> If on my theme I rightly think
> There are five reasons why men drink,
> Good wine, a friend, or being dry,
> Or lest we should be, by and by,
> Or any other reason why.

It was at Christ Church in the 1920s that fastidious **Harold Acton** noted how, among the self-consciously stylish, 'cocktails were substituted for Amontillado'. You may wish to continue to Folly Bridge to drink in the **Head of the River**. Alternatively head back up St Aldate's and turn right into Blue Boar Street and left into Alfred Street to find **The Bear**. Reputedly Oxford's smallest pub, it claims to date back to 1242 and features an extraordinary collection of neckties. From the Bear go down Bear Lane and through Oriel Square to Merton Street. Pass Merton College which was already brewing its own ale by 1284. At the end of the street is the **Eastgate Hotel**, which has a pleasant bar. Go left into the High Street and cross into Queen's Lane, passing Queen's College, which was still brewing its own beer until 1939.

Continue into New College Lane. You will pass the rear of All Souls where Archbishop Bancroft, visiting in 1609, was shocked by the strength of the beer and beyond that the rear of Hertford College where the routine trashing of aesthetes' rooms, invariably prefaced by 'the sound of the upper classes baying for broken glass' was so vividly described in Evelyn Waugh's *Decline and Fall*. Just before the Bridge of Sighs find a narrow passage-way on your right which leads down to the **Turf Tavern**, immortalised in Hardy's *Jude the Obscure* and featured in the *Inspector Morse* TV series. With its low ceilings and gardens overshadowed by medieval city walls the Turf Tavern has been described as 'what people imagine Oxford pubs to be like, except for the shortage of locals'. Leave the Turf Tavern via Bear Place to emerge into Holywell Street opposite the Music Room. Turn left for a very short walk to the busy, often noisy, **King's Arms** (aka the K.A.). From there a walk of similar brevity will take you along Broad Street past the New Bodleian to the White Horse, next to Blackwell's. From the White Horse continue along Broad Street to pass Trinity College, where Dr Kettell held firmly that 'the houses that had the smallest (i.e. weakest) beer had most drunkards, for it forced them to go into town to comfort their stomachs'. The future Cardinal Newman was appalled by the consumption of alcohol he encountered as a freshman, 'if any one should ask me what qualifications were necessary for Trinity College I should say there was only one, Drink, drink, drink'. Pass Balliol to turn right into St Giles and reach St John's College. Cross St Giles to find the **Eagle and Child**. Dating from 1650, this was the favoured watering-hole of C.S. Lewis and J.R.R. Tolkien. Beyond the city centre the energetic walker is recommended to **The Perch** at Binsey, a thatched pub with gardens, to **The Trout Inn**, Godstow Road, Wolvercote, in an idyllic Thameside setting and to **The Victoria Arms** at Old Marston, a riverside pub much favoured by the punting fraternity.

Architectural Contrasts

This is quite a long walk. Starting from Carfax walk down Queen Street to see **St George's Tower** and **Nuffield College**. Turn right up Worcester Street to reach Worcester College where the medieval cottages of **Gloucester College** face **Clarke**'s handsome classical facade and Richard MacCormac's 1983 Sainsbury building offers yet another striking contrast. Pass along neo-classical Beaumont Street and cross St Giles to reach St John's College and another contrast between Laud's **Canterbury Quad** and MacCormac's 1994 **Garden Quad**. Continue north along St Giles into Banbury Road, then right into Keble Road and right again into Parks Road to view the High Victorian Gothic of Butterfield's **Keble College** and the contrasting Hayward and De Breyne Building of 1973–7 by Ahrends, Burton and Koralek, a swirling wall skilfully shoe-horned into a narrow site. Opposite stands the **University Museum**. Turn left along South Parks Road to see **Rhodes House**. Continue past Linacre College into St Cross Road pass the striking St Cross building (1961–4) by Leslie Martin, Professor of Architecture at Cambridge. At medieval St Cross church left again into Manor Road to reach Arne Jacobsen's **St Catherine's College**. Return to St Cross Road and turn left to go down Longwall Street and cross the High Street to view **Jackson's Examination Schools**. Then turn round to admire the superb frontage of **Queen's College**. Cross back over the High Street and continue to Radcliffe Square to see the **Radcliffe Camera** and **All Souls College**. At the north end of the square enter the courtyard of the Bodleian Library to admire the light, airy interior of the Divinity School and the Tower of the Five Orders (of architecture). Exit beneath this to cross Catte Street and view Jackson's Hertford College and Bridge of Sighs before turning left and left again to see Hawksmoor's **Clarendon Building**, Giles Gilbert Scott's **New Bodleian**, the **Old Ashmolean** and Wren's **Sheldonian Theatre**. Architectural enthusiasts with stamina and a map may also wish to see such other outstanding modern buildings as Wolfson College (beyond the Dragon School – see Trips from Oxford, Walking section, North Oxford), Queen's College's Florey Building by James Stirling (off St Clements' Street, beyond Magdalen College), the Jacqueline du Pré Concert Hall and Garden Building at St Hilda's, the only Oxford building by the influential Alison and Peter Smithson, Lutyens'

Campion Hall in Brewer Street and Templeton College (south of South Hinksey). (I am indebted for the selection of modern buildings to Geoffrey Tyack, author of *Oxford: An Architectural Guide*.)

Looking for Paradise: A Garden Walk

The English word 'paradise' comes from the Persian for an enclosed garden and Oxford's are quite as much an expression and reinforcement of collegiate pride and identity as a chapel, library or hall. Kellogg College has a roof garden. Green College, very appropriately in view of its medical orientation, has a 'Physic Garden'. In Oxford gardening as an art was pioneered by monks and **friars** cultivating herbs for their medical and culinary use, flowers for chapel altars and vegetables for the refectory kitchen. The earliest college gardens also consisted of haphazard but utilitarian herb and vegetable plots to supply the kitchens, complemented by orchards with walks. The concept of a garden designed for aesthetic as well as practical value was primarily a Renaissance innovation. Paul Hentzner, visiting in 1598, observed as a distinctive feature of Oxford life that after meals students were free 'to walk in the college garden, there being none that had not a delightful one'. The indiscriminate cutting down of trees for fuel and fortifications during the **Civil Wars** necessitated much subsequent replanting, as at Magdalen's Grove in the 1680s. **Celia Fiennes**, visiting Oxford in the 1690s, remarked particularly on the abundance of 'greens of all sorts, Myrtle, oringe and Lemons . . . growing in potts of Earth and so moved about from place to place and into the air sometimes'. The title story of Henry James's *A Passionate Pilgrim* (1875) describes the gardens of New College, St John's and Wadham. Mavis Batey's delightful and authoritative *Oxford Gardens* (Scolar Press 1982) provides a superb survey of the subject, deftly integrated with the story of the university itself.

Starting from Carfax go down St Aldate's to reach the gates of **Christ Church** Memorial Gardens, created in 1926 in honour of alumni killed in **World War I**. As an entrance way to Christ Church Meadow this remains readily accessible to the public without payment of the college admission fee. As you follow the path, keeping the college wall on your left, look out over Christ Church Meadow and imagine what it would be like if a city-centre relief road had been built there in the 1960s. Also note the avenue of trees, leading down to the river, planted by **Dean Liddell** as rowing became the cult sport of Victorian Oxford. At the turning into Dead Man's Walk go through the gate to reach Merton Street and turn left to ask at the porter's lodge of **Corpus Christi** if the garden is open to visitors. (For usual college visiting hours see page 315). Corpus was early noted for its swarm of bees. Its feature terrace, constructed against the city walls in 1623 and surmounted by a vast beech, affords a fine view across Christ Church Meadow and a chance to peep across to the Canon's and Dean's gardens at Christ Church, closed to the public but for ever associated with **Alice** and the Cheshire Cat. Leaving Corpus walk up Merton Street and turn right to reach the **Botanic Gardens** on your right. Just in front of the archway to the right is a small garden created in honour of **Howard Florey** and the research team which developed penicillin. From the Botanic Gardens cross the road to reach **Magdalen College** whose fifteen hectares of grounds constitute Oxford's largest college garden. Originating as the gardens of the Hospital of St John, they had a formal avenue of trees as early as the fifteenth century. Its picturesque deer park dates from the seventeenth century and was practical in its origin – to supply fresh venison for the college kitchen. Addison's Walk commemorates prose stylist Joseph Addison (1672–1719), whose rooms overlooked the then Water Walk. Addison, deploring the artificiality of topiary and the potted plants admired by Celia Fiennes, was the pioneering campaigner for the 'natural landscape' style which, displacing geometrical arrangements of symmetrical parterres, became the distinctively English norm in the course of the eighteenth century. Magdalen's Great Plane Tree dates from 1801; its wych-elm, which blew down in 1911, was thought to be the largest tree in Britain. Magdalen's water meadows are famed for fritillaries. From Magdalen turn back up the High Street and right into Queen's Lane to reach **New College**, which once used the **city wall** itself to effect to grow vines against it, though now it backs a modern herbaceous border. New College also developed a cloister garden and raised an artificial mound as a striking feature. This seems to have originated as a purely practical solution to dumping five hundred wagon-loads of demolition wreckage in 1529–30 but was later embellished with winding paths to ease the ascent to the top on which, in Celia Fiennes's day, there was a summer-house. When Florence Nightingale visited the college she was given a bouquet of climbing roses from the college cloisters. In more recent times the gardens at New College have benefited from the attentions of garden writer Robin Lane Fox. From New College follow New College Lane to Catte Street, turn left, cross Radcliffe Square to your right and go down Brasenose Lane. At the junction with Turl Street turn right to find **Exeter College** on your right. The Fellows' Garden has a mound, affording a splendid prospect towards Radcliffe Square. From Exeter continue north to enter Broad Street, go right and then left at the King's Arms to find **Wadham College** on your right. At Wadham the clipped yews, statuettes and parterres described by Evelyn were banished under John Wills, (Warden 1783–1806) to be replaced by a 'romantic' garden created by Shipley, the gardener of **Blenheim Palace**. The Fellows' garden at Wadham, planned in the 1790s, features a great copper beech. From Wadham return to Broad Street and turn right past Trinity and Balliol to turn right again for **St John's College**. The groves planted at St John's in 1712–16 included pleached elms but a thorough remodelling in 1770–78 created a landscape style garden in just four acres, winning the acclaim of George III in 1785 that 'his dominions did not contain another specimen of gardening to match it'. St John's in the 1890s pioneered the rock garden, a project of one of its own Fellows, H.J. Bidder. An outstanding post-war gardener was Geoffrey Blackman (1903–80), Sibthorpian Professor of Rural Economy (1945–70), a pioneer in the then novel field of ecology and an expert on herbicides. Apart from revolutionising agronomy in the university he created outstanding woodland gardens at West Wood House, Bagley Wood and Wood Croft, Boar's Hill. As Keeper of the Groves at St John's he used mountains of leaf mould to transform its lime-soaked soil. From St John's cross St Giles and go down Beaumont Street to reach Worcester College. The only college with a lake, this is regarded by less lofty but possibly more learned critics than George III as the city's one true landscape garden, laid out by its then youthful Bursar Richard Greswell (1800–81) in 1827 to take advantage of the possibilities created by the completion of the Oxford canal.

Other gardens further afield worth visiting include the **University Parks** area, Templeton College, **St Catherine's** and St Hugh's. 'Specimen trees' are a pronounced future of the University Parks which nevertheless pledged not to detract 'from the natural beauty of the indigenous by an excess of the exotic'. Its *Crataegus durobrivensis* was found for the first time in 1900, growing beside the Genesee River in New York State and the nearby Dawn Redwood in Szechwan in 1945, after centuries of being known only as a fossil. Trees – pyramidal hornbeams, Norwegian silver birch, fast-growing Lombardy poplars and a stately cedar of Lebanon – are also a special feature of the grounds of Templeton College. Built on the site of a former dairy farm, the college planted 12,000 to screen itself from Oxford's ring road. The garden of St Catherine's was designed by Danish architect Arne Jacobsen as an integral aspect of his designs for the college buildings. It features formal yew hedges and includes a water garden, an eighty foot concrete bell-tower and a sculpture by Barbara Hepworth. It is intended to be at its best in May/June when the iris beds and bush and climbing roses are in flower – a fond memory for those about to depart? – and in October when berried plants and autumnal trees are major features, providing a blazing welcome to the newest intake of undergraduates.

St Hugh's garden was the creation, virtually from scratch, of the redoubtable **Annie Rogers**, a disciple of Gertrude Jekyll. Its fourteen acres include The Dell, a Victorian fernery, a nut walk, a wilderness and a magnolia dating from 1918. Annie Rogers is remembered by a commemorative sun-dial, though perhaps there should have been a memorial in the shape of an umbrella. She was renowned for carrying a particularly capacious one, into which she was alleged to slip unauthorised cuttings, thus prompting the charge that the most common plant at St Hugh's was 'snitchwort'.

COLLEGE OPENING HOURS AND CHARGES

Many colleges are open to visitors, usually from 2.00 p.m. until 4.00 or 5.00 p.m. Some are open in the mornings for groups accompanied by an official guide. Most put restrictions on the size of groups and/or require notice of them. Christ Church charges £4 (£3 to concessions) but that includes Oxford Cathedral. Magdalen and New College charge £2 (£1 to concessions). Trinity College charges £1.50 per person, and Balliol (term only) and Brasenose, charge £1. All Souls, Corpus, Exeter, Harris Manchester (chapel only), Hertford (open 10.00–12.00), Jesus, Keble, Kellogg (open from 9.00), Lady Margaret Hall (open from 10.00), Linacre (check times at Porter's Lodge), Lincoln, Merton (grounds; library tours £1), Nuffield (open from 9.00), Oriel, St Anne's (open from 9.30), St Catherine's (open from 9.00), St Hilda's, St Edmund Hall (open daylight hours), St Hugh's (open from 10.00), St John's (open from 1.00), St Peter's (open from 10.00), Wadham (open from 1.00 and 10.30 in vacations), Wolfson (gardens only in daylight hours) and Worcester are free. Pembroke, Queen's and Somerville are only open to groups accompanied by an official guide and by prior appointment. Official functions, examinations etc. may lead colleges to close themselves to visitors at little notice or none. The following are not normally open to the public: Campion Hall, Regent's Park College, St Anthony's College, St Benet's Hall, St Cross College and Templeton College.

Trips from Oxford

(For further information on references in bold use the index.)

Walking

North Oxford, Jericho and the University Parks area are a short distance from the city centre. The other destinations may take an hour or more, depending on your pace and weakness for diversions en route.

NORTH OXFORD

Starting from the **Martyrs' Memorial** walk up St Giles on the right-hand (east side) passing **St John's College** to enter the Banbury Road. Opposite **St Anne's College** bear right to enter Norham Gardens which features houses (1,5,7,11,13) by local architect **William Wilkinson**. **Sir William Osler** lived at No. 13. At the end is **Lady Margaret Hall**. Unless you wish to visit the college turn left into Fyfield Road (2, 3 and 4 by Wilkinson) and cross Norham Road (14–26 and 30–35 by Wilkinson) to reach the path running past the **Dragon School**. Turn left into Bardwell Road and left again into Banbury Road. The first turning, Park Town, offers a circular diversion to view the very different Italianate style of S.L. Seckham. Continue back down the Banbury Road to return to the Martyr's Memorial.

JERICHO

Cafés and curio shops now enliven this former working-class area, where **Hardy**'s doomed hero, Jude Fawley, had lodgings. To reach it, starting from Carfax, go up **Cornmarket Street** and turn left down Beaumont Street. At the bottom you may wish to visit **Worcester College** before turning right up Walton Street. This will take you past **Ruskin College** and the handsome **Oxford University Press** building. **Somerville College** and **St Aloysius** church, which has a memorial to **Gerard Manley Hopkins**, are off Little Clarendon Street to the right, while turnings to the left lead down to **Oxford canal** and the church of **St Barnabas**. At the northern edge of Jericho is St Sepulchre's cemetery (disused) where **Benjamin Jowett** is buried.

UNIVERSITY PARKS

From Carfax go up Cornmarket Street as far as St Mary Magdalene, right along Broad Street and then, at the King's Arms, left into Parks Road to pass **Wadham College**, the **University Museum** and **Keble College** before reaching the Parks over on your right. To return by a different route leave the Parks at the eastern end of the University Science Area and pass **Linacre College** to enter St Cross Road which will take you to twelfth century St Cross church and adjacent Holywell cemetery, the last resting-place of such Oxford luminaries as **Acland**, **Pater** and **Bowra**. St Cross Road leads into Longwall Street which ends at the High Street. Turn right to return to Carfax.

Osney

Osney Town is in fact an island, just south-west of the railway station, developed for housing from 1851 onwards. Shaped like a belt-buckle, 'Oxford's Little Venice' features mid-Victorian terrace housing and, in summer, canal boats lined up along its banks. The church of **St Frideswide** on Botley Road features a door panel relief of the saint at prayer, carved by **Alice Liddell**.

Binsey

This small farming hamlet has a renowned riverside pub, The Perch. The little late Norman church of St Margaret has associations with *Alice in Wonderland* and **Frideswide** through the ivy-covered Treacle Well just beyond its west end. Start from Oxford railway station and follow the Thames Path north-west.

Godstow

This can be reached by following the Thames Path beyond Binsey through meadows. A fifteenth century bridge leads to the ruins of **Godstow Abbey**, where **Fair Rosamund** was buried. The Trout Inn, a former fisherman's inn rebuilt in 1737, is famous for the peacocks in its riverside garden and has a back bar dedicated to Inspector Morse. For an alternative return route take the Godstow Road to the **Oxford Canal** and follow the towpath, skirting Jericho, back to Hythe Bridge.

Boar's Hill

This would be a much longer walk, going beyond Osney, through **North Hinksey** and then cross-country via Chilswell House (Priory) to pass through **Youlbury** Wood. The Jarn Mound raised by **Sir Arthur Evans** in 1931

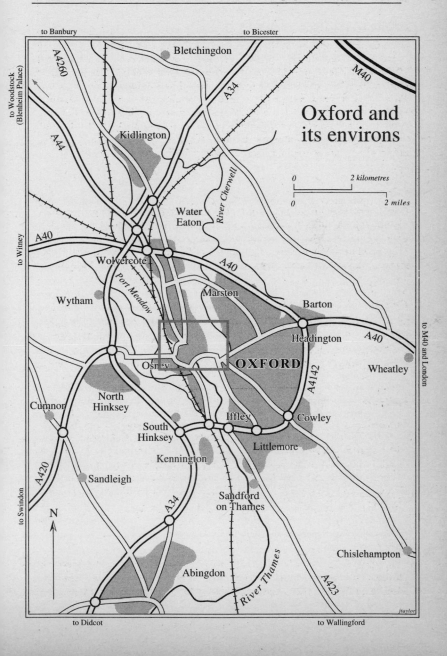

to Banbury · to Bicester

to Woodstock
(Blenheim Palace)

A4260

Bletchingdon

A34

M40

Oxford and
its environs

Kidlington

A44

to Witney

A40

River Cherwell

0   2 kilometres
0   2 miles

Water
Eaton

Wolvercote

A40

Port Meadow

Marston

Barton

A40

to M40 and London

Wytham

Headington

Osney

OXFORD

A4142

Wheatley

Cumnor

North
Hinksey

Iffley

Cowley

South
Hinksey

Littlemore

A420

Kennington

to Swindon

Sandleigh

A34

Sandford
on Thames

N

Chislehampton

Abingdon

River Thames

A423

jtaylor

to Didcot · to Wallingford

affords the classic view of Oxford's 'dreaming spires' some three miles away to the north-east. To the south-west is an extensive vista over the Vale of the White Horse. The less intrepid may prefer a twenty-minute bus ride by Stagecoach service No. 44 from St Aldate's to Boar's Hill via North Hinksey, followed by lunch at The Fox.

By Car to Stratford-Upon-Avon

Shakespeare's birthplace lies thirty miles (48 kms) north-west of Oxford but there are several locations en route which justify diversions.

ROUTE 1

The most direct route between Oxford and Stratford is along the A44. **Woodstock**, the first major settlement, was the birthplace of Edward III's son, the Black Prince and was famous for fine gloves in medieval times; there is still a glove factory in Harrison's Lane. Woodstock is now a major tourist attraction thanks to Blenheim Palace, which was the birthplace of Sir Winston Churchill and is designated by UNESCO as a World Heritage site. Designed by Sir John Vanbrugh, it was presented by a grateful nation to John Churchill, Duke of Marlborough, Winston Churchill's direct ancestor, in recognition of his victory over the army of Louis XIV at Blenheim (Blindheim) in southern Germany in 1704, the first time the French had been beaten in a major engagement in forty years. To my mind Blenheim's exuberant Baroque pile is much grander than Buckingham Palace and well worth the visit – even the website is majestic. The interior features work by Laguerre, Thornhill, Gibbons and Rysbrack. American visitors will be intrigued to learn about the contributions to the life of the house made by three successive American duchesses. The 2,000 acre grounds, landscaped by Lancelot 'Capability' Brown, make a fittingly grand complement to the house, with a superb artificial lake, a maze and a Column of Victory 134 feet high, surmounted by a statue of the duke. Blenheim also bottles and sells its own mineral water. A branch of Oxfordshire County Museum is housed in Fletcher's House in Park Street, which leads up to the triumphal archway entrance to the Palace. There are two celebrated historic inns, The Bear and the Feathers, both renowned for their cuisine.

    Bladon is a small village on the southern edge of the Blenheim Palace estate, unremarkable except for its churchyard, where the modern Churchills lie in a family plot, Winston a few steps from his controversial father, Lord Randolph, and his adored American mother, Jenny.

DIVERSION

Great Tew lies beyond Enstone where the A34 meets the B4022. In the seventeenth century Lord Falkland's house, Tew Park, served as a salon for such luminaries as Hobbes and **Clarendon**. Falkland was killed fighting for the royalists at Newbury in 1643 but is commemorated in The Falkland Arms pub. The village was landscaped and partly Gothicised in the early nineteenth century under the influence of the pioneering gardening writer J.C. Loudon. The absence of modern buildings and survival of the village stocks reinforce the effect of an arcadian time-warp. St Michael's church contains a fine monument by Francis Chantrey. To prolong the diversion continue along the B4022 to the A361 to take a left and then a right to reach pretty Swerford. Beyond that lies **Hook Norton** noted for its Victorian brewery, home of the celebrated beer known as 'Hooky'. Notice the curious eighteenth century hinges on the door in the thirteenth century church porch. West of Hook Norton, beyond the rose-clad village of Great Rollright and on the western side of the A44 are the **Rollright Stones** (aka King's Men). Forming a circle a hundred feet across and dating from 3500 BC they are ranked next in importance to Stonehenge and Avebury but are far less well known. A quarter of a mile away the upright Whispering Knights are the remnants of a vanished burial mound. The location affords panoramic views of the area.

Staying on the A44 would enable you to make a much shorter diversion to **Chipping Norton**, which grew rich on the wool trade. Fifteenth century St Mary's church is approached via gabled seventeenth century almshouses and has fine tombs and brasses. There are extensive ruins of a Norman motte and bailey castle. The striking Bliss Tweed Mill of 1872 has now been converted to smart apartments. To reach Stratford-Upon-Avon you need the A3400 via Shipston-on-Stour, which once hosted a large market for sheep (hence the name) and still has a number of historic inns.

ROUTE 2

This route offers an incursion into the Cotswolds, passing through a series of pretty and prosperous market towns and villages, well supplied with handsome coaching inns, antique shops and honey-coloured houses. The Cotswold region is the England's largest officially designated 'Area of Outstanding Natural Beauty', covering seven hundred and ninety square miles, 80 per cent of it farmland. The area has one of the lowest population densities in England, with a population of 85,000 – which may be part of its attraction to the 38,000,000 who visit it each year. Leave Oxford by the A40 to head westwards.

Eynsham (pronounced Insham) has a fourteenth century cross, an arcaded hall in the town square and a handsome toll bridge of 1777. Remains of a rare flash lock are visible nearby.

Witney is a substantial market town whose name is synonymous with blankets. Its Blanket Hall dates from 1721. Witney has a branch museum, a soaring church spire, a long green set with limes and a Butter Cross of 1668 with a clock-turret of 1683 and a sundial. A mile south east of the town centre, off the B4022, **Cogges Manor Farm Museum** combines a medieval manor house with Victorian farm buildings and rare breeds to present a thousand year panorama of rural life, with daily demonstrations of practical skills. **Wood-green** is an elegant eighteenth century residential suburb. Five miles north-east is **North Leigh Roman Villa**, a fourth century complex of sixty rooms grouped around a courtyard.

Minster Lovell on the B4047 merits a short diversion. The romantic ruins of fifteenth century Minster Lovell Hall and Dovecote stand beside the River Windrush, spanned by a fifteenth century bridge. There are two grisly legends associated with the ruins. The Old Swan Inn incorporates a mill of 1526.

Continue on the A40 to reach **Burford** ('Gateway to the Cotswolds'), which consists of a steep main street lined with historic properties. The town's story is told in the Tolsey Museum, housed in a sixteenth century building once used as a toll-house. The Bay Tree Hotel was once the home of Sir Lawrence Tanfield, Lord Chief Baron of the Exchequer to Elizabeth I. In 1649 Cromwell locked three hundred and forty mutinous soldiers in the large and handsome church for three days and nights and then had three of them shot to death in the churchyard. The nearby **Cotswold Wildlife Park** has one of England's foremost wild animal collections.

Turn north on the A424/A429 to reach **Stow-on-the-Wold** whose market square is crowded in by inns and some fifty-plus antique shops and art galleries. There is also a Toy and Collectors Museum. Stow-on-the-Wold is a good base for exploring the Cotswolds as half a dozen roads converge here, though happily not at the town centre. Continue on the A429 to reach **Moreton-in-Marsh**, whose broad main street is actually a section of the ancient Fosse Way. The Curfew Tower incorporates an old lock-up. **Charles I** slept at the White Hart in 1643. The Tuesday market has up to two hundred stalls. Jacobean **Chastleton House** (1612) a few miles away to the south-east has exciting associations with the Gunpowder Plot and the **Civil Wars**. More peacefully it is the birthplace of croquet and now in the care of the National trust. **Batsford Arboretum** and the **Cotswold Falconry Centre** are also nearby to the north-west. To reach Stratford continue along the A429 until you bear off left on the A3400.

Alternatively **Broadway** and **Chipping Campden** both merit a further diversion along the A44. Broadway's Lygon Arms hosted both Charles I and **Cromwell**. Antique shops are now much in evidence. In Victorian days the village was a favoured summer retreat of an artistic clique including John Singer Sargent and Edwin Austin Abbey. Nowadays custom-made furniture is an important local manufacture and there are over a dozen antique shops. The Folly Tower of 1799 on Fish Hill marks the highest point in the Cotswolds, 1,024 feet above sea level, affording views much admired by **William Morris**. South of Broadway is **Snowshill Manor**, an organic cottage garden with stunning views. The house is stuffed with an extraordinary collection of tools (local), models (ships), lamps (Persian), armour (Japanese), scrolls (Tibetan) etc.

From Broadway the B 4632 offers a further diversion to **Chipping Campden**, which has a majestic Market Hall of 1627, excellent brasses in the late medieval church, and a museum in Woolstaplers Hall. Stay on the B 4632 to reach outstanding **Hidcote Manor Gardens** in the village of Hidcote Bartrim. Developed from 1907 by American horticulturalist Major Lawrence Johnstone, Hidcote pioneered the notion of a garden as a series of roofless 'rooms'. Follow the B 4632 for a back way into Stratford.

A Thames Excursion

The A34 going south leads to Abingdon; turn off to take the A4183. (Alternatively you could make an eight mile walk along the river bank or take a river cruiser from Folly Bridge or a Stagecoach bus, routes 33 or 44 from St Aldate's.) Until 1870 **Abingdon** was the county town of Berkshire but in that year that status was transferred to Reading and in 1974 Abingdon suffered the further indignity of being incorporated into Oxfordshire. Fragmentary remains of its once great abbey, founded in 675, still survive, as does a three-in-one arched fifteenth century bridge 150 yards long. Unusually the town grew up entirely on one bank of the river. At the Bell Inn Charles I took leave of his French queen, Henrietta Maria, for the last time before sending her abroad. The grand colonnaded Town Hall was built by **Wren**'s master mason, Kempster, in 1677–82. The County Hall of 1683 houses a museum. The unusual thirteenth century church of St Helen's with five aisles is wider than it is long and flanked on three sides by almshouses dating from the fifteenth to eighteenth centuries.

From Abingdon continue on the A34 to branch left onto the A 4130 to reach **Didcot**. This important junction town is now very appropriately home to a Railway Centre which pays homage to the glory days of the GWR – I.K. Brunel's Great Western Railway (aka God's Wonderful Railway). There are over twenty locomotives on display and more than forty coaches. From Didcot there is a possible diversion to **Long Wittenham** where the Pendon Museum has lovingly crafted miniature re-creations of the local countryside as it was in the 1930s.

From Didcot follow the A4130 to reach **Wallingford**, a riverside town of fine Georgian houses. There is Saxon stonework in St Leonard's church and the remains of Saxon earthworks. There are Gainsborough portraits in the unusual seventeenth century Town Hall which is mounted on stone pillars. The Thames is spanned by an ancient bridge of fourteen arches.

From Wallingford go north on the A 4074. You may feel like a short diversion off this along the B 4009 to reach **Ewelme**, the most picturesque of Chiltern villages, notable for its almshouses and the church where **Chaucer**'s daughter is buried inside (get down on your knees to view the horrific cadaver concealed within a tomb of staggering splendour) and **Jerome K. Jerome** is buried outside. Henry VIII chose Ewelme for his honeymoon with teenage Catherine Howard. **Sir William Osler** had a residence in the almshouse. The main street is bordered with streams which traditionally grew watercress.

The A 4074 leads on to **Dorchester**. The Abbey Church of St Peter and St Paul is all that remains of the major twelfth century Augustinian abbey but retains many intriguing features, most notably its windows. One depicts the Tree of Jesse. Another was restored in 1966 by 'American Friends' of the church as a memorial to Churchill. There is also a thirteenth century Crusader effigy and a rare Norman lead font. Near that note the fascinating epitaph to twenty-nine year old Sarah Fletcher who hanged herself on discovering her husband's intended bigamy with an heiress.

Return to Oxford via **Nuneham Courtenay**, a model village whose main street is lined with identical double cottages built by the **Harcourt** family in 1761 – after demolishing the old village, which would have spoiled the view from their new residence, Nuneham House. The medieval church was replaced by a classical church-cum-temple designed by James 'Athenian' Stuart and the grounds landscaped by Capability Brown. This drastic demonstration of the power of the rich inspired Goldsmith's poem *The Deserted Village*. For nature-lovers there is England's oldest arboretum, created in 1835 specifically to cultivate North American trees such as redwoods. It is now an out-station of the University of Oxford's **Botanic Gardens**. The Palladian house is now a Global Retreat Centre attached to the Brahma Kumaris World Spiritual University, which is based in India.

By Train

Most railway services from Oxford are run by Thames Trains. The following excursions are possible. Journey times (minimum in brackets in minutes) vary depending on the number of intermediate stops). Careful perusal of timetables is essential. What would seem like a relatively straighforward journey to Stratford Upon Avon could take from sixty-five minutes to just under three hours!

1. The line to Stratford Upon Avon. En route are ancient **Warwick** (44) and elegant **Leamington Spa** (36). Warwick's imposing castle is well geared to tourist visitors, perhaps a little too well for those who like their history raw. Leamington has gracious gardens and good shopping.
2. **Bicester** (pronounced Bister) (55) has a major factory-shop centre with sixty retail outlets (clothes, homewares, ceramics), much favoured by Japanese visitors.
3. The line to the cathedral city of **Worcester** (69) gives access to **Moreton-in-Marsh** (33) from which there are buses to more distant Cotswold delights such as **Stow-on-the-Wold**, **Bourton-on-the-Water**, **Chip-**

ping **Campden** and **Broadway**, which are quite as pretty as they sound. Beyond Moreton-in-Marsh are delightful **Evesham** (48) and **Pershore** (65).
4. The line to **Bristol** (79) gives access to **Didcot** (10), **Swindon** (34) (which also has a GWR heritage centre; plus a factory-shop mall), the market town of **Chippenham** (49) and the city of **Bath** (65), with its impressive Roman Baths and Abbey.
(NB Thames Trains carries cycles free but with restrictions in rush hours.)

By Bus (the main bus station is at Gloucester Green)

The Oxford Bus Company runs services to Abingdon and Didcot.

Swanbrook runs a service to Gloucester which has intermediate stops at Witney, Minster Lovell, Burford, Northleach and Cheltenham. (Cycles carried for one pound.)

Stagecoach runs services to Bicester, Abingdon and Didcot. Its service to Stratford Upon Avon has intermediate stops at Woodstock, Chipping Norton Moreton-in-Marsh and Shipston-on-Stour. Another service runs through Eynsham, Witney, Minster Lovell, Burford and Shipton Under Wychwood.

Bus service X39 from Oxford Railway station goes through Nuneham Courtenay to Wallingford and Ewelme.

Cycling

Oxford is a hub of the Sustrans National Cycle Network and the meeting-point of Route 5 (London-Reading-Stratford-upon-Avon) and Route 51 (Oxford-Milton Keynes). The Tourist Information Centre has maps of the Oxfordshire Cycleway which circles the county on minor roads and lanes. Oxford City Council proclaims itself pro-cycle – it certainly doesn't like cars. There are more than a dozen cycle shops in the city. CycleCity Guides produce an Oxford Cycling Map (ISBN 1-900623-01-3) which covers the city centre on one side and Oxfordshire on the reverse. Oxford University Cycling Club (founded 1873) organises social events as well as races. Its website (http://users.ox.ac.uk/~cycling/) has route directions to dozens of locations including Woodstock, Witney, Burford, Stow-on-the Wold, Moreton-in-Marsh, Hook Norton, Shipston-on-Stour, Broadway and Evesham. Oxford Popular Cycling Front organises informal weekly cycle rides in and around Oxford, normally by way of a public house.

Sport

The first mention of 'Real' (i.e. royal) tennis at Oxford dates from 1450. Magdalen's founding statutes forbade its inmates from keeping 'a Harrier, or other Hound of any kind or Ferrets, or a Sparrow-hawk or any other Fowling Bird'. The Laudian statutes of the 1630s likewise reveal the common undergraduate pastimes by what they forbade. Down-market 'ball play' and ferreting were outlawed but bows and arrows were exempted from the general ban on weapons on the archaic grounds that archery was still of military value.

Swimming at Parson's Pleasure, a stretch of river bank later notorious for nude bathing and sun-bathing by dons, was certainly practised by the seventeenth century; the legendary venue was finally closed in 1992. Eighteenth century recreations were those favoured by the country gentry from which the student body was then drawn – riding to hounds, fishing and shooting. More brutalised tastes were catered for by a bull-baiting club which survived until 1826.

Sport was formalised by the Victorians who established permanent clubs and teams, with codified rules, regularised membership, organised competitions and the iconographic paraphernalia of glory in the shape of uniforms, blazers, 'colours', club ties and team photographs. Participants in a full inter-varsity competition became entitled to wear a dark blue blazer. 'Blues' became the sporting aristocracy of Oxbridge life. Major sports such as rowing, rugby, cricket and soccer were ranked as Full Blue events. There are currently fourteen for men and fifteen for women. Minor sports rank as Half Blues and now include such arcane and exotic pursuits as Eton Fives, Rugby Fives, Lifesaving, Orienteering, Powerlifting and Taekwondo.

Sport became a – for some *the* – central feature of university life for about a century. *The Handbook to the University of Oxford*, published in 1932, devoted a longer chapter to Sports than to Women's Education, Religion and Music added together. In the long run, however, Oxford could not compete with the rise of professionalism from the 1880s onwards. The cult of 'effortless superiority' was eventually exposed by superiority of effort.

The second major factor in Oxford's sporting eclipse was the proliferation of other universities as rival centres of excellence in the post-1945 period. There are now a hundred and fifty plus members of the British Universities Sports Association. In terms of overall rankings in 1998–9 Oxford stood second in women's sports, seventh in men's. Between 1998 and 2001 Oxford claimed the status of national collegiate champions in American Football, Basketball (Male and Female), Dancesport, Fencing (Women's), Lacrosse (Women's), Rugby Union (Women's), Squash (Men's Individual) and Ultimate Frisbee. The keynote of sport at Oxford has become differentiation, both in terms of range, from aikido to yachting, and level, from fumbling fresher beginners at college level to top-notch national standard. At collegiate level the major competitive feature of university sporting life is the series of inter-collegiate knockout competitions known as 'Cuppers'. In 1999 the Oxford University Sports Federation came into being to promote sport across the board and at all levels.

ROWING

The Thames made rowing an obvious candidate for inter-collegiate endeavour. The first Bumping Races were held in 1815 and the first Boat Race against Cambridge in 1829, though it was not at first the annual, climactic event that it became. The initial encounter was rowed at Henley and the second, at Westminster, did not occur until 1836 when the celebrated Oxford dark blue (from Christ Church) and light blue (from Eton) colours were first adopted by the respective sides. The University Boat Club was founded a decade later, facilitating the organisation of competitions for Pairs (1839), Fours (1840) and Sculls (1841) and inspiring the celebration of the first Henley Regatta (1839) and subsequently (*c.*1846) a domestic Oxford Regatta. Timed or 'signal' racing was introduced in 1851 and from 1856 onwards the inter-varsity race became an ongoing event. The first international match, against Harvard, was rowed in 1869, the course being the traditional inter-varsity run along the Thames from Putney to Mortlake; Oxford won by more than three lengths. Henry James, visiting Oxford that same year, was completely seduced by the siren call of the oar: 'As I walked along the river I saw hundreds of the mighty lads of England, clad in white flannel and blue, immense, fair-haired, magnificent in their youth, lounging down the stream in their punts or pulling in straining crews and rejoicing in their godlike strength.'

The racing boats of the day were very different from their sleek modern counterparts, being readily convertible to passenger carriers with a capacity of twenty. The less arduous and non-competitive pastime of punting evolved simultaneously in the mid-Victorian era, the original craft being working boats, propelled by watermen with a sixteen foot pole and used for fishing and ferrying passengers and light goods. By the 1860s they were being built out of mahogany, making them much lighter and thus easier to propel and manoeuvre. Cambridge was slow to catch on, not introducing punts onto the Cam until the Edwardian era. By then the annual varsity rowing race on the Thames

The victorious Oxford University Boat Race crew of 1894

had become a national event, inspiring ardent partisanship throughout a sport-mad nation, most of whom had no other connection with either university. 'Boat Race Night' was traditionally celebrated in the capital by troupes of drunken undergraduates smashing street-lamps and seeking trophies in the form of policemen's helmets, the aftermath of which was frequently a cursory appearance in Bow Street Magistrates' Court, a caution and a nominal fine from a bench inclined to indulge the 'high spirits' of the *jeunesse d'orée*.

More seriously the two varsity clubs henceforth supplied the core of successive British Olympic teams. Although recruitment widened subsequently Oxford can still take pride in the achievements of Matthew Pinsent, three times winner of Olympic gold in the Pairs. (Oxford Brookes oarsmen also notched up three golds at the Sydney Olympics.) The annual Putney to Mortlake combat no longer inspires nationwide passion but is still regarded as a major sporting event, referred to universally and simply as 'The Boat Race'. The presence of a substantial transatlantic element in both teams has often led to caustic speculation about 'whether our Americans can beat their Americans'. Rowing remains a top sport at Oxford itself. Regular races are held in the Michaelmas term for novices to test their aptitude and in the Hilary term for the hardy or foolhardy to test their fortitude. Eights Week in Trinity term attracts crowds of ten thousand plus to the river.

ATHLETICS

Oxford University Athletic Club evolved from a core of steeplechasers based in Exeter College. It was formally established in 1860. Early in the field of authenticated achievement, its members claimed numerous 'firsts' in the matter of world records, most notably the first six foot high jump, achieved in 1876; as a university record it was not bested for seventy-two years. Like rowing and cricket in their eighteenth century origins competitive athletics attracted heavy betting. The 1866 varsity meeting broke up in a free-for-all when punters, bookies and undergraduates set to over a disputed dead-heat. In 1880 three members of the OUAC, determined to 'clean up' the sport convened a meeting at the Randolph Hotel which led to the formation of the Amateur Athletic Association, a landmark in the history of athletics in Britain.

Undoubtedly the most significant event in Oxford's sporting history took place on 6 May 1954 when Roger Bannister, paced by Christopher Brasher and Christopher Chataway, stormed round the track of the Iffley Road University Sports Centre to complete a mile in three minutes fifty-nine point four seconds, thus becoming the first runner to beat the four minute barrier. Bannister, a President of Vincent's, went on to become a Master of Pembroke College and Chairman of the Sports Council. Chataway, who set a new 5,000 metre world record that same year, became a TV presenter and Conservative MP. Brasher, a Cambridge man, went on to win a gold for the 3,000 metres steeplechase in 1956 and become the organiser of the London Marathon.

CRICKET

Although a first inter-varsity match was played against Cambridge at Lord's in 1827 the Oxford University Cricket Club was not founded until 1862. The Lord's match became one of the occasions of the London social season. It attracted those with little interest in cricket as such as an opportunity for undergraduates to meet their friends' sisters. The club's greatest triumph was probably to beat the Australian touring side in 1884. OUCC veterans include controversial Douglas Jardine, the England captain who managed to bring the country to the brink of war with Australia by his use of intimidatory 'bodyline' bowling and Sir Colin Cowdrey, who was already playing for Kent when he captained Oxford in 1954. Unlike other university clubs it has continued to command the talents of future world class players including M.J.K. Smith and Pakistan's Imran Khan. New College also produced in the late Brian Johnston a radio commentator whose voice became synonymous with the game. In 1993 the decision of the new editor of *Wisden*, the canonical cricket annual, to omit the time-honoured list of that year's Oxbridge Blues provoked outrage among traditionalists but was defended on the grounds that it would cure those universities of 'clinging to the illusion that they are playing first-class cricket' (i.e. of professional, county standard). In its efforts to regain that level OUCC has merged with Oxford Brookes to create a stronger player base.

RUGBY

The university's rugby club was founded in 1869 over a year before the Rugby Football Union came into existence as the organising body for the sport. For half a century or more the Oxford Club played a major role in fostering the game nationally and overseas. The annual Varsity Match, played at Twickenham since 1921, is still a major national fixture, attracting crowds of 40,000 or more. Gate receipts at rugby matches were long the main source of financing all other sports at the university since few could exist without subsidy, a further subvention being made from the colleges in proportion to their own club memberships.

SOCCER

Oxford University Association Football Club was founded in 1871 and won the FA Cup in 1874. Pegasus FC, founded in 1948, drew on players from both Oxford and Cambridge and won the Amateur Cup Final in 1951 and 1953. The city's professional team, Oxford United, originated as the Headington village club, which finally turned professional in 1949, changed its name in 1960 and gained entry to the Football League in 1962. Its most distinguished player has been captain 'Big Ron' Atkinson, who took it into Division 2 in 1968 and later became manager of Manchester United. In 1986 Oxford won the 'Milk Cup' trophy.

Who Whom?

In sport, as in other areas of university life, women struggled to gain acceptance. The earliest intakes of 'undergraduettes' played croquet, badminton and tennis. Hockey and 'recreational rowing' were added by the 1890s. The Women's Boat Club was founded in 1926 but it was not until 1981 that an Oxford team was steered to victory in the Boat Race – by a whopping eight lengths – by a woman cox, Susan Brown. Anomalies remain. Both sexes are eligible for Full Blues in athletics, soccer, squash, swimming and tennis but only men can qualify for cricket and golf. And whereas Fencing and Modern Pentathlon rank as Full Blue sports for women, they count as only a Half Blue for men. The emergence of mixed sports such as canoeing, croquet, kendo, polo and lacrosse doubtless points to an increasingly gender-blind future. Scarcely less revolutionary than the gender revolution has been the development of Town vs Gown competitions since 1980, starting with six-a-side cricket. By 1985 fifteen sports were being played, by 1996 thirty-five. Overall Town has proved the more consistent victor.

Chronology

727	Traditional date of the foundation of St Frideswide's Priory
	c. 735 Death of St Frideswide
912	Oxnaforda first mentioned in the *Anglo-Saxon Chronicle*
919	Oxford known to be fortified with walls
1002	Oxford's Danish population massacred on St Brice's Day
1005	Dedication of St Ebbe's church
1035	St Martin's, Carfax granted to Abingdon Abbey
1050	Saxon tower of St Michael, Northgate built
1071	Robert d'Oilly builds Oxford castle
1086	Domesday survey includes first record of St Peter in the East
1096	First evidence of teaching at Oxford
1100	St Aldate's church in existence. St Cross, Holywell built
1122	First recorded Mayor of Oxford; All Saints church founded; St Frideswide's re-founded
1123	St Giles church begun
1129	Osney Abbey founded
1130–3	Henry I builds Beaumont Palace
1133	Godstow nunnery and Rewley Abbey founded
1142	Queen Matilda flees from Oxford castle
c. 1155	Henry II confirms the guild merchant
1167	English students migrate from Paris
1187	Visit of Giraldus Cambrensis
1190	Emo of Friesland becomes Oxford's first known overseas student
1191	Oxford granted a borough seal and control of its markets
1193	Golden Cross Inn opened
1199	Charter granted by King John
1209	Earliest recorded town-gown riot; Migration of students to Cambridge
1214	Papal Legate's ordinance, the earliest charter of university rights

1221	Arrival of Dominican friars
1224	Arrival of Franciscan friars
1231	Henry III orders all students to be enrolled with a master
1244	Chancellor acquires jurisdiction over student debts
1248	Town-Gown riot; Mayor required to swear to respect university privileges; Office of proctor first recorded
1249	University College endowed
1252	Arrival of Augustinian friars
1255	University acquires rights to regulate the sale of food and drink
1258	Parliament meets at Oxford
1263	Balliol College first mentioned
1264	Merton College first statutes promulgated
1280	University College statutes; Rewley Abbey founded
1283	Gloucester College founded (re-founded as Worcester)
1286 ? 1291	Durham College founded (re-founded as Trinity); Arrival of Trinitarian friars
1295	Oxford sends burgesses to Parliament for the first time
1300	Mitre Inn opened
1314	Exeter College founded
1320	Tackley's Inn built
1326	Oriel College founded by Adam de Brome and Edward II
1334	Temporary migration of Oxford scholars to Stamford
1341	Queen's College founded
1348–9	Black Death devastates Europe
1355	St Scholastica's Day riots
1362	Canterbury College founded (later absorbed into Christ Church)
1370	University independence from the Bishop of Lincoln's jurisdiction confirmed
1379	New College founded by William of Wykeham
1396–7	First reference to stone quarries at Headington
1410	All students are required to live in a recognised hall of residence
1427	Lincoln College founded
1435	St Mary's Hall founded
1437	St Bernard's College founded (later to become St John's)
1438	All Souls founded
1458	Magdalen College founded; Duke Humfrey's Library opened
1478	Oxford's first printed book
1488	Duke Humfrey's library completed; Henry VII visits Oxford
1489	Papal bull confirms university independence from all external ecclesiastical jurisdiction

1571 Jesus College Founded

1496	John Colet returns to Oxford from Italy
1499	Erasmus arrives in Oxford
1502	Lady Margaret Professorship of Divinity established
1509	Brasenose College founded
1517	Corpus Christi College founded
1518	Plague outbreak
1525–9	Wolsey begins the building of Cardinal College
1535	Dissolution of Oxford's religious houses
1538	Shrine of St Frideswide desecrated; Friars are dispersed
1542	Diocese of Oxford created
1546	Regius Professorships established in Divinity, Civil Law, Medicine, Greek, Hebrew; Christ Church founded
1549	Edwardian statutes promulgated to regulate university teaching
1555	Trinity College founded
1555	St John's College founded; Burning of Oxford Martyrs; Latimer and Ridley
1556	Burning of Thomas Cranmer
1559	Ejection of Catholic appointees in favour of Protestants
1566	State visit of Elizabeth I
1571	Jesus College founded; Epidemic outbreak
1577	Epidemic outbreak
1578	Ralph Agas publishes a map of Oxford
1580	Convocation requires all students to reside in a college or hall
1581	All students are required to subscribe to the Thirty Nine Articles
1584	Dr Thomas Cogan's *The Haven of Health* prescribes advice on student lifestyles
1592	State visit of Elizabeth I
1598	Visit of Paul Hentzner
1602	Opening of the Bodleian Library
1604	University secures the right to elect its own burgesses to Parliament
1605	Visit of James I; King's Arms public house built in his honour
1610	Stationers' Company promises the Bodleian a free copy of every new book; Water is piped from Hinksey Hill to Carfax conduit
1610–13	Wadham College founded and built
1613	Schools Quadrangle at the Bodleian built
1617	Visit of James I
1619–26	Establishment of Savilian Professorships of Astronomy and Geometry, Sedleian Professorship of Moral Philiosophy,

	Camden Professorship of Ancient History, Tomlins Lecture (later Professorship) in Anatomy and Heather Professorship in Music
1620	Visit of James I; Foundation of the Physic Garden
1624	Pembroke College founded; Navigability of the Thames improved
1630	Archbishop Laud elected Chancellor
1631	Hebdomadal Board established
1632	Physic Garden opened
1633	First meeting of the Board of Delegates of the Press
1636	Archbishop Laud reforms the university statutes; Canterbury Quad completed at St John's and opened by Charles I
1642	Charles I establishes his headquarters in Oxford
1644	Fire devastates central Oxford
1646	Oxford surrenders to Parliamentary armies
1647–9	Parliamentary purge of Heads of Houses
1649	Cromwell visits Oxford
1650	Cromwell elected Chancellor
1660	Ejected Heads of Houses reinstated
1663–9	Sheldonian Theatre built
1665	Charles II establishes his temporary court, fleeing the plague
1668 or 1669	A 'flying coach' makes the first journey to London in a day
1670	University establishes a coach service to London
1674	*History and Antiquities of the University of Oxford* by Anthony A. Wood; First *Oxford Almanack* published
1675	*Oxonia Illustrata* by David Loggan
1681	Charles II summons and dismisses Parliament at Oxford
1681–2	Tom Tower built at Christ Church
1683	Ashmolean Museum opened
1687	Fellows of Magdalen reject a Catholic royal nominee as President
1691–2	*Atheniae Oxonienses* by Anthony A. Wood
1700	All Saints' Church collapses (rebuilt 1706–8)
1710	Visit of Z.C. von Uffenbach
1714	*The Antient and Present State of the University of Oxford* by John Ayliffe; Worcester College founded
1724	Establishment of the Regius Professorship of Modern History
1729	John Wesley establishes the Holy Club
1733	*Oxonia Depicta*
1737	Licensing Act bans performances of plays within five miles of Oxford
1737–49	Radcliffe Camera built
1740	Hertford College founded

1748	*The Foreigners' Companion through the Universities of Cambridge and Oxford* by Thomas Salmon; Holywell Music Room opened
1753	*Jackson's Oxford Journal* begins publication
1758	Blackstone lectures on laws of England
1763	James Boswell visits Oxford
1770	Radcliffe Infirmary opened
1771	Bocardo lock-up closed; Mileways Act improves local roads
1772	North and East Gates removed
1774	The Covered Market is established
1778	New Magdalen bridge completed; Oxford linked to Banbury by canal
1782	C.P. Moritz visits Oxford; Morrell's brewery opens in St Thomas's Street
1784	James Sadler's balloon ascent
1786	Manchester College; George III visits Oxford
1788	Haydn composes his Oxford symphony (No.92)
1790	Oxford Canal link to the Midlands canal system completed
1791	Haydn awarded honorary Doctorate of Music
1802	First examination Honours list published
1805	County Gaol built; Hertford College dissolved
1806	Newdigate Prize established
1809	Money is distributed to 7,000 to mark the 50th anniversary of the accession of George III
1810	Regent's Park College
1814	The Prince Regent visits Oxford; *History of the University of Oxford: Its Colleges, Halls and Public Buildings* published by Rudolf Ackermann
1815	Brasenose crew is the first to be recorded as Head of the River
1818	Gas street-lighting introduced
1819	Oxford Choral Society established
1822	Beaumont Street laid out
1825	The Oxford Union is established
1826	Bull-baiting club suppressed; OUP begins to move to Walton Street
1827	First varsity cricket match
1829	First Oxford vs Cambridge boat race, held at Henley
1832	Princess Victoria visits Oxford; Reform Bill riots; Cholera epidemic
1833	Keble's Assize Sermon starts the Oxford Movement
1834	The Duke of Wellington is elected Chancellor
1835	Municipal Reform Act enfranchises local ratepayers
1836	University colours adopted for second Boat Race against

	Cambridge; New Theatre (now the Apollo) founded in George Street
1837	*Oxford (City and County) Chronicle* founded
1839	Oxford Archaeological and Historical Society founded
1841	Newman publishes Tract XC; Martyrs' Memorial built (to 1843); Oxford population 24,258
1843	Great Western Railway reaches Oxford; *Original Views of Oxford, its Colleges, Chapels and Gardens* by William de la Motte
1844	Oxford railway station opened
1845	New Ashmolean Museum opened; Newman quits Oxford
1849	Cholera epidemic
1850	Royal Commission investigates the organisation of the university; Honour Schools of Natural Science and Law and Modern History founded
1851–4	University Galleries opened
1852	Last coach ran from Oxford to Birmingham
1853	Park Town laid out; First class lists in Natural Science and Law and Modern History
1853–7	*The Adventures of Mr Verdant Green* by Cuthbert Bede (E.Bradley)
1854	Parliamentary Act passed to reform Oxford; Cholera epidemic
1855	Nathaniel Hawthorne visits; St John's begins developing North Oxford
1856	Ralph Waldo Emerson visits
1857	Delegacy of Local Examinations established; Matthew Arnold elected Professor of Poetry
1858	Salter Bros boatbuilding business established at Folly Bridge
1860	University Museum completed; Huxley and Wilberforce debate evolution
1861	*Tom Brown at Oxford* by Thomas Hughes
1862	First professing Jew graduates; St Philip and St James consecrated
1864	Abolition of the Laudian Statutes; First varsity athletics match
1865	Oxford School of Art founded; *Alice's Adventures in Wonderland*
1866	Randolph Hotel opened
1867	Grenadier Guards summoned from Windsor to put down a Town-Gown brawl
1868	Oxford Police Act merges town and university forces; *Munimenta Academica* by Henry Anstey Henry; Taunt's shilling photographs; Delegacy of Non-Collegiate Students founded
1869	Oxford wins its first international rowing race, against Harvard; St Barnabas church opened

1870	Keble College founded; University *Gazette* founded; First class list in Theology
1871	Last religious tests abolished; Second Royal Commission of Inquiry appointed
1872 ? 8	University College celebrates its millennium; First varsity rugby match; Honour School of Jurisprudence established
1873	Oxford and Cambridge Schools Examination Board founded
1874	Cooper's Oxford marmalade first sold; Ruskin's Hinksey Road project; First varsity soccer match; Hertford College re-founded
1875	Oxford High School for Girls founded; Indian Institute founded
1876	World's first recorded six foot high jump achieved at Oxford; Sir Thomas Jackson pioneers the use of Clipsham stone
1877	Colleges obliged to contribute to a Common University fund; Cowley barracks opened
1878	Lady Margaret Hall founded; Wesley Memorial church opened; City of Oxford High School for boys opened
1879	Somerville College founded; Society of Home Students founded; Blackwell's bookshop opened at 50 Broad Street
1880	Amateur Athletic Association founded at the Randolph Hotel
1881	Horse-drawn trams introduced
1883	New faculty organisation introduced; *Oxford Magazine* founded
1884	Oxford Historical Society, Oxford University Dramatic Society established
1886	St Hugh's College founded; Mansfield College
1887	First class list in Oriental Languages
1888	*Robert Elsmere* by Mrs Humphrey Ward
1889	Oxford becomes a county borough
1890	Oxford Electric Company founded
1891	Oxford School of Art becomes Oxford City Technical School; Pitt Rivers Museum completed
1892	Day Training College for Teachers established; *Isis* founded
1893	Society of Home Students becomes St Anne's College; St Hilda's College founded; C.B. Fry equals the world long jump record; Women's names printed in class lists
1894	New Ashmolean opened
1895	Visit of Jacques Bardoux; St Martin's, Carfax demolished; BLitt and BSc degrees introduced
1896	Campion Hall founded; Oxford Bach Choir formed; William Morris establishes his business at 48 High Street; *Jude the*

	Obscure by Thomas Hardy; St Martin's, Carfax closed and demolished
1897	St Benet's Hall; Oxford Town Hall opened; First class list in English
1898	Morris Garages opened
1899	Ruskin College established
1901	Male student population of Oxford 2,537, female students 239
1902	Rhodes Scholarships established
1905	University School of Forestry established; First class list in Modern Languages
1909	*Principles and Methods of University Reform* by Lord Curzon
1910	Greyfriars Oxford Electric (Cinematograph) Theatre opened
1911	*Zuleika Dobson* by Max Beerbohm; Population of Oxford 62,000
1912	William Morris manufactures his first motor car
1913–14	Bridge of Sighs built at Hertford College; Barnett House established
1917	DPhil degree introduced
1918	Influenza epidemic
1919	Third Royal Commission established; Women admitted to full university membership
1920	First government subsidy accepted; *Cherwell* begins publication; Women are awarded degrees; Politics, Philosophy and Economics (PPE) degree introduced
1921	Population of Oxford 67,000
1922	Cowley motor works established
1923	University accepts first block grant from the Treasury; First class list in Politics, Philosophy and Economics; Oxford Playhouse opened
1924	Museum of the History of Science opened
1926	Pressed Steel Company opened
1927	Oxford Preservation Trust established
1928	*Oxford Mail* begins publication
1929	St Peter's College founded
1930	Delegacy of Non-Collegiate Students becomes St Catherine's Society; Oxford Society formed
1932	*Oxford's College Gardens* by Eleanour Sinclair Rohde; First section of ring road opened
1933	Apollo Theatre rebuilt; First class list in Geography; Oxford Union votes not to fight for King and Country
1934	Royal Oxford Hotel built

1935	*Gaudy Night* by Dorothy L.Sayers; Institute of Economics and Statistics established; Cutteslowe walls built
1936	*Oxoniensa* begins publication
1937	Nuffield College founded
1938	Population of Oxford 94,000; Department of Surveying and Geodesy established; Oxford Playhouse occupies new premises on Beaumont Street; *An Oxford University Chest* by John Betjeman
1939	First class list in Agriculture
1940	New Bodleian Library completed
1941	World's first use of penicillin at the Radcliffe Infirmary
1942	Oxfam founded
1944	Music Faculty established
1945	First class list in Forestry Maison Française established; *Brideshead Revisited* by Evelyn Waugh
1946	King George VI opens New Bodleian Library; Institute for Colonial Studies established; Maison Française opened
1948	St Anthony's College founded by Antonin Besse; Pergamon Press founded as Butterworth–Springer; Thomas Sharp's 'Oxford Replanned' proposes a road through Christ Church Meadow
1949	First class list in Psychology, Philosophy and Physiology
1951	First class list in Biochemistry; Population of Oxford 97,000
1952	First class list in Music
1952	Morris and Austin merge to form the British Motor Corporation
1954	Roger Bannister runs the first sub-four-minute mile
1955	St Giles School of English founded
1956	Oxford adopts a Green Belt planning policy
1957	St Edmund Hall becomes independent; Clarendon Hotel demolished; Oxford Historic Buildings Fund established; Blackbird Leys estate begun
1958	Nuffield College completed
1959	Cutteslowe Walls demolished; Clarendon Laboratory achieves world record low temperature; Oxford Instruments Group founded; Morris 'Mini' car launched
1962	Linacre College founded; Oxford United FC promoted to the Football League
1963	St Catherine's Society becomes St Catherine's College; Oxford's Mayor becomes a Lord Mayor; Women are allowed to take part in Oxford Union debates
1964	Norrington Table first published; Franks Commission appointed; New College proposes the admission of women

1965	St Cross College established
1966	Franks Report published; Centre for Criminological Research established; *Dr Faustus* starring Richard Burton and Elizabeth Taylor at the Oxford Playhouse; Wolfson College founded; Museum of Modern Art opened; Oxford ring road completed
1967	Simon House night shelter opened
1968	Oxford city police absorbed into Thames Valley force
1969	Religious Experience Research Unit established
1970–2	Westgate Shopping Centre built
1970	College of Technology becomes Oxford Polytechnic; Radio Oxford begins broadcasting
1971	All Saints Church converted into a library for Lincoln College
1972	Counselling Service established; Wellcome Unit for the History of Medicine; Transport Studies Unit Centre for Postgraduate Hebrew Studies; Centre for Socio-Legal Studies; Installation of new 'Emperors' Heads' sculpted by Michael Black
1973	First class list in Experimental Psychology; Oxford city introduces 'park and ride scheme'
1974	Reorganisation of local government ends university representation on the City Council; Admission of women to Brasenose, Hertford, Jesus, Wadham, St Catherine's
1976	Museum of Oxford opened in the former public library
1978	University Computing Service established
1979	Green College established
1981	Oxford population 99,000; Wolfson College established; Nissan Institute of Japanese Studies; *Brideshead Revisited* televised; Susan Brown becomes the first female member of an Oxford Boat Race crew
1982	Oxford Institute for Energy Studies
1983	First class list of Bachelors of Fine Arts
1984	Templeton College established; Stanford University opens a centre in Oxford
1985	New entrance examinations introduced – public school intake falls below 50 per cent; Women accepted at Oriel, the last all-male college; Congregation votes to deny Margaret Thatcher an honorary degree
1986	Oxford United FC promoted to the First Division; Second class degrees divided into upper and lower classes
1987	Oxford Playhouse closes; Congregation approves an equal opportunities policy
1988	First Class list in Mathematics and Computation;

	Development Programme for Oxford launched; 'The Oxford Story' opens
1989	Second edition of Oxford English Dictionary completed
1990	Rewley House becomes Kellogg College
1994	Honorary degree conferred on US President Bill Clinton; BMW buys Rover Group
1996	Wafic Said offers £20,000,000 to establish a Business School
1999	Oxford University Sports Federation established
2001	Said Business School Opened; Research Assessment Exercise ranks eighteen Cambridge departments at 5 and thirty at 5★ – Oxford seventeen at 5 and twenty-five at 5★; Undergraduate applications to Oxford rise by 17.5 per cent
2002	Oxford University Press launches Oxford Reference Online website of 130,000,000 words

Further Reading

For Reference

T.H. Aston, R. Evans and J.I. Catton *The History of the University of Oxford: II Late Medieval Oxford* (1992)

T.H. Aston and B. Harrison (eds) *The History of the University of Oxford: VIII The Twentieth Century* (1994)

T.H. Aston, L.S. Sutherland and L.G. Mitchell (eds) *The History of the University of Oxford: V The Eighteenth Century* (1986)

M.G. Brock and M.C. Curthoys *The History of the University of Oxford: VI Part 1 The Nineteenth Century* (1998)

M.G. Brock and M.C. Curthoys *The History of the University of Oxford: VII Part 2 The Nineteenth Century* (2000)

J.I. Catto (ed) *The History of the University of Oxford: I The Early Oxford Schools* (1986)

J.I. Catto and T.A.R. Evans *The History of the University of Oxford: II Late Medieval Oxford* (1992)

E.H. Cordeaux and D.H. Merry *A Bibliography of Printed Books Relating to the University of Oxford* (1968)

E.H. Cordeaux and D.H. Merry *A Bibliography of Printed Works relating to the City of Oxford* (1976)

V.H.H. Green *A History of Oxford University* (1984)

C. and E. Hibbert *The Encyclopaedia of Oxford* (1988)

J. McConica (ed) *The History of the University of Oxford: III The Collegiate University* (1986)

N. Tyacke (ed) *The History of the University of Oxford: IV Seventeenth Century Oxford* (1997)

Victoria County History of Oxfordshire *Vol III The University of Oxford* (1954)

Oxfordshire

U. AYLMER *Oxford Food* (1995)
JAMES BOND and JOHN RHODES *The Oxfordshire Brewer* (1985)
H.A. EVANS *Highways and Byways in Oxford and the Cotswolds* (1905/1994)
JOHN STEAD *Oxfordshire* (1996)

General Accounts

JOHN BETJEMAN *An Oxford University Chest* (1938/1979)
JOHN DOUGILL *Oxford in English Literature:The Making and Undoing of 'the English Athens'* (1998)
WILLIAM GAUNT *Oxford* (1965)
CHRISTOPHER HOBHOUSE *Oxford: As it was and as it is today* (1939)
J.A.R. MARRIOTT *Oxford: Its place in National History* (1933)
J.C. MASTERMAN *To Teach the Senators Wisdom or an Oxford Guide-Book* (1952)
J. MORRIS *Oxford* (1965)
Oxfordshire Museum Service *The Story of Oxford* (1992)
J. PREST (ed) *The Illustrated History of Oxford University* (1993)
A.L. ROWSE *Oxford in the History of the Nation* (1975)
EDWARD THOMAS *Oxford* (1903, reprinted 1983)

Anthologies/Pictorial

JUDI CATON *Oxford in Old Photographs* (1988)
MALCOLM GRAHAM *A Century of Oxford: Events, People and Places Over the Last 100 Years* (1999)
NANCY HOOD *Literary Oxford: Britain in Old Photographs* (2000)
J. MORRIS *The Oxford Book of Oxford* (1978)
W.A. PANTIN *Oxford Life in Oxford Archives* (1972)
JOHN RHODES *Oxford: The University in Old Photographs* (1988)

Guide Books

DAVID BRAMWELL *The Cheeky Guide to Oxford* (2000)
MICHAEL DE-LA-NOY *Exploring Oxford* (1991)
A.R. WOOLLEY *The Clarendon Guide to Oxford* (5th ed 1983)

Colleges

PAULINE ADAMS *Somerville for Women: An Oxford College 1879–1993* (1996)
GEOFF ANDREWS, HILDA KEAN and JANE THOMPSON *Ruskin College: Contesting Knowledge, Dissenting Politics* (1999)
JOHN BUXTON and PENRY WILLIAMS *New College, Oxford 1379–1979* (1979)
HOWARD COLVIN and J.S.G. SIMMONS *All Souls: A College and Its Buildings* (1989)
MILES JEBB *The Colleges of Oxford* (1992)
ELAINE KAYE *Mansfield College, Oxford: Its Origin, History and Significance* (1996)
G.H. MARTIN and J.R.L. HIGHFIELD *A History of Merton College* (1997)
C.S. NICHOLLS *The History of St Antony's College, Oxford 1950–2000* (2000)
ERIC H.F. SMITH *St Peter's: The Founding of an Oxford College* (1978)

Architecture and Topography

MAVIS BATEY *Oxford Gardens: The University's influence on garden history* (1982)
J.C. BUCKLER *Drawings of Oxford* (1979)
H.M. COLVIN *Unbuilt Oxford* (1983)
COLIN HARRISON *Turner's Oxford* (2000)
TANIS HINCHCLIFFE *North Oxford* (1992)
PETER HOWARD and HELENA WEBSTER *Oxford: An Architectural guide* (1999)
Royal Commission on Historical Monuments *City of Oxford* (1939)
JENNIFER SHERWOOD and NIKOLAUS PEVSNER *The Buildings of England: Oxfordshire* (1974/1996)
GEOFFREY TYACK *Oxford: an Architectural Guide* (1998)

Museums

A. MACGREGOR *Tradescant's Rarities* (1983)
R.F. OVENELL *The Ashmolean Museum 1683–1894* (1986)

The City of Oxford

RUTH FASNACHT *A History of the City of Oxford* (1954)
MARY PRIOR *Fisher Row: Fishermen, Bargemen and Canal Boatmen in Oxford 1500–1900* (1982)
Victoria County History of Oxfordshire *Vol IV: The City of Oxford* (1979)
R.C. WHITING *The View from Cowley: The Impact of Industrialization upon Oxford 1918–39* (1983)

Education

A.J. ENGEL *From Clergyman to Don: The Rise of the Academic Profession in Nineteenth Century Oxford* (1983)

LAWRENCE GOLDMAN *Dons and Workers: Oxford and Adult Education since 1850* (1995)

JACK MORRELL *Science at Oxford 1914–39: Transforming an Arts University* (1997)

JOSEPH A. SOARES *The Decline of Privilege: The Modernization of Oxford University* (1999)

TED TAPPER and BRIAN SALTER *Oxford, Cambridge and the Changing Idea of the University: The Challenge to Donnish Domination* (1992)

Specific Periods and Aspects

N. BARKER *The Oxford University Press and the Spread of Learning 1478–1978* (1979)

HUMPHREY CARPENTER *Ouds: A Centenary History of the Oxford University Drama Society 1885–1985* (1985)

D.G.H. EDDERSHAW *The Civil War in Oxfordshire* (1995)

W.N. HARGEAVES-MAWDSLEY *Oxford in the Age of John Locke* (1973)

ANTHONY KENNY (ed) *The History of the Rhodes Trust 1902–1999* (2001)

GRAHAM MIDGLEY *University Life in Eighteenth Century Oxford* (1996)

P. SUTCLIFFE *The Oxford University Press: An Informal History* (1978)

RICHARD SYMONDS *Oxford and Empire: The Last Lost Cause?* (1986)

Biographies

J.A.W. BENNETT *Chaucer at Oxford and Cambridge* (1974)

ANN BROWN *Arthur Evans and the Palace of Minos* (1983)

MORTON S. COHEN *The Selected Letters of Lewis Caroll* (1982)

SIR ROY HARROD *The Prof* (1959)

C.H. JOSTEN *Elias Ashmole 1617–1692* (1966)

DIARMAID MACCULLOCH *Thomas Cranmer* (1996)

I. KER *John Henry Newman* (1988)

FIONA MACCARTHY *William Morris* (1994)

GWYN MACFARLANE *Howard Florey: the making of a great scientist* (1980)

ADAM SISMAN *A.J.P. Taylor* (1994)

EVELYN WAUGH *Ronald Knox* (1959)

A.N. WILSON *C.S. Lewis: A Biography* (1990)

Reminiscences and Memoirs

MURIEL BEADLE *These Ruins Are Inhabited* (1961)
MAY WEDDERBURN CANNAN *Grey Ghosts and Voices* (1976)
G.V. COX *Recollections of Oxford* (1868)
J. BRETT LANGSTAFF *Oxford – 1914* (1965)
K.M.E. MURRAY *Caught in the Web of Words* (1977)
MARK PATTISON *Memoirs of a Don* (1885/1988)
PETER SNOW *Oxford Observed: Town and Gown* (1992)
REV. W. TUCKWELL *Reminiscences of Oxford* (1901)
CHIANG YEE *The Silent Traveller in Oxford* (1944)

Critiques

ROSA EHRENREICH *A Garden of Paper Flowers: An American at Oxford* (1994)
WALTER ELLIS *The Oxbridge Conspiracy* (1994)
RACHEL JOHNSON (ed) *The Oxford Myth* (1988)

Glossary

Act   Degree-giving ceremony and festivities marking the ending of the academic year until its replacement by *Encaenia*; Handel played in the Sheldonian at the last Act in 1733

Admissions   The decision to admit a person to a course of study rests with individual colleges

Aegrotat   Official permission to miss, but still pass, an examination, usually occasioned by serious illness

Aesthete   Non-sportsman, opposite of hearty

Ashmolean   University museum first opened in 1683

Bachelor   Person who has passed the university's first level degree in most subjects (including sciences), usually after a three year course of study; the status is signified by the letters BA (Bachelor of Arts) written after the name

Balls   Organised on a college basis at the end of the summer (Trinity) term; tickets (£100+) are sold for couples and 'black tie'/ball gown is traditionally *de rigueur*; less formal affairs are known as 'Events'

Batells   College bills

Blackwell's   Oxford's biggest bookshop; the main branch is located in Broad Street

Blue   Award given to a person who has represented Oxford at a sport in an official inter-university competition; major sports (e.g. cricket, soccer, rugby, athletics) rank as Full Blues, minor ones as Half Blues

Boat Race   Annual rowing competition between two teams of eight representing Oxford and Cambridge on the River Thames between Putney and Mortlake

Bod, the   Bodleian Library

BNC   Brasenose College

Broad, the   Broad Street

Bulldog   Nineteenth century slang for a university policeman appointed to assist the Proctor in enforcing discipline over undergraduates. Traditionally they wore dark suits and bowler hats, as the porters at Christ Church still do

Bumping races   Because the river is too narrow for boats to compete in line abreast, races are run by starting at equidistant points and rowing to bump (overlap with but not necessarily hit – in Cambridge you do hit) the boat in front (see Eights Week)

Bump supper   Celebratory dinner to mark success in bumping races; crew members keep an oar as a memento (usually elaborately painted with college coat of arms, names of crew etc.); an old boat might be burned as part of the festivities which were invariably drunken and often rowdy

Burgesses   Normally citizens of a borough with political rights, e.g. to vote and hold public office. Confusingly Members of Parliament elected to represent Oxford in the House of Commons were traditionally known as burgesses

Canon   Clergyman living at or attached to a cathedral; the six canons of Christ Church are members of Oxford Cathedral and serve on the governing body of the college

Carfax   Crossing where the High, St Aldate's, Queen Street and Cornmarket Street converge

Chair   Academic post held by a professor; endowed chairs (e.g. Regius, Chichele, Savilean) are held by a succession of occupants; 'personal' chairs may be created for a particular scholar and lapse on their retirement

Chancellor   Originally the administrative head of the university but since the Restoration largely an honorific post, held for life. (Lord) Roy Jenkins, a former politician and distinguished biographer was elected Chancellor in 1987 and, unusually, is not an absentee

Cherwell   Tributary of the River Thames, much favoured for punting; also a student newspaper

Class   Group of students under formal instruction; also the rank achieved in a degree examination – first, second (since 1986 divided into upper second, a 2:1, or lower second, a 2.2), third or, until its abolition in the 1960s, fourth

Clerk   Person in minor orders, hence technically a priest and therefore subject to and protected by the canon law of the Church; before the Protestant Reformation all students ranked as clerks

Collections   Beginning of term examinations, supposedly to check on work done during vacations; also, confusingly, an end of term report/ticking off

College   A self-governing corporation for purposes of teaching and research; collectively the colleges constitute the major component of the university but are conceptually distinct, and to a varying extent financially independent, from it

Come up   To arrive as a student; (see Down)

Commemoration   Traditionally a week-long celebration at the end of Trinity Term marking the closure of the academic year and consisting of degree ceremonies, balls, rowing-races and commemorative services honouring founders and benefactors

Commoner   Undergraduate student who does not hold a scholarship; traditionally those with a scholarship received their 'commons' (meals) free, whereas commoners had to pay for them

Common University Fund   Fund originally established as a result of the University Reform Act of 1877 to receive levies from the income of the wealthier colleges for the benefit of the university as a whole; it additionally serves as a mode of transferring money from the university to the colleges

Congregation   Meeting of resident Masters of Arts involved in university work which serves as the university's legislature; it meets in the Sheldonian Theatre and attendees must wear gowns

Convocation   Meeting open to all Masters of Arts, resident or not; in the past opponents of change used it to mobilise former students to constitute a blocking mechanism against reform; it is now restricted to the election of honorific appointments, including the Chancellor and the Professor of Poetry

Daily Information   Daily (in term time) news sheet appearing on college notice boards

Dean   Title borne by the head of Christ Church; also – without the capital D – title of a college fellow responsible for discipline and academic advising

Delegates   Members of the university appointed to manage a specific function such as the University Press, schools examinations etc.

Doctor   At Oxford a holder of one of the highest degrees, such as the Doctorate of Letters or Civil Laws, which are regarded as more prestigious than the Doctor of Philosophy (see DPhil) degree routinely awarded for postgraduate research

Dons   Generic term for a university teacher; from Latin *dominus*, lord; until the reforms of the nineteenth century dons were unmarried (until 1878, unless they were a head of house or a professor), untrained and virtually unsackable

Down   Not at Oxford; undergraduates leaving voluntarily, e.g. during vacations or at the end of their degree course, 'go down'; those who are ejected as a punishment for some misdemeanour have been 'sent down' ('Oxford is up, everywhere else is down, except Cambridge, which is nowhere'.)

DPhil   What other universities call a PhD

Eight   A rowing boat with eight oarsmen (and a cox who steers)

Eights Week   Four days of intercollegiate rowing races, a highlight of the social calendar, when spectators sport fancy striped blazers and straw hats and consume copious quantities of strawberries and Pimms; crews consist of eight oarsmen and a cox, who steers; boats race at timed intervals, aiming to bump the boat in front and thus take its place in the order of precedence the following day; the crew at the top of the first division is known as Head of the River and starts from that position the following year, with the rest following in the sequence achieved by their predecessors

Encaenia Ceremony for giving honorary degrees, originally held in the university church of St Mary's but since 1669 in the Sheldonian Theatre

Examination Schools Building used for university examinations and at other times for lectures

Exhibition See scholarships

Faculty University department of study and the staff which comprise it; modern faculties, governed by boards date from 1883

Fellow Constituent member of a college, with the right to vote on its affairs and normally with teaching and administrative duties; most college tutors are Fellows. Honorary and Emeritus Fellows are normally excluded from teaching and administration but may enjoy the hospitality of the college.

FRS Fellow of the Royal Society

Finals Examinations taken at the end of the course of study for the Bachelor of Arts degree which determine the class of degree awarded

First See Class

Freshers Students newly arrived at the university

Freshers' Fair Held in the Examinaton Schools at the start of the academic year; clubs and societies set out stalls and attempt to recruit new members

Gated Confined to college as a punishment

Gaudy College reunion banquet, usually held at intervals of seven or ten years; from Latin *gaudere*, to rejoice

Gentleman commoner Undergraduate of élite social rank to whom special privileges were accorded between the Reformation period and the reforms of the mid-nineteenth century

Go down See Down

Gown Literally an academic robe; metaphorically the university as in 'Town vs Gown'

Graduate Either any non-resident person with a first degree or, more particularly, a resident one working for a higher degree

Great Tom Removed from Osney Abbey in 1546 and recast in 1680, this huge bell (85 inches diameter, weighing just under eight tons) hangs in Wren's Tom Tower at Christ Church and is rung a hundred and one times nightly at 9.05 p.m., the number signifying the original number of scholars at The House

Greats Name for *Literae Humaniores*, also the final examination taken at the end of that course of study

Hall The dining-hall of a college, formerly also one of the scores of halls of residence occupied by students; to add to the confusion some colleges are still called Hall

Head of House Head of a college; the title varies as follows:

  Principal – Brasenose, Hertford, Jesus, Lady Margaret Hall, Linacre, St Anne's, St Edmund Hall, St Hilda's, St Hugh's, Somerville

Warden   – All Souls, Green, Keble, Merton, New, Nuffield, St Antony's, Wadham

President – Corpus Christi, Magdalen, Rewley House, St John's, Templeton, Trinity, Wolfson

Master   – Balliol, Pembroke, St Catherine's, St Cross, St Peter's, University

Provost   – Oriel, Queen's, Worcester

Rector   – Exeter, Lincoln

Dean   – Christ Church

Heads of Houses usually occupy a separate Lodging, often with a walled, or at least private, garden

Hearty   Keen sportsman, especially rower

Hebdomadal Board   Supreme decision-making body of the university, meeting weekly and consisting entirely of heads of colleges, instituted by Archbishop Laud in 1631; in 1854 it was superceded by the Hebdomadal Council consisting of elected representatives of heads of houses, professors and masters

High, the   High Street

High Table   Table set on a dais at the end of a college dining hall and reserved for dons and their guests

Higher degrees   Are normally taken by those who already have a bachelor's degree and may take one year (Master of Studies, Master of Science) or two (Master of Letters, Master of Philosophy) or three (Doctor of Philosophy)

Hilary   The spring term

Honours   Rank of degree introduced in 1801 to reward academic merit above the mere pass level; all graduates are now normally honours graduates

House, The   From *Aedes Christi*, ('House of Christ') i.e. Christ Church (never referred to as Christ Church College); strictly speaking only members of Christ Church were supposed to refer to it as 'The House'

Isis   The river Thames (in Latin *Tamesis*) although the name is now obsolete; also a student magazine

JCR   Junior Common Room, literally a place of refreshment and recreation, metaphorically the undergraduate population of a college

LMH   Lady Margaret Hall

Literae Humaniores   The study of Greek and Latin literature, history and philosophy, a four year course divided into Mods and Greats

Long Vac   Long vacation, summer break; traditionally assumed to have been instituted so that students could help with the harvest, it has also given opportunities for study and travel

Manciple   Medieval catering manager

Masters   At Oxford (and Cambridge) holders of a Bachelor of Arts degree need take no further examination to acquire a Master of Arts (MA) degree seven years after matriculation, though a small administration fee is payable; in academic terms the distinction is now meaningless, whereas in the medieval period the Master's degree constituted a licence to teach

Matriculation   Having a person's name registered as a member of the university; from Latin *matricula*, a roll

May Morning   Oxford festivity in which the first day of summer is marked by a gathering at 6 a.m. at the foot of Magdalen College Tower, on top of which choristers sing an invocation in praise of the season. The custom dates back to the sixteenth century. From Victorian times it was often accompanied by drunken roistering in punts but this has been replaced by busking, Morris dancing, street theatre etc.

Mercury   Famous statue in Tom Quad, Christ Church

Michaelmas   The autumn term

MCR   Middle Common Room, for graduate students (see JCR)

Moderations   Aka 'Mods', traditional first public (i.e. university rather than collegiate) examination, variously taken after two, three or five terms, depending on faculty; results are classified but do not affect the final degree result either way

Newdigate Prize   University competition for English verse competition, established in 1806; the Professor of Poetry chairs the panel of judges and the winning entry is recited at *Encaenia*. Past winners include Ruskin (1839), Matthew Arnold (1843) Oscar Wilde (1878) John Buchan (1898) and the present Poet Laureate, Andrew Motion (1975)

OED   Oxford English Dictionary

Oxford University Dramatic Society   (OUDS, pronounced 'owds') Founded 1884, it flourished especially under the guidance of Nevil Coghill

OUP   Oxford University Press; the main offices are in Walton Street and there is a shop for OUP books in the High Street

Oxbridge   Oxford and Cambridge; 'Camford' has never caught on

Oxfam   Oxford Committee for Famine Relief

Oxon.   Abbreviation of Latin *Oxoniensis*, of Oxford

Oxonian   An Oxford graduate

Parks, The   University park located north of the Science Area; rare trees, cricket etc.

Parson's Pleasure   Nude bathing place (now defunct) for dons

Pimms   Cocktail mix to be drunk with lemonade, ice, mint, fruit bits

Playhouse, The   Theatre in Beaumont Street

PPE   Politics, Philosophy and Economics, aka 'Modern Greats'

Plough   Fail an examination

Porter   College servant responsible for security, post etc.; traditionally an embodiment of college tradition and not infrequently an *eminence grise* in college affairs; invariably enshrined in a lodge guarding access to the college

Praelector   A senior fellow

Prelims   In some faculties a first (i.e. preliminary) public examination, taken after one or two terms

Proctors   The university's police officers; recently they have developed a role as tribunes, acting on behalf of the teaching staff to pose challenging questions to the university about its administration

Professorship

Regius   – chair founded by the Crown, which is still usually involved in the appointment

Chichele   – chair attached to All Souls College; the college was founded by Henry Chichele but the chairs are of more recent creation; the same applies to Waynflete (attached to Magdalen), Wykeham (attached to New College) and Canon (attached to Christ Church)

Poetry   – honorary post, established in 1708, originally tenable for ten, now five, years holders are elected by Convocation and may have no formal connection, past or present, with the university. They have included Matthew Arnold (1857–67), Cecil Day-Lewis (1951–6), W.H. Auden (1956–61), Edmund Blunden (1966–8), and Nobel Laureate Seamus Heaney (1989–94)

Punt   Flat-bottomed boat, roughly 1 metre wide × 8 metres long, propelled by a pole

Quad   Quadrangle, a college courtyard

Rag Week   Period of licensed idiocy during which students dress up, cavort, experiment with fire-eating etc. ostensibly and incidentally to raise money for charity

Reader   Professor-in-waiting, sometimes eternally

Rhodes scholarships   See pages 233–4

Rustication   Temporary expulsion from the university for a limited period; from the Latin for 'living in the country' (see also Down)

St Giles's Fair   Traditional fair held on the first Monday and Tuesday of September in St Giles

Scholarships   A scholarship may also be known as a bursary, demyship, exhibition or studentship

Scholasticism   Intellectual mode of discourse of medieval universities, compounded of Christian theology and Aristotelian philosophy

School   In the university context either a room or building for the teaching of a specific subject or a course of study prescribed by a faculty

Schools   Final examinations and the building in which they take place, the Examination Schools

Science Area   Main concentration of science facilities, located between the Parks and South Parks Road

Sconce　To demand a forfeit (usually drinking an excessive amount of alcohol traditionally a yard of ale – at an excessive pace) of a fellow diner for an offence against table etiquette

Scout　Traditionally a male college servant, usually attached to a staircase or group of staircases; duties might include laying fires, waiting at table, making beds, clearing up after parties, running errands, cleaning clothes etc.; in modern times replaced by a cleaner/bedmaker

SCR　Senior Common Room, for dons (see JCR)

Sent Down　See Down

Servitor　Student receiving board and tuition in return for waiting on college fellows

Sporting the oak　Closing the outer door to a college room as a sign of wishing not to be disturbed

Stacks　The Bodleian Library's system of book-shelves on rollers

Statutes　Legally binding rules for the government of the university or colleges

Student　With a capital S, this means a Fellow specifically of Christ Church

Subfusc　Formal dress worn for taking examinations and degree ceremonies – dark suit, white bow tie, gown; from Latin *subfuscus*, dark brown, which is not permitted

Subscription　Affirming belief in the Thirty-Nine Articles of Religion drawn up in 1571 to define the Anglican faith

Teddy Hall　St Edmund Hall

Terms　Sub-divisions of the academic year, lasting eight weeks – Michaelmas (autumn), Hilary (winter) and Trinity (spring/summer); undergraduates are required to 'keep terms' by being in residence for at least six weeks of each term

Terrae Filius　Licensed jester who participated in degree ceremonies until the office was suppressed in the eighteenth century

Trinity　Third university term; also a college

Turl, the　Turl Street

Tutorial　A one-to-one or one-to-two (at most one-to-three) hour-long weekly encounter between tutor and undergraduate in which the former hears and comments on an essay. Now thought to represent the essence of Oxford teaching, the tutorial only dates from the nineteenth century and actually originated among 'crammers', i.e. private tutors not employed by the university

Undergraduate　Term traditionally used at Oxford (and Cambridge) for a matriculated student who has not yet passed his final examinations for the Bachelor's degree

Union Society　The university's debating society, which follows rules of Parliamentary procedure; not to be confused with the Students' Union (OUSU) which is quite separate

Univ. Abbreviation for University College, not the university

Up The route to Oxford; whatever the starting-point undergraduates 'come up' to Oxford at the beginning of each term

Vac. Vacation, as in Long Vac.

Varsity Slang term for university, especially in connection with sporting activities

Vice-Chancellor Effective administrative head of the university, holding office for a four year term

Visitor Outsider appointed to make periodic inspections of a college in the interests of probity and efficiency; the Visitor may sometimes act as arbiter in cases of dispute between college members

Viva *Viva voce*, with the living voice; an oral examination, still usual as part of the procedure for earning a doctorate; also used in borderline cases

WEA Workers' Educational Association, founded in 1913 by Albert Mansbridge, it organised adult education evening classes with a cultural/social rather than vocational bias and initially held its meetings in Toynbee Hall.

Index